Peace for Lebanon?

Published in association with the
Canadian Institute for International Peace and Security

Peace for Lebanon?

From War to Reconstruction

edited by
Deirdre Collings

Lynne Rienner Publishers • Boulder & London

Published in the United States of America in 1994 by
Lynne Rienner Publishers, Inc.
1800 30th Street, Boulder, Colorado 80301

and in the United Kingdom by
Lynne Rienner Publishers, Inc.
3 Henrietta Street, Covent Garden, London WC2E 8LU

Library of Congress Cataloging-in-Publication Data
Peace for Lebanon? : from war to reconstruction / edited by Deirdre
   Collings.
     p. cm.
   Includes bibliographical references and index.
   ISBN 1-55587-367-7 (alk. paper)
   ISBN 1-55587-501-7 (pbk.) (alk. paper)
   1. Lebanon—History—1975– I. Collings, Deirdre, 1962– .
DS87.P43 1994
956.9204'4—dc20   93-39746
                                      CIP

British Cataloguing in Publication Data
A Cataloguing in Publication record for this book
is available from the British Library.

Printed and bound in the United States of America

The paper used in this publication meets the requirements
of the American National Standard for Permanence of
Paper for Printed Library Materials Z39.48-1984.

Contents

Part 3 Toward Socioeconomic Stability

Part 4 Toward Sociopolitical Stability

Preface

———————— . ————————

Between September 1990 and November 1991, the Canadian Institute for International Peace and Security (CIIPS) conducted a series of intensive workshops on the conflict in Lebanon. This volume represents one product of that series.

The institute decided to undertake a comprehensive project on Lebanon in 1989, during some of the most destructive fighting the country had witnessed, when a delegation of twelve Lebanese Canadians representative of Lebanon's various communities met with then Secretary of State Joe Clark to express, with a united voice, their concern about the deteriorating situation. Partly as a result of Secretary Clark's interest, the institute undertook a major study of the conflict.

The Lebanon Project was organized to examine the political, economic, social, and human aspects of the conflict, and to assess the impact of the domestic, regional, and international environment. Seventy-two formal presentations were prepared for the project, and participants engaged in more than 120 hours of vigorous discussion. In addition, two public sessions were held in conjunction with the workshops. This book consists of revised and updated versions of the most provocative of these original papers. Arabic terms and names are generally written in a common English form. Where diacritical marks are conserved, both the 'ayn and the hamza are represented by a prime mark (').

The Lebanon Project would not have been possible without the dedicated assistance of many people. The institute consulted with a wide advisory network during the planning and execution of the project, and we would like to express our sincere appreciation to all who responded. Five individuals formed the core of this network, and were called upon heavily for their input and guidance: Hani Faris, Georges Corm, Atif Kubursi,

Mahmoud Ayoub, and Samir Khalaf. We are deeply grateful for their time, expertise, and sage advice throughout the process. The project also drew on talents of many members of the institute's staff. Very special mention goes to Doina Cioiu, project administrator; Jill Tansley, rapporteur and cowriter of the working paper; Marcel Langlois; Philip Lemieux; and of course, Bernard Wood, former head of CIIPS.

I would also like to thank the copyeditor, Benjamin Hardy, and the many people at Lynne Rienner Publishers for their care with the manuscript, particularly Martha Peacock and Michelle Welsh.

Extra special recognition goes to Rafal Rohozinski, who provided extensive assistance throughout the production of the book manuscript, including computer troubleshooting, full production backup, and highly useful editorial advice.

Publication of the book encountered some delay because of the federal government's unfortunate decision, prompted by austerity measures, to cut CIIPS's funding. Despite the institute's pending closure, the Department of External Affairs concurred that publication of this volume should proceed, and agreed to its funding. The Political Science Department of Carleton University and John Sigler deserve special credit for ensuring that this work saw the light of day, by way of the university's generous institutional support to complete the project.

This book, the last product of CIIPS, is dedicated to the late Norma Salem, whose vision initiated the project, and to the former staff members of CIIPS, each of whom contributed in some way to the success of this endeavor.

Deirdre Collings

Lebanon's Strategic Situation, July 1993

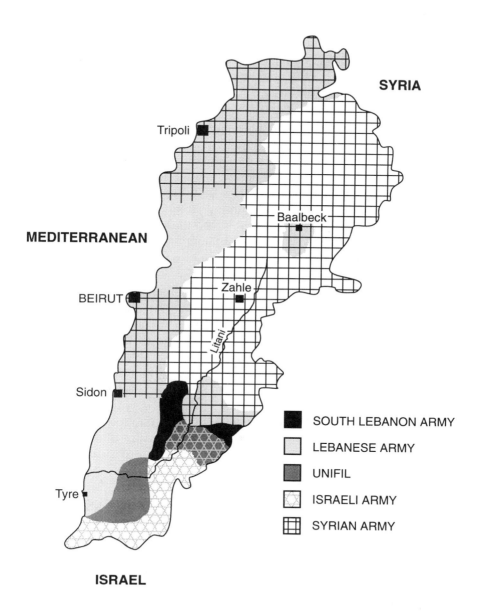

Source: Lebanese Center for Policy Studies, Beirut. Adapted by Rafal Rohozinski.

Introduction

·

Deirdre Collings

For over fifteen years, the conflict in Lebanon frequently commanded the attention of Western news media. The blood, the destruction, the possibility that Lebanon might spark another major Arab-Israeli war, all made for newsworthy headlines and action-packed images. Then, in August 1990, a peace plan for Lebanon—the Ta'if Accord—was set in motion. As the fighting diminished and the security situation improved, Lebanon disappeared from nightly newscasts. "Lebanon at war" was a story; "Lebanon in the absence of war" was not. Indeed, it seemed many members of the international community assumed that the cessation of overt bloodshed meant Lebanon's conflicts were sufficiently resolved.

The Ta'if Accord marked a definite turning point in the fifteen year conflict. As a first step, the accord managed to reestablish a modicum of security in much of the country. This alone was a remarkable feat. Whether Ta'if has ushered in an era of long-term, self-sustaining peace for Lebanon, however, remains the subject of considerable debate. There are important questions, for example, concerning the foundations of Lebanon's newfound security: Is it based on genuine domestic reconciliation? Does it mean that the roots of the conflict have been thoroughly excised?

Observers agree that the war itself did not resolve the divisive issues that prompted its eruption, nor were these issues resolved in the negotiations leading up to Ta'if.[1] The accord does address a number of major issues inherent in Lebanon's past difficulties and future peace, but its provisions do not automatically translate into the necessary political will and latitude to pursue their implementation fully. As one longtime observer noted: "Perhaps the Ta'if recipe itself is not so bad, but the 'cooks' and the constraints of the kitchen are another matter."

By acknowledging many of Lebanon's longstanding problems, the accord created the expectation that at least some would be constructively

1

addressed. To date, however, there has been little improvement in Lebanon's longstanding and overlapping political, socioeconomic, and regional predicaments. Unraveling this tangle is no easy task.

It is not the purpose of this volume to reexamine the roots of the conflict—many other studies have addressed these issues in detail[2] (although no consensus exists concerning the exact process that led to Lebanon's war). It is, nevertheless, useful to sketch some of the principal conflicts whose convergence proved explosive in the mid-1970s, leading to Lebanon's long-term destabilization. These conflicts include domestic disagreement over Lebanon's identity and role in the region (i.e., differing perceptions of Lebanon's raison d'être and, by extension, its foreign policy orientations), domestic disagreement over the sectarian-based power-sharing arrangements of the political system, domestic socioeconomic discontent, and mounting pressures imposed by external players (notably the Palestinians and Israel).[3]

To outline the domestic disagreement over Lebanon's "identity" can involve a long, complicated, and controversial discussion. Let us briefly say, therefore, that at the time of Lebanon's independence and the promulgation of the 1943 National Pact, not all members of the Lebanese political establishment shared the same vision of their country's identity and its role in the region.[4] The essence of this disagreement centered on the question: Is Lebanon Arab or not?

Before explaining this point, a brief aside is warranted. Too often, the war in Lebanon has been described as one between Muslims and Christians. This simplified explanation is highly misleading, however, and obscures more than clarifies the reason for the conflict. As Georges Corm stressed in CIIPS's workshops: "It is too simplistic to label all Arab nationalists as Muslims and all Lebanese nationalists as Christians. Furthermore, the so-called Maronite establishment is not representative of the entire Maronite community; there were Christian supporters of both the Palestinian and national movements, and there was a definite class aspect to the crisis, which transcended the sectarian divide. . . . Moreover, there was a fantastic rivalry among competing groups *within* the so-called Christian bloc, and *within* the so-called Muslim bloc. . . . Quarrels within the movements and within the sects have been much more intensive than the 'Christian-Muslim' problem." Workshop participants agreed that, especially at the beginning of the crisis, there was *not* a strict line of intersectarian division. After the violence erupted, however, group identity became an increasingly divisive issue, principally because of militia actions: the warlords employed sectarian-based violence to compel Lebanese civilians to take refuge, both psychologically and physically, in sectarian ghettos that were "protected" by same-sect militias. In this way, militia leaders appropriated the mantle of legitimacy through the appearance of popular support. (See the chapter by Corm in this volume.)

Prior to 1943, certain elements of Lebanon's Christian population would have preferred continuation of the French Mandate. Their stance emanated from their belief that the French presence in Lebanon guaranteed both their protection (in relation to the large Muslim population of the region) and their privilege: under the French mandate system, Lebanese Christians were considered the political majority and Muslims, the minority. In contrast, a large segment of the population—most Muslims as well as many Christians—welcomed independence, viewing it as a step toward Lebanon becoming a more integral part of the Middle East.

By 1943, however, most conservative Christians had come to accept the formalization of the Lebanese state. The National Pact permitted Maronite Christians to retain control over key political, security, and military offices (the presidency, head of public security, and commander of the army, for example). For many Maronites, these guarantees—perceived to be important because pan-Arab nationalist sentiments were running high in the region, including among certain segments of the Lebanese population—helped alleviate their fears concerning Lebanon's ability to remain autonomous following its independence.[5]

Although the National Pact embodied a domestic understanding that allowed Lebanon to proceed to independence, pro-West versus pro-Arab orientations continued to divide the Lebanese on the question of their state's identity and, by extension, its foreign policy.[6] These domestic differences, containable in 1943, became increasingly explosive as various conflicts erupted across the Middle East (i.e., the Arab-Israeli conflict [1948 and after], the various inter-Arab cold wars, and the U.S.-USSR Cold War [with its posturing by proxy in the Middle East]). These regional conflicts often required Lebanon to side with one or another of the protagonists, but any such foreign policy decision almost always caused disagreement among the Lebanese and sometimes escalated to open conflict (as in the 1958 civil war).

By 1970, this particular issue had become volatile because of the increasingly militant Palestinian presence in Lebanon.[7] Following its expulsion from Jordan in September 1970, the Palestine Liberation Organization (PLO) relocated its headquarters to Beirut, and Palestinian armed organizations began to form a state within a state in Lebanon. Palestinian actions, which also attracted massive Israeli retaliation on Lebanese soil, fed a sense of insecurity among conservative Christian Lebanese, who thought that Lebanon's sovereignty was being intolerably compromised. Nevertheless, many Lebanese, Muslim and Christian, supported the Palestinian cause as the standard bearer of Arab nationalism. The Palestinian issue polarized domestic debate; as the regional situation turned increasingly volatile, so did the Lebanese domestic scene.

Part of Lebanon's internal rift, therefore, was fashioned by different perceptions of Lebanon's security needs and its foreign policy directions—

especially its obligations to Arab causes.[8] This cleavage was overlaid by another contentious debate concerning political representation and power sharing.

The 1943 National Pact, which had helped define the power-sharing arrangements of Lebanon's sectarian-based political system, had more than guaranteed a privileged position for Maronites; it had also elevated the political status of Muslims—especially because it awarded Lebanon's prime ministership to the Sunni community. In addition, the confessional political system had instituted power sharing based on the demographic weight of each confessional community, meaning that Muslim (especially Sunni) political status became more acceptable than it had been during most of the French Mandate.[9]

Within three decades, however, substantial socioeconomic and demographic change had spawned contentious new viewpoints concerning the fairness and "representativity" of the confessionally based system.[10] For example, differential rates of population growth among Lebanon's communities had produced a clear Muslim majority—one comprising, moreover, many Shi'ites. By the 1970s, Lebanon's leaders were divided. In particular, traditional Muslim leaders questioned the continuation of Maronite political privilege given Lebanon's altered demographic balance and lobbied to reform the confessional system to reflect the new reality. Other Lebanese, especially conservative Christian leaders, considered the call for reform to be a ploy aimed at instituting Muslim domination of the state. Such conservative Christians, who would later join to form the Lebanese Front,[11] viewed the preferential status of the Maronites as the only way to ensure the security of their community; thus, they were committed to preserving the system and its confessional ratios for power sharing. (Dissenters argued that Maronite privileges resulted in Maronite control of the state, to that community's advantage.) By 1975, another group had coalesced: a left-wing counterelite composed of both Muslims and Christians, and embodied in the Lebanese National Movement (LNM).[12] The LNM asserted its disaffection for sectarian quotas by including deconfessionalization of the political system among its proposed domestic reforms.

Discontent arising from socioeconomic imbalances become intertwined with these issues of identity, security, foreign policy, power sharing, and ideology. The chapters in Part 3 of this book make explicit the linkages between these socioeconomic issues and Lebanon's destabilization and restabilization. Although Lebanon's free-enterprise economy was highly successful, the country's "miraculous" growth did not benefit all Lebanese. Three major features fed socioeconomic discontent: rapid but unbalanced socioeconomic growth, lack of social content in Lebanon's economic successes and government programs,[13] and centralization of economic activities in greater Beirut to the neglect of outlying areas. The transformation of Lebanon's rural economy, beginning in the 1960s, provides an illustration.

As cash-crop agriculture (owned by city dwellers) replaced traditional farming practices and crops, small rural farmers went bankrupt. Their livelihood lost, lacking alternate employment, and facing inadequate rural social and physical infrastructure, thousands of farming families succumbed to the lure of Beirut's economic promises; most ended up impoverished in Beirut's suburban slums, known as the "Belt of Misery." In South Lebanon, the Palestinian presence and consequent Israeli bombardments exacerbated rural-to-urban migration. Beirut's miserable periphery festered with discontent; its residents became prime quarry for militia recruiters once hostilities broke out.

Throughout the 1970s, therefore, Lebanon's governing elite faced two mounting challenges: rising political, social, and economic discontent and increasing disruptions caused by external actors (especially the Palestinians and Israel). These proved more than Lebanon's fragile political system could manage.[14] The rigidity of Lebanon's political organization—its sectarian quotas and its inability to allow for peaceful change—rendered it unstable and contributed to both the war's eruption and continuation.

Moreover, the sectarian system contributed more to the state's weakness than to its strength. Rather than bolstering Lebanese citizens' allegiance to the state, the sectarian system encouraged the Lebanese to identify with their sects, or alienated them altogether. This tendency, in combination with high levels of internal dissatisfaction and the historical ties linking Lebanon's communal groups with outside powers, prompted many sectarian and political groups to look to foreign sponsors for backing in domestic power struggles. Concomitantly, foreign patrons pursuing their own regional or international agendas were eager to sponsor Lebanese clients. In brief, this perilous patron-client symbiosis resulted in a proliferation of substate foreign policies that embroiled outside powers in Lebanon's domestic turmoil and entangled Lebanon in wider regional conflicts. Lebanon's vulnerability to regional influences, as Lebanese clients and their foreign patrons joined (often very briefly) to pursue their own shifting agendas, contributed substantially to the war's complexity and intractability.

When fighting broke out in 1975, two basic coalitions formed. On one side was a conservative alliance (which became the Lebanese Front in 1976) that was antireform and pro–status quo in terms of power sharing; it demanded restoration of Lebanon's sovereignty and, therefore, the elimination of Palestinian militancy and freedom of action in Lebanon. In opposition was a broad-based alliance, the LNM, demanding pervasive socioeconomic and political reform, including deconfessionalization of the political system. Domestic irreconcilability only increased when the LNM, intent on its quest for reform, forged an open alliance with Palestinian armed organizations in Lebanon.

Once the war commenced in earnest, Lebanon's longstanding divisive issues became more intractable. Militia-orchestrated "ethnic cleansing" erected barriers of both fear and geography between Lebanon's confessional groups. The domestic debate concerning security versus reform became enmeshed in the debate over Lebanon's "Arab" identity and obligations. As the war continued, the number of Lebanese actors increased, as did the number of external "patrons"; Lebanon's prosperous economy became devastated and its structural imbalances more pronounced. Ultimately, the war developed an insidious life of its own as the militia-run "war system," dominated by those with weapons, patrons, and a vested interest in Lebanon's continued destabilization, became firmly entrenched.

This overview provides some sense of the issues that coalesced into uncontainable conflict in the 1970s, issues that must be addressed if Lebanon is to secure lasting stability in the 1990s. Although Lebanon after Ta'if is no longer at war, it is not yet at peace. Lebanon's future remains hostage to myriad interconnected political, socioeconomic, psychological, and regional challenges. The need to surmount these challenges—despite Lebanon's "peace"—is the reason why the Canadian Institute for International Peace and Security supported the effort that resulted in this volume.

PLAN OF PRESENTATION

This book presents various assessments of post-Ta'if Lebanon as well as certain prescriptives for its long-term stabilization. Our contributors provide forward-looking analyses; they assess Lebanon's current conditions, but also its future needs. Their thoughts regarding the future have benefited from analytical understanding of the past. Most of the chapters reflect this past-present-future perspective.

The volume's division into four parts is, at one level, highly artificial. No single factor caused the war in Lebanon, nor did any particular factor cause it to protract. It was the dynamic interaction of many complex factors that pushed Lebanon beyond the point of contained conflict into open warfare and kept it there for over fifteen years. For analytical purposes, some dissection is necessary, as the four-part division of this book suggests; nevertheless, the interconnectedness of Lebanon's dilemmas is attested by the cross-referencing of chapters. Indeed, some chapters are cross-referenced across all four sections.

Part 1 considers how and why the Ta'if Accord came about and reviews certain events that occurred in the accord's aftermath: What factors have allowed Ta'if to endure where so many other agreements failed? Does Ta'if embody the recipe for achieving lasting peace based on national reconciliation? Do the 1992 parliamentary elections represent a culmination of the reconciliation process?

After 1975, numerous initiatives to settle Lebanon's troubles were launched, but the 1989 Ta'if Accord was the first to be signed, ratified, and implemented (a process still unfinished). The chapter by Hani Faris provides insight concerning the foundation on which Ta'if was built with an overview of Lebanon's traditional (prewar) conflict management methods and of the reasons why the principal peacemaking attempts failed after 1975.

Joseph Maila conducts an analysis of the Ta'if Accord itself. While some observers (especially in the West) are quite euphoric concerning the peace that Ta'if has wrought, Maila's analysis—on the nature of that peace—leaves him quite pessimistic. Maila accepts that the accord represents a radical turn in the Lebanese crisis but disagrees that it represents real constitutional and political progress. He also argues that the accord's exact text is perhaps not as important as its implementation: in his judgment, "Lebanon's peace was achieved at the price of her independence. . . . True reconciliation among the Lebanese is yet to be achieved."

Augustus Richard Norton and Jillian Schwedler analyze a crucial political event in post-Ta'if Lebanon, the 1992 parliamentary elections. Their examination of the context in which the elections were held, the issues at stake, and the electoral results suggests that the electoral process, as it materialized, has served more to deepen the domestic divide than to catalyze national reconciliation. Nevertheless, the 1992 elections also reveal a number of important trends that will significantly shape Lebanon's future direction and stability.

The chapters in Part 2 examine the enduring roles of important regional actors in Lebanon's post-Ta'if environment—the Palestinians, Israel, and Syria—as well as Lebanon's future relationship with the United States. Paul Salem introduces Part 2 with a reflective look at the relationship between Lebanon's national security and its foreign policy. Salem assesses Lebanon's past foreign policy predicament (and the multiplicity of foreign policies spawned by substate actors) before analyzing how Ta'if has modified this predicament. Demonstrating how Lebanon's foreign policy, domestic policy, and future stability remain integrally linked, Salem cautions that careful management is needed lest Lebanon's post-Ta'if foreign policy spark sharp domestic disturbances, and so unravel the peace.

Rex Brynen and Rosemary Sayigh both deal with a set of actors who are significant in Lebanon's landscape, but about which the Ta'if Accord is silent: the Palestinians. Ironically, the one thing that most Palestinians in Lebanon share with most Lebanese is the desire that Palestinian refugees "go home." However, given the settlements likely to emerge from the regional peace talks, fulfillment of this shared desire is doubtful at best. Return to their original villages is highly dubious (most fled from the Galilee region of present-day Israel); and return to a newly autonomous West Bank and Gaza is far from guaranteed. Thus, it is probable that a large Palestinian community will remain in Lebanon for some time. Rex Brynen focuses on the changing political dimension of Palestinian-Lebanese relations, elucidating the three main factors that shape it: Lebanese attitudes toward the Palestinian movement, the evolution of PLO strategy and aims, and the shifting currents of regional politics. Examining the present and future uncertainty of the Palestinian-Lebanese political dynamic, Brynen emphasizes the Palestinians' vulnerability in Lebanon: Their weak political position is compounded by extreme socioeconomic disadvantage. Rosemary Sayigh tackles this latter issue—the status and future of the Palestinians in Lebanon—with a useful socioeconomic profile of their situation. By highlighting their lack of rights and their deteriorating situation, Sayigh raises perplexing issues that Lebanese authorities will inevitably have to face.

Israel's influence over Lebanon is not what it was a decade ago. Nevertheless, it still occupies a self-declared "security zone" in South Lebanon and engages in fairly frequent attacks against Hizballah and Palestinian targets. Don Peretz's historical overview of Israel's involvement in Lebanon notes that Israel's foreign policy makers have always been divided over their objectives there. He identifies four main factors that, in different combinations, have shaped Israeli actions with respect to Lebanon: security of Israel's northern border, alliances with the Maronite community, Israel's relations with Syria, and Lebanon's water resources. Peretz focuses on the regional and security dimension of Israel's current interest in Lebanon, leaving the issue of Lebanon's water resources to a later chapter (Amery and Kubursi in Part 3).

Although a number of contributors deal with Syria's post-Ta'if presence in Lebanon (e.g., Maila, Salem, Saidi, Norton), As'ad Abukhalil looks at the motives behind that presence and outlines its basic characteristics. He contends that Syria's interventions in Lebanon were propelled not by expansionist dreams, but by the Syrian regime's obsession with maintaining control over what was happening in Lebanon, and he suggests how, in post-Ta'if Lebanon, this goal has been comprehensively realized.

In the final chapter of Part 2, Michael Hudson considers the future of relations between Lebanon and the United States. Reviewing the evolution of this relationship, Hudson observes that its rekindling will take some effort, given the extreme reversal in the 1980s. He contends, however, that this effort is in Lebanon's best interest, given that in the post–Cold War, post–Gulf War world, the United States is the "key external actor . . . shaping Lebanon's future." Hudson is optimistic that Lebanon can recreate itself in American eyes, but underlines the importance of internal reconciliation, reform, and leadership in this task.

The Ta'if Accord speaks directly of the need for extensive socioeconomic and administrative reform. As Ta'if brought greater security, it also induced increased rhetoric about the need to reconstruct the country for *all*

Lebanese. However, as one skeptic notes, "Despite all the talk of economic regeneration, the Lebanese were left holding the invisible hand in 1992."[15] All contributors to Part 3 make a compelling case for transforming the rhetoric into reality.

Hassan Charif describes how Lebanon's outlying regions (to the north, east, and south of Beirut) were left out of the socioeconomic mainstream following the country's creation in 1920. Emphasizing that this neglect was a principal factor contributing to the 1975 war, he argues that Lebanon's goal now must be to correct its past mistakes: reconstruction must not focus solely on Beirut at the expense of outlying regions. Charif concludes with recommendations for regional development actions and policies that would ensure Lebanon's sustained restabilization.

Expanding the scope of Charif's discussion, Ahmed Sbaiti reflects on Lebanon's prewar socioeconomic imbalances, its wartime reconstruction attempts, and its future reconstruction imperatives. He focuses on the role of the Council for Development and Reconstruction (created by the Lebanese government in 1976), reviewing its proven weaknesses and strengths before outlining the challenges it now faces in postwar Lebanon. He concludes that Lebanon's future stability can only be achieved through comprehensive policies and programs that "balance reconstruction with development and economic recovery with some measure of public benefit."

Hussein Amery and Atif Kubursi substantiate this "stability-through-development" correlation with a hard look at the relationship between Lebanon's regional development needs, the Litani River's resources, and Israel's potential designs on these resources. Their analysis provides a concrete illustration of the linkage between the socioeconomic, political, and regional aspects of Lebanon's dilemmas. From Lebanon's perspective, they conclude, both political and socioeconomic imperatives preclude sharing water with Israel. They warn, however, that Israel's present and projected water needs indicate it may harbor a different agenda for the Litani's waters and that its continued occupation of South Lebanon could well be a function of hydrostrategic goals.

Rounding out Part 3, Nasser Saidi proposes a holistic program for Lebanon's successful modernization and reconstruction. Lasting peace, he asserts, must be grounded in the effective management of three sets of issues: those that gave rise to the war, those that emerged during the war, and those that will face Lebanon as it moves into the twenty-first century. Although touching on issues of political, social, and administrative reform, Saidi's focus is economic, reflecting his belief that "economic recovery and growth can act as the single most important unifying force in restoring Lebanon's battered national fabric." In addition to prescribing a rich array of reforms for addressing medium- and long-term economic policy issues, Saidi recommends strategies to ensure Lebanon's prosperous development in a changing regional context.

The final section of the book, Part 4, examines the manifold issues intrinsic to Lebanon's struggle for sociopolitical stability. Georges Corm begins with a penetrating look at the militia-orchestrated "war system" in Lebanon, exposing the totalitarian foundations of militia activities: their usurpation of state revenues; their use of sectarian-based terror against the population; and their creation of sectarian ghettos to "legitimize" their power bases. Corm's study shows that, in many ways, Lebanon's militia phenomenon was merely a horrific extension of the sectarian-based logic underpinning Lebanon's political system. The "brutal realism" of the Ta'if Accord, he notes, is that it rewards the champions of communal violence by formally inducting them into the government. Corm challenges this realism, asking why the Lebanese should be expected to ignore militia crimes against the population and, more important, questioning whether the communal identity of leaders guarantees their ability to effectively administer the state.

The remaining chapters undertake a more conceptual look at Lebanon's sociopolitical prerequisites for stability, examining the cardinal debate over Lebanon's sectarian-based political system. Raghid el-Solh introduces the conceptual debate with an analytical survey of perspectives on the relationship between religious identity and sense of citizenship in Lebanon. Whereas some analysts see Lebanon's confessional system as a wonder of democratic representation, others consider it the root of all Lebanon's suffering—producing weak government as well as perpetuating sectarian identification, politics, and agendas, rather than encouraging national allegiance, thus rendering Lebanon ripe for external interference. These different interpretations of Lebanon's political system, he observes, are related to the larger sociological question of the true social reality of Lebanon's social fabric: Is its sectarianism organic or fabricated, liberating or alienating? One's position on this question defines the parameters for further analysis, setting the limits and possibilities for one's views concerning the role of identity-based differences in causing the conflict, the means to achieve "democratic" governance in Lebanon (i.e., should it be based on the rights of sectarian groups or the rights of individual citizens?), the viability of the Lebanese state, and the prescriptions for changes to ensure future stability. El-Solh's framework provides a backdrop to the chapters that follow.

Mahmoud Ayoub argues that plans for Lebanon's future stability should not require the abolition of religion from the people's daily lives. Focusing on the evolution of the Maronite community in Lebanon, he argues that Lebanon's sectarian difficulties are largely the result of a long history of outside interference that destroyed the social mosaic of Middle Eastern society: It is not diversity of religious belief that caused Lebanon's troubles, but manipulation of these beliefs that pitted one communal group against another. Ayoub agrees to the abolition of political sectarianism, but contends that this should not translate into Lebanon's secularization or Westernization.

Reflecting on means to consolidate Lebanon's fragile peace, Salim el-Hoss (a former prime minister) asserts that the road to future stability "can only be a democratic one." His analysis suggests that democracy—defined as the constitutional, legal, and institutional framework for the exercise of freedoms in a society—is what Lebanon needs, but has yet to attain. Lebanon, he argues, has never been truly democratic. Rather, the country's political system was riddled with antidemocratic features: unequal opportunity, lack of resilience, and the near-complete absence of political accountability. El-Hoss concludes with recommendations he believes will set Lebanon firmly on the road to peace through political deconfessionalization and comprehensive encouragement of democratic development.

Daoud Khairallah resolutely propounds that political deconfessionalization alone will not secure Lebanon's future. He highlights the dual aspects of confessionalism that underly its embodiment in both the political and the judicial systems: "Personal status laws, and the institutions through which these laws are applied, are under the exclusive control of the religious authorities of Lebanon's seventeen officially recognized sects." If democracy is to take root, he argues, complete secularization of both the political and judicial systems must occur; otherwise, the different personal status laws will continue to "cement the individual to his sect" and prohibit the emergence of a coherent sense of citizenship among Lebanese: "Only secular democracy can provide a guarantee against the recurrence of fratricide."

Samir Khalaf considers the prospects for Lebanon's sociopolitical stability through a slightly different lens: the restoration of civility in Lebanon. Khalaf focuses on two disturbing symptoms resulting from the legacy of psychosocial trauma suffered during the war: "retribalization" and "collective amnesia." Exploring ways by which these psychosocial wounds can be healed, Khalaf contends that the reconstitution of Lebanon's society is "much too vital to be left to politicians and vengeful militias." Rather, the process of transcending the disintegrative effects of the war requires broader talents. Khalaf points to both culture and urban design as tools for restructuring Lebanon's pluralism and reconstituting its political tolerance.

In the final chapter I reflect on what our authors have to say about peace for Lebanon. While acknowledging the important external factors that will definitely affect Lebanon's quest for peace, I argue that these are largely beyond the control of the Lebanese. My focus, therefore, is on Lebanon's domestic environment and the issue identified by our authors as vital to Lebanon's move toward a more stable sociopolitical order: deconfessionalization of its political system. My purpose is to render more explicit some of the differing ideas raised by our authors in Part 4, to explore their positions on the relationship between deconfessionalization and democratization, and, in so doing, to offer some perspective on Lebanon's prospects for realizing these objectives.

Lebanon's newfound calm furnishes opportunities to begin the process of fixing, healing, and developing for lasting stability. This process, however, will be both fragile and lengthy. Our purpose here is to illuminate some of the complex issues confronting Lebanon as it embarks on the precarious journey from protracted war to enduring peace.

NOTES

1. See the chapter by Maila in this volume.

2. For important works in English see: Michael Hudson, *The Precarious Republic: Political Modernization in Lebanon* (New York: Random House, 1968); Walid Khalidi, *Conflict and Violence in Lebanon: Confrontation in the Middle East* (Cambridge, Mass.: Center for International Affairs, Harvard University, 1979); Marius Deeb, *The Lebanese Civil War* (New York: Praeger Publishers, 1980); Samir Khalaf, *Lebanon's Predicament* (New York: Columbia University Press, 1987); Kamal Salibi, *A House of Many Mansions* (Los Angeles: University of California Press, 1990); and Robert Fisk, *Pity the Nation: Lebanon at War,* 2nd ed. (London: Andre Deutsch, 1992). Two particularly useful edited volumes are Nadim Shehadi and Dana Mills (eds.), *Lebanon: A History of Conflict and Consensus* (London: Centre for Lebanese Studies, I. B. Taurus and Co., 1988); and Halim Barakat (ed.), *Toward a Viable Lebanon* (Washington: Croom Helm in association with Center for Contemporary Arab Studies, Georgetown University, 1988).

3. These four aspects were the ones identified (and more or less accepted) by most CIIPS workshop participants, although participants held different opinions concerning the relative importance of each aspect. The overview in this introduction is grounded in the discussion contained in the institute's workshop report, *Peace for Lebanon: Obstacles, Challenges, Prospects,* Working Paper no. 43 (Ottawa: CIIPS, May 1992).

4. Lebanon's present international borders were drawn in 1920 when France added to Mount Lebanon the contiguous Ottoman provinces to the north, south, and east. Discussion of the historical factors influencing different domestic perceptions within this new Lebanon can be found in the chapters by Charif, Ayoub, and Salem in this volume. For extensive discussion see Kamal Salibi, *A House of Many Mansions.*

5. See Kamal Salibi, *A House of Many Mansions.* It is important to emphasize that not all Maronites feared Lebanon's independence or were pro-West in their outlook.

6. For further detail on this interplay, see the chapter by Salem in this volume.

7. In the first Arab-Israeli war of 1948, many Palestinians crossed the border to take refuge in Lebanon; a second wave followed in 1967. After the 1967 war and the 1969 Cairo Accord, Palestinian armed organizations became increasingly active in Lebanon, launching raids into Israel across Lebanon's border.

8. See the chapters by Salem and by el-Solh in this volume.

9. Under the French Mandate, Christians enjoyed the status of a political majority; Muslims were designated a political minority. After independence, the

confessional system allotted political power according to the demographic weight of Lebanon's principal sects, blurring this Christian-Muslim political divide: Maronite Christians came first, followed by Sunni Muslims, Shi'ite Muslims, Greek Orthodox Christians, Druze, and so on.

10. See the chapters in Part 4, as well as those by Faris, Maila, Salem, and Saidi.

11. Formed in 1976, the Lebanese Front was a conservative, predominantly Maronite Christian coalition whose members included Pierre Gemayel's Phalange Party and Camille Chamoun's National Liberal Party. The Lebanese Front did have some support from certain sectors of the traditional Muslim leadership, especially those who opposed the radical changes advocated by the Lebanese National Movement (see note 12). The militias of the groups comprising the Lebanese Front officially united in 1976 as the Lebanese Forces. For detailed discussion see Raymond G. Helmick, "Internal Lebanese Politics: The Lebanese Front and Forces," in Halim Barakat (ed.), *Toward a Viable Lebanon,* pp. 307–323.

12. The Lebanese National Movement was a broad-based, multisectarian coalition (encompassing groups of various ideological orientations) led by Kamal Jumblatt, a Druze leader and head of the Progressive Socialist Party (PSP). Many of its members came out of the Muslim left, although it initially also had a significant Christian membership.

13. An important exception was President Fouad Shehab's major socioeconomic reform program following the 1958 civil war.

14. In 1975 some factions saw war as the only way to change an unfair political system that could not accommodate change from within. See the chapter by Faris and the final chapter by Collings in this volume.

15. Michael Young, "Rewinding Lebanon in 1992," *The Lebanon Report* vol. 4 no. 1 (January 1993), p. 4.

Part 1

·

From War to the "Peace" of Ta'if: Reconciliation Attempts, 1975–1992

1

The Failure of Peacemaking in Lebanon, 1975–1989

Hani A. Faris

"Lebanization" refers to a process whose outcome is the total collapse of state authority and the disintegration of civic society into a Hobbesian state of nature. The media have often employed the term to describe conditions in Iraq, Afghanistan, Bosnia-Herzegovina, Somalia, and some of the former Soviet republics. Not long ago, however, Lebanon appeared a relatively stable, essentially democratic society whose citizens enjoyed a high degree of individual freedom. Many observers considered its social system to be resilient, capable of coping with the challenges of development and modernization. The radical transformation that took place raises two fundamental questions: (1) Why did the political process fail to arrest or contain the violence that erupted and (2) What were the conflict issues and societal forces responsible for destabilizing the political order? This chapter examines Lebanon's traditional mechanisms for dealing with conflict, and argues that they served only to mitigate overt conflict by containing divisive issues rather than resolving them; traditional means of conflict avoidance had inherent limitations that rendered them incapable of coping with new challenges. The chapter then examines the major peace initiatives undertaken during the fifteen years of war and explores why they failed to settle the conflict.

MITIGATING CONFLICT BEFORE THE WAR: COMPROMISE AND CONTAINMENT

The National Pact of 1943, an unwritten agreement between Maronite leader Bishara al-Khoury and Sunni leader Riad al-Solh, laid the foundation of modern Lebanon. The pact's authors committed their respective

17

communities not to seek alliances with, or protection from, Western powers, and not to involve the country in any merger schemes with other Arab entities. Lebanon was to participate in the collective Arab and international systems without compromising its autonomy. Al-Khoury and al-Solh also reconfirmed certain sectarian-based political practices, assigning the post of president to a Maronite and that of prime minister to a Sunni, and distributing electoral seats and appointments to the civil service and the cabinet according to sectarian proportions.[1] Essentially, the Lebanese political system (as envisioned by its architects) would promote stability through accommodation, representation, and co-optation: it would reconcile the two opposing orientations within the country over the issues of identity and foreign policy, stabilize expectations among the sects by defining the manner in which power was to be distributed, and co-opt the leadership of the various sects through a system of power sharing based on sectarian representation.

These three principles—accommodation, representation, and an overarching cross-sectarian elite—allowed the country to proceed to independence, and contributed to its relative stability during the next three decades.[2] In retrospect, however, these fundamental principles failed to provide a sufficiently strong basis on which to build a viable entity. Although they succeeded in containing overt conflict for a time, ultimately they were unable to moderate or resolve the underlying issues that produced social conflict (as post-1975 developments attest). Each of the three principles had limited utility in dealing with emerging challenges in Lebanon and in the region.

The principle of accommodation defined what policies should not be followed without providing direction as to the policies Lebanon should pursue.[3] In the absence of a national consensus, the intent was to bypass differences over fundamental issues in order to allow the various groups to collaborate in the struggle for independence. When independence was achieved, the continued success of this policy of avoidance was predicated on two conditions being met at all times, namely, that the Lebanese refrain from invoking their differences over fundamental issues, and that regional and international powers refrain from exploiting these differences as a means to influence the country's foreign policy orientations or internal makeup. By the mid-1970s, both conditions were being seriously violated.

Similarly, the policy of sectarian representation outlived its utility as a stabilizing force: by the late 1960s, the policy itself had become a source of instability. Originally, it had been adopted as a temporary measure, to calm the fears prevalent among Lebanese Maronites that their security, identity and status would be jeopardized in a united and independent Lebanon divorced from France.[4] The policy also had an additional benefit. By allowing representatives of all sects to participate in government, it helped ensure their loyalty, and that of their followers, to the new entity.

Following the country's independence, this policy, which was supposed to serve as a transitional measure, assumed a life of its own. Communal associations, political parties, and leaders with clear sectarian agendas flourished, increasingly appropriating to themselves the role of intermediary between the citizen and the state. They also exploited governmental structures to promote the use of a citizen's sectarian affiliation as his primary source of identification. Gradually, appointments to all levels of government became governed by fixed sectarian quotas. The policy of sectarian representation became a vehicle for privilege and corruption, and produced a rigid political organization incapable of adapting to changing circumstances. As demographic changes radically altered the sectarian proportions of the Lebanese population, the 1926 arrangements for sectarian representation became outdated. Gradually, the sectarian political system became less fair and less representative; its legitimacy eroded as it held stubbornly to old formulas.

Likewise, the political elite was not suited to dealing with the issues that fueled the 1975 crisis. Traditionally, this elite had played a key role in settling differences. It had helped mitigate incipient conflicts by venting sectarian frustrations and demands (without undermining the sectarian system), by providing services to citizens (bypassing bureaucratic rigidity), and by channeling government benefits to followers and regions. Overall, this elite had facilitated the integration of Lebanese society through their shared attitudes and approach to politics. By the late 1960s and early 1970s, however, a process of rapid social change in Lebanon was undermining the elite's role. As a nondoctrinaire group, its members were ill-equipped to counter the effects of the ideological movements that spread in a dramatic fashion throughout the Arab world following the 1967 Arab defeat. The activities of these movements led to the maturation of a new, multireligious, secular, alienated, and activist counterelite, opposed to Lebanon's political arrangements, but debarred from participation in the formal system.[5] The emergence of this counterelite weakened the support base of the traditional elite, especially among Lebanese Muslims. Meanwhile, widespread corruption in Suleiman Frangieh's administration further eroded the traditional elite's image and effectiveness. With few exceptions, most traditional leaders became a marginal force shortly after the start of the war when they failed to agree on a course of action to deal with the crisis and, in the process, lost their former solidarity.

An inexorable impetus toward the outbreak of violence was developing by the spring of 1975. Two sets of deeply dividing conflict issues were creating concurrent, superimposed, and mutually reinforcing cleavages. The first set related to Lebanon's domestic problems: socioeconomic imbalances, regional disparities, sectarian rivalries, and ideological conflicts that had been simmering for a number of years.[6] The assassination on 25 February 1975 of Ma'rouf Sa'd, a former member of Parliament and local

Sunni leader in Sidon, was indicative of the explosive nature of these unresolved and interrelated issues.[7] The incident was followed by widespread
disturbances and clashes between Lebanese Army units and armed civilians. Both public opinion and the traditional elite split over the role of the
military establishment. Traditionally, Muslims had been suspicious of the
army and opposed its use for internal security.[8] The resurfacing of this controversy in public life undermined the state's ability to restore public order.
The voices demanding a redefinition of the country's power distribution
arrangements grew louder.

The second set of conflict issues involved Lebanese-Palestinian relations. After 1967, Lebanon had become a major support base for
Palestinian activism.[9] Repeated attempts by the Lebanese Army to break
the Palestinians' power and bring them under its control (for example, in
April 1969 and May 1973), in combination with Israel's unrelenting and
vastly destructive military raids on Palestinian refugee camps, prompted
the Palestinians to form alliances with Lebanese opposition forces in order
to secure their presence in Lebanon. These alliances inevitably led to hostilities with the Maronite establishment, which feared that the Palestinian
presence was threatening the balance of power in the country.

The dust had not yet settled on the Sidon incident when an incident in
the Beirut suburb of 'Ayn al-Rumaneh (13 April 1975) sparked massive
clashes between the Phalangist militia and the Palestinians. These clashes
caused the various Lebanese factions to take sides and to be drawn into the
fighting. Gradually, a schism developed in Lebanese society between pro-
and anti-Palestinian resistance organizations, which was superimposed in
turn on a longstanding, unresolved issue that had divided the Lebanese
since independence: Lebanon's identity and role in the region and the
extent of its "Arab" obligations. Thus, long-simmering domestic disagreements over Lebanon's identity and foreign policy—disagreements that
Lebanon's traditional mechanisms for dealing with conflict had contained,
but never resolved—erupted into the open. Lebanese political movements
split between two coalitions: the "progressive" Lebanese National
Movement (LNM) and the "conservative" Lebanese Front (LF).[10] Each
side, fearing destruction at the hands of the other, forged external alliances
to support its political and military programs. In the process, foreign powers exploited Lebanon's factionalized body politic to promote their own
interests.

ATTEMPTS AT PEACEMAKING, 1975–1989

The Lebanese war raged for the next fifteen years. Scores of attempts to
settle the conflict were initiated during this time. There were peace confer-

ences at both local and regional levels, and foreign powers were involved in mediation efforts. Attempts at settlement ranged in form and substance from unilateral to multilateral, formal to informal, short- to long-lived, and piecemeal to comprehensive. Some sought genuine reconciliation among the various warring factions; others promoted plans that imposed conditions favorable to their foreign sponsors; still others were empty gestures; all failed.

The most serious attempts to settle the conflict merit analysis. They were the National Dialogue Committee (1975), the Constitutional Document (1976), the Arab summit conferences at Riyadh and Cairo (1976), the Geneva-Lausanne Conference (1983, 1984) and the Damascus Tripartite Agreement (1985).

The National Dialogue Committee, 25 September–24 November 1975

The National Dialogue Committee, formed at Syria's prodding following a highly destructive and inconclusive round of fighting, comprised prominent traditional sectarian leaders and a small number of noncontroversial, accomplished professionals.[11] From the start, however, the committee faced two insurmountable obstacles: the inability of its members to agree upon a common agenda, and the collapse of elite solidarity, traditionally a vital component for conflict avoidance.

Lacking a clearly defined mission, mandate, or agenda, committee members had totally different expectations. The veteran Maronite politicians wanted the committee to reestablish law and order in Lebanon, thereby postponing consideration of any proposal to introduce serious domestic reforms; they continued to deny the need for change in the country's constitutional arrangements. Their position seems to have been based on the consideration that the outcome of any negotiations with the traditional Muslim leaders or the LNM to change the political system would not be in their favor unless the Palestinian armed presence in Lebanon was ended. In retrospect, it seems that at the time the committee was meeting, Maronite leaders were hopeful that their militias, with the support of the army and external allies, could effect a favorable military outcome to the conflict. The veteran Muslim politicians, on the other hand, insisted on the priority of reform. Many of these leaders had lost much status and prestige in their communities to a counterelite, the LNM.[12] Thus, traditional Muslim leaders could only justify their participation in the committee if they obtained meaningful concessions from the Maronite politicians on longstanding demands for a new power-sharing arrangement. In other words, the success of the committee depended on the willingness of traditional leaders on both sides to compromise, and on their ability to reach consensus concerning fundamental issues such as identity, secularization, and power sharing—

issues they had not been able to agree on before. Needless to say, circumstances in the country did not favor such an outcome.

A second obstacle to the committee's success was its membership. The conferees were asked to find a way out of a crisis that was, to some extent, of their own making. Some of them, such as Pierre Gemayel, Camille Chamoun, and Kamal Jumblatt, were leaders of militias and broad coalitions that had already chosen to fight out rather than peacefully resolve their disagreements, and were determined to bypass the governmental apparatus. The success of the committee was predicated on their cooperation, which was not forthcoming. The elite solidarity that had allowed for consensual politics in earlier times had cracked, and the committee was fated to fail.

Although the committee met in nine sessions and formed three subcommittees to deal with political, financial, and socioeconomic reforms, it proved an exercise in futility. It was dubbed a dialogue of the deaf with participants talking at, rather than to, each other. They were not able to agree on a single substantive issue. A close reading of the committee minutes indicates that neither side had the intent of breaking the deadlock: each was convinced that it would prevail on the battleground. The committee disbanded, leaving the country to face an uncertain future.

The Constitutional Document, 14 February 1976

Military offensives and counteroffensives waged in January 1976 resulted in the rough demarcation of boundaries in a de facto partitioning of Lebanon. This formed the backdrop to the Constitutional Document. In addition to battle lines, the January events defined the array of forces on both sides. Maronite militias, backed by the Lebanese Army, faced an armed alliance made up of the LNM militias, Palestinian armed organizations, and Syrian irregulars (i.e., units of the Palestine Liberation Army [PLA] and Sai'qa dispatched by Syria). Maronite leaders, confronted by this open alliance between the LNM and the Palestinians, and concerned about the possibility of alienating Syria, decided to concede to some reforms championed by the traditional Muslim leaders. In return, the Maronite leaders demanded guarantees from Syria that PLO activities in Lebanon would be curtailed. Accordingly, with the knowledge of the country's sectarian leaders, a reform program was worked out between President Frangieh and Syrian foreign minister Khaddam. This seventeen point program, announced by President Frangieh on 14 February, became known as the Constitutional Document.[13]

The compromise embodied in the Constitutional Document set the tone for all succeeding discussions of constitutional change.[14] It upheld the sectarian distribution for the three posts of president, prime minister, and speaker of parliament, but proposed that parliamentary seats be distributed equally between Christians and Muslims (i.e., it proposed to replace the 6:5

ratio that favored the Christians with an equal 5:5 ratio). Moreover, it called for the election of the prime minister by a simple parliamentary majority, the election of the president by a parliamentary majority of 55 percent (after the first ballot), and abolition of the sectarian distribution of government jobs (except for senior civil service posts, which would be divided equally between Muslims and Christians). In light of these reforms, the document suggested amending the electoral law to ensure better representation for all citizens, and called for decentralization of the civil administration. Finally, the document provided for establishment of a supreme council for the trial of presidents and ministers, a supreme constitutional court to decide on constitutionality of laws and ministerial decrees, and a higher council for planning and development.

The Constitutional Document's significance lies in the compromise it proposed: Christians would relinquish some of their powers in return for consent by the Muslims to maintain the confessional system and not to demand a share of political power commensurate with their demographic majority. This compromise formula was challenged twice. First, it was rejected by Kamal Jumblatt, who sought the total secularization of the political system. Later, it was opposed by Bashir Gemayel, who wanted to secure a position of unchallenged hegemony for the Maronite community. Both figures were assassinated, and the formula survived. Although never enshrined in law, the Constitutional Document established the direction and parameters for a future agreement.

The conflict settlement plan envisioned by the document had a major flaw. It did not provide a credible mechanism for enforcing its provisions; rather, it assumed that the authority of the president, the institutions of the state, and the backing of the traditional elite would be sufficient. All three traditional power brokers, however, had been seriously weakened. Moreover, the document was not approved by the LNM, the most powerful force inside Lebanon at the time. The opposition of Gemayel as well as Jumblatt sealed the Constitutional Document's fate.

The Riyadh-Cairo Arab Summit Conferences, October 1976

Prior to the Syrian Army's entry into Lebanon in June 1976, the LNM and the PLO opposed efforts of the Lebanese Front leadership to involve Arab and Western powers. The LNM felt that internationalization of mediation efforts would relieve the pressure on the Lebanese Front to offer meaningful concessions. Following Syria's military intervention on behalf of the Lebanese Front and the mending of Syrian-Egyptian relations,[15] a summit meeting attended by Saudi Arabia, Kuwait, Egypt, Syria, Lebanon, and the PLO was convened in Riyadh to consider the Lebanese conflict and the crisis in Syrian-Palestinian relations. Decisions taken at the Riyadh Summit were endorsed by a full Arab Summit conference held in Cairo.[16]

The two summits established a sizeable Arab Deterrent Force (ADF) to assist the Lebanese government in reasserting its authority. A committee composed of representatives from Syria, Egypt, Saudi Arabia, and Kuwait was formed to supervise the application of the 1969 Cairo Agreement between Lebanon and the PLO. In addition, it was decided that the combatants should declare an immediate cease-fire, withdraw to pre-April 1975 positions, and surrender their heavy weapons to the ADF. Although the summits called on the Lebanese to reconcile their differences, they did not offer any substantive recommendations.

The Riyadh-Cairo resolutions assumed that an Arab consensus and the formation of the ADF would effectively dissuade Arab governments from supporting local factions and would provide the Lebanese government with a credible military force stronger than any combination of Lebanese and Palestinian paramilitary organizations. After a promising start, two developments undermined this assumption: Sadat's trip to Jerusalem in November 1977 and the Lebanese Forces' expanded collaboration with Israel. The Arab world viewed Sadat's trip and the Camp David agreements as achieving U.S. and Israeli policy objectives, namely, to have Egypt conclude a separate peace with Israel and abandon its responsibilities concerning the Arab-Israeli conflict and the Palestinian issue. This situation, in turn, led the Syrian leadership to mend relations with the PLO while its relations with the Lebanese Forces deteriorated. Syrian contingents of the ADF began to clash frequently with the Lebanese Forces and the Lebanese Army. Israel's March 1978 invasion and its creation of a "security zone" in South Lebanon ended all hopes for implementation of the Riyadh Summit's resolutions.

Throughout the next six years (1976–1982), various Arab summits attempted to revive an Arab peace plan for Lebanon. All attempts were thwarted, however, by both regional and internal developments. Regionally, Arab assistance to Lebanon depended upon the coordinated effort of key Arab states. However, the inter-Arab discord that accompanied the Camp David process devastated Lebanon's prospects for peace. This discord also limited the capability of the Arab system to insulate Lebanon from Israeli acts of aggression. Internally, the proliferation of actors made the task of reaching an agreement much more difficult.[17] As traditional leaders weakened, a younger, more militant generation emerged to assume leadership of the militias, and it was during this time that the "war system" in Lebanon became entrenched.[18]

The Geneva-Lausanne Conference,
31 October–4 November 1983 and 12–20 March 1984

In 1983, the signing of the Lebanese-Israeli May 17th Agreement left the Lebanese government in a predicament. The agreement had the support of the United States, but was rejected by a majority of Lebanese and strongly opposed by several Arab countries, especially Syria. Renouncing the agreement would strain relations with the United States and allow continued Israeli occupation of Lebanese territory. Its ratification, however, would renew the civil war and elicit a hostile Syrian response. To deal with the impasse, President Gemayel accepted a Saudi-Syrian initiative and formed a Committee for National Reconciliation composed of himself and nine other prominent political figures. Politically, the participants divided into four blocs: the Front for National Salvation (Rashid Karameh, Suleiman Frangieh, and Walid Jumblatt), the Lebanese Front (Camille Chamoun and Pierre Gemayel), the Amal Movement (Nabih Birri), and independents (Saeb Salam, Adel Osseiran, and Raymond Eddé).[19] With the exception of Nabih Birri (leader of the Amal militia) and Walid Jumblatt (who had succeeded his father as leader of the Progressive Socialist Party), the appointed members were longstanding veterans of the Lebanese establishment. Representatives from Syria and Saudi Arabia were also invited to attend. The participants were to discuss issues concerning Lebanon's identity, Israel's occupation, comprehensive reform measures, and the role of the military.[20]

From the outset, the Geneva meeting was stalemated. The Muslim participants and Frangieh, with encouragement from the Syrian representative, insisted on the abrogation of the May 17th Agreement and on forcing Israel's withdrawal before attending to Lebanon's domestic conflict issues. The meeting's only accomplishment was the definition, by consensus, of Lebanon's identity as an independent and sovereign Arab state.

During the Lausanne meeting, convened following the abrogation of the May 17th Agreement in March 1984, two visions of Lebanon were discussed. Members of the Lebanese Front proposed the establishment of a federal system composed of confessionally homogeneous units. Muslim participants submitted a joint settlement plan that proposed elimination of political sectarianism, administrative decentralization, limiting the powers of the president and expanding the powers of the council of ministers. Clearly, the leadership of the Lebanese Front was demanding political decentralization (a federal system) to counter the demands of the Muslim leadership for the elimination of political sectarianism. (Abolishment of political sectarianism would undermine the Maronite leaders' privileged status in the political system and relegate them to a minority position.) Similarly, Muslim participants were demanding the complete elimination of the sectarian system to counter the Maronite establishment's resistance to any reform. During the deliberations, it became evident that agreement was possible on a broad number of necessary reforms. Unfortunately, differences over the relative powers of the president, on the one hand, and the council of ministers and prime minister, on the other, prevented participants from approving an accord that could have settled the civil war. On this issue, participants divided along religious lines.[21]

The Geneva-Lausanne Conference was the only forum that Lebanon's leading political figures attended in person, and in which they had an opportunity to fully articulate their positions in uninterrupted negotiations. This occasion was also the closest that Lebanese leaders ever came to reaching an agreement. Although the conference disbanded without adopting a mutually acceptable agreement—testimony to the continued strength of sectarian rivalries and suspicions—the common ground between the various factions had expanded.

The Damascus Tripartite Agreement, 28 December 1985

The deadlock reached at Lausanne signaled an end to hopes for national dialogue and reconciliation at the hands of the traditional elite. Lebanon's most prominent oligarchs proved unable, or unwilling, to make the concessions required to resolve internal differences. In the aftermath of the Lausanne conference, fighting erupted on many fronts and among various factions, including former allies.[22] Syria attempted a new approach to peacemaking. The leaders of the three major militias, Elie Hobeiqa (Lebanese Forces), Nabih Birri (Amal), and Walid Jumblatt (PSP), met in Damascus to negotiate a settlement plan.

The resulting Tripartite Agreement departed radically from former peace plans in several areas, especially in its call for the abolition of the sectarian system and for the definition of a special relationship with Syria.[23] Following a transitional period, the sectarian system of representation in the legislative, executive, and judiciary branches of government would be totally abolished. Even the three highest offices—president, prime minister, and speaker of the parliament—would no longer be apportioned on a sectarian basis. A senate would be created, and each *mohafazah* would become an electoral district. With respect to Syria, the agreement considered the establishment of distinctive relations with Syria to be the test of Lebanon's "Arabism," and called for strategic complementarity between the two countries.

The Tripartite Agreement, however, was short-lived. Two weeks after its signing, Samir Ja'Ja' led a rebellion that removed Elie Hobeiqa from the leadership of the Lebanese Forces, and annulled the accord. Nevertheless, the plan's two new elements (phased abolition of sectarianism and special relations with Syria) became key issues that any future settlement would have to address.

CONCLUDING REMARKS

On 22 October 1989, the Lebanese Parliament adopted the Document of National Understanding, better known as the Ta'if Accord. Gradually, institutions of the state revived and a measure of stability and peace reappeared.

It took fifteen years of savage fighting and devastation of the country before a settlement agreement was implemented. Prior to Ta'if, various combinations of international, regional, and Lebanese domestic circumstances had contributed to the failure of every peacemaking effort. Internationally, the Cold War had exacerbated the conflict through competition between the two superpowers for influence in the Middle East. Regionally, landmark events such as the 1967 and 1973 wars with Israel, the 1970 civil war in Jordan, and the Camp David process had intensified inter-Arab quarrels; this had prompted some Arab governments, as well as Israel, to exploit the opportunities offered by Lebanon's factionalized body politic. Foreign sponsors had used Lebanese groups to promote their own narrow interests. Meanwhile, Lebanese factions had exploited Arab government infighting to forge external alliances to support their political and military programs. The whole country was victimized by this relationship between the regional powers and local groups.[24] Moreover, at times these foreign sponsorships played into the longstanding domestic disagreement over Lebanon's identity within the region (and its loyalties with respect to the Arab-Israeli-Palestinian conflict), further complicating the conflict.

Domestically, Lebanon's traditional mechanisms for dealing with conflict were no longer able to contain the interlocking conflict issues that surfaced during the 1967–1975 period. As the war unfolded, these issues became even more intractable because Lebanon's traditional elite became marginalized and the number of armed domestic actors (and their foreign sponsors) proliferated. Moreover, some leaders had a vested interest in continuing the conflict. Finally, the level of violence dramatically highlighted the need for internal reform, but also heightened sectarian consciousness and fears, which greatly hampered the Lebanese leaders' ability to agree on reforms or implement peace plans.

Following the outbreak of violence in 1975, Lebanese leaders were faced with three alternative courses of action concerning domestic political reform (the one area that they themselves could control): preservation of the status quo, abolishment of the sectarian system, or adoption of reform measures that would allow for some readjustment of power-sharing arrangements.[25] Championing of the first alternative was suicidal: it meant ignoring fundamental socioeconomic and demographic changes that could not be reversed. Advocating the second alternative in a crisis atmosphere proved to be unrealistic. The third alternative, which called for a negotiated compromise, eluded the feuding parties until the Ta'if Accord.

Ta'if became possible largely because of the relaxation of tensions at both the international and regional levels. Following the collapse of the Eastern bloc, the United States ceased to view the Lebanese conflict in the context of its confrontation with the Soviet Union. It was subsequently more willing to concede a role for Syria in Lebanon and less supportive of Israeli interventionist policies. At the regional level, the Arab League revived its peace initiative and secured the cooperation of Syria, Iraq, and Egypt with its efforts. Domestic developments were also important to the success of Ta'if. Lebanon's economy was rapidly deteriorating, threatening the welfare of all sectors and regions. Several key leaders advocating maximalist demands had passed from center stage. Some militias had lost their foreign sponsors, and most were weakened and exhausted by factionalization and infighting. Most also realized that no actor was capable of imposing its will on the others. Moreover, widespread domestic disenchantment with the militias increased the public's passive resistance to militia hegemony.

Although Ta'if is the first negotiated accord since 1975 that has endured, the settlement it embodies did not evolve in a vacuum; rather, it rests on principles discovered during the earlier, unsuccessful searches for peace. The Ta'if Accord, however, cannot be the final blueprint for a future Lebanon: The country still needs new political institutions and processes that promote social cohesion, that protect citizens rather than sectarian interests, if it is to avoid another descent into chaos. The people and their leaders need more than a Ta'if Accord if they are to prevent "Lebanization" from ravaging Lebanon again.

NOTES

1. Article 95 of the 23 May 1926 Constitution, promulgated under the French Mandate, institutionalized the latter arrangement; it was amended by the Chamber of Deputies on 9 October 1943.

2. The events of 1958 were a major exception to Lebanon's relative level of stability during this time.

3. See the chapter by Salem in this volume.

4. Prior to 1943, some Maronites feared the intensity of pan-Arab nationalist sentiment in the region and its possible implications for a newly independent Lebanon. The National Pact assuaged these fears by guaranteeing Maronite control over key political, security, and military positions in the new Lebanon. For detailed discussion, see Kamal Salibi, *A House of Many Mansions* (Los Angeles: University of California Press, 1990).

5. The political process essentially debarred secularists and opponents of the sectarian system from employment in the civil administration and the security services, and from membership in representative institutions. Recruitment to the civil service depended heavily on a candidate securing the *wasta* (patronage) of a traditional *za'im* (member of the elite). Understandably, the price for obtaining the wasta was political allegiance to the za'im and the establishment. Moreover, the electoral system was biased in favor of the country's politically established families. The use of the list system within multiple-seat electoral districts dominated by one sect helped to perpetuate political dominance by the traditional elite.

6. Further discussion of these issues can be found in other chapters by Salem, Charif, Sbaiti, Saidi, el-Solh, Ayoub, el-Hoss, Khairallah, and Norton in this volume.

7. Sa'd was assassinated while heading a demonstration staged by Sidon's local fishermen. The demonstrators were protesting the government's approval of a commercial fishing fleet operation that they feared would threaten their livelihood. Because former president Camille Chamoun, a Maronite from Mount Lebanon, was behind the new enterprise, the affair assumed regional, sectarian, and ideological dimensions in the assassination's aftermath, in addition to the original socioeconomic aspect.

8. Recruitment to the army, unlike that for other governmental agencies, was not subject to review by the Civil Service Council. Hiring practices had ensured an overrepresentation of Christians in the officer corps, a situation that aroused suspicion and fear among those Muslims who tended to view the army as a hostile institution intended to maintain and promote the interests of the Maronite establishment. In this context, the wisdom of General Fouad Shehab is noteworthy: His refusal to allow the army to intervene in the 1958 civil war in Lebanon saved the institution from disintegration and contributed to the country's speedy recovery. For an informative account of differences between Muslim and Christian politicians over the role and structure of the army during the administration of President Elias Sarkis, see Salim el-Hoss, *Zaman al-amal wa al-khaybah: Tajarib al-hukum ma bayna 1976 wa 1980* (The Time of Hope and Disillusionment: Experiences in Government Between 1976 and 1980) (Beirut: Dar al-'ilm lil malayeen, 1992), pp. 97–132.

9. For further discussion of the Palestinians in Lebanon see chapters by Brynen and Sayigh in this volume.

10. A brief statement of this complicated issue can be found in the introduction to this volume.

11. The minutes of the meetings were published in *al-Tariq,* nos. 1–8 (January–August 1976).

12. The Lebanese National Movement had succeeded in establishing a strong presence in most areas outside the control of the Lebanese Forces.

13. For the Arabic text of the Constitutional Document, see *al-Nahar,* 15 February 1976. For an English translation, see Walid Khalidi, *Conflict and Violence in Lebanon,* Appendix 11 (Cambridge, Mass.: Harvard Center for International Affairs, 1979), pp. 189–191.

14. See also Hani Faris, "Political Institutions of the Lebanese Republic," in Altaf Gauhar (ed.), *Third World Affairs, 1988* (London: Third World Foundation for Social and Economic Studies, 1989), p. 137.

15. Syrian-Egyptian relations deteriorated shortly after the Arab-Israeli war of October 1973 and ended when Sadat—ignoring Syrian security interests—agreed to negotiate the disengagement of forces on the Egyptian front with the United States and Israel. In the three years that followed, Syria and Egypt supported different factions within Lebanon.

16. For the text of the resolutions adopted at the Riyadh and Cairo summits see *al-Nahar,* 18 and 27 October 1976.

17. In the 1976–1982 period, the Lebanese Forces militia rebelled against the authority of the Lebanese Front, while the Shi'ite Amal militia (the military wing of the Movement of the Deprived) declined to join the National Movement. Meanwhile, various local leaders established separate militias to pursue their own agendas.

18. For further discussion of the "war system" see the chapter by Corm in this volume.

19. Eddé declined membership in the committee and did not attend any of its meetings.

20. The minutes of the Geneva-Lausanne Conference are published in *Geneva-Lausanne: al-mahadir al-siriya al-kamila* (Geneva-Lausanne: The Complete Secret Minutes) (Beirut: al-markaz al 'arabi lil-ma'lumat, 1984).

21. Frangieh sided with the Lebanese Front on this issue although he was politically allied with Karameh and Jumblatt.

22. See the chronology in this volume.

23. For the text of the Damascus Tripartite Agreement, see *al-Nahar,* 29 December 1985.

24. This explains why some refer to the Lebanese war as a series of proxy wars.

25. Of course, reform of the sectarian system was not the only difficulty facing the Lebanese, but it was perhaps the issue that the Lebanese had the most control over in terms of resolving (unlike the issue of the Palestinians, for example). Many analysts agree that the sectarian system was a significant factor in the prolongation and destructiveness of the war, because of its relationship to foreign sponsorship of Lebanese militias (see the chapters by Salem, Corm, and Khairallah in this volume). Had the Lebanese been able to reform their system themselves, they might have curtailed their proclivity to seek foreign sponsors, and the conflict might well have been defused at an earlier date.

2

The Ta'if Accord:
An Evaluation

Joseph Maila

The Document of National Understanding concluded in al-Ta'if, Saudi Arabia on 22 October 1989 occupies an important place in the history of modern Lebanon. The Ta'if Accord did more than end Lebanon's fifteen-year war by establishing the internal conditions for peace; it also implicated important regional and international players—specifically Israel, Syria, and the members of the United Nations Security Council. The regional and international dimensions of the Lebanese conflict, which substantially compounded the seriousness and tragic human consequences of the war, serve to underline the particularity and importance of the Document of National Understanding agreed to by the Lebanese deputies.

The Ta'if Accord, however, is not as innovative and original as some may believe. Certain of its basic assumptions are far from new.[1] Indeed, Lebanese history is replete with pacts, accords, and agreements that attempted to achieve an intercommunal equilibrium.[2] The Ta'if Accord embraces this consensual, sectarian logic, and accepts its dictates concerning the necessity and value of procedures that distribute public offices among the various communities, that provide the communities with a veto, and that regulate conflicting sectarian interests. In this way, the Ta'if Accord is rooted in a well-established "tradition" that renders Lebanon more of a contractual, consociative country than one based on a constitution. According to this tradition, the formal, legal framework is always subordinate to a pragmatic, consensual approach to mitigating conflict within the country, and to managing national and communal strains.

Fifteen years of war did not alter this equation or this particular political culture; this is perhaps the war's major lesson. If one community had emerged victorious during the war, it would probably have signaled the end of Lebanon's communal contract; presumably, the victorious community

31

would have claimed dominance over the others by virtue of its military and political superiority. The verdict of Lebanon's many battles, however, was always "no victor, no vanquished." Maintaining the peace, therefore, was and is a matter of maintaining a balance—of sharing power—and of preserving the rights of communities that view themselves as the bedrock on which the Lebanese state is constructed. The Ta'if Accord embodies this general philosophy.

A DIFFICULT BIRTH

Although the war did not banish faith in the need to "balance" Lebanon's communities, it did upset the balance. Restoration and redefinition of Lebanon's equilibrium required numerous attempts to devise proposals for reconciliation—all of which failed—before the warring communities finally accepted a proposal for communal compromise (despite their laborious struggle to destroy the compromise option).[3]

As far as immediate factors are concerned, the Ta'if Accord sprang from the conjunction of three major failures: the failure of General Aoun's war of liberation against Syria; the failure of Syria to impose a solution acceptable to all of Lebanon's communities, especially the Maronite Christians; and finally, the failure of attempts to resolve the conflict through international intervention.

Had General Aoun succeeded in his uprising against Syrian forces in Lebanon at a time when he was interim leader (though his authority was contested by the former prime minister, Salim el-Hoss), the Ta'if Accord might never have materialized. Aoun's recourse to arms, however, proved ineffective on both the military and diplomatic levels. On the military front, General Aoun's Lebanese Army units, supported at that time by the Lebanese Forces militia, could not match Syrian firepower. On the diplomatic level, international outrage—expected to force a Syrian retreat— failed to materialize. Moreover, Aoun further miscalculated when he concluded that Lebanese Muslims would rally to his call for a war of liberation against Syria. Internally, Lebanon remained a country of communitarian alliances rather a community of alliances.

Paradoxically, the second major failure leading to Ta'if was Syria's. Syria was not, of course, defeated by General Aoun and his followers, but events in the spring of 1989 foiled its longstanding objective of transforming Lebanon into a Syrian protectorate.

Syria did not fully articulate its objectives toward Lebanon until the 1983 Tripartite Agreement.[4] A Syrian-sponsored treaty between Lebanon's main militia leaders, the agreement provided firsthand clarification of the Syrian-approved vision of Lebanon. Point by point, Syria's preferences were clearly pronounced: the expected "privileged relations," the strategic, economic, social, and cultural "complementarity" of the two countries, and the expected stationing of Syrian troops. Implementation of the Tripartite Agreement, however, never materialized, as tumult inside the Lebanese Forces militia compelled its abrogation.[5] This turn of events scuttled Syria's attempt to settle and normalize its relations with Lebanon free of any third-party intervention.

By 1988, Syria's free hand in Lebanon had become somewhat curtailed by other Arab regional players who took active interest in Lebanon's predicament. When the Lebanese Parliament failed to elect a successor to President Amine Gemayel, the resulting power vacuum prompted the Arab League to intervene once again in Lebanese affairs. The league turned the Lebanese question over to a commission chaired by Kuwait, effectively side-stepping Syria.

When General Aoun declared his war of liberation against Syria on 14 March 1989, he set in motion events that led directly to the resolutions adopted by Arab leaders at the Casablanca Summit on 26–29 May 1989. These resolutions provided for creation of a Tripartite Arab High Commission comprising the kings of Morocco and Saudi Arabia and the president of Algeria; notably, Syria was excluded. On 30 July 1989, the commission released a report criticizing Syria as an obstacle to the restoration of Lebanese sovereignty. Syria's protest appeared to doom the Arab mediation effort.

At the beginning of September 1989, however, the commission resumed its effort, conducting negotiations in Beirut and Damascus (and to some extent between Beirut and Damascus) before convening a meeting of Lebanese deputies on 30 September in Ta'if, Saudi Arabia. At Ta'if, the Lebanese deputies examined a draft agreement that was proposed as a basis on which to end the war.

The third failure that factored into the signing of the Ta'if Accord relates to the international community's longstanding inability to effect a settlement to the war in Lebanon. Throughout the Cold War, the bitter rivalry between the United States and the Soviet Union—particularly in the Middle East—precluded an international solution to the Lebanese problem. When Soviet power collapsed, leaving the United States as the sole superpower in the Middle East, a U.S.-sponsored solution, effected through a close and reliable Arab ally, became possible. Although purely fortuitous, the choice of Saudi Arabia as site for the Lebanese reconciliation meetings did symbolize a significant change.[6] Saudi Arabia's role as host and sponsor of the talks signified, in effect, a shift in general political influence away from the Syrians and toward the Saudis.

Saudi Arabia was not a new player on the Lebanese scene. Throughout the war, Saudi Arabia had acted as a force for compromise and had played a useful mediating role. It was at the Arab League summit in Riyadh (17–18 October 1976) that the Arab Deterrent Force (ADF) was created as part of an Arab effort to help restabilize Lebanon; Saudi Arabia initially contributed troops to ADF ranks, and, as a contributor to ADF, participated in the 1978 conference at Beit Eddin convened to address the growing crisis in Lebanese Christian–Syrian relations. It also formed part of the quadripartite Arab Vigilance Committee responsible for implementing the resolutions on Lebanon passed at the Arab summit in Tunis, 20–22 November 1979. By the time of Lebanon's 1989 crisis, Saudi Arabia was well positioned to step again into the Lebanese arena, taking full advantage of its reputation as a privileged mediator.

Saudi Arabia was motivated to act because of its longstanding investment in Arab peace: it had devoted considerable energy to ensuring rapprochement and cooperation among the often-divided countries of the Arab League. Moreover, its 1989 intervention was generally supported because it was perceived as the only Arab regional force capable of providing a counterweight to Syria. With an international solution to Lebanon's difficulties unlikely, and a purely Syrian solution rejected, an internationally supported Arab solution via the Saudis seemed to offer a midpoint between two extremes.[7]

However, the ambiguity inherent in the Ta'if process meant that it and the resulting compromise document were subject to different interpretations. Some considered the Ta'if Accord to represent an "international" solution, thinly veiled as or merged with an "Arab" solution because of the proxy role assigned to Saudi Arabia by international and Arab powers. Others believed the Ta'if Accord merely provided an Arab cover to Syria's dominant role in Lebanon. This view, based upon the inevitability of Syria's involvement in any search for a solution to Lebanon's problems, contended that Damascus, by definition, would be more closely involved than any other Arab country. Syria, therefore, would become the ultimate beneficiary of any Arab-orchestrated process to restore Lebanon's peace; labeling the Ta'if process an Arab solution would merely legitimize Syrian armed actions in Lebanon, despite the protests of many Lebanese. Contributing to this view is the precedent established by the ADF, which was originally to be Arab but ended up entirely Syrian. The transformation of the ADF demonstrated the weakness of the Arab regional system and its susceptibility to subversion by individual countries, depending on the balance of forces.

It is important to note that at the time of signing, the Ta'if text could be understood in both ways. The specific way in which the text came to be interpreted and understood was determined by subsequent events and their consequences for inter-Arab relations.

CONSTITUTIONAL REFORMS AND
THE WITHDRAWAL OF FOREIGN FORCES

The Ta'if Accord contains a number of key principles that establish (or reestablish) the foundations on which the Lebanese state is built.[8]

From an internal point of view, three points are especially important. First, in a statement of general philosophy, the Document of National Understanding reaffirms that Lebanon is a country where various communities coexist. Basic principles that the war may have obscured are again set forth: independence, unity, sovereignty, a liberal, parliamentary democracy, Arabness, and the definitive nature of a "Lebanese homeland for all her sons." Once these points of history and general identity have been recalled, so to speak, the document proclaims a principle (which could be described as a structural regulation) that reads as follows: "There shall be no constitutional legitimacy for any authority which contradicts the 'pact of communal coexistence' (*al aysh al mushtarak*)."[9]

This solemnly stated principle is crucial to understanding the nature of the Lebanese political system: the legitimacy of authority in Lebanon is grounded in the agreement of the various communities to live together. This agreement is the foundation of political power and its ultimate aspiration, for if any authority were to prove incapable of protecting or reinforcing this desire to live together, its legitimacy would be annulled; its authority would be de facto only. This principle is capable of very broad application. It could be marshaled to condemn Lebanon's partitioning along communal lines, or the seizing of political power by one community. Coexistence implies the sharing of power. Any authority that sought to undermine this solemn national and constitutional commitment to intercommunal amity would thereby make itself illegal.

In regard to institutions, the Ta'if Accord called for the expected changes: equality of seats for the Christian and Muslim communities in the parliament, transfer of executive powers (which had rested constitutionally with the president of the republic) to the council of ministers, and strengthened parliamentary powers; as an interim step, the accord also provided for a one-time government "appointment" (*sic*) of deputies to achieve religious balance in the parliament and to increase the number of deputies from 99 to 108. It provided for a new electoral law that redrew electoral districts on the basis of the *mohafazah,* with its larger and communally mixed electorates. It included provisions to establish a supreme court (whose creation was first envisioned in the constitution of 1926), a constitutional court, and an economic and social council. It upheld the principle of administrative decentralization, increasing the importance of Lebanon's outlying regions. If implemented well, a transfer of administrative authority to regional departments (*mohafazat*) could help depoliticize decisions of the central authorities.

The third point, crucial on the internal level, is the abolition of sectarianism. This question has dominated Lebanon's political life since its birth. The principle of a state based on the various sectarian communities appeared as early as 1926, in Article 95 of Lebanon's constitution. From its inception, however, this sectarian system was described as transitional only. Even the 1943 National Pact—which consecrated the principle of a confessional distribution of public offices and positions in the government and the bureaucracy—called for the eventual elimination of the sectarian system. The Ta'if Accord reiterates this idea that Lebanon's sectarianism is transitional only, but goes somewhat further than previous statements by proposing certain steps to abolish it. For example, the accord's text eliminates sectarian criteria for recruitment of public servants, except for posts at high levels. Similarly, it eliminates all mention of religion on identity cards. Responsibility for devising further measures for the eventual, complete eradication of sectarianism is entrusted to a national committee chaired by Lebanon's president.

The Ta'if Accord also contains important security and foreign policy provisions. In regard to security, the accord provides for dissolution of militias and collection of their arms. The cessation of internal conflict clears the way for the conversion of militiamen to civilian life, or their enrollment in the army or the internal security forces through conscription. The security plan's ultimate aim is for the state to "extend its authority over all the territory of Lebanon by means of its own forces," although Syrian forces "shall assist the legitimate Lebanese forces" in this task.[10]

With respect to Lebanon's relations with Syria, the accord sets forth two key measures. First, two years after the adoption of constitutional reforms, Syrian forces should redeploy to the Bekaa Valley, but also to "any other position" decided upon by a Lebanese-Syrian military committee. A Lebanese-Syrian agreement would determine the size of the remaining Syrian forces and the duration of their stay on Lebanese soil. Ta'if states that the Tripartite Arab High Commission would assist the two governments in concluding this agreement, "if they so desire."

The second measure embodies the accord's primary symbolic and political message: the establishment of "privileged relations" with Syria. Lebanon and Syria are expected to undertake and maintain close relations "in all areas." The two states are expected to reinforce this cooperation in the area of security in particular.

Finally, with respect to Lebanon's relations with Israel, the basic principle is very simple: Ta'if calls for implementation of UN Resolution 425 that demands the withdrawal of Israeli troops. In so far as Lebanon's legal relations with Israel are concerned, Ta'if calls for the resurrection of the

1949 Israeli-Lebanese armistice. In the interim, "all necessary steps will be taken to liberate Lebanese territory from Israeli occupation."

As this brief overview suggests, the Ta'if Accord is an extremely important document, from the extent of the matters it deals with to the array of questions that it attempts to settle. However, two of its general features are of special note.

First, the Ta'if Accord is a package deal in which the internal and external aspects of the Lebanese crisis are inextricably linked. Although the internal question of reform and the external question concerning the status and future of foreign forces in Lebanon are dealt with separately, they are basically articulated within a single scheme that must be implemented in its entirety for the Lebanese crisis to be definitively resolved. This observation is enlightening because, although many believed that the conflict was based solely on internal factors, the Ta'if Accord highlights the conflict's very strong regional dimension.

Second, the accord establishes an Arab mechanism for supporting Lebanon's transition to peace. On 24 October 1989, the Tripartite Arab High Commission issued a communiqué reiterating its determination to "help Lebanon emerge from its crisis" and to "restore the sovereignty of the state." The communiqué repeated the provision contained in the Ta'if Accord stating that Syrian troops, following their two-year mission, should "confer all their responsibilities for security to the constituted Lebanese armed forces" and redeploy. It also proclaimed the commission's willingness to serve as an intermediary during Lebanese-Syrian negotiations over the duration and size of the Syrian troop presence in Lebanon. This Arab guarantee, although more declarative than definitive and predicated on the willingness of both states to agree, nevertheless seemed a decisive factor in ensuring agreement to the accord at the time of signing. It provided assurance, particularly to the factions in Lebanon hostile to Syria, that their country would not be left alone to negotiate one-on-one with Damascus.

CONSTRAINTS AND CHANGES

The Ta'if Accord represents a radical turn in the evolution of the Lebanese crisis. Does it also represent real constitutional and political progress and a change in attitude?

It is, of course, too early to answer this question. Although reforms have been introduced, the continuation of foreign occupation makes Lebanon a country *sous influence,* where democratic responses and even free political competition are subject to tight controls. There is some room, however, to evaluate the changes that have occurred so far, beginning with the Ta'if Accord itself—in terms of the context in which it was born and the direction that this has set.

First, from a formal point of view, the elements embodied in the accord's provisions had occasionally been debated even before the war, and, after 1975, were intensively discussed in various arenas.[11] In this sense, the Document of National Understanding is the fruit of many previous efforts and debates. For this reason a close reading of the accord, whose general outline was originally prepared by the Tripartite Arab High Commission, does not occasion any surprises—except that of finding ideas, scattered throughout the text, that are contained in various other documents.[12] Ta'if's lack of surprises is certainly understandable given that, like all intercommunal agreements, it was the product of a compromise, and that the number of possible compromise solutions is limited.

These observations concerning the formal origins of the accord have implications for its substance as well. The Lebanese deputies, who attended the Ta'if conference as individuals, had a very limited margin of maneuver. Although they could freely debate the proposed constitutional reforms, they could not venture far from the original text: cobbling together an alternative compromise formula would have been most difficult to accomplish.

There was another matter, moreover, on which discussion appeared virtually impossible or even forbidden, namely the chapters dealing with Syria's "redeployment" and Lebanese-Syrian relations.[13] The text relating to these points had been determined in advance by way of prior Syrian-Arab negotiations. Those Lebanese deputies who asked Saud al-Faisal, the Saudi minister of foreign affairs, to mediate one last time with Hafez al-Asad may have obtained a few improvements in the wording, but no substantive changes to the spirit of the text were possible. This preordination will undoubtedly be subject to much critical commentary by future historians and specialists in constitutional law. The supreme irony in all this is that the national will of a people was smothered through the voices of its own representatives. In the end, the argument that carried the vote was that the treaty was a whole and had to be either accepted or rejected in its entirety. The law recognizes situations like this with the term "national will abduction."

In regard to the content of the accord, the reforms adopted at Ta'if helped modify the constitutional aspect of the political system. Under the new system, legislative power has been strengthened: It is practically impossible to dissolve Parliament unless it decides to do so itself. Most important, however, are the changes at the executive level, where powers previously held by the president have been transferred to a council of ministers that meets as a collegial body. This change to Article 17 of the constitution prompted some to comment that Lebanon had now entered its Second Republic.

The constitutional changes do indeed put a new face on the Lebanese political system. Under the amended constitution, the president no longer controls the government; he is responsible instead for ensuring the proper functioning of its institutions and for safeguarding the constitution. His role is to be more a representative of political and moral authority than to become involved in political activities and the day-to-day management of governmental affairs.

Nevertheless, by confirming that Lebanon is a country of various sectarian communities that wish to live together, the Ta'if Accord aims to enshrine cooperation and intercommunal consensus on the institutional level. It could reasonably be expected, therefore, that political practice will take communal balancing into account in ways that are not explicitly outlined i₁ the constitution. Lebanon's new situation is comparable to, though the reverse of, its position in the pre-Ta'if era, when the president held full authority from a legal point of view but, because of tradition, was constrained by a collegial decisionmaking process. What the constitutional law seems to imply in this regard is "corrected" to some extent by communal political practices. Lebanon's legal institutions are thus governed and regulated by the law of communal coexistence and the distribution of public offices among the various communities. The way in which the Ta'if Accord has been applied in the first few years confirms this impression. "Waiting to abolish sectarianism"—this, it seems, continues to be the basic law of the republic.

The ideal situation according to the Ta'if agreement would be to carry out someday the political deconfessionalization of Lebanon.[14] The war has badly damaged the possibilities for achieving this legitimate aspiration. A great deal of optimism is needed to foresee any genuine separation of religion and politics in Lebanese society—unless, of course, it were to be imposed by force. If Lebanon were to deconfessionalize through force, however, it would obviously mean that no consensual agreement had been reached on the matter. The result, therefore, could well be renewed violence. The special committee created by the Ta'if Accord to deal with this issue will perhaps shed some light on practical methods for defusing communal ardor. In the meantime, the accord restricts itself to binding together the threads of Lebanese society, threads that are frayed by many years of sectarian-based violence.

What direction will Lebanon's political system take once social and intercommunal ties have been reestablished? The answer to this question will depend primarily on developments in three key areas: the abolition of sectarianism, the maintenance of a collegial executive, and the implementation of planned administrative decentralization. If confessionalism is abolished, it is very possible that with the creation of a senate where the spiritual families are represented (as foreseen in the Ta'if Accord), the Lebanese political system will embark on the long journey toward a secular state. In that case, Lebanon would truly set its course in the direction of a Second

Republic or even a third. On the other hand, if sectarianism is not abolished and if political power remains the product of consensus and cooperation among community representatives, the post-Ta'if political system will look very much like the pre-Ta'if system, with an increased danger of instability due to the fine balance that must be maintained among communities when each must always be watchful of the other. If a consensual, collegial exercise of power is sustained, combined with extensive decentralization (even if only administrative), then it is quite possible that Lebanon's political system could eventually reorient itself along quasi-federal lines.[15]

These possible outcomes of the Ta'if Accord are largely hypothetical. In reality, the fate of the Lebanese Ta'if Accord will, paradoxically, be determined outside Lebanon, elsewhere in the Middle East.

THE FUTURE OF TA'IF'S PEACE IN LEBANON

The goal of the Ta'if Accord was to establish the foundation for a Lebanon that was both "new" and—of primary importance at the war's end—independent. The government's resumption of power, the Lebanese Army's reconstitution, and the agreement to confer eventual responsibility for maintaining law and order to the Lebanese government's own forces, all attest to the intent that Lebanon regain its liberty. In this regard, however, the situation is highly complex, depending not only on the good will and cooperation of the Lebanese themselves but also on the complicated regional situation.

The Document of National Understanding discusses Lebanon's restoration to sovereignty and independence with reference to the presence and status of the two foreign armies in the country: those of Israel and Syria. While the accord appeals to the United Nations to pressure the Israeli government into withdrawing, its approach to the question of Syria is quite different. Syria is not a foe but a friend, one with whom Lebanon is expected to forge close ties. As a result, there is no mention anywhere in the text of a Syrian "withdrawal" from Lebanese soil: the word simply does not appear. All that is mentioned is a "redeployment" of Syrian troops to the eastern part of Lebanon.

The paradox of the Ta'if Accord is that its full implementation depends upon two powers not formally parties to it. Israel is bound only by the decisions of the UN and Syria by the promises it gave to the Tripartite Arab High Commission. In this light, nothing could be more instructive for understanding the future direction of the accord than to observe how it has actually been applied.

Two major events shaped the initial implementation of the Document of National Understanding. The first was General Aoun's opposition, buoyed by the considerable popular support that rallied to his call. This groundswell of popular opposition, however, was soon exhausted by the inter-Christian war of the spring of 1990, and the fallout from the Persian Gulf crisis delivered the final blow to Aoun's "intifada." The second major event was the crisis in the Gulf, which began in the summer of 1990. In Lebanon, it had the effect of greatly accelerating events. Reaping the full benefits of its membership in the anti-Iraq coalition, Damascus had the Lebanese Parliament pass the constitutional proposals contained in the Ta'if Accord on 21 August 1990. One month later, the president of the republic promulgated the new constitutional amendments. The main proposals of the Ta'if Accord thus became the constitutional law of the land. Less than one month later, on 13 October 1990, Syrian troops—supported by forces loyal to President Hrawi as well as, amazingly, by both Samir Ja'Ja's Lebanese Forces and Elie Hobeiqa's militia—seized the presidential palace in Baabda. All resistance was thereby crushed; senior officers loyal to Michel Aoun were arrested, numerous atrocities were committed against his soldiers, and Dany Chamoun and his family were murdered. It is these incidents that place the implementation of the Ta'if Accord in its actual context.

Following Aoun's ouster, events proceeded very quickly. In full control both politically and militarily, Syria had Ta'if's proposed reforms implemented in a manner that suited its own purposes. Roads were opened, militias disbanded, and heavy arms confiscated; an armistice was declared and deputies were appointed, thereby normalizing the situation in Lebanon. Taking advantage of inter-Arab divisions resulting from the Gulf War, Syria signed with Lebanon the Treaty of Brotherhood, Cooperation and Coordination on 22 May 1991 and the Pact of Defense and Security on 1 September of that year. Thus, at Syria's initiative, the future of the two countries became intimately entwined. A Lebanese-Syrian upper council was created to "decide upon general cooperation and coordination policies between the two countries."[16] Notably, the Tripartite Arab High Commission had been completely squeezed out of the political equation. Left to deal with Syria alone, Lebanon was unable to prevent Damascus from turning the Ta'if Accord into an instrument applied in ways that suited Syrian interests.

The Ta'if Accord's implementation effectively ended the violence in Lebanon. It restored a certain peace to the country by silencing the cannons and enabling civilian society to reconstitute itself, but the accord, as implemented, failed to ensure Lebanon's independence. Lebanon's peace was achieved at the price of its independence.

Three years after the conclusion of this "inter-Lebanese" accord, Lebanon remains under occupation, its wishes and its future not decided in its capital city. Owing to regional considerations (i.e., in view of the resistance struggle against Israel), the scheme to disarm the militias has left Hizballah intact. Between October 1989 and October 1992, four governments of "national union" (*sic*) were formed, all inspired by Damascus. It does not seem to matter that a large portion of Christian opinion, and some Muslim, has been paradoxically and systematically excluded from these "unions" and from the government. The Lebanese elections that Syria wanted were held in August, September, and October 1992. The electoral participation rate of less than 20 percent was not sufficient to give full representativeness to the parliament. In certain regions, the whole process was absurd, as some deputies were elected with a grand total of a few hundred votes (in one case, forty-one). The changes to the electoral law provided for in the Ta'if Accord were not fully honored, as—in the most perfect submission to old-style politics—constituencies were gerrymandered to ensure political victory for certain candidates. The so-called "state" electoral lists that were issued were worthy of authoritarian political regimes. Accusations of electoral fraud were raised by even the most faithful supporters of the Ta'if Accord, notably Hussein al-Husseini, the former speaker of parliament. Moreover, the intelligence and security services unleashed a savage campaign of repression against the supporters of General Aoun, despite the Ta'if Accord's explicit prohibition of involvement by these services in politics.[17]

Despite all these dire occurrences, many people continue to believe that the Ta'if Accord is the best means by which to restore the state of Lebanon and to liberate its territory. Others think that the tragedy of the accord lies in the subjugation of Lebanon—the voluntary servitude to which the Lebanese must agree in order to live in peace, free of violence. The ultimate paradox is that precisely at a time when so many oppressed peoples are recovering their liberty, Lebanon is entering a period of guardianship. The Ta'if Accord has effected only an authoritarian peace. National reconciliation and independence, with dignity and liberty, are ideals yet to be achieved.

NOTES

1. For example, Ta'if incorporates the assumptions that (1) any solution to the crisis in Lebanon must be grounded in the 1943 National Pact and, (2) agreement among the various sectarian groups is a prerequisite for a new social compact in Lebanon.

2. For example: the 1943 National Pact, the various Druze-Christian agreements on Mount Lebanon, the nineteenth-century *a'miat* (assemblies of peasants that gave birth to various coalitions), or the numerous unwritten agreements that underpinned Islamic-Christian coexistence in Lebanon and settled incipient conflicts such as those in 1958 and 1969.

3. See the chapter by Faris in this volume.

4. Syria's goals in Lebanon were evident long before 1983. For example, Syria's 1976 intervention in Lebanon was guided by the strategic objective to reestablish Lebanon's stability in a way that would serve Syrian regional interests.

Syria was unable, however, to achieve this objective during the mandate of President Sarkis, whose term ended with the 1982 Israeli invasion of Lebanon and a Syrian military setback. Nevertheless, the collapse of the Israeli-Lebanese treaty of 17 May 1983 opened new avenues: Shortly after Israel's retreat to its self-declared "security zone" in southern Lebanon, Damascus was busy sponsoring a "tripartite" agreement among the three dominant Lebanese militia leaders: Nabih Birri of Amal (Shi'ites), Walid Jumblatt of the Popular Socialist Party (Druze) and Elie Hobeiqa of the Lebanese Forces (Christians). The conclusion of the Tripartite Agreement represented the first time since the war commenced in 1975 that an agreement (not simply a proclamation or a plan) was reached—under Syrian sponsorship and inspiration—that set forth specific constitutional reforms to be undertaken and, most important, that revealed Syria's desiderata concerning its relations with Lebanon.

5. An intifada inside the Lebanese Forces militia ousted Elie Hobeiqa from the leadership, replacing him with Samir Ja'Ja'. Ja'Ja's ascension forced the abrogation of the Tripartite Agreement that Hobeiqa had signed.

6. In September 1978, U.S. president Carter made two declarations calling for an internationally brokered solution to the Lebanese crisis. At that time, the Soviet Union opposed the idea, but after 14 March 1989 the Soviet position came very close to that of the French (see the declarations by France's prime minister on 18 April 1989 and by Foreign Minister Roland Dumas on 23 April). The Franco-Soviet approach would have involved the Arab League and the Secretary-General of the United Nations (see the joint Franco-Soviet declaration of 5 July 1989, at the time of Mr. Gorbachev's visit to Paris).

7. Nevertheless, the Ta'if Accord is affected by both international and Syrian interests. The international dimension was limited to the Security Council's declaration on 31 October 1989 that strongly supported the inter-Lebanese agreement reached in Saudi Arabia in the name of the Tripartite Arab High Commission. Despite the fact that the accord was not concluded under Syrian aegis, Syria's stamp was evident because the Ta'if meeting assigned an essential role to Syria in Lebanon's pacification, and recognized it as a "privileged" partner in Lebanon's external relations. Further clarification of this point follows.

8. The Ta'if Accord is divided into four parts: (I) General Principles and Reforms, (II) The Extension of Lebanese Sovereignty to All the Territory of Lebanon, (III) The Liberation of Lebanon from Israeli Occupation, and (IV) Lebanese-Syrian Relations. For a comprehensive analysis of Ta'if's clauses see Joseph Maila, "Le Document d'entente nationale: un commentaire," *Cahiers de L'Orient* 16–17 (1989–1990). (English translation: "The Document of National Understanding: A Commentary" in *Prospects for Lebanon* 4 [Oxford: Centre for Lebanese Studies, 1992]).

9. Part I, subsection J of the Ta'if Accord.

10. Part II, Preamble and section 5 of the Ta'if Accord.

11. See the chapter by Hani Faris in this volume.

12. The main sources of inspiration for the Ta'if Accord were the 1985 Syrian-sponsored Tripartite Agreement (among the three militia leaders), and discussions that took place between Damascus and Beirut toward the end of the term of President Amine Gemayel at the time of an American mediation effort led by April Glaspie of the State Department.

13. That is, parts II and IV of the Ta'if Accord.

14. The Ta'if Accord speaks not of secularism, but of the abolition of political sectarianism.

15. The Ta'if Accord excludes, however, any form of political partition or even a federation.

16. For an analysis of the Treaty of Brotherhood, Cooperation and Coordination, see my article in the *Cahiers de L'Orient* 24 (4th quarter 1991), pp. 75–88.

17. See Part II, subsection 3e of the Ta'if Accord.

3

Swiss Soldiers, Ta'if Clocks, and Early Elections: Toward a Happy Ending?

Augustus Richard Norton
& Jillian Schwedler

IMPLEMENTING TA'IF

Dashed Hopes

For many in North America and Europe, violence in Lebanon during the 1970s and 1980s became so normal that all but the most egregious incidents passed virtually unnoticed. "The weather is balmy, the stock market is up twelve points, there was a car bombing in Beirut, and let's see what is on the tube tonight." Lebanon became a nonstory, and although the slaughter, the maiming, and the cruelty were depicted in graphic detail through the magic of television, no one much noticed, after a point, except the Lebanese. The tragedy of Lebanon has been described in many ways, but the fact that violence in Lebanon became routine (so routine as to be reported yet pass virtually unnoticed) is a profound marker of the tragedy.

Lebanon's neighbors, particularly Israel and Syria, were more engaged, if not implicated, by the daily violence in Lebanon. For these two geopolitical rivals, however, Lebanon was less the object of their actions than the locale. Israel's attempt to shape Lebanon politically ended in failure, and in the debris Israel now maneuvers and manipulates, reluctant to take Lebanon seriously as an independent state. Syria has blundered in Lebanon, but Damascus seems to have found a recipe for influencing the policy of the government in Beirut. Neither Israel nor Syria has been reluctant to pursue tacit bargains that undermine Lebanon's sovereignty and chip away at the government's autonomy.

Lebanon is a small country. Even in its best days, its army was dwarfed by the military power of its neighbors; its politics, despite the country's small size, have been more the product of the periphery than of a coherent center. Indeed, the Beirut government, especially since 1975, has been a study in frail authority. Many Lebanese, especially among the political elite, awaited a foreign savior to rescue them from their morass, but their wait was in vain. At the end of the day, the Lebanese would have to save themselves.

After years of so many cease-fires that most of us lost count somewhere between 150 and 200, the civil war in Lebanon formally came to an end in 1990 by way of the Ta'if Accord and a firm Syrian push. The Lebanese, replete with dashed hopes from previous peace failures, were joined in disbelief: There was a surprising lack of elation and no dancing in the streets. This was not a peace to be celebrated, but one to be considered with suspicion and caution. In fact, foreign observers and western diplomats were far more exhilarated by the prospects for peace than were the Lebanese themselves. As events were to show, the Lebanese had good reason to be concerned: Peace was not carried on the wings of doves but on the shoulders of Abdul Halim Khaddam, the Syrian vice president whose name brings shivers of fear to most Lebanese. Lebanon is a portfolio that Khaddam handles with dexterity and confidence, much like a veteran imperial proconsul.

If the Lebanese public was wary of the peace, members of the government were not. Many of these men had invested courageously in the framework for ending the war, and now they felt vindicated. Buoyed by early successes in disarming the militias during the first half of 1991, the government was confident of its momentum. In the spring and summer of 1991 President Elias Hrawi called for the withdrawal of Israeli forces from southern Lebanon. By July 1991, government forces had moved southward, bringing most of the armed Palestinian positions under governmental authority, much to the surprise of many observers. The remaining disarmament tasks, however, were too daunting for the new government. In the South, the Israeli-proxy militia led by General Antoine Lahad went unchallenged and Hizballah, the self-proclaimed core of the Islamic resistance to Israel's continuing occupation, retained its arms. Hizballah's attitude was guaranteed by way of an understanding between Iran and Syria to which Lebanon was only a bystander. Powerful patrons, namely Israel and Iran, were not to be challenged.

The summer of 1991 was extraordinary by all accounts. Press reports indicate that hundreds of thousands of Lebanese returned. Middle East Airlines flights were booked solid, and even Lebanese with *wasta* (or "connections") were unable to translate their influence into a coach seat to Beirut International Airport. However, the visitors were voyeurs, returning only to catch a glimpse of home, smell the summer, sip some *arak,* enjoy the food, and then leave.

Most visitors left very little behind; the situation was too risky for investment, peace too precarious, and life too hard to justify moving back to Lebanon. One would hear stories from Lebanese about the sky-high price of land, as though land prices reflected something other than the lack of confidence among the Lebanese in their banks, their currency, and their economy. As the most conservative of investments, land is a hedge against uncertainty, and its stellar prices were more a symptom of the sickness in the economy than an indicator of its latent health.[1]

Overall, we can only be relieved that the Ta'if Accord has provided a basis for ending the carnage that took approximately 150,000 lives over fifteen years.[2] There is, however, still reason for concern about Lebanon's future. This chapter provides perspective on some of those concerns by examining one of the major post-Ta'if political events: the 1992 parliamentary elections. The fact that elections were held, the way the electoral process was conducted, and the results of that process are all important factors shaping the future of Lebanon's Second Republic. At face value, the electoral process might have served to catalyze genuine national reconciliation by providing the Lebanese people—newly freed from the militia hegemony that ruled their lives for fifteen years—the opportunity to say who should be empowered to resurrect their country. This potential, however, was not fully or clearly realized. Indeed, some would argue that the electoral process, as it materialized, served to alienate certain sectors of the population rather than draw all into a consensual fold. In order to understand how the promise of elections was compromised in Lebanon, some background context relating to the Ta'if Accord, the Syrian presence, and the Lebanese Parliament is necessary.

Ta'if and the "Swiss Problem"

The accord that brought a formal end to the fighting in Lebanon was signed in al-Ta'if, Saudi Arabia, in November 1989. The Saudis, as well as their Arab League partners in mediation, the Algerians and the Moroccans, deserve substantial credit for overseeing and shepherding the agreement. Nonetheless, and this comment is not intended in any way to diminish the success of the mediators, the stunning reality is that the Ta'if Accord's provisions for domestic reforms are not dramatically different from those of the Constitutional Document mediated by Syria in 1976.

Perhaps the key aspect of the agreement is that it seals the principle of Muslim-Christian parity, whereby parliamentary representation is split on a fifty-fifty basis. Implicitly, the accord rejects the idea that parliamentary seats need to be reallocated periodically to adjust for disparate rates of population growth among the major confessional groups. Instead, the principle of parity provides the basis of a historic compromise meant to underscore the fact that Lebanon is a country shared by Christians and Muslims. Despite the decline of Maronite power and the relative gains of the Shi'ite Muslims, the extent to which Maronite prerogatives have been preserved and the central political authority of the Sunnis buttressed is striking, while

Shi'ite gains have been minimal. In general, the looming salience of Lebanon's Shi'ites has been greatly exaggerated: external players, especially Saudi Arabia, are Shi'ite-phobic, and the Shi'ites are riven among themselves.

Although Syria deferred to Saudi Arabia during the negotiations in al-Ta'if, the accord's implementation has proceeded under the aegis of the Syrian government. Indeed, Syria is playing the role of a bullying big brother, although most Lebanese would choose a more colorful term. There is an old joke in Lebanon about a fellow, call him Ahmad, who meets his friend Samir in Beirut: "Ahmad, you look very angry." "By God, I am angry. I was stopped at a checkpoint and a Swiss soldier stole my Syrian watch." "What? Ahmad, you must mean that a Syrian soldier stole your Swiss watch." "Samir, you said it, not me!" Plenty of Lebanese complain these days about "the damn Swiss," and everyone understands that they are not talking about watchmakers.

In the vernacular of informed Lebanese one also hears frequent references to "the bourse," meaning the Beirut-Damascus highway frequently traveled by Lebanese politicos who flock to the Syrian capital to share secrets and rumors, and to check their moves with "the Swiss." In short, little is done by the Beirut government without rehearsing the move with "our Syrian friends."[3]

"Swiss" influence is also very much in evidence on the ground in Lebanon, in the form of 40,000 Syrian soldiers and assorted secret service agents. An armed Syrian presence was seen as a necessary condition for proceeding with the implementation of certain of the Ta'if Accord's provisions (specifically the disarming of the militias); however, Syrian troops were not accepted as a permanent fixture on the Lebanese landscape. According to the timetable set forth in Ta'if—Syrian prevarication and reinterpretation notwithstanding—the Syrian forces in Lebanon were to be redeployed to the Bekaa Valley two years after the accord's implementation, a stipulation clearly understood and expressed as such by the participants in the Ta'if negotiations. Saudi officials reportedly conveyed assurances of Syria's intention to redeploy within that time frame, and even to withdraw all of its forces eventually from Lebanon. Because the implementing legislation was passed in September 1990, the "Ta'if clock" specified a September 1992 Syrian redeployment.

Unquestionably, it would help a great deal if the Arab-Israeli peace process that began in 1991 worked to the benefit of Lebanon. With its population of 400,000 Palestinians, its strategic importance to both Syria and Israel, and its troubled border with Israel, there is no mistaking the fact that Lebanon is a captive of the Arab-Israeli conflict. None of the belligerents is anxious to release the hostage. There should be little confusion that continuing Israeli occupation of the South undermines the forces of moderation in Lebanon and skews the maneuvering room of the Beirut government. Some of us hoped, a few years ago, that it might even be possible to start the peace process in the South. Now it is clear that Lebanon will probably be the last stop for the peace train. From the standpoint of Tel Aviv, the "security zone" in southern Lebanon is a success, and there is no reason to tamper with success. Transparently, Syria sees the situation in the South as a bargaining chip and a rationale for maintaining forces in Lebanon. In fact, from the bargaining perspective, there was no reason for Syria to redeploy in September 1992 and thereby give the Israelis an unreciprocated gift. The peace process is inching forward, though, and Lebanon may, in the end, be a beneficiary; however, many Lebanese fear they will be the meal at the *sulha* banquet.

Ta'if and the Parliament

The last general elections for the Lebanese Parliament prior to 1992 were held in 1972. Like the Lebanese Army, which also maintained an administrative vitality, the parliament remained nominally intact throughout the civil war, and its members represented Lebanon in the Ta'if negotiations. Though frail and diminished in numbers by natural and unnatural deaths, Parliament played its constitutional role by electing René Muawwad president in 1989 and, following his assassination seventeen days later, elected Elias Hrawi to the office. Equally important, the deputies passed legislation ratifying Ta'if's provisions in September 1990, thereby sealing the pact that was the basis for restoring tranquility to the country and for implementing political reforms.

As part of the process of national reconciliation, the parliament needed to replenish and expand its membership—to reach its full Ta'if-ordained complement of 108 members equally split between Muslims and Christians.[4] In total, forty new members were needed: thirty-one seats were vacant due to death or resignation; nine others had been added to achieve Muslim-Christian parity. The Ta'if Accord included a provision for an exceptional procedure to fill the vacant parliamentary seats, namely the appointment of deputies. On the face of it, appointing deputies to an elected representative body is an anomalous procedure, and the prospect of commencing Lebanon's national reconciliation with this procedure caused considerable dissent. Although no one questioned the need to rejuvenate Parliament, it was feared that appointive deputies would only weaken the parliamentary body by infusing it with members of the war elite and agents of Syrian influence.

As an alternative to appointing deputies, some observers thought that the elections, if conducted with integrity, could serve as an affirmation that the Ta'if process would lead to genuine national reconciliation. These observers proposed holding parliamentary by-elections under international supervision. Their view, that by-elections held early in the post-Ta'if period would catalyze the reconciliation process, stood in contrast to that of many Lebanese politicians who did not envisage elections until the peace wrought by Ta'if was well entrenched.

Although the by-election idea created a brief flurry of interest among those engaged in peaceseeking, Damascus had no interest in an electoral process that would undermine its influence in Lebanon, and the United States was quietly satisfied with the appointment of deputies. Given that these were the two players who mattered in post-Ta'if Lebanon, the by-election idea was a nonstarter. Thus, in 1991, forty deputies were appointed, some of whom were widely respected. Nevertheless, domestic resentment did not relent and Lebanese criticism of the process became louder and more widespread than before the appointments. When Parliament extended its own mandate for three years, it seemed that Lebanon's first postwar general elections would not be held until 1994.[5]

Ta'if and the Electoral Process

To the surprise of both the Lebanese and many foreign observers, elections were being discussed—with Syrian prodding—by early 1992. The frenzied preparations caused some observers to conclude that the elections could not possibly be conducted before the autumn. They were wrong.

Possibly, the stinging criticism concerning the deputy-appointment process, especially by major foreign powers like France, may have found its mark. It is unlikely, however, that a realpolitik impresario like President Hafez al-Asad would press for general elections merely to accommodate criticism of the appointment process. A more plausible explanation is that Asad and Khaddam were intent on ensuring that a compliant legislative body would be in place prior to the Syrian redeployment as mandated by the Ta'if clock (in case Syria might be compelled to respect the September 1992 deadline, which, in the event, it was not).[6]

The Ta'if Accord also addressed the question of districting during the parliamentary elections. As stipulated in the accord, a new electoral law would eliminate parliamentary elections by *qada'*, or local district (plural: *aqda*), and redraw the electoral boundaries on the basis of the six provinces, or *mohafazat*. The provinces are the North, Beirut, the Bekaa, Mount Lebanon, the South, and Nabatieh. The last was added in 1975, although governmental services for the Nabatieh province remain largely centered in Sidon, the capital of the province of the South.[7] Treating the mohafazat as electoral constituencies was intended to "ensure: a) coexistence among the Lebanese communities; b) political representation for all classes and age-groups in the population; and c) the effectiveness of that representation."[8] This measure was aimed at reversing the 1953 electoral law which divided the country into twenty-six aqda, most of which were uniconfessional areas.

Nonetheless, the new electoral law, which was passed on 16 July 1992, suspended the Ta'if stipulation for the upcoming parliamentary elections. Since the Ta'if Accord clearly stated that elections were to take place on the basis of the mohafazat, the new electoral law represented "official" gerrymandering of the districts. This districting worked to the benefit of several of the traditional warlords. In Mount Lebanon, Walid Jumblatt won in the Shouf, and Elie Hobeiqa won in Baabda.

Amal leader Nabih Birri and other leading pro-Syrian candidates shrewdly insisted that the mohafazat of the South and of Nabatieh be treated as a single district rather than constituting an electoral district for each mohafazah, or using the aqda as the basis for districting. Birri reasoned that the smaller districts would favor the local, traditional notables, whereas treating the two provinces as a single constituency would favor his massive list of twenty-two candidates. Birri's electoral strategy also reflected the conclusion that the administrative gain of having two Shi'ite-dominated provinces was outweighed by the clout of one large, formidable province. Thus, Nabatieh was politically reunited with Sidon while the administrative division of the two provinces survived. (The unification of Nabatieh and the South was cited by Christian critics of the elections as one of several major irregularities in the conduct of the elections.)

The electoral law also increased the number of parliamentary seats to 128 from 108, the twenty additional seats being shared equally between the leading Christian and Muslim sects. As a result, the political power of the smaller sects was further diluted. It is noteworthy that the Druze did not benefit from the additional increment, since the ten new Muslim seats were split between the Shi'ites and the Sunnis. The allocation of the 128 seats is shown in Figure 3.1.

The new constitution contained another measure intended to ensure the elections were free and fair: It called for the establishment of an independent constitutional council (Article 19) which was to investigate accusations of ballot tampering, fraud, and disruption of the polling. Although the government had drafted and passed the law to create the council, Parliament did not approve the measure in time for the 1992 elections. Events demonstrated that such a council proved necessary as numerous incidents—mounted with varying success—threatened to disrupt the electoral process. In the North, three journalists representing the newspaper *al-Diyar,* owned by Charles Ayyoub, a candidate on the opposition list of Ahmad Karameh, were beaten by armed supporters of Omar Karameh. Three days after the elections, eight unsuccessful candidates from the North questioned the results and demanded the creation of the independent council specified in the new constitution. This call for official inquiry into the legitimacy of the election process highlights an important mechanism that was skipped over in the rush to set the elections in motion. Instead, electoral disputes were to be brought before a special commission composed of

Figure 3.1 Distribution of Seats in Parliament

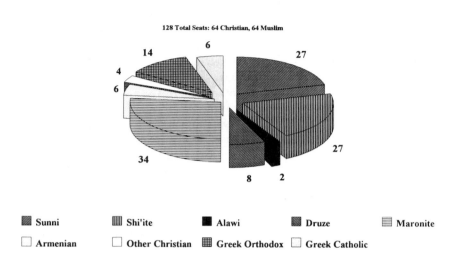

128 Total Seats: 64 Christian, 64 Muslim

▨ Sunni ||||| Shi'ite   ■ Alawi   ▨ Druze   ☰ Maronite

☐ Armenian   ☐ Other Christian   ▦ Greek Orthodox   ☐ Greek Catholic

the new parliamentarians, who, as the focus of many of the accusations, were unlikely to jeopardize their own political futures.

Finally, the Ta'if Accord stipulated the redeployment of Syria's 40,000 troops within two years. Because this period would have expired at the end of September 1992, the Syrian withdrawal should have been well under way by late August, when the first round of elections was held in the North. A continued Syrian presence could only bolster the campaigns of pro-Syrian incumbents. Although the accord did not stipulate the withdrawal as a precondition for holding parliamentary elections, the continued Syrian presence was seen as a major threat to Lebanon's independence by its large Christian community, which subsequently boycotted the three rounds of polling.

THE PARLIAMENTARY ELECTIONS[9]

Preelection Arrangements

As plans for the August/September elections began to crystallize, many foreign observers questioned the conditions under which the polling would be conducted. Several respected nongovernmental organizations explored the possibilities for international monitoring of the elections with Lebanese political figures at a conference in Oxford, England.[10] The international supervision of elections is a well-practiced function, having been conducted in Central America, Asia, and Africa, but election monitoring is usually carried out at the official request of a government. Judging from those who were consulted, the Lebanese favored both the postponement of the elections (until after the Syrian redeployment) and an international role to ensure the integrity of the process. Nevertheless, it is hard to visualize a Beirut government, pliant to Syrian interests, either postponing the elections or officially requesting international monitoring. No monitoring of the elections was requested; however, elements of civil society in Lebanon purposefully mobilized to observe and report accurately on the elections.[11]

Preparations for the elections were pushed forward by the government; voter lists, which had not been updated for twenty years, were hurriedly assembled, and an electoral process by stages was scheduled to begin by August 1992. Lebanon uses a list system for elections whereby the elector casts his or her ballot for multiple candidates. For example, in the constituency of Aley, five seats are at stake: two for Maronites, one for Greek Orthodox, and two for Druze. The elector, therefore, casts a total of five votes, allocated, respectively, among the Druze, Maronite, and Orthodox candidates. To ensure victory, candidates try to assemble (or join) a slate that will appeal across confessional lines. While voters are not obliged to cast their votes for an entire slate, they often do. Thus, the selection of candidates and the construction of electoral coalitions is really a key phase of the election that takes place weeks or months before election day. If this phase is subverted or contorted—for instance, through the "advice" of Syrian security officials—the choice before the voter may be more apparent than real.

Consequently, the list system means that electoral manipulation is not simply a matter of registering the dead to vote and other predictable techniques of electoral corruption, but can be part and parcel of the process of building electoral lists, a process that takes place out of view and before the actual balloting. Despite the West's fascination with election-monitoring, the fact is that the real content of elections precedes the balloting. Monitoring on election day, therefore, might only serve to validate or certify a corrupted process. Several Lebanese attending the Oxford meeting, themselves well-practiced in the task of winning elections, noted that because of the structure of Lebanon's electoral system, ballot monitoring would not be enough to guarantee the integrity of the process.

Syrian Influence and the Christian Boycott

The parliamentary elections of 1992 illustrate the extent of Syrian influence as well as the depths of anti-Syrian sentiments, especially in the Maronite community. Pro-Syrian candidates gained considerably, helped by the creation of the super constituency in southern Lebanon, and aided, indirectly, by the Christian boycott. Impressive though the Christian efforts were in protesting and boycotting the Syrian-steered electoral process, the Christian efforts were truly a double-edged sword. The boycott served to underscore the dubious prospect of really free elections while Syrian troops remained in Lebanon, but the absence of many Christian voters denied victory to many moderate Muslim candidates who might have tempered the victory of more radical Muslim candidates.

With the backing of the Maronite Church, various Christian leaders[12] demanded the elections be postponed until Syria withdrew its 40,000 troops, as required by the Ta'if Accord. For example, Maronite Patriarch Nasrallah Boutros Sfeir, Kata'ib Party chief George Sa'ade, and Lebanese Forces commander Samir Ja'Ja' stated that they supported the boycott not because they rejected the Ta'if Accord (à la exiled General Michel Aoun), but because they believed that the presence of Syrian troops would guarantee a pro-Syrian parliament.

The movement to boycott the elections gathered momentum within the Maronite and Greek Catholic communities. In the weeks preceding the polling in Mount Lebanon, five Maronite deputies called for the elections to be postponed, and two resigned when the process moved forward as scheduled. Of the three who retained their candidacy, one was pressured to remain off any list, while another's car was bombed. More withdrawals followed those of the two Maronite deputies; even candidates who would have won their bid by default pulled out. In the end, the many withdrawals meant that some candidates ran unopposed.

In the North, the Kata'ib organization had been struggling to present itself as a nationalist rather than Christian political party. As the elections approached, however, Kata'ib sought to distance itself from the illegitimacy surrounding the government, first by criticizing elections scheduled before Syrian troops were redeployed, and ultimately by withdrawing from the race.

The goal of the Christian boycott was to deny the imprimatur of legitimacy to a parliament that was likely to be malleable to Syrian interests. If the Syrians were able to subordinate Lebanese sovereignty to Syrian influence, then the least Syria's opponents might do would be to avoid complicity in the electoral charade. In the event, the boycott was a remarkable technical success, although the wisdom of the boycott is questioned—privately—by some Lebanese Christians, who note that the boycott provided a parliamentary membership skewed in Syria's favor and with precious little scope for the active protection of civil rights.

The Islamists' Nonsectarian Strategy

The elections illuminated substantial changes in the Lebanese political climate, including election platforms that appeared to indicate a widespread move away from sectarianism. Prominent leaders of Hizballah, Amal, and Jama'ah al-Islamiyyah (as well as several Christian factions) portrayed their parties and candidate lists as nationalist and nonreligious, focusing instead on economic, social, and political reform. Of special note in this regard was the behavior of Hizballah, which reflected a highly sophisticated campaign strategy. Building on its extensive social outreach programs, which included feeding the poor, rebuilding damaged homes, and providing fuel for heat during the harsh winter months, Hizballah sought to mobilize the lower classes across a united front, thereby supplanting traditional ties with a new patronage. This strategy (which was also used by Jama'ah al-Islamiyyah, and to a lesser extent by Amal) resulted in great gains at the ballot box— across sectarian lines—particularly in Beirut and the South (see Figure 3.2). As more than a symbolic component of this strategy, most Islamist candidates dropped Islamic titles from their names during the campaign, favoring the neutral "Doctor" to the religious "Sheikh."

Hizballah's success was abetted by the Christian-led boycott. Although both the boycott and Hizballah's nonsectarian campaigning were widely effective, low turnout at the polls also signaled voter apathy. The legitimacy of the process was widely questioned, with blame generally placed on

Figure 3.2 Voter Turnout by Region and Affiliation

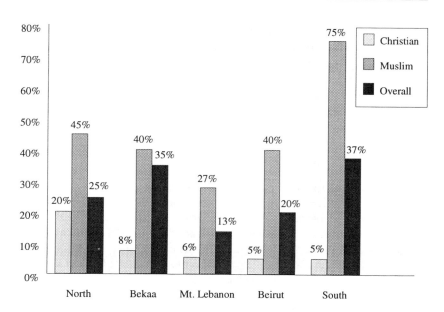

Sources: Statistics represent estimated figures that the authors derived from a variety of sources surveyed following the elections (August–October 1992) including *The Lebanon Report, The New York Times,* and *The Washington Post.*

officials rather than on election tampering. Nevertheless, inaccurate electoral lists, ballot box tampering, and improper tallying were evident countrywide.

Election Results by Region

The first of the three scheduled rounds of voting took place on 23 August in the Bekaa Valley and in the North, where the Islamists won a decisive victory in a predominantly Christian region, despite the fact that Christians in the North did not publicly associate themselves with the election boycott, and overall only 25 percent of the electorate voted. Moreover, the boycott did reverberate in the area, as several prominent candidates withdrew, significantly Boutros Harb, minister of education under Karameh; George Sa'ade, head of the Kata'ib Party; and four other Kata'ib members.

A notable result of the election was that two members of Jama'ah al-Islamiyyah eclipsed the candidates offered on the official list of Omar Karameh. One of these, Fathi Yakan, won his seat on a platform of social and political reform, a technique adopted by Hizballah and Amal elsewhere in Lebanon. Yakan was one of many Islamic candidates who dropped the title "Sheikh" during the campaign.

In the Bekaa, the results of Hizballah's social services strategy were dramatic. The list presented by Speaker of Parliament Hussein al-Husseini was overwhelmingly defeated by the Hizballah list. Al-Husseini managed to retain his own seat, but grabbed only the fifth largest number of votes. The Sunni and Christian candidates on his list lost outright to counterparts presented by Hizballah. Several other candidates faced embarrassing defeats: Albert Mansour, the defense minister in the government that ousted General Aoun two years earlier, did not win a seat despite his prominent position on the al-Husseini list; and President Elias Hrawi's son Roy lost to his nephew Khalil, further weakening the position of the existing government.

*   *   *

During the second round of elections, on 30 August in Mount Lebanon and Beirut, the Christian boycott proved extremely successful, resulting in highly irregular electoral results. In the Jubayl district, Maha Khoury Asad won her seat with forty-one votes from an electorate of 60,000, in part because citizens refused to allow election officials entrance to buildings to conduct polling. (Some resourceful officials erected polling stations in tents and car trunks.) In other instances, the abstention of Christian voters and candidates meant that many opposition candidates prospered in regions where their victory would normally be unlikely. For example, in predominantly Christian Mount Lebanon, Hizballah gained one of two Shi'ite seats in the district of Baabda when Ali Ammar (of Hizballah) ran virtually unopposed by any Christian-backed moderate. The boycott was so effective in Kisrawan that the ballot for the district's five seats listed only one candidate. (The five seats were filled in a by-election in October.)

The boycott was also felt in Beirut, where most voting took place in the western, mainly Muslim quarters of the city. Two major lists dominated the six in circulation: the "official" list, headed by Prime Minister Rashid al-Solh, and an opposition list headed by former prime minister Salim el-Hoss. The official list did not fare well against that of the opposition, which had all but two of its candidates elected. An important component of al-Solh's strategy was to court the Armenian electorate by including on his list three of the community's most popular leaders for the Armenian Orthodox seats. The Armenians, al-Solh figured, would turn out in record numbers and would vote his entire list, giving him the necessary edge over el-Hoss. However, el-Hoss's sophisticated counterstrategy triumphed; by not including any Armenian candidates, el-Hoss neutralized the Armenian vote by ensuring their candidates' victory, regardless of whether Armenian voters turned out. Thus, the second round of elections may be characterized by a high level of sophistication in campaign strategy, and by the success of the Christian boycott. Voter turnout ranged from 6.5 percent in Jubayl, where only 0.55 percent of the Christian electorate voted, to about 40 percent in Muslim West Beirut.

*   *   *

The third round of the elections was held in the South on 6 September, despite repeated threats by South Lebanon Army leader Antoine Lahad to bomb polling stations. Participation in the South was officially placed at 37 percent overall, with the massive Christian boycott (approximately 5 percent voted) offset by the high Muslim turnout (estimated as high as 75 percent in Shi'ite areas).

The list led by Amal leader Nabih Birri was wildly successful. Birri's list comprised a peculiar patchwork of important alliances representing Amal, Hizballah, Rafiq al-Hariri's sister Bahiyya al-Hariri, members of traditionally prominent Shi'ite families of the South, Syrian allies, and independent Christian candidates. All twenty-two candidates on Birri's strong list easily won their seats. The success of this list was certainly due to the candidates' shrewd decision to join in tactical (and popular) alliance, and to the treatment of the mohafazah of the South as a single electoral district. Other factors also swayed votes. First, both Hizballah and some members of Amal had garnered some popular support by way of their "resistance" attacks against Israel. More important, their popularity at the polls was a reflection of the basic services strategy marshaled by both Hizballah and Amal to the benefit of voters in the South—one of the most neglected areas of the country. Indeed, government institutions and social services are effectively nonexistent in the South.[13]

Moreover, this longer-term social strategy was backed by tactical support on election day: Hizballah provided transportation for voters via 5,000–7,000 cars, and gave away gasoline to motorists heading for the polls. Clearly, financial resources played a role in the success of the alliance. Nevertheless, despite their sweeping victory, the absence of ideological unity among the alliance led the group to fracture soon after the elections.

Two landslide victories belonged to decidedly non-Islamist candidates, Bahiyya al-Hariri and Mustapha Sa'd. Like Hizballah, they owed their victories to the social services they provided, particularly during the harsh winter of 1991–1992, and to the creation of a single electoral district in the South, which weakened local notables. Many of the successful candidates, in the South as elsewhere, criticized the government without proposing tangible alternative economic programs.

Although the Birri list did enjoy genuine popularity, the electoral process in the South (as in the other districts) was not pristine. While there seems to have been very little tampering with actual ballots, some voters reported that upon entering the polling places they were urged simply to cast their vote for the entire list. Conscientious voters wishing to strike off a few names or add a few others would wish to go behind the curtain intended to ensure a secret ballot. The voting official might ask, "Why do you need the curtain?" The query was, of course, a means of exerting unmistakable pressure.

Nevertheless, many voters did signal their nonacceptance of the coalition by crossing out candidates they did not support and penciling in alternates. In part, this protest resulted from the South's unification into a single region: voters were often faced with choosing candidates about whom they knew little. While scratching out certain candidates indicated voter dissatisfaction with the structure of the elections, it may also be interpreted as voter acceptance of the electoral process in general.

*   *   *

On 11 October, by-elections were held in Kisrawan, the predominantly Maronite district which postponed its original polling when all but one candidate pulled out of the race for five seats. The Maronite patriarchy, questioning the legality and legitimacy of the new parliament, continued to call for a boycott. The opposition's resolve, however, clearly lost steam as twenty-six candidates came forward soon after the third round of elections in the South. By October, only four had dropped out, leaving voters with twenty-two choices to fill the five seats. A significant blow was leveled against the boycott movement when ex–foreign minister Fares Bouez, son-in-law of President Hrawi, abandoned their ranks to lead three corunners to victory. The fifth seat went to the head of a rival list. Much like the candidates' defections from the boycott, voters also participated in greater numbers. In some towns participation was nearly 50 percent, in others, nil. Overall estimates of turnout range from 18 percent to 25 percent.

Anticipating trouble during the by-elections, the government deployed some 10,000 soldiers to prevent disruptive incidents at polling sites. Boycott supporters constructed several roadblocks to prevent ballot boxes from reaching polling sites, and antielection activities were widespread in Ghazir, a small town where supporters of exiled General Aoun paraded through the streets with Lebanese flags. At the end of the day, however, the final members of the new parliament were elected.

THE SECOND REPUBLIC OF TA'IF: A NEW ERA?

The Lebanese participants in the Ta'if negotiations were not alone in viewing elections as a key component in a national process of healing and reconciliation. Many friends of Lebanon as well thought of elections as a catalyst for peace. Instead, the elections have underscored some of the country's divisions, and, some would argue, widened those divisions.

The Christian Boycott and Michel Aoun

While the Maronite-inspired boycott managed to keep a sizable portion of the electorate from the polls, it also allowed Islamists to enter the government in record numbers, at the expense of more moderate Muslim candidates favored by the Christians. Moreover, almost immediately following the elections, the Christian opposition showed few signs of maintaining the unification which prevailed during the boycott. Indeed, alienated Christian leaders hinted at a willingness to reenter the system as illustrated by the numerous candidates who stepped forward in the Kisrawan by-elections, in stark contrast to the solid support for the original boycott. These leaders hoped to salvage what influence they could in the shaping of a new Lebanon. Moreover, several prominent Christian leaders, including exiled General Michel Aoun, expressed interest in cabinet positions, so long as conditions such as the withdrawal of Israeli and Syrian troops from Lebanon were met. Their hopes were dashed, however, when Rafiq Hariri, appointed prime minister in October, announced that his cabinet would not include supporters of the boycott.

Thus, although the boycott undercut the legitimacy of the electoral process, it also left the Maronite community intensely insecure and faced with a severe crisis of leadership. When the war society reigned in Lebanon, both the Kata'ib and the Lebanese Forces garnered wide support.

Now, however, in the post-Ta'if period, civil society is struggling to regain its footing; public services are being restored, albeit exceedingly slowly, and the government in Beirut is rediscovering its authority. On the surface, life in Lebanon appears to be returning to a pattern that is more or less normal, but the long dominant Maronite community has shrunk in numbers due to largescale emigration, Maronite political prerogatives were whittled in the Ta'if Accord, and Syria casts a long shadow, even in the fastness of Mount Lebanon.

In this climate, it is not surprising that the banished Michel Aoun, who stood up to Syrian power until his stronghold in Baabda was reduced to rubble in the autumn of 1990, has recaptured an impressive following, especially among Lebanese Christians. Aoun's message rings true in the ears of his admirers: The Ta'if Accord is a cover for conceding Lebanese sovereignty to Syria. Aoun rejected the terms of the accord, arguing that it should not be ratified until Syrian troops left Lebanon. When Syria failed to withdraw in September 1992, Aoun's following was further buttressed, and his prediction that Ta'if was a recipe for Lebanon's annexation by Syria was, so some thought, vindicated.

Michel Aoun T-shirts have been reported in Hazmiyya and other East Beirut suburbs. His cassettes are easily smuggled into the country, and pamphleteers regularly circulate materials by him and supporting him. Following Lebanon's independence day on 22 November 1992, some 200 of his followers were arrested by the Lebanese authorities. When a number of those arrested were treated brutally in captivity, it only corroborated Aoun's critique of the government.

The phenomenon of Michel Aoun may be transitory, but this depends on the wisdom of Lebanon's newly empowered politicians. For years, it was appropriate to criticize the government in Beirut for neglecting a large segment of its population, which happened to be Shi'ite Muslim. For Lebanon to be whole, it was argued, the Shi'ites must be brought into the political system, not as *zilmis* (clients) but as players. When this simple wisdom was not followed, as after the star-crossed Israeli invasion of 1982, the result was disaster. May we hope that a similar mistake is not made vis-à-vis the Maronite community?

Hizballah Enters the Fold

Although Muslim voters turned out at a much higher rate than many of their Christian compatriots, the overall turnout was sufficiently low to suggest that a number of Muslim voters, especially in Beirut, also stayed away from polling stations. The highest rate of turnout was among the Shi'ite Muslims, for whom the election represented a real choice between the traditional *zu'ama* and notables who had dominated Shi'ite politics for decades, and a new class of counterelites. Arguably, the choices made by

Shi'ite voters authentically represented the changing political views of the Shi'ite community. In southern Lebanon, as we have seen, Amal leader Nabih Birri's insistence on a single electoral district, in combination with a number of other strategic and tactical elements, yielded a comprehensive victory for Birri's list and an unmistakable loss for various local notables. Significantly, in this regard, the venerable Kamal al-Asad went down to an ignominious defeat.[14]

The election marked another watershed for the Shi'ite community, namely the integration of Hizballah into the Lebanese political system. Hizballah spokesmen had roundly condemned the Ta'if process and deemed any attempt to reform the extant political system as fundamentally flawed. The government was, Hizballahi commentators were wont to note, rotten to the core. Only the erection of a new system would really address the fundamental flaws. In contrast to these stated criticisms, Hizballah ran in the elections—implicitly accepting the extant political system as legitimate— and did quite well.

It remains uncertain whether the striking victory of the Islamist bloc will redirect the future of Lebanon. The Islamists did not, as some expected, gain a position in Hariri's new cabinet. Regardless of whether the Islamist bloc proves to be committed to the provisions of the Ta'if Accord and to the democratization of the political process, participation in the electoral process is a positive step toward political normalization and liberalization. The Islamist bloc may not yet be swimming in Lebanon's political mainstream, but the water will clearly be tested.

Even ephemeral support of democratic processes may well unleash forces that will not be easily derailed even should the Islamic bloc attempt to impose its societal vision upon Lebanon. In the South, where the Amal-led list brought several victories by Hizballah candidates, one cannot help but recall the image of voters—perhaps even those transported to the polls in Hizballah-owned vehicles—who crossed out certain list candidates and penciled in other names. The average Lebanese voter is not easily manipulated. On the contrary, the election results demonstrated that despite reputed voter apathy, many Lebanese cast a vote for social and economic reform, and for a better life, and it is not insignificant that the Islamists have shown savvy in addressing the needs of a sizable portion of the Lebanese citizenry.

On a comparative note, Lebanon may prove a very interesting test case for the integration of Islamist voices in the political process. One should be dubious about claims that Lebanon is a microcosm of the Middle East. The Lebanese state is much weaker than most Arab states, and Lebanese society is more culturally diverse than all but one or two other countries in the region (viz., Iraq and Israel). Nonetheless, it should be instructive to observe the behavior of the Hizballah deputies elected to office in 1992. The growth of Islamist populist movements across the Middle East is often labeled a totalitarian phenomenon by Arab rulers and Western policy elites. Certainly, the coup d'état of January 1992 in Algeria (although many supporters of the coup have now had second thoughts), was defended as a fitting riposte to the ambitions of the Islamic Salvation Front, which, it was feared, would impose an Islamic dictatorship in Algeria were it allowed to proceed to taste the power it had won at the ballot box. Although the Lebanese example leaves unanswered the behavior of an Islamist parliamentary majority, much may still be learned by watching the parliamentary process unfold in Beirut. In a nutshell, will idealism succumb to pragmatism when Islamists are brought into the give and take world of politics?

Hariri's Enterprise and Post-Election Politics

Despite the questions surrounding both the elections and the new parliament, the fact is that the process has gone forward, and the parliament has met regularly since its first session in October 1993. Further, there is significant evidence that the government of Prime Minister Rafiq Hariri is moving deliberately and with integrity toward the reconstruction of Lebanon. Nevertheless, real concerns remain: Financing is slow in coming, and there are fears that Hariri will treat Lebanon like a business acquisition and simply add the country to his hefty portfolio. His cabinet, filled with financiers, businessmen, and some of his close aides and advisers, has been described as more of a board of directors than a cabinet of ministers. To be fair, Hariri has acted with real backbone, and, if he survives politically and physically, he may succeed in being the father of the reconstruction of Lebanon. Certainly, his staunch refusal to accept the 400 expelled Palestinians in December 1992 introduced a new element into the diplomatic equation in the region.

There even seems to be movement in Washington since the convening of the new parliament. In a symbolically important move, U.S. secretary of state Warren Christopher swooped down into Lebanese Army headquarters in Yarze on 22 February 1993, and emphasized Washington's commitment to Lebanon's independence. In fact, he said little that was new. Nonetheless, Christopher's visit to Yarze may indicate a shift in U.S. perceptions. Unlike the Bush administration, which still revealed evidence of trauma for the Reagan administration's disastrous and amateurish venture in saving Lebanon, the new players may be willing to turn a new leaf. The tragedy of the hostages is over, and a new political generation—unscarred by Lebanon—is in charge in Washington.

CONCLUSION

Overall, Lebanon's new parliament represents a significant break with the country's recent political history. Only fifteen of the 1972 incumbents were reelected, and about 60 percent of the MPs elected in 1992 have no previous experience in public office. (In November, this ratio was echoed when the new cabinet was created: twenty of the thirty ministers are newcomers to political office.) Although the outcome may have been quite different had the Christian boycott been less effective, the shift to nonsectarianism in the platforms of both Christian and Muslim candidates and the voters' increased penchant to hold the new parliament accountable may mark a significant shift in the political scene.

The elections exemplify the deradicalization of many players within Lebanese civil society. The importance of implicating Hizballah in the formal political process is extraordinary, and the actions of discriminating voters—the boycott notwithstanding—are equally heartening. This is not to suggest sectarianism in Lebanon has slid off the plate. In significant measure, the attitude of individual Lebanese to the elections was largely predicted by confessional identity, although this statement needs to be conditioned: An overwhelming majority of Lebanese believed the elections were held too hastily. In fact, regardless of their political views vis-à-vis Syria, most Lebanese perceived the elections to reflect Syrian pressures rather than an autonomous Lebanese decision. Nevertheless, the fact that a significant percentage of Lebanese citizens were legitimately engaged in the electoral process, combined with the self-mobilization of various elements of civil society for the purpose of monitoring the process, indicates that the roots of democracy run deeply in Lebanon, more deeply than many observers recognize.

The Islamists, who are now incorporated into the political system, focused their electoral campaigns on social reform. Actions speak louder than words, and Hizballah social and welfare activities in the South and around Beirut demonstrate that the Islamists have become an important part of Lebanon's resurgent civil society. Many Christians now shy away from sectarian politics. True, nonsectarianism does not equate to civil society, any more than sectarianism and civil society are necessarily incongruent. A healthy civil society is marked by toleration, civility and the spurning of parochial interests in favor of the general good, and this implies that the identification of the Lebanese with Lebanon must be deepened rather than hijacked by narrow "tribal" interests. This also implies that the government must be capable and competent to play the role of rule setter, referee, and judge, because without a vigorous and legitimate government civil society is impossible.

Platitudes aside, the fact remains—and herein lies the hope for Lebanon's future—that civil society in Lebanon is reviving. Civil society proved its resilience throughout the civil war, and it has already shown that it can check the arbitrary actions of the government, while also providing a basis for building ties and alliances across confessional lines. An obvious illustration of this point occurred in 1991 when the rejuvenated labor union federation initiated demonstrations that felled the government of Omar Karameh.

To be sure, serious obstacles litter the future, and big questions condition Lebanon's fate. Can Hariri produce the combination of confidence and economic reform necessary to boost Lebanon's sagging economy? How will the Islamists respond down the road if future elections do not bring comparable victories (as might be the case if the Christians actively contest the next parliamentary election)? Will Syria cease to find excuses to continue its massive deployment in Lebanon? And, the biggest question of all, what results will emerge from the peace process, where Lebanon may be last in the queue, behind the Palestinians, Jordan, and Syria?

Lebanon is only now consolidating its Second Republic. Perhaps, as former Prime Minister Salim el-Hoss has noted, only when Lebanon moves purposefully toward a truly democratic and independent Third Republic will the country be secure and immune to the horrors that marked its recent history.

NOTES

1. A graphic economic indicator of Lebanon's uncertain peace is the post-Ta'if value of its currency: the Lebanese pound experienced its most precipitous decline after 1990 (see Appendix B). This is especially noteworthy given that the pound was relatively stable throughout most of the war. Although the fighting seriously disrupted and even destroyed much of Lebanon's secondary and tertiary economic sectors, the war itself was a business. As relatively vast inflows of currency kept the economy afloat, the pound's value (against the U.S. dollar) deteriorated only slightly from 1975 into the 1980s. Although its value declined sharply after the mid-1980s, the real plummet began after 1990.

2. These figures for the 1975–1990 period were released by the Lebanese police on 9 March 1993, and reported in the *New York Times,* 10 March 1993. The report indicated over 144,000 Lebanese killed, nearly 200,000 wounded, and 17,415 missing, of which 13,968 had been kidnapped by militias. Most of the kidnapped are presumed dead. The figures exclude 6,630 killed and 8,000 wounded in incidents involving Palestinians; 857 Palestinians and Lebanese killed in the Sabra and Shatila camps in September 1982; and 3,781 people killed in fighting between Amal and the PLO during the "War of the Camps."

3. Syria's influence over Lebanon is transparent in the peace process: the Lebanese do not stray very far from the Syrian lead. Lebanon has been a participant in the bilateral negotiations launched in Madrid in October 1991, but Lebanese negotiators appear to take nary a move without checking with their Syrian counterparts. When the multilateral component of the negotiations convened in Moscow in January 1992, Syria boycotted the meeting and Lebanon followed. Both countries continue the boycott.

4. See Augustus Richard Norton, "Lebanon after Ta'if: Is the Civil War Over?" *Middle East Journal* vol. 45 no. 3 (Summer 1991), pp. 457–473; and a letter updating the article, ibid. vol. 45 no. 4 (Autumn 1991), pp. 739–740.

5. If elections had been delayed until 1994, Syria's overt presence in

Lebanon might have been diminished—provided, of course, that Syria had abided by the Ta'if provision for Syrian troop withdrawal.

6. In fact, there is every indication (in 1993) that Syria intends to remain widely deployed in Lebanon for the foreseeable future.

7. The authors are indebted to Ambassador Simon Karam, Lebanon's envoy to the United States, who shared his deep knowledge of Lebanon's administrative organization in a telephone interview with A. R. Norton on 13 July 1993.

8. This passage was taken from an English translation of the Ta'if Accord published in *The Beirut Review* vol. 1 no. 1 (Spring 1991).

9. This section draws on the valuable accounts in *The Lebanon Report* vol. 3 no. 9 (September 1992) and no. 10 (October 1992).

10. The meeting was held in May 1992, cosponsored by the International Peace Academy and the Norwegian Institute of International Affairs in cooperation with the Centre for Lebanese Studies in Oxford.

11. For example, the Ford Foundation sponsored a comprehensive study of the elections by the Lebanese Centre for Policy Studies, led by Paul Salem, for release in 1993.

12. Various leaders made different pronouncements condemning the elections, including those of the Lebanese Forces, followers of exiled General Aoun, the National Liberal Party, the Phalangist Party, and Raymond Eddé's National Bloc.

13. See the papers by Charif, Amery, and Saidi in this volume.

14. "Kamil-bey" is the Shi'ite za'im who many reform-minded Shi'ites view as the epitome of what is wrong with the old system (although he retains a core of supporters in the South). His defeat marked the passing of a long phase of Shi'ite history in Lebanon, during which the Shi'ites were supplicants rather than men and women with political rights.

Part 2

Enduring Regional and
International Dimensions

4

Reflections on Lebanon's Foreign Policy

Paul Salem

FRAMING THE ISSUE

To trace the foreign policy of small states is always a difficult task; to do so for a divided and penetrated state like Lebanon is doubly hard.[1] What is foreign policy and what is domestic policy in a country thoroughly dominated by foreign forces? Can we truly speak of policy at all in a state that has very little independence? When we speak of foreign policy, do we mean only the foreign policy of the central government, or do we refer also to the foreign policies of the various communal subgroups that make up the Lebanese polity?

Let us look at some of these questions more closely. First, instead of asking the usual question, "Can a polarized and dominated country like Lebanon have a foreign policy?"[2] let us ask the more interesting question: Does Lebanon have anything but a foreign policy? With most of the country under domination by outside powers and the state having virtually no area of uncontested jurisdiction, all policy, even that which would otherwise be considered domestic, must be negotiated and cleared through outside channels. In a sense, all policy is foreign policy.

The presence of foreign armies is not the only reason for the excessive importance of foreign policy. Historically, for example, Lebanon's internal divisions prompted many Lebanese factions to seek foreign sponsorship to further their domestic agendas, and, because of regional and international polarization, they found willing foreign sponsors. Also, the strength of substate actors (i.e., confessional parties or militias) often compelled the state to resort to foreign support to impose its authority. Furthermore, the media and general public encouraged this orientation. Foreign policy always held the promise of a deus ex machina,[3] while all that could be expected on the domestic front was slow and uninspiring change.

The problem, then, is not, Does Lebanon have a foreign policy? but, Does it have a domestic policy? Indeed, Lebanon's challenge is to limit the scope of foreign policy by recapturing a domestic sphere in which the state can truly be sovereign and can implement policy on its own terms. Only then can a legitimate foreign policy, properly defined, be said to exist.

Although the foreign relations of several substate communities in Lebanon stretch back many centuries, it is difficult to speak of the foreign relations of a recognizable Lebanese state before the establishment of Greater Lebanon and, more important, before its independence in 1943. Nevertheless, some nationalists trace historical elements of Lebanese foreign policy all the way back to Fakhr al-Din, the mythologized seventeenth-century Druze prince and unruly Ottoman Wali who is popularly credited with laying the foundations for an autonomous—and eventually independent—Lebanon.[4] These nationalists argue that Fakhr al-Din's close relations with Italian merchant cities and his military pact with Tuscany in 1608—conceived to fend off Turkish influence and avoid domination by either France or Spain—support their contention that Lebanese foreign policy, while receptive to close commercial cooperation, is designed to preserve Lebanese independence and nonalignment through obedience to this maxim: Lebanon should avoid close association and alliance with potentially dominating powers.[5] The story of independent Lebanese foreign policy, however, is interspersed with long and significant periods of foreign domination, most notably Turkish, Egyptian, and French.

Properly speaking, modern Lebanese foreign policy was born in 1943 when it became necessary for the newly independent state to *have* a foreign policy. With conflicting domestic pro-French and pro-Arab tendencies, the outline of a Lebanese foreign policy was set (like so much else in Lebanese politics) in the National Pact negotiated between Bishara al-Khoury and Riad al-Solh.[6] With respect to the country's foreign affairs, the pact was like a marriage built on a double divorce, a double negation: No to close alliance and protection from France, and No to merger with a larger Arab entity. It outlined what policies were *not* to be followed, without indicating what policies were to be followed. It represented a giving up of positive options held by internal players in favor of negative options imposed by the necessity for compromise.

Naturally, the double negation suggested some form of nonalignment or neutrality; such nonalignment was a principal theme of Lebanese foreign policy over the decades.[7] The problem, however, was that neither the internal nor the external environments of the state encouraged or harmonized with a nonalignment option for Lebanon. Internally, the communities and parties that made up the polity pursued conflicting regional and international alliances. Externally, the increasingly polarized regional and global environments made nonalignment a decreasingly viable option. This is to say nothing of the wisdom of nonalignment per se as a foreign policy in a region beset by conflict. In this respect, a conspicuous warning in Machiavelli's *The Prince* is worth citing:

> Irresolute princes, in order to avoid present dangers, most of the time follow the road of neutrality, and most of the time they are ruined . . . for if two of your neighbours come to blows they will be of such quality that, when one of these wins, you will either have to fear the victor or you will not. And in either of these cases it will always be more useful for you to disclose yourself and wage a good war; for, in the first case if you do not disclose yourself you will always be the prey of the victor, with the pleasure and satisfaction of the one who has been conquered; you will have no excuse nor anything else which can defend you and no one to receive you; for the victor will not want to have suspect friends who did not aid him in adversity; and he who lost will not receive you, because you did not want to risk his fortune with arms in hand.[8]

This advice holds much resonance regarding Lebanon's position in the Arab-Israeli conflict, in inter-Arab conflicts, and in the Cold War. Lebanon suffered from all three and benefited from none.

Moreover, Lebanon mustered no commitment to nonalignment or neutrality—for example, armed neutrality—as a positive national policy. It was policy by default. The absence of commitment in foreign policy was typical of the low level of commitment that the Lebanese state exhibited in most policy areas. This laissez-faire approach to policy could only encourage a low level of commitment by the population to the state, as the state was not perceived to be pursuing any meaningful ends, and this would cause domestic weakness and political decay. Indeed, a robust stand in foreign policy often has politically salutary results domestically. International conflict often has a socially cohesive function; identifying an enemy without may help cement national unity within. Also, building an army and preparing for war have easily identifiable integrative effects in developing countries.

The principle of nonalignment suggested by the National Pact left many questions unanswered. Although the 1943 pact addressed the conflict between pro-French and pro-Arab orientations—a conflict that would soon become outdated with the collapse of French colonial power—it had nothing to say about conflicts yet to emerge: the Arab-Israeli conflict, the U.S.-Soviet Cold War, and the various inter-Arab cold wars that ebbed and flowed from the 1950s to the 1990s. If Lebanese foreign policy was based on the double negation of nonalignment, did this mean that Lebanon should be nonaligned in the Arab-Israeli conflict? Could it afford to be nonaligned in the superpower Cold War, or even, more important, in the Arab cold wars? Without clear internal agreement on such basic tenets of foreign policy, Lebanon was buffeted by conflicting winds, now siding with the United States, now with Gamal Abdul Nasser, now with Syria, and so on. It made firm allies nowhere and grew increasingly isolated and bereft of foreign partners.

The instability of this vague nonalignment position was compounded by the fact that no coherent theoretical model underpinned it. Michael Chiha, one of the main framers of the Lebanese nationalist idea, spoke of Lebanon as somehow a "bridge" between East and West; but, what that exactly meant in policy terms, and how a state was to behave as a bridge without being thoroughly trampled upon, was—and remains—unclear. Others spoke of "neutrality" without considering the host of international treaties and agreements that went into the establishment of neutral states in Europe. Conceptions of Lebanon as a "buffer" state also offered little promise other than the unsavory prospect of being interminably squeezed. Lebanon as a fulcrum upon which regional and international forces would be delicately balanced could only work if, as the pivot point, the Lebanese state were strong enough to sustain the weight of the forces it was trying to balance; otherwise, the pivot itself would be crushed, as indeed happened. Describing Lebanon as a Hong Kong or a Switzerland only appealed to the vanity of the Lebanese without clarifying policy options.

However, Lebanese foreign policy had problems beyond those mentioned above. Prime among these was the multiplicity of Lebanese foreign policies; while the central government pursued one foreign policy, various internal parties and communities pursued their own foreign policies. This, of course, undermined the authority of the state and provided opportunities for outside intervention. There are several reasons for the prevalence of these substate foreign policies.

First, Lebanon's communal groups have historical links with outside powers. The Maronites have ancient ties to Rome and France;[9] the Sunnis are heirs of several Muslim empires; the Shi'ites have 500-year-old ties to Iran; the Druze are closely tied to their coreligionists in Syria and Israel;[10] even the Greek Orthodox are now reviving old ties with Russia interrupted by seventy years of Communist rule. These foreign ties have existed for centuries and have important religious, cultural, and political dimensions that cannot be easily erased. Second, the double negation of the National Pact contributed to the frustration of national subgroups. Unable to pursue their foreign interests through the central government, they pursued foreign links on their own, be it with Gamal Abdul Nasser, Hafez al-Asad, France, or Khomeini's Iran.

The third reason for the prevalence of substate foreign policies is the high level of internal dissatisfaction within the political system. To put it in simplified terms, most Muslim leaders and political groupings felt grossly underrepresented in government and complained of unequal distributions of power and wealth; in the 1970s they turned to the Palestinians for support in trying to redress this complaint. Many Christians, consequently, suffered from the equally serious complaint of insecurity in the face of a strong and largely Muslim Palestinian armed movement; this led them to call for outside help from Syria, Israel, the United States, and even Iraq. Both concerns, unfairness and insecurity, provided fertile ground for development of substate foreign policies. Both, if redressed, would help to curtail substate foreign policies. The Ta'if Accord has largely redressed the sense of unfairness among the Muslims; it has not, however, effected a decrease in the sense of insecurity among many Christians.

The present-day configuration of these substate foreign policies is roughly as follows. The Maronites are currently divided. After the waning of their traditional patron, France, they looked for other sponsors. Over the past two decades they have tried Israel, the United States, Iraq, and Syria. Currently there are two main camps, one represented by President Hrawi and the Frangieh clan, which relies strategically on Syria, and another led by exiled General Michel Aoun and others, which rejects the close Syrian alliance but has no viable strategic alternative. The pro-Israel camp, strong in the late 1970s and early 1980s, has declined.

Among the Sunnis there are also several factions. A staunchly pro-Syrian faction, based in Tripoli, is led by a former prime minister, Omar Karameh. In another, pro-Saudi, faction Prime Minister Rafiq al-Hariri plays a prominent role. A third, pro-PLO faction was strong before 1982, but has now all but disappeared. The Shi'ites have a pro-Syrian wing led by Amal leader and Speaker of Parliament Nabih Birri, as well as a pro-Iranian wing led by Hizballah. The Druze have a primary alliance with Syria, but maintain important relations with Israel through the Druze community there. The Greek Orthodox have a pro-Syrian wing in the Syrian Social Nationalist Party, but some Orthodox leaders have pro-U.S. or pro-French leanings.

All these substate foreign policy orientations do not make life any easier for the central government; given the related problem of outside domination, the state's difficulty in formulating and implementing foreign policy is readily understandable. Both in theory and practice, Lebanese foreign policy is remarkably elusive.

OUTLINES OF LEBANESE FOREIGN POLICY

Let us turn to a more historical and traditional description of Lebanese foreign policy at the state level. After independence and the National Pact, the outlines of applied Lebanese foreign policy began to take shape through various agreements entered into by the government, most notably the 1944 inter-Arab Alexandria Protocol and the 1945 Charter of the League of Arab States. These, in addition to the 1950 Arab Common Defense and

Economic Cooperation Pact, gave official content to the Arab aspect of Lebanese foreign policy. Through these agreements, Lebanon committed itself to defending Arab causes and to coordinating its foreign and defense policies with the community of Arab states.

The equivocal spirit of Lebanon's participation in these agreements, however, was reflected in a number of provisions. For example, the Alexandria Protocol included—at the insistence of the Lebanese delegation—a special decree in which Arab states vowed to respect and support "the independence and sovereignty of Lebanon" within its present boundaries. Moreover, the Charter of the League of Arab States accepted—also after Lebanese insistence—that decisionmaking within the League be by consensus and not by majority vote.

Lebanon's prominent role in laying the foundations of common Arab policymaking was counterbalanced early on by its equally visible role in founding the United Nations and its help in drafting the UN Charter and the Universal Declaration of Human Rights. In the U.S.-dominated postwar atmosphere of the late 1940s and early 1950s, Lebanon's heavy involvement in the UN had unavoidable political overtones. The pro-Arab orientation of Bishara al-Khoury and Riad al-Solh contrasted with the more Western orientation of the equally vigorous Charles Malik, Lebanese ambassador to the United States and to the UN, and onetime president of the UN General Assembly.

Nevertheless, in line with general Arab policy—especially that of Syria and Egypt—the Lebanese government rejected U.S. proposals for the formation of a Middle East Defense Organization (MEDO) in 1951, refused participation in the 1955 Baghdad Pact, and threw its modest weight in support of the Arab-Palestinian cause. Increasing U.S. influence, however, and heightened Lebanese Christian fears about the growth of Nasserism and Arab nationalism, soon led to a change. In 1957 President Camille Chamoun and newly appointed Foreign Minister Charles Malik shifted gears to place Lebanon more squarely in the U.S. camp through official acceptance of the Eisenhower Doctrine, designed to combat Soviet and Nasserist influence in the region.[11] This foreign policy shift was poorly received in Muslim circles and became an important factor in the deterioration of the internal political consensus that led to the brief civil war of 1958. When President Fouad Shehab assumed power in 1958 as a compromise candidate with support from Abdul Nasser, he pursued a careful foreign policy—toeing the Nasserist line in regional political affairs while pursuing close technical and economic relations with the West, especially France. This foreign policy was undergirded by a vigorous domestic policy of etatism. However, Shehab's policy of maintaining close relations with the West internationally, while pursuing close relations with the Soviet Union's allies regionally, contained obvious internal contradictions.

Lebanon's next president, Charles Helou, meant to continue Shehab's policies but was soon overtaken by events. The Arab defeat in the 1967 war prompted the militarization of the Palestinian cause and the Palestinian presence in Lebanon. Thus, the previously foreign policy issues of Palestine and the Arab cause were transformed into Lebanese domestic issues with direct repercussions for the country's national security and sovereignty. The 1969 signing of the Cairo Agreement, granting Palestinian refugees the right to carry arms, patrol their own camps, and prosecute a guerrilla war against Israel from Lebanese soil, marked a fatal crack in Lebanese national security; the distinction between foreign and domestic policy was no longer viable. From that point on, with the Lebanese state thoroughly penetrated by external forces, foreign and domestic policy would become hopelessly entwined. The Frangieh administration came to power in 1970 enjoying good relations with Syria and brandishing a get-tough policy toward the Palestinians. Foreign and domestic policies soon clashed, leaving the Frangieh government paralyzed.

With the collapse of the state in 1975, Lebanon's foreign policy shattered into a number of confessional pieces. As the war progressed, different communities developed separate relations with Israel, Syria, Iran, Libya, Iraq, and the Soviet Union. The state, meanwhile, having lost virtually all of its independence, authority, and sovereignty, fell under foreign domination and lost the capacity to formulate foreign policy autonomously. Reflecting this reality, the official policies of the administration of President Elias Sarkis (1976–1982) in foreign affairs feebly echoed those of Damascus.

The Israeli invasion of 1982 overturned the status quo of 1976–1982 but introduced its own complications. With the decline of domestic support in Israel for an extensive military presence in Lebanon and with the scaling back of Israel's territorial occupation of Lebanon, Israel's patron—the United States—was left holding the political cards in Beirut. Amine Gemayel's administration, with its meager domestic resources and overdependence on the United States vis-à-vis both Syria and Israel, closely followed the U.S. lead in foreign affairs during its first two years in office (1982–1983). As in 1958, when Muslim and Nasserist opposition to the state's pro-U.S. policy provoked a violent crisis, the Gemayel administration's pro-U.S. leanings evoked disapproval in Muslim circles, this time with support from Syria and Iran, and led to the intifada (uprising) of 6 February 1984 that split the army, brought down the government, and ended the state's brief period of control over the nation's capital.

Between 1984 and 1988 the Gemayel administration attempted, without success, to reestablish close relations with Syria, after both U.S. and Israeli power in the country had ebbed. Meanwhile, substate actors deepened their foreign links. The newly formed Hizballah introduced a strong Iranian influence into the country, Amal consolidated its links with Syria, the Druze Progressive Socialist Party fastened its ties with Syria and the

Soviet Union, while the Christian Lebanese Forces—disillusioned with
Israel—explored links with Iraq. In the North, the influential Karameh and
Frangieh families worked closely with Damascus, while in the South, the
Israeli-backed South Lebanon Army ensured Israeli control over its self-
declared "security zone."

With the end of Gemayel's term and the emergence of rival governments under General Michel Aoun and Dr. Salim el-Hoss, domestic and
foreign policies became further intertwined. In a complex and multifaceted
set of crises, tensions between the two governments escalated into a military showdown involving Syria and Iraq on opposite sides. In a series of
developments that have now become familiar,[12] the Arab League, with
encouragement from the United States, moved to defuse the crisis and, after
consultation with Syria, invited the Lebanese deputies to Ta'if, Saudi
Arabia in September 1989 for talks that led to the elaboration of the
Document of National Understanding—the Ta'if Accord. Implementation
of the Ta'if Accord, however, had to await the Iraqi invasion of Kuwait and
the subsequent green light from the United States for Syria to go ahead and
uproot General Aoun (who opposed the accord) from Baabda and the small
enclave he controlled.

Given the text of the Ta'if Accord and Syria's virtually unchallenged
dominance over the country after October 1990, the foreign policies of
President Hrawi and his successive councils of ministers and prime ministers have all been thoroughly pro-Syrian. Whether this foreign policy flavor
will continue if and when Syrian influence on the ground ebbs, remains to
be seen.

THE POST-TA'IF FRAMEWORK

The 1989 Ta'if Accord proposed a radical break from the old National Pact
in foreign policy matters. In place of the double negation is an unambigu-
ous alignment with Syria. The agreement talks of distinctive Lebanese-
Syrian relations, common strategic, political, and economic interests, and
the necessity to coordinate policy at all levels. This was formalized in the
May 1991 Treaty of Brotherhood, Cooperation, and Coordination and the
September 1991 Pact of Defense and Security. In addition, the National
Pact's equivocal reference to Lebanon as an independent country with an
"Arab face" is replaced in the Ta'if Accord by the definitive affirmation
that Lebanon is "Arab in its identity and association."[13] In other words, the
neither-nor position between the Arabs and the West has been erased in
favor of final identification with the Arabs; the absence of alignment has
been replaced by explicit alignment with Syria.

How can this new foreign policy arrangement be assessed? First, what
does it mean exactly? Does foreign policy "coordination" with Syria mean

that Lebanon no longer has a foreign policy of its own and that Lebanon's foreign policy will be handled on its behalf by Syria, or does it mean that Lebanon's foreign policy can still be autonomously formulated but must be pro-Syrian? So far, the former arrangement has prevailed, but as the state regains its vigor, the latter arrangement may become the relevant one.

Second, is the Ta'if-derived foreign policy orientation a stable one? To a certain extent, general recognition of Syria's importance by all parties in Lebanon, and the necessity of good relations this implies, will probably be a feature of Lebanese foreign policy in the foreseeable future. Indeed, it is possible to argue that the risks (outlined previously) involved in Lebanon's nonalignment and noncommitment in foreign policy may be avoided through this new alignment. The aloofness from Syria and the Arab hinterland, implied in the first National Pact, is no longer viable. However, the extent of the closeness to Syria built into the new arrangement was based on particular internal and external conditions that could change and hence cause the relationship to unravel.

Internally, Syrian ascendancy was made possible by the bloody infighting within the Christian right wing, Syria's traditional opponents. The divisions between Aoun's army and Samir Ja'Ja's Lebanese Forces militia allowed Syria to play the role of power broker, increasing its influence accordingly. Large sections of the Christian community, however, viewed the Syrian entry in October 1990 as a conquest and will be likely to try to shake off the Syrian alliance when the opportunity presents itself.

Externally, Syrian ascendancy was favored by particular regional developments, especially the emergence of the 1990–1991 Kuwaiti crisis and the U.S. need for Syria to join the anti-Saddam coalition. This ascendancy has already begun to wane with the end of the Gulf War, the poor showing of Soviet arms in Arab hands in the Gulf, the final collapse of Soviet power, and the increasingly secure U.S. position in the Middle East. Both internally and externally, there are reasons to expect that this new foreign policy orientation may be challenged—perhaps violently—from within or without.

Putting those possibilities aside, what should Lebanon's relations with Syria be like? To be sure, good relations with Syria are axiomatic. The two countries are immediate neighbors and have significant common interests. However, Syria's involvement in the Lebanese war since 1976 has left many scars on the relationship.[14] As Lebanese groups fought with each other and with the Palestinians, so too did some fight against or with the Syrians. As bad blood developed among the Lebanese themselves, so too did some develop between Lebanon and Syria. This must be openly recognized and treated. The fact that the Lebanese and Syrians are described by some as "brothers" does not mean that they did not come into serious conflict with one another. The fact that they came into conflict, however, does not preclude resumption of "fraternal" relations.

Just as reviving peace in Lebanon requires a process of profound national reconciliation among the Lebanese, so too does reestablishment of close relations between Syria and Lebanon require reconciliation. This is not taking place. The state-to-state rapprochement that one sees today expressed in treaties and pacts might be, in a sense, a good thing, because all states should organize their relations clearly and formally and not leave them open to chance and misinterpretation. Nevertheless, a stable and lasting rapprochement must be more profound. Conflicts with enemies can be resolved in treaties and pacts, but differences within the family, so to speak, require much more openness and good will. Until the treaties and pacts are translated into mutual understanding and trust, Lebanese-Syrian relations will continue to be problematic.

Most important, both sides must be more understanding and accommodating of one another. The Syrians, for example, must understand Lebanese fears. First, the Syrian Army is large and powerful and, naturally, not always Syria's best ambassador. Second, Syrian political and economic systems differ radically from those of Lebanon; the Lebanese systems are much more liberal and freewheeling. Close coordination between the two countries may not be altogether possible without turbulent systemic change. Third, Lebanon is an open country with important ties to many countries in the West and the East; the cliché that Lebanon is the meeting place of East and West, Christendom and Islam, is overused, but remains very relevant. Syria must respect this role if Lebanon is not to lose its particular identity.

The Lebanese also must understand Syrian fears. Unlike the Lebanese state, the Syrian state has taken its security very seriously. Although it invests immense resources in defending against external aggression and internal sabotage, it is still insecure in the face of Israeli strength and the existence of other external and internal foes. Damascus itself is strategically insecure, located in a militarily penetrable desert only miles from Israeli positions. From this Damascene perspective, Lebanon, despite its divisions and weaknesses, is a security threat. Lebanon covers the entire western horizon of the Syrian capital and contains the strategic higher ground. A political vacuum in Lebanon is menacing to Syria, as is the alignment of internal groups with Israel, or Iraq, or any of Syria's other opponents. Syria cannot afford these security threats. Lebanese alignments that are threatening to Syria naturally meet with a violent preemptive response.

Indeed, it is in the interest of the Lebanese to understand Syria's security fears and try to address them. This is not done, as is the case today, by merely pledging fealty to Syria—compliance is not alliance. It is done, more effectively, by building a strong Lebanese Army in control of its territory that can play a role in promoting both Lebanese and Syrian security, not a role hostile to Syria. In a sense, Lebanon's mistake in the past was its failure to realize that in order to defend Lebanon vis-à-vis other Arab states, it should have helped more in their defense. Lebanon's nonalignment or neutrality backfired. It kept away neither Lebanon's enemies nor its friends.

Beyond Syria, the Gulf countries have emerged as a focus of Lebanese interests. The 1990 Gulf War confirmed the irrelevance of the already eclipsed slogans of Arab nationalism and represented a baptism by fire of the *raison d'état* logic of contemporary inter-Arab politics. With the rise of the oil-rich states, especially Saudi Arabia, and the decline of the heavily militarized former Soviet allies, the structure of Arab power has drifted increasingly away from the ideological toward the economic. The explicit Arab orientation of Lebanon's post-Ta'if policy will be less divisive than in previous years: While many Lebanese disagree over the politicized and ideological formulations of Arabism, they agree on necessary economic closeness with the Arab world.

Iran, meanwhile, is playing the same destabilizing role that populist and revolutionary Arab regimes played in the 1950s and 1960s. By arming local parties and providing regional cover for the existence of a state-within-a-state in Lebanon, the postrevolutionary regime in Iran has placed a serious obstacle in the way of regaining state sovereignty and establishing stable foundations for domestic peace. So far, the Iranian presence has been sanctioned by Syria, and, like almost everything else in Lebanon today, any negotiations with Iran over the future size and nature of its intervention in Lebanon will have to be conducted through Damascus. The Lebanese government's current policy of supporting Ta'if and the disarming of militias while opposing the disarming of the Hizballah militia (and conducting relations with Iran as if this were not a serious issue) is untenable.

The issue of Hizballah is, of course, closely linked to the Israeli occupation of a large portion of South Lebanon. Since the beginning of the Madrid peace process, Lebanon's position at the negotiating table has consisted of demanding the immediate implementation of UN Security Council Resolution 425 that calls for an unconditional Israeli withdrawal from Lebanon. This demand has been rejected by the Israelis, who have responded with demands that Lebanon and Syria disarm Hizballah, subdue resistance activities, and prepare security guarantees regarding Israel's northern border. Understandably, the talks have gone nowhere. Meanwhile, both parties have tolerated an escalation of military confrontations in South Lebanon in the hope that pressure on the ground will lead to concessions at the negotiating table. Syrian involvement in the Lebanese-Israeli negotiations is in some ways helpful insofar as it redresses the massive power imbalance between Lebanon and Israel. The danger in three-way negotiations, however, is that Lebanon might end up on the table rather than at it. Indeed, in the Arab-Israeli peace process, Lebanon faces a complex challenge. Much skill, courage, and luck will be required if Lebanon is not to lose the peace as it has already lost several wars.

Internationally, with the end of the Cold War and the consequent expansion of U.S. military influence in the Middle East—as evidenced, for example, by the 1990–1991 Gulf War—Lebanon and Syria will both have to make their peace with the "new world order." It is important, however, that U.S. influence not be employed as a divisive force in Lebanon. The Ta'if Accord was concluded after the end of the Cold War with heavy U.S. encouragement; it is crucial, therefore, that the United States remain involved in the Ta'if process and see it through to its completion, lest the formidable obstacles lead to an unraveling of Ta'if's precarious peace. Lebanon should look to the United States not as a strategic ally as in 1957–1958 or 1982–1984, but as an influential power that can help in completing the Ta'if Accord and nursing Lebanon back to health.

With regard to the United Nations—appeals of well-meaning internationalists notwithstanding—Lebanon must not seek a special place among the nations, for that place, as recent history has shown, is likely to be especially wretched. Lebanon should strive to become a state like any other, not the ward of any international organization. The UN cannot provide Lebanon with the protection and support it needs. Lebanon's security must be acquired through domestic strengthbuilding and regional alliancemaking. The UN will always be a friend to Lebanon, but to accede to political maturity, Lebanon—like all other states—must make the hard political choices necessary to establish a meaningful and useful alliance-and-adversary foreign policy structure closer to home.

LOOKING AHEAD

The future of stability and foreign policy in Lebanon depends on several critical factors: domestic consensus, regional peace, and responsible policy-making on the part of both the Syrian and Lebanese governments. Domestically, although the text of the Ta'if Accord represents a large common ground among most Lebanese groups, the way the accord has been implemented and the orientation of post-Ta'if governments have left large sections of the population—especially within the Christian community—discontented. If this serious discontent is not addressed, the pro-Syrian and pro-Arab foreign policy orientation of the Ta'if Accord may become threatened by sharp domestic disturbances. The example of the fragmentation of the Soviet bloc and the independence of small ethnic groups in Eastern Europe—even the ethnic and religious breakup of Iraq—has not been lost on Lebanese Christian separatists.

Progress or failure in regional peace talks will, of course, have a direct bearing on Lebanon. A region at peace, stabilized by a set of bilateral and multilateral agreements and supervised by one superpower, would provide ample room to reinforce Lebanon's precarious peace and to strengthen its state institutions. A region drifting back into confrontation would, almost inevitably, tear Lebanon apart again. Despite Lebanon's best efforts, the country is still a sparring ground for Syria and Israel; if they cannot resolve their differences at the negotiating table, they are likely to pursue their politics by other means in the Lebanese arena.

The burden of Lebanon's future, however, hinges on the policies of the Lebanese and Syrian governments. If they can make their close alliance work in the interest of both states, then this new foreign policy orientation will be a popular and stable one, stable enough to withstand conditions of both war and peace. If the alliance proves to be dysfunctional—for Lebanon as a whole or for any one of its principal communities—then its domestic foundations will weaken and eventually crumble. Nothing succeeds like success. It is important for officials in both countries to act quickly to redress the imbalances that have emerged and to develop the alliance into a system of open cooperation and friendship free of the tensions of previous years. Indeed, after fifteen years of war, Lebanon can scarcely afford another foreign policy failure or another giant step backward in the long process of rebuilding its national security.

NOTES

1. The definitive study on Lebanese foreign policy has yet to be written. As domestic and foreign policies in Lebanon are closely interwoven, such a study could not be undertaken without detailed historical attention to the intricacies of Lebanese domestic politics. The present chapter is offered as a thought-piece on Lebanese foreign policy, with special attention paid to an examination of the wisdom of pursuing a neutral, or nonaligned, foreign policy. It is based on remarks presented at the CIIPS conference on Lebanon held in Ottawa, Canada in October 1991.

2. Ghassan Salame, "Is a Lebanese Foreign Policy Possible?" in Halim Barakat (ed.), *Toward a Viable Lebanon* (Washington: Georgetown University Press, 1988), pp. 347–360.

3. For example, the foreign interventions of 1831 (Egypt), 1860–1861 (France), 1917 (Allied Powers), 1920 (France), 1958 (Egypt and United States), 1969–1975 (Palestinians), 1976 (Syria), 1978 and 1982 (Israel), and 1990 (Syria).

4. See Richard van Leeuwen, "Fakhr al-Din and His Place in Lebanese History," *The Beirut Review* no. 4 (Fall 1992).

5. See Fuad Dakrub, *Lebanon's Foreign Policy* (Beirut: Dar al-nashr al-arabiyya, 1959), p. 16, or Halim Abu Izzidin, *Lebanon's Foreign Policy: Principles, Systems, and Documents* (Beirut: Dar al-ilm lil-malayin, 1966), p. 15. Both articles are in Arabic.

6. See Farid el-Khazen, "The Communal Pact of National Identities: The Making and Politics of the 1943 National Pact," *Papers on Lebanon* no. 12 (Oxford: Centre for Lebanese Studies, 1991), 68 pp.

7. Throughout this essay, the term "nonalignment" is to be understood in its general sense—of "not being aligned, or allied, with any particular state." It is not to be associated with the positions or policies of the officially institutionalized

Nonaligned Movement that emerged in the 1950s and of which the Lebanese state was a member.

8. Niccolo Machiavelli, *The Prince,* trans. Leo Paul S. de Alvarez (Irving, Tex.: University of Dallas Press, 1980), pp. 133–134.

9. See Joseph Mouawad, "The Image of France in Maronite Tradition," *The Beirut Review* no. 4 (Fall 1992).

10. See Robert B. Betts, *The Druze* (New Haven: Yale University Press, 1988).

11. See Lebanon, Ministry of Foreign Affairs, *Documents on the Foreign Policy of Lebanon* (Beirut, 1958).

12. See for example Karim Pakradouni, *Le Piege* (Paris: Grasset, 1991), or P. Salem, "Two Years of Living Dangerously: General Aoun and the Unlikely Rise of Lebanon's Second Republic," *The Beirut Review* no. 1 (Spring 1991), pp. 62–87.

13. See texts of the Treaty and the Pact in *The Beirut Review* no. 2 (Fall 1991), pp. 115–118, 132–133, and an annotated text of the Ta'if Agreement in *The Beirut Review* no. 1 (Spring 1991), pp. 119–172. For a detailed analysis of the Ta'if Agreement, see Joseph Maila, "Le Document d'entente nationale, un commentaire," *Les Cahiers de l'Orient* no. 16–17 (1989), pp. 135–217, and his "L'Accord de Taef, deux ans après," *Les Cahiers de l'Orient* no. 24 (1991), pp. 13–69.

14. For a review of Lebanese-Syrian relations (in Arabic) see *Lebanese-Syrian Relations, 1943–1985: Events, Bibliography, and Documents* (Antelias, Lebanon: Lebanese Centre for Documentation and Research, 1986). For an analysis of the Syrian role in Lebanon after the outbreak of war see Adeed Dawisha, *Syria and the Lebanese Crisis* (London: MacMillan, 1980), and Naomi Weinberger, *Syrian Intervention in Lebanon* (Oxford: Oxford University Press, 1986). Kesrouan Labaki, in *Des idees pour le Liban* (Antelias, Lebanon: Publishing and Marketing House, Maison du Futur, 1984), pp. 89–90 offers some interesting additional insights into the dynamics of the relationship.

5

Palestinian-Lebanese Relations: A Political Analysis

Rex Brynen

In July 1991, units of the Lebanese Army moved to deploy into Palestinian-held positions around the southern cities of Sidon and Tyre. Palestinian fighters briefly resisted their advance, but then retreated to the nearby refugee camps. Shortly thereafter, they surrendered their heavy weapons to the army. By the end of the year, Fatah—the largest group within the Palestine Liberation Organization—had ordered the demobilization of all of its regular military forces in Lebanon, leaving only refugee camp militias in place of what had once been a powerful Palestinian armed presence.

These events seemed to mark the end of an era in relations between the Palestinian nationalist movement and the Lebanese government. More than two decades earlier, the Cairo Agreement (November 1969) had granted the PLO a degree of local autonomy within Palestinian refugee camps, and the right to engage in armed struggle against Israel from military bases in South Lebanon. Following Jordan's suppression of the PLO in 1970–1971, Lebanon became the PLO's primary civil operational base and political center of gravity. With this came growing Israeli retaliation, mounting criticism from the Lebanese right, and an inconclusive clash with the Lebanese Army in 1973. After the eruption of the Lebanese civil war in 1975—and the effective collapse of central authority—the PLO's military resources rendered it one of the most powerful actors in the country; not only Palestinian camps but also large areas of West Beirut and southern Lebanon were under its de facto control. This situation only changed after Israel's 1982 invasion of Lebanon, the consequent destruction of much of the PLO's organizational and military infrastructure, and the evacuation of thousands of PLO personnel from Beirut.[1]

This chapter explores the changing political dimension of contemporary Palestinian-Lebanese relations, and the factors shaping it. It also attempts to assess the future trajectory of this relationship, and its implications for Palestinian and Lebanese political development.

FACTORS IN THE TRANSFORMATION
OF PALESTINIAN-LEBANESE RELATIONS

As noted above, the 1982 war in Lebanon initiated a dramatic transformation in Palestinian-Lebanese relations, the effects of which continue to be felt more than a decade afterwards. Nevertheless, changes in the Palestinian movement's political position in Lebanon cannot be attributed to the Israeli invasion alone. Rather, these changes must also be seen against a backdrop of additional factors that have shaped Palestinian-Lebanese relations in the past and which will continue to do so through the 1990s, namely, Lebanese attitudes toward the Palestinian movement, the evolution of PLO strategy and aims, and the shifting currents of regional politics.

The Palestinians in Lebanese Politics: Emergence of a Consensus

One of the most important elements in the changing position of the Palestinian nationalist movement in Lebanon has been the emergence of a Lebanese consensus that strongly opposes any return to the pre-1982 era of Palestinian influence. Today this consensus cuts across ideological and confessional lines, including almost all segments of the Lebanese political spectrum.

It was not always so. In the late 1960s and early 1970s, the Palestinian nationalist movement enjoyed strong popular support, primarily in the various Muslim communities but also among a significant portion of the Christian communities.[2] Such popularity constrained the capacity of the Lebanese government to suppress the growth of Palestinian guerrilla groups after the 1967 Arab-Israeli war. Indeed, this popular support—as well as Palestinian activism and Arab pressures—led the Lebanese government to accept the autonomy of Palestinian refugee camps and certain types of PLO military activities on Lebanese soil in the 1969 Cairo Agreement.

During this period, the presence of a radical and nonsectarian Palestinian nationalist movement (in a Lebanon that was neither) also served to accelerate the growth of anti–status quo forces within the country's political system. For the parties of the Lebanese National Movement (LNM), the Palestinian movement served as both a popular rallying point and partial protection against the threat of suppression by the Lebanese state and its conservative supporters. Later, with the eruption of civil conflict, the LNM sought the active support of Palestinian military forces. The PLO was generally happy to oblige, perceiving that a close alliance with the LNM would minimize the prospects for the sort of reversal it suffered in Jordan in 1970–1971. In short, initial Palestinian involvement in Lebanese politics was driven as much by the "pull" of Lebanese actors seeking Palestinian support as by the "push" of PLO policy.

Over time, however, this situation began to change. The strongest initial opposition to Palestinian nationalist activities had been voiced by the conservative establishment, which feared the destabilizing consequences of Palestinian radicalism. Although the Arab nationalist orientation of their constituents deterred many Sunni politicians from active criticism of the PLO, most Maronite leaders were critical from the outset. As their criticism of the Palestinian threat to Lebanese sovereignty mounted, Christian public opinion also grew more hostile. Periodic clashes and a brief military confrontation in April 1973 heightened tensions. When the war erupted in 1975, this estrangement became irreconcilable amid political polarization and a bitter legacy of atrocities by both sides.[3]

Palestinian-Lebanese relations were equally a casualty of the growing cycle of Palestinian guerrilla raids and Israeli military preemption or retaliation. Critics of the Palestinian armed presence argued that Lebanon was too weak to bear the costs of confrontation with Israel. In the South, the mounting toll of destruction alienated a large portion of the local population, including not only Maronites along the border but also the Shi'ite peasantry whose villages, crops, and families generally bore the brunt of the violence.[4]

Finally, Palestinian-Lebanese relations were also undermined by aspects of PLO policy itself, as well as by the behavior of some Palestinian guerrillas. Prior to 1975, the PLO honored the Cairo Agreement or other Palestinian-Lebanese agreements as much in the breach as in the observance. Theft, assault, corruption, and extortion by ill-disciplined guerrillas became all too common amid the chaos of war. The Palestinian militias were, of course, hardly the only ones to commit such acts; in the Hobbesian anarchy of the time, criminality also flourished in the ranks of Lebanese parties and militias. However, Palestinian *tajawuzat* (excesses) attracted particular opprobrium, partly because of the scale of the Palestinian military presence, but even more so because they were committed by non-Lebanese. The buildup of Palestinian military capabilities (spurred by the civil war and confrontation with Israel), and the expansion of PLO service institutions (constructed to meet growing community needs), exacerbated this still further.[5] In the eyes of many Lebanese, the PLO had become a state within a state, and Lebanon, a Palestinian *watan badil* (alternative homeland).

Combined, these factors contributed to the sharp decline of the Palestinian nationalist movement's image through the 1970s and into the 1980s. Indicative of this, the Lebanese Parliament reopened discussion of the Palestinian presence following Israel's 1978 invasion of the South. Over PLO objections, it passed resolutions that effectively called for an end to Palestinian military activities and the reestablishment of Lebanese authority over the Palestinian camps.[6]

Along the border, Israel organized a proxy militia among (predominately Christian) villagers opposed to the PLO and LNM.[7] Elsewhere in the South, Shi'ite villagers—often acting under the umbrella of the Amal movement—armed themselves to resist Palestinian military deployments near their villages. Clashes between the two inevitably followed. Even within the PLO-LNM alliance itself some tensions were present, evident in factional clashes or LNM pressures on the PLO to suspend cross-border attacks and restrict the scope of its political intervention in Lebanese affairs.

The PLO leadership could not, of course, be held wholly responsible for the decline of its position in Lebanon. Within the Shi'ite community, as in the Maronite community before it, political leaders often fanned tensions so as to strengthen their own positions among their coreligionists. Israel pursued an active program of covert destabilization of the PLO presence in conjunction with its Lebanese allies. Arab intelligence services were also active through their own local proxies, further complicating the picture. Wherever the blame might be apportioned, however, it was clear that the popular position of the Palestinian movement was slipping. Moreover, the PLO was often insensitive to the Palestinian responsibility for this decline, instead responding to challenges with an increasingly heavy military hand, a move that only further undermined the movement's popularity.

The implications of a Palestinian position in Lebanon dependent on force majeure became amply evident during and after the 1982 Israeli invasion. The vast destruction caused by that war—over 19,000 dead and 30,000 wounded, hundreds of thousands displaced or rendered homeless—confirmed the widespread impression that the Palestinian movement had become an unbearable burden for Lebanon.[8] The successive Lebanese administrations of Bashir and Amine Gemayel spoke openly of the need not only to eliminate the Palestinian armed presence and reassert control over the refugee camps, but also to reduce the size of the Palestinian civilian presence by removing all but the 1948 refugees. Even the PLO's erstwhile allies in the LNM clearly stated their opposition to any sort of return to the pre-1982 era. In May 1987, the Lebanese Parliament—with the support of virtually all political and confessional groups—officially abrogated the Cairo Agreement.

Over the same five years, various Lebanese militias took advantage of the PLO's new weakness to settle old scores. In Beirut, the Lebanese Forces massacred hundreds of Palestinian civilians in the Sabra and Shatila refugee camps in September 1982. In the South, the South Lebanese Army terrorized local Palestinian populations during the Israeli occupation of Sidon and Tyre. In 1985–1987, the War of the Camps saw Amal launch a series of bitter assaults against Palestinian refugee camps, resulting in a death toll of perhaps 3,000 and the destruction of tens of thousands of homes.

During this period, the Palestinian movement did succeed in forging or reforging political alliances with a range of actors, from Hizballah to General Michel Aoun. However, these were at best tactical and opportunistic, shaped by the shifting coalition politics of the continuing war and motivated by the desire of Lebanon's various warring parties to secure support from whatever sources available.[9] Of the major Lebanese parties, only Hizballah spoke in favor of armed struggle against Zionism from South Lebanon, yet even its activities focused on the Israeli presence on Lebanese soil, while its political relationship with the PLO was soured both by the latter's moderate foreign policy and by its military intervention in Amal-Hizballah clashes in Iqlim al-Tuffah during 1990–1991.

With the initiation of national reconciliation and the diminution of military conflict, even prospects for opportunistic alliances faded. Although the Ta'if Accord of October 1989 made no explicit mention of the Palestinians, the question of the Palestinian armed presence was nonetheless seen to be an important test of the accord's commitment to "reinstating the authority of the Lebanese State over all Lebanese territory" and "disbanding all Lebanese and non-Lebanese militias and surrendering their arms to the Lebanese State."[10] Mindful of the tragic consequences of past vulnerabilities—Dubaya, Jisr al-Basha, Tel al-Za'atar, Nabatieh, Sabra, Shatila, and the recent War of the Camps—the PLO was reluctant to entrust the security of refugee camps to the Lebanese government or disarm its remaining military forces in Sidon and Tyre. Lebanese political elites were, however, virtually unanimous in insisting that it must.[11] This domestic consensus played an important role in fortifying the Lebanese Army, which in earlier confrontations with the Palestinians in the 1970s had found its resolve sapped by internal political-confessional divisions.[12] Thus, by the summer of 1991, the stage was set for the showdown in the South.

Lebanon in Palestinian Strategy and Politics

Just as Lebanese attitudes to the Palestinian presence in Lebanon changed over the years, so too did the role of Lebanon within Palestinian nationalist strategy. These changes, moreover, not only affected PLO policy in Lebanon but also, to a very substantial degree, were shaped by events there.

When Palestinian guerrilla activity began in the mid-1960s, Lebanon's primary role in Palestinian strategy was as a military sanctuary from which raids against Israel could be launched. With the explosive growth of the Palestinian movement after the 1967 war, the Cairo Agreement of 1969, and the PLO's expulsion from Jordan in 1970, Lebanon's importance for such activities grew sharply.[13] The mystique of the *fida'i* (guerrilla) consequently dominated Palestinian policy, with the PLO generally resisting efforts by the Lebanese government to limit its military freedom of action against Israel.

By the mid-1970s, however, Palestinian goals and strategy began to change. The movement's initial emphasis on the liberation of all Palestine gradually gave way to acceptance of the idea of a Palestinian state in the West Bank and Gaza; similarly, its early commitment to the exclusivity and primacy of armed struggle was replaced by an increasing emphasis on political and diplomatic means. With this, the objective importance of cross-border attacks declined, transcended by Lebanon's importance as a diplomatic and informational base, and as an autonomous political haven wherein Palestinian institutions could develop and Palestinian decision-making could be exercised—all relatively free from the tutelage of Arab states.

The implications of this shift for Palestinian policy in Lebanon were fundamental; however, actual Palestinian behavior was equally shaped by the movement's internal dynamics. Divided by ideology, personalities, the crosscurrents of Arab politics, and the complexities created by geographical dispersal, Palestinian politics has long been factionalized and intensely competitive. Because of its access to nationalist institutions and its relative political freedom compared with populations in the occupied territories or other Arab countries, the Palestinian community in Lebanon represented perhaps the most important constituency for competing groups from 1970 through the early 1980s. Rejectionist organizations, opposed to the increasing moderation of the PLO's political line, often sought to demonstrate their militant nationalist credentials through armed attacks on Israel from Lebanese soil, forcing Fatah to follow suit even when local or international circumstances dictated the wisdom of slowing or suspending military actions. The development of sizable Palestinian armed forces created a further internal, institutional constituency for armed struggle, sustaining its appeal even after its practical role in Palestinian strategy had sharply declined.

Thus, through the 1970s and well into the 1980s, the major political battles within the Palestinian movement were substantially fought out in Lebanon, in part through debates over Lebanese policy. Gradually, however, the internal balance of power shifted from the proponents of militant rejectionism to the pragmatic orientation of the PLO/Fatah mainstream. At the same time, the scale of Israeli military retaliation—and the very grievous damage it caused to the status of the Palestinian movement in Lebanese public opinion—further underscored the costs of military action. Thus, in the wake of Israel's 1978 invasion, the PLO accepted the deployment of the United Nations Interim Force in Lebanon (UNIFIL) in South Lebanon. In July 1981, after two weeks of cross-border fighting, the PLO went so far as to agree to a U.S.- and UN-negotiated de facto cease-fire with Israel. Both of these decisions prompted accusations that the PLO leadership had sold out the liberation struggle. Nonetheless, both were ultimately upheld, whether by political persuasion or physical enforcement.

It was against this backdrop that, in 1982, Israel invaded Lebanon. The war had several critical effects. First, it shattered the PLO's military infrastructure in Beirut and South Lebanon, calling into question the continued viability of a military option.[14] Second, it exacerbated internal divisions in the PLO, resulting in an open split in 1983. The Syrian-backed rebellion by Fatah dissidents weakened the PLO, but also partially liberated the PLO mainstream from rejectionist constraints and accelerated the growth of Palestinian moderation. Finally, the destruction of both Palestinian nationalist institutions in Lebanon and the PLO's protective umbrella severely weakened the political voice of the Palestinian community there. Prior to 1982, Palestinians in Lebanon had been at the center of the nationalist movement. After 1982, events in Lebanon—in particular, the acute insecurity of the Palestinian community there—continued to occupy a central place in Palestinian political discourse. Increasingly, however, the political and organizational attentions of the nationalist movement became focused on the West Bank and Gaza.

This latter shift hastened, and was hastened by, the eruption of the Palestinian uprising in December 1987. The intifada confirmed the new centrality of the occupied territories, and hence the political eclipse of the Palestinian community in Lebanon. For example, Palestinian financial resources, which had been deployed to reestablish the PLO's influence and position in Lebanon, were increasingly diverted to support the uprising. The intifada was also critical in confirming the PLO's commitment to a negotiated two-state solution to the Palestinian-Israeli conflict. This commitment was made explicit in the Palestine National Council's November 1988 declaration of Palestinian independence and Yasir Arafat's subsequent recognition of Israel. Believing that cross-border attacks would both divert world attention from the uprising and undercut the PLO's diplomatic and public opinion campaigns, Fatah effectively suspended its external military action against Israel.[15] Palestinian regular military forces were downgraded and—in the case of Lebanon—eventually demobilized altogether.[16]

The Impact of a Changing Regional Environment

In addition to the specific interests and policies pursued by various Palestinian and Lebanese actors, Palestinian-Lebanese relations were always profoundly affected by external factors. Israel, Syria, Algeria, Egypt, Iraq, Jordan, Kuwait, Libya, Morocco, Saudi Arabia, France, the United States, Soviet Union, and United Nations—to name only the most salient examples—have at one time or another played a significant role in shaping the Palestinian-Lebanese relationship (by providing material aid to the PLO and its allies, or by providing similar aid to the PLO's opponents, or by pressuring Syria or Israel, or by participating in diplomatic processes concerning the Lebanese conflict). The most influential players by far, however, have been Israel and Syria.

Israeli foreign policy interests in Lebanon are old and complex, long predating the emergence of the modern PLO.[17] Its specific interests regarding the Palestinian presence, however, were clear: to inhibit the ability of Palestinian groups to use Lebanon as a base of operations for either military or political (mass mobilization, diplomacy, information, leadership) activities. This goal was pursued, in part, through massive retaliatory and punishment attacks, both overt and covert, on Palestinian and Lebanese targets. These not only disrupted or destroyed the infrastructure and capabilities of Palestinian groups, but also raised the cost to Lebanese decision-makers of tolerating Palestinian nationalist activities. The attacks also eroded public support (or stoked public antipathy) toward the Palestinian presence. A second policy mechanism was the provision of direct material support to the Palestinians' Lebanese opponents. From the mid-1970s, Israel began to supply significant amounts of arms or funding to the National Liberal Party, the Phalange, the Lebanese Forces, and Major Sa'd Haddad. Both policies came together when, following Israel's 1978 invasion of South Lebanon, the Israeli Defense Forces (IDF) handed control of a strip of Lebanese border territory to Haddad's militia to act as a barrier against Palestinian infiltration attempts. The same pattern was repeated after the 1982 war on a slightly grander scale: First Israel used military force to install a friendly Phalangist government in Beirut, and later established a self-declared "security zone" in the South under the control of the IDF and South Lebanese Army (SLA).

Syria has loomed as an equal or even greater intervening variable in Palestinian-Lebanese relations. Its primary interests have been to maximize its influence in Lebanon (a goal for which the Palestinian movement has served both as vehicle and obstacle) while assuring strategic security and stability on its western flank. Equally important, Damascus has sought to use its position in Lebanon to increase its influence over the Palestinian movement, thereby increasing its leverage in the broader Arab-Israeli conflict. However, the particular impact of Syrian policy on the PLO's position in Lebanon has varied markedly over the years. In 1969, Syrian support for the PLO was an important factor in the conclusion of the Cairo Agreement; four years later it helped to abort Lebanese Army efforts to suppress the guerrillas. Although Damascus again lent support to the PLO at the start of the war in Lebanon, it soon reduced and reversed this position. By June 1976, Syria was militarily intervening against the PLO and LNM. Between 1977 and 1982, Syrian-Phalange relations deteriorated and, as the Camp David process raised a regional challenge, PLO-Syrian relations improved somewhat. However, this did not prevent Damascus from covertly seeking to isolate or undermine the PLO's position in Lebanon from time to time so as to decrease the latter's influence over Lebanese events or increase its dependence on Damascus.

Shortly after the 1982 war, PLO-Syrian relations collapsed completely. In an effort to extend its influence over the Palestinian movement, Damascus actively assisted the 1983 Fatah rebellion, with the rebels driving loyalist forces from the Bekaa Valley and seizing control of Palestinian refugee camps in the North. Later, in a further bid to blunt the resurgence of the mainstream PLO, Syria supported Amal's attacks on Palestinian refugee camps in Beirut and the South in 1985–1987, and assaults by radical Palestinian groups that drove Fatah forces from the Beirut camps in the summer of 1988. Finally, Damascus gave its blessing to Lebanese abrogation of the Cairo Agreement.

In recent years, the impact of regional actors on Palestinian-Lebanese relations has shifted once more. The Ta'if Accord's implicit but clear commitment to the disarmament of the Palestinian community and reassertion of Lebanese control in Palestinian-controlled areas was strongly backed not only by Saudi Arabia and Syria, but also by almost every other Arab state (except Iraq), and by the bulk of the international community. The eruption of the 1990–1991 Gulf War further increased the pressures on the Palestinian movement: Iraq was no longer able to provide significant support to the Palestinian position, Saudi Arabia and the other Gulf states were seriously alienated by the PLO's position during that crisis, and Syrian intervention against the forces of General Michel Aoun (an act facilitated by Syria's participation in the anti-Iraq coalition) further tilted the Lebanese balance of power against the PLO.

In the wake of the war, a sharp decline in Arab financial support for the PLO has seriously undercut its erstwhile financial influence in Lebanon. The decline and eventual collapse of the Soviet Union further aggravated the situation, eliminating one of the PLO's most important sources of military supply and diplomatic support. The strong post–Cold War, post–Gulf War regional influence of the United States, coupled with its particular support for the reassertion of Lebanese government authority and hostility toward the PLO, has served to weaken the Palestinian position in Lebanon still further.

CONCLUSION: WHERE NEXT?

All of the factors discussed above—the process of Lebanese national reconciliation, the emergence of a Lebanese political consensus in favor of strictly limiting Palestinian activities, the loss of external Palestinian allies and resources, and strong support for the reassertion of Lebanese authority from Syria, other Arab states, the United States, and the rest of the international community—were amply clear as the Lebanese Army prepared to deploy in Palestinian-controlled areas in the summer of 1991. In 1969, 1973, and throughout much of the civil war, the PLO had proven able to counterbalance pressures in Lebanon by securing internal and external allies, playing upon the rivalries and contradictions of both Lebanese and inter-Arab politics. This time, however, Palestinian appeals for support fell on deaf ears. Palestinian fighters—who had earlier vowed to defend their positions at all costs—were demoralized by the apparent hopelessness of their position, and were quickly compelled to accommodate the new realities of their disadvantaged position.

Looking ahead, the future of Palestinian-Lebanese relations remains highly uncertain. In the immediate future, much will depend on the development of Lebanon's own national reconciliation process. Should the Ta'if process fail and Lebanon once more collapse into open political and military warfare, the practical demands of civil conflict may lead Lebanese actors to ally again with the Palestinian movement. As before, Palestinian groups would doubtless find opportunities to enhance their local position through forging tactical and opportunistic ties with various combatants. Should this scenario be realized, the Palestinians might reestablish a degree of their pre-1991 (although certainly not their pre-1982) political and military influence in the South. However, the constraints on even this are enormous; the very threat of a Palestinian reassertion would invite a powerful counterresponse by local and regional actors anxious to abort any such eventuality. Moreover, the Palestinian community is at present far too weak to guarantee its own defense against such an assault.

In short, the Palestinian insecurities that would be generated by the rekindling of Lebanese domestic conflict would outweigh Palestinian political gains. Should conflict continue to be avoided, the Lebanese consensus regarding the subordination of a disarmed Palestinian presence to central government authority will undoubtedly be sustained. The Palestinian movement is in no position to resist this openly unless galvanized by direct and precipitate Lebanese Army action against the refugee camps. Instead, the PLO is likely to procrastinate and prevaricate as long as possible, attempting to delay indefinitely further action against the camps while hoping that local and regional circumstances take a turn for the better.

In the meantime, the Palestinian leadership will continue to seek to negotiate better political and socioeconomic terms for its community in Lebanon. Prior to the Army's deployment, the PLO clearly hoped that the authorities' desire to avoid a confrontation would bolster their negotiating position. Since then, there has been some effort to turn Palestinian weakness into a strength, with the PLO implicitly suggesting that the marginalization of Palestinian power now allows the Lebanese government to relax legal restrictions on Palestinian residents without fear. Certainly, some Lebanese officials have spoken of Beirut's capacity to be magnanimous in its victory.[18] Others, however, seem to suggest that the central authorities no longer need consider Palestinian demands (or, in the present context of Palestinian powerlessness, requests).[19] Instead, they say, it is now time to bring the full weight of Lebanese law to bear, whether by demolishing "unofficial" housing or by deporting all Palestinians save the 1948 refugees and their descendants.[20]

Such hostility hardly reassures an insecure Palestinian community that, as Rosemary Sayigh observes elsewhere in this volume, today finds itself not only vulnerable and politically weak, but also economically and socially disadvantaged. Indeed, in an ironic way the Palestinians are making an important contribution to the reunification of Lebanon—not as political actors, but as common targets for Lebanese blame in an emerging revisionist historical memory. By acting as a scapegoat upon which most of the responsibility for the war can be placed, the Palestinians implicitly absolve the war's primary participants of their own culpabilities, facilitating future cooperation among Lebanese leaders by allowing them to jettison the baggage of their previous (and often murderous) domestic conflicts.

The future of Palestinian-Lebanese relations is also likely to be shaped by the future development of the Palestinian movement itself. Within the movement (and especially within Fatah) a variety of factors—adverse local conditions, declining financial support, the suspension of cross-border operations, and the PLO's diplomatic flexibility—have all generated growing discontent among a significant portion of the PLO's Lebanese cadres. Critics of the PLO mainstream have sought to capitalize upon this, seeing in Lebanon an important source of opposition to the peace process. To a substantial degree, however, the mainstream PLO leadership seems to view Lebanon as a lost cause. Within the broader dynamics of Palestinian nationalist politics, Lebanon's once influential community now clearly plays a secondary role, eclipsed by presently more salient constituencies within the occupied territories (and, to a lesser extent, within Jordan).

Finally and perhaps most importantly, the future evolution of Palestinian-Lebanese relations will be fundamentally shaped by regional developments, and specifically by the Arab-Israeli negotiating process. Clearly, stalemate or failure in the peace process will have negative repercussions, exacerbating the tensions of the present situation. Lebanese concern over permanent resettlement of the refugees will grow.[21] This may well lead to increasingly harsh and discriminatory measures against the Palestinian community as the central authorities seek to limit its size and disrupt its sociopolitical organization. Palestinian vulnerabilities will be compounded by hopelessness and despair, further undercutting the position of the mainstream nationalist movement.

On the other hand, paradoxically, diplomatic progress may also hold its dangers. Should the negotiating process appear to lead to a bilateral Israeli-Syrian (and, presumably, a parallel Israeli-Lebanese) agreement without equivalent progress on Palestinian-Israeli issues, Lebanese concern over Palestinian resettlement will be magnified still further. For their part, Palestinian groups may (as in the late 1970s) seek to abort a diplomatic process inimical to their interests by stoking the level of military confrontation in South Lebanon or by attempting to sabotage any proposed Israeli-Lebanese confidence- and security-building measures. By contrast, should the Israeli-Palestinian track proceed at a faster rate than Syrian-Israeli negotiations, Syria may seek to influence Palestinian decisionmaking through Lebanon, whether by supporting the growth of rejectionist elements or by exerting political and physical pressures against the Palestinian community there. It might also encourage attacks against Israel or its self-declared "security zone" in South Lebanon, hoping thereby to derail diplomatic progress. In either case, significantly asymmetric developments in the peace process could have conflictual or destabilizing implications for Lebanon, in the short run at least.

Indeed, even if the negotiating process leads to a comprehensive regional settlement, problems will remain. The common interests of the PLO, Syria, and Lebanon in sustaining any agreement would certainly weaken the position of rejectionists and lessen the likelihood of violence. Some Palestinians in Lebanon would choose to return or relocate to a Palestinian entity in the West Bank and Gaza. Many others—perhaps from areas within Israel's pre-1967 border, perhaps born and raised in Lebanon, perhaps with family or economic ties there, or perhaps simply too poor to move—would undoubtedly not. At present, the question of this population is obscured by Lebanese opposition to resettlement and Palestinian emphasis on the right of return. Nevertheless, this question will necessarily arise, and have to be dealt with, in the context of any regional settlement.

NOTES

The financial assistance of McGill University, the Inter-University Consortium for Arab Studies (Montreal) and the Social Science and Humanities Research Council of Canada in support of this research is gratefully acknowledged.

1. For a detailed examination of this period, see Rex Brynen, *Sanctuary and Survival: The PLO in Lebanon* (Boulder: Westview Press, 1990).

2. Commentators—particularly Lebanese commentators—often ignore the extent of initial public support for the Palestinian armed presence in Lebanon. In one November 1969 survey, 46 percent of Lebanese expressed "complete support" and another 40 percent indicated "reserved support" for the Palestinian movement, while 62 percent expressed complete or reserved support for Palestinian guerrilla activities from Lebanese soil. Similarly, a study of Lebanese student attitudes found that 94 percent of Muslims and 55 percent of Christians supported the Palestinian resistance movement (*al-Nahar*, 17 November 1969; Halim Barakat, "Social Factors Influencing Attitudes of University Students in Lebanon Towards the Palestinian Resistance Movement," *Journal of Palestine Studies* vol. 1 [Autumn 1971], p. 112).

3. These include the destruction of Palestinian refugee camps at Dubaya, Jisr al-Basha, and Tel al-Za'atar by the militias of the conservative Lebanese Front, and the sacking of the predominately Christian town of Damour by joint PLO-LNM forces.

4. The cumulative extent of this destruction was evident in figures released by the Lebanese government in 1981: 1,300 Lebanese civilians dead, 8,000 invalids, and 10,000 orphans; 259,000 persons displaced; 10,000 homes destroyed, along with 132,000 dunums (hectares) of crops. *Middle East Reporter* (Beirut, 4 April 1981), p. 9.

5. For a discussion, see: Yezid Sayigh, "Palestinian Armed Struggle: Means and Ends," *Journal of Palestine Studies* vol. 16 (Autumn 1986); Cheryl Rubenberg, *The Palestine Liberation Organization: Its Institutional Infrastructure* (Belmont, Mass.: Institute of Arab Studies, 1983); Rex Brynen, "The Politics of Exile: The Palestinians in Lebanon," *Journal of Refugee Studies* vol. 3 (1990).

6. Text in *Arab Report and Record*, 16–30 April 1978, p. 288.

7. Beate Hamizrachi, *The Emergence of the South Lebanon Security Belt* (New York: Praeger, 1988).

8. Casualty figures as reported by Lebanese government, in *Race & Class* vol. 24 (Spring 1983), p. 341.

9. Following the first round of the War of the Camps in 1985, the Progressive Socialist Party—despite its rhetorical opposition to Arafat—was bribed to allow Fatah temporary use of its port facilities at Khalde. During the second and third rounds in 1986–1987, some Hizballah units (opposed to both Syria and Amal) supported the PLO, although others fought alongside Amal. Fatah was also able to bribe some Amal officials into providing intelligence and other assistance. The Lebanese Forces, also motivated by conflict with Damascus, provided Fatah with transit routes for personnel and supplies between 1986 and 1988. Subsequently, Arafat lent his support for Michel Aoun, particularly after he launched his direct challenge to Syria in 1989. Aoun reciprocated by providing transit routes through areas controlled by the Lebanese Army. In fighting at Iqlim al-Tuffah in 1990–1991, Fatah tactically allied with Amal to blunt the growth of Hizballah.

10. Text of Ta'if Accord, in Deirdre Collings and Jill Tansley, *Peace for Lebanon? Obstacles, Challenges and Prospects* Working Paper 43 (Ottawa: Canadian Institute for International Peace and Security, May 1992).

11. This consensus spanned ideological and confessional lines. President Elias Hrawi (Maronite) declared that "We assure the Palestinian people that they will be looked after by the Lebanese government, which will preserve their rights. But we will not allow an armed presence, because only the legitimate weapons of the state must remain." Speaker of Parliament Hussein al-Husseini (Shi'ite) complained that Yasir Arafat "still seemed to be living in the era before 1982," and that as a result "We pay no heed to statements by the PLO. Lebanese law must apply to outsiders before Lebanese." Amal leader Nabih Birri (Shi'ite) stressed that "What applies to Lebanese must apply to Palestinians." The Lebanese Forces' Roger Dib (Maronite) asserted that in the past, "Lebanese government institutions collapsed because of Palestinian weapons." Defense Minister Michel al-Murr (Greek Orthodox) argued that "The excuse that Palestinian weapons must be kept under the pretext of liberating Palestine is false because weapons have not liberated a single inch of Palestinian soil but have destroyed Lebanon and displaced the Lebanese from their lands. . . . Under no circumstances will we allow the Palestinians to use their weapons to establish a state within our state." A similar view was expressed by Interior Minister Sami al-Khatib (Sunni): "Resistance against Israel must not be an excuse for creating a state within a state" (*Middle East Reporter,* 12 January 1991,

p. 11; 6 April 1991, pp. 2, 5–6). See also *New York Times,* 4 April 1991, p. A13; *Voice of Lebanon,* 1 April 1991 (in *Foreign Broadcast Information Service–Near East and South Asia,* hereafter *FBIS-NES*).

12. *Middle East Reporter,* 13 July 1991, p. 10. In an address to the Army prior to its confrontation with the Palestinians, then Defense Minister Michel al-Murr had emphasized that "all the Lebanese people" blessed their "march of salvation and deliverance" (*Voice of Lebanon,* 2 July 1991 [*FBIS-NES*]).

13. Within Israel, the number of incidents near the Lebanese border grew from two incidents in 1967 to 410 in 1970 (*Middle East Record,* 1969–1970 [Jerusalem: Israel Universities Press, 1977], p. 215).

14. Palestinian groups did play a part in the resistance against Israeli occupation in South Lebanon. Moreover, from the mid-1980s the PLO did reestablish some significant military infrastructure in and around the refugee camps of West Beirut (until driven out by pro-Syrian groups in 1988), Tyre, and especially Sidon. None of this, however, approximated the scale of Palestinian military infrastructure prior to the 1982 war.

15. A March 1990 report by the U.S. State Department confirmed Fatah's noninvolvement in cross-border attacks, placing the blame for most on rejectionist groups. Indeed, Ahmad Jibril of the Popular Front for the Liberation of Palestine–General Command complained that ". . . Arafat and his organs are obstructing factions that want to engage in armed struggle . . . [going] so far as to put security barriers before some of these operations" (U.S. State Department, "Report on PLO Compliance with Pledges Concerning Terrorism," 19 March 1990, in *Journal of Palestine Studies* Vol. 19 [Summer 1990], pp. 180–182; *al-Quds Palestinian Arab Radio,* 25 August 1989 [*FBIS-NES*]).

16. *al-Hayat* (London), 20 December 1991, pp. 1, 4.

17. See Peretz's chapter elsewhere in this volume.

18. *Middle East Reporter,* 18 July 1992, p. 8.

19. President Elias Hrawi himself suggested that there was "no cause" for a formal Palestinian-Lebanese dialogue, since the Lebanese government's directorate of refugee affairs dealt with the issue (*Voice of the Mountain,* 12 July 1991 [*FBIS-NES*]). Although an official Palestinian-Lebanese dialogue was begun in late July 1991, the government quickly ruled out a formal Palestinian-Lebanese agreement; subsequently, the dialogue was suspended by Lebanon "pending the outcome of the Middle East peace conference" (*Wakh* [*Manama*], 18 July 1991, [*FBIS-NES*]; *Middle East Reporter,* 3 August 1991, pp. 7–9; 19 October 1991, pp. 8–9; 1 February 1992, p. 13.)

20. In a memorandum submitted to a February 1992 conference of the Arab League's Committee for Palestinian Refugee Affairs, the Lebanese government noted that it "approves of reconstruction of the camps to exactly what they were before the civil war" but "utterly rejects plans to enlarge existing camps or build new ones." It also emphasized that Lebanese law must apply to this process— including, presumably, previous laws that severely restricted the size and permanence of refugee camp dwellings. With regard to unregistered Palestinians, the government stressed that "it can only recognize Palestinians who fled to Lebanon before 1948 [and their descendants]." Earlier, Lebanese officials had suggested that as many as 100,000 Palestinians were illegally resident in the country. *Middle East Reporter,* 1 February 1992, pp. 12–13.

21. The sensitivity of this issue was underlined in September 1992, when efforts by the United Nations Relief and Works Agency to conduct a census and issue new Palestinian refugee identity cards provoked widespread Lebanese concern that the international community had decided to "resettle" Palestinians in Lebanon. *New York Times,* 23 September 1992, p. A13.

6

Palestinians in Lebanon: Uncertain Future

Rosemary Sayigh

THE POLITICAL BACKGROUND

The Lebanese state and much of the political class have, from the beginning, viewed the Palestinian refugee presence as an unfair burden and a threat to Lebanon's existence.[1] Given U.S. backing for Israel's refusal to repatriate the refugees, there was little hope that their numbers could be lessened through this channel. More than once, Maronite leaders proposed that the Palestinian refugees be redistributed among the Arab countries; but such proposals were rejected outright by the Muslim/progressive opposition, and, even if the Lebanese state had pressed the matter in the Arab League, it would have found no response. Many members of the Lebanese political class hoped that Palestinian emigration to the oil-producing countries would solve the problem.[2] The Gulf states, however, were not ready to give the emigrants nationality and, by the late 1970s, recession prompted cutbacks in both jobs and entry permits. Forced to contain a growing body of refugees, the Lebanese state developed its own methods of management, including nondefinition of Palestinian refugee status and rights, Lebanese Army control of the camps, encouragement of migration, and (occasionally) violence. Meanwhile, Palestinians have pursued an equally tenacious struggle for official Lebanese recognition of their national and civic rights.

The status of the refugees has always been a central issue in Lebanese-Palestinian negotiations. It is useful, therefore, to begin with a brief review of this question. It was not until 1962, fourteen years after the Palestinian refugees arrived, that a decree issued by the Lebanese Ministry of the Interior implicitly classified them as a special category of foreigners, obliging them to apply for work permits for all but casual or self-employment.[3] Before this, their status remained unclear, supposedly in line with Arab

League recommendations that advised host governments to grant Palestinian refugees civil rights, but not nationality. In Lebanon, leading government figures assured the Palestinians in 1948 that they would not be treated as foreigners, but by 1951 the minister of social affairs had issued a decree forbidding their employment without work permits.[4] In 1969, after a series of camp uprisings supported by the Lebanese National Movement, the Lebanese government recognized Palestinian national and civic rights in the Cairo accords. The accords, however, were never ratified by the Lebanese Parliament and in June 1988 they were unilaterally annulled. In April 1991, when Lebanese government–PLO relations were resumed in the context of the Ta'if Accord's provisions to disarm all militias in Lebanon, the Palestinians again raised the issue of status and rights. However, the negotiations were frozen by the Lebanese soon after they began.

Members of the ministerial committee set up to deal with the Palestinians have said that the government is prepared to discuss only the issues of Palestinian residence and work rights, and that Lebanon's interests would come first in any such discussion.[5] Such agenda-setting dismisses Palestinian political demands—reopening of the PLO office, autonomy for the camps, media freedom, and the right to national struggle. PLO representative Shafiq al-Hout does not expect to gain Lebanese concessions on the critical issue of employment, especially given the current economic crisis.[6] Among official reasons given for the freezing of the negotiations is the need to await the outcome of the Arab-Israeli peace talks (commenced in October 1991 in Madrid). There are two other, unspoken, reasons, however, that prompted the government's disinclination to continue the talks: the ease with which the Lebanese Army took control of the areas around the Palestinian camps in Sidon in July 1991 (signaling a decline in the PLO's strategic interests in Lebanon); and Syrian policy toward the Palestinians in Lebanon, itself tied to the peace talks.

Syria's policy toward Lebanon has never been easy to decipher. Certain moves undertaken by the Syrian regime during 1991–1992 suggest that Damascus feels the need to improve its relations with the Palestinians (for example, the release of almost all Palestinian prisoners, and an ending of arrests). These actions suggest that Syria may want to keep the Palestinians as an active force in Lebanon, to put pressure on Israel and the United States in the peace negotiations. Other moves, however, suggest that Syria's main concern is to avoid any provocation or confrontation. Among the signs that reinforce this interpretation are the redeployment of all pro-Syrian Palestinian resistance-group military personnel to the Bekaa; the absence of Syrian pressure on the Lebanese government to permit the reopening of the PLO's Beirut office; and the continuing encirclement of Palestinian camps in Beirut by Syrian Army units at a time when, under

U.S. pressure, Syrian military presence in Beirut has been considerably reduced.

A small but significant sign that Syria may be prepared to shift its hard-line stand on the Palestinian refugee issue can be found in a remark made by Lebanese Foreign Minister Fares Bouez during the parliamentary election campaign in Kisrawan in early October 1992. Bouez stated that the permanent settlement of 50,000–100,000 Palestinians in Lebanon should be viewed as acceptable.[7] This remark is significant because, as President Hrawi's son-in-law, Bouez represents the pro-Syrian bloc within Maronite politics. Moreover, the government's success in holding elections despite Patriarch Sfeir's call for Maronite nonparticipation (particularly in Kisrawan), suggests that Maronite opposition to the permanent settlement of Palestinians may no longer be an insuperable obstacle to U.S. plans to settle the Middle East crisis. The uproar that erupted in Lebanese political circles and media around the issue of *towteen* (implantation, i.e., permanent settlement in the country of refuge) before any clear outcome of the Washington talks was visible, suggests that the Lebanese state is making moves to "solve" the refugee issue independent of a final Middle East settlement, and that Syria is not vetoing such moves.

Rejection of towteen unites (at least verbally) the Lebanese government, all Lebanese parties and sects, and all Palestinian resistance groups. Rashid al-Solh, a former prime minister, stoutly declared the government's opposition.[8] Speaking on behalf of the Lebanese Ministerial Committee for Palestinian Affairs, Shawki Fakhoury said that Palestinian settlement is "a real danger against which we must struggle no matter what the cost."[9] Lebanese political forces across the board have declared their absolute refusal of Palestinian implantation.[10] Nevertheless, skeptics contend that Saudi financial inducements will smooth over many objections, and that the Lebanese government will not be given the option to refuse Palestinian settlement. Rather, the government will be faced with questions of How many, Which ones, and Is it wiser to give them Lebanese nationality or preserve their refugee identity? Furthermore, given the cooling of both pro- and anti-Palestinian feeling, it is conceivable that Lebanese opposition to towteen could be handled using methods similar to those used against the Maronite opposition to the 1992 elections.

The current U.S.-brokered peace process, with its possibility for final settlement of the Middle East conflict (and therefore of the Palestinian refugee issue) has further politicized the question concerning the exact size of the Palestinian community.[11] United Nations Works and Relief Agency (UNWRA) statistics give a figure of 317,376 registered refugees (March 1992), a figure much lower than that cited by Lebanese Minister Shawki Fakhoury who placed their number at 400,000–500,000, and lower than that cited by the Palestinian Red Crescent (nearly 600,000, including

70,000 outside Lebanon). The Directorate of Palestinian Refugee Affairs (DPRA) reports a figure of 350,000 resident Palestinians. However, all these figures are problematic because (1) there are Palestinians in Lebanon who are not registered with UNWRA,[12] and (2) neither UNWRA nor the DPRA keep the records of Palestinian migration. (It should be noted that until the 1980s most Palestinian migration from Lebanon was temporary, for work or study.)

The possibility of a final, imposed settlement to the refugee issue also explains Palestinian suspicion and anger in September 1992 when UNWRA began issuing new identity cards. Because these cards had to be collected in person by household heads, the operation took on the complexion of a census. The conflict with UNWRA dragged on, with strikes and demonstrations against the new cards. As of January 1993, few refugees had applied for them, but it is expected that refusal to collect the new cards will be met by a withholding of UNWRA or state services.

Meanwhile, longstanding as well as more recent state measures are adding to Palestinian insecurities in Lebanon, increasing the pressure on them to migrate. Between 1982 and 1992, no work permits were issued to Palestinians. With the new Hariri government (October 1992), new Ministry of Labor decrees require all Palestinians to apply for work permits even for casual, daily rate labor. Their living space is restricted by the state's refusal to allow new camp sites to replace those destroyed by war,[13] and by its prohibition of "horizontal expansion" (i.e., building on empty land around camp perimeters). Between 25,000–50,000 Palestinians displaced during the war are threatened with eventual eviction from "illegal" accommodations.[14] Another recent measure targeted Palestinian residence rights: the DPRA has been removing the names of Palestinians who have obtained a second nationality from its list of Palestinians with resident rights; 40,000 names are said to have been eliminated so far.

The one certain point in this scenario of uncertainties will be Palestinian resistance to the myriad pressures for settlement or migration. Refusal of settlement outside Palestine has been the cardinal point of the national movement in exile—the primary mobilizing element of a struggle that has cost thousands of lives. Nevertheless, many regional, internal political, and economic factors are collaborating to limit the scope for resistance. U.S. domination of the Middle East has radically transformed the Arab environment of the Palestinian struggle. PLO involvement in the peace talks implies its acceptance, however reluctant, of resettlement "outside" Palestine for diaspora Palestinians. Popular resistance to such a fate by Palestinians residing in Lebanon will have little support from the PLO. Indeed, in early October 1992, the growing rift between the PLO leadership and local cadres of the Palestinian Resistance Movement was signaled when Salah Salah, head of the Palestinian political leadership in Lebanon, accused the PLO of collaborating with UNWRA and the Lebanese state in reducing the situation of the Palestinians in Lebanon to a level where they can choose only between "bad and worse."[15]

THE ECONOMIC AND SOCIAL SITUATION

For the majority of Palestinian refugees, the urgency of their civil rights has become more compelling given the ever increasing harshness of their social and economic situation. The refugees' plight is worsened by the spiraling inflation of the Lebanese economy on the one hand, and substantial Palestinian unemployment on the other. During the first six months of 1992, Lebanon's national currency depreciated by 60.4 percent against the dollar, while the cost of basic commodities and medical services rose by 68.8 percent.[16] Because most basic commodities (e.g., foodstuffs, fuel, medicine) are imported, they are priced in terms of dollars; ordinary people, however, are paid in Lebanese pounds. Although all middle- and lower-income strata of the population are suffering a drastic drop in living standards, the Palestinians have been hit the hardest because of the legal constraints on their employment.

A survey conducted by the PLO Statistical Bureau (Damascus) in 1989/90 gives some idea of Palestinian employment and unemployment levels. The survey found that only 33.1 percent of the Palestinian labor force was employed. Although the survey probably missed many kinds of casual and part-time labor, it accurately points to the main structural feature of refugee Palestinian labor in Lebanon: Palestinian participation in the Lebanese economy is restricted to agricultural and construction labor; opportunities for professional, salaried work are restricted to employment with UNWRA and the "national sector" (i.e., the social institutions of the PLO and Palestinian Resistance Movement [PRM], as well as fighters and cadres). An important factor contributing to unemployment is insecurity; attacks against Palestinian workers by the Lebanese Forces and Amal militias during the 1980s left a legacy of confinement of most economic activity to the camps.

Traditionally, UNWRA has been a large employer of Palestinians, especially teachers, who form its single largest sector.[17] Before 1982, however, the largest part of the Palestinian labor force (65 percent, according to one reliable estimate) was employed by the PLO and resistance movement in their large complex of productive, social, and cultural services, as well as political offices and fighting forces. It is impossible to estimate how much employment the PLO and resistance groups still generate, but it is said to be shrinking, with salaries often months in arrears. A third source of professional employment is provided by the small number of independent

Palestinian and Lebanese social institutions that operate in and around camps.

A recent UNICEF survey of 1,600 families in eight camps and five displacement centers found that only 37 percent of men and 8 percent of women aged fifteen to forty-nine were employed. The survey also found that most employment was located inside, or on the periphery of, camps and that most employers were Palestinian associations.[18] As yet unencumbered by the need for work permits, camps generate a great deal of economic activity in the form of crafts and petty commerce. However, because of the low levels of capital accumulation and high levels of war destruction, these activities yield little income.

The almost total closure of the Lebanese economy to Palestinians is a long-term trend that now coincides with other negative developments, including the dwindling of PLO/resistance services, subsidies, and employment opportunities; cutbacks in UNWRA support;[19] a decline in foreign government and international nongovernmental organization (NGO) support (because the conflict in Lebanon is perceived to be over); and the termination of private and public transfers from Palestinians working in the Gulf. The cutbacks in PLO employment and services are especially serious because they are unaccompanied by any national plan to retrain demobilized fighters or set up income generating projects.

Given this framework it is not surprising that, according to one welfare administrator, around 60 percent of Palestinians in Lebanon are living below the UN-designated poverty level. It is impossible to give overall data on income levels, but some idea of the situation can be derived from the records of social institutions that help "hardship cases." As of July 1992, UNWRA had 9,483 families (39,055 persons) classified as "special hardship cases." However, in interpreting this figure it is important to note that the number of people eligible for help is restricted by a budgetary ceiling, eligibility criteria can be exclusive (barring, for example, a widow who has a son over eighteen), and aid is restricted.[20] Similarly, the aid programs and statistical records of other institutions serving the needy are neither comprehensive nor complete. For example, the PLO Institute for Martyrs' Families, which gives allowances to families of men killed in war, will not reveal the number of families it helps; although its allowances vary, families in the largest category receive $9.50 a month, a sum that barely covers the cost of bread. Another institution that helps orphans in needy families, Beit Atfal al-Sumood, recognizes that its list of 1,272 orphans (March 1991) does not include all orphans; its assistance does not exceed $18 per child per month. Whether with respect to female-headed households, or large households dependent on a single wage earner, the incidence of hardship has not been fully surveyed by any of the social institutions working with Palestinians in Lebanon.

Displacement

The displaced form a special category within the refugee population. A survey carried out in 1988 found a total of 4,468 Palestinian families (around 25,334 individuals) scattered over eighty-seven locations.[21] Most were displaced during the 1985–1987 War of the Camps, but others had been displaced since the early 1970s. Of the surveyed families, 75.2 percent had been displaced more than once, 19.7 percent more than three times. A more recent survey found nearly 6,000 displaced families, of whom 50.4 percent were located in or near Sidon and 28.1 percent in Beirut.[22] Most are living in shacks on "empty" land or in half-built or derelict buildings. When the day comes for all war refugees to return to their homes, displaced Palestinians will face a crisis, since they have no homes to return to, and cannot afford to rent.

The material and social conditions endured by the displaced vary with location, but are invariably worse than in camps. Visiting Shatila families scattered through West Beirut, I have found them in the ruins of the American embassy, in high-rise buildings without electricity, piped water, or proper sewage, and (in two of the largest buildings occupied) without separate toilets or kitchens. The distance of these displaced families from UNWRA- and PLO-run services such as schools and clinics, mostly located in camps, is a problem because of the cost of transportation. Distance from friends and kin disrupts social ties.

Many families have been living in such abnormal conditions since the War of the Camps. The resulting effects on health, education, and family relations are very visible in individual cases. Among mothers in particular, stress-related conditions—heart abnormalities, asthma, diabetes, insomnia, kidney and thyroid problems—are very much in evidence. Among children, overcrowding produces a high incidence of respiratory, stomach, and skin infections.[23] A further result of the prolonged stay in displaced locations, as the chairman of Camp Popular Committees in Lebanon has noted, is *tafakuk usari* (family breakup). The demoralization of adolescent boys, mostly out of school, without training programs and unemployed, is also particularly noticeable.

Health, Sickness, and Disability

The ever rising cost of private medical services in Lebanon (where there is virtually no public health sector) has caused a major crisis for UNWRA's health department and the community it serves. UNWRA's health care system is based on general and specialized clinics.[24] Cases requiring hospitalization are generally contracted to Lebanese hospitals. According to UNWRA's annual report, in 1991 the number of contracted beds was reduced by 36 percent. Palestinians report that UNWRA now helps only with cases of open heart surgery and cancer.

There are other bodies besides UNWRA that offer medical services primarily to Palestinians. The Palestinian Red Crescent Society, for example, has a larger infrastructure than UNWRA (ten hospitals and forty-six clinics),[25] but is so underfunded that much of it is nonoperational. The Norwegian People's Aid (NPA) operates a physiotherapy center in Mar Elias camp (Beirut); Medical Aid for Palestinians (MAP) is active in the South; and Popular Aid for Relief and Development (PARD) runs a mobile clinic serving the displaced. What is essentially lacking so far, however, is a general health profile of the Palestinian population. Doctors who work among Palestinians speak of a rise in stress-related illnesses and breakdowns,[26] and drug addiction is reportedly becoming a problem, but the lack of systematic data means that the extent of health-related problems, or incipient problems, in the Palestinian community is not clearly known.

Surveys are beginning to be carried out, however, on the Palestinian handicapped population in Lebanon—a necessity because of years of fighting. A detailed survey in Bourj al-Barajneh camp found ninety-seven serious cases of physical or mental disability in a population of around 12,000.[27] Of these nearly half were war injured; sixteen were amputees. A number of NGOs run small projects that care for the handicapped.[28]

Health and sickness are so closely tied to economic conditions that further decline in income levels will inevitably have its first repercussions in the field of health. Palestinians feel the economic squeeze most sharply when illness or accident hits. Social institutions are constantly besieged by people seeking help with surgery and hospital bills.[29]

Education

In the past, high levels of education enabled Palestinians to compete for jobs even though they were disadvantaged as nonnationals. Educational achievement was also a source of collective pride and individual motivation—an interim substitute for a country and a passport. Today, after years of destruction and disruption, Palestinians in Lebanon are facing an educational crisis. Its symptoms include a fall in educational standards, a rise in the number of school dropouts, and a sharp decline in the number of students continuing beyond the preparatory level. What people fear most, however, is the likelihood that even if their children succeed in obtaining professional qualifications, they will not find jobs. The education crisis thus has two aspects, one scholastic, the other economic.

War has been the main cause of decline in the standards of free UNWRA schooling, through damage to buildings, loss of study time, and the effects of trauma on children's ability to concentrate. For example, children living in combat areas during the War of the Camps lost three years of schooling. People also blame the resistance movement for decline in standards because it drew teachers and students into politics, leading to a loss of motivation and achievement. Whereas before 1982, many families in camps could afford to put their children in private (tuition-paying) schools, the present-day economic squeeze is forcing a return to a deteriorated UNWRA school system. UNWRA points to budgetary shortfall as the reason it cannot expand or upgrade its schools.[30] Teachers in UNWRA schools say that comprehension and language competence have declined, an observation confirmed by poor examination results. Parents and teachers complain of buildings that are "like prisons," denuded of everything that could facilitate learning.

The number of school-age children who do not attend school is unknown, mainly because the size of the refugee population is unknown. A limited UNICEF survey found high dropout rates in thirteen low-income areas. At the preparatory level (ages thirteen through fifteen) the rate of dropout was 36.6 percent, a startling rise over the 6.2 percent rate for 1978. The rate was higher for boys than for girls (43.1 percent versus 29.6 percent), a clear sign of economic pressures. The dropout rate was higher among displaced Palestinians than those in camps (48 percent versus 33 percent), and was higher in war zones, Beirut, and the South, than in the North and the Bekaa. A small number of school-age children (2.4 percent) had never attended school.[31]

What makes the situation even more critical is the rising cost of private education and the inaccessibility of Lebanese public schooling and vocational training to Palestinian refugees. Accessing secondary schooling has always been essential for Palestinians, in order to bridge the gap between free UNWRA schooling and low-cost universities. Between 1985 and 1991, private school fees increased by a factor of fifteen.[32]

Overshadowing all these issues of ends and means looms a larger, more critical, uncertainty: Where and in what capacity will "Lebanese" Palestinians be allowed to work (whatever certificates they obtain)? What kind of education does their situation demand?

Local NGOs

Palestinian and Lebanese social organizations have played a special role in the development of camp communities. Unlike UN or other international agencies, these institutions are autonomous, directed to local needs, and aimed at offering employment and training to Palestinians living in the camps.[33] In addition, there are PLO social institutions that, however reduced, still could play a role in community development. If Lebanese-PLO negotiations remain stalled, however, these local and PLO institutions may face problems. The Lebanese government could insist on a stricter application of certain regulations. For example, Lebanese labor law requires a majority of people employed in associations and companies to be Lebanese nationals; also, all employers should contribute to the social security fund (from which Palestinians cannot benefit). Services could also be redirected, through the imposition of a quota for Lebanese beneficiaries. Any of these changes would disrupt the basic aims (and painfully balanced budgets) of these associations.

CONCLUSION

The Palestinian refugee community in Lebanon faces an unknown future in which none of the likely alternatives is encouraging. There are three possible outcomes to the ongoing Middle East peace process: (1) autonomy for West Bank and Gaza Palestinians as a stage toward eventual sovereignty of these territories; (2) breakdown or inconclusive dragging out of negotiations; and (3) autonomy in the West Bank and Gaza with restrictive conditions concerning the diaspora Palestinians, such as prohibition of their rights to nationality and repatriation (among other limitations on sovereignty). Of these three possibilities, the best but least likely outcome is the first, i.e., sovereignty, with an eventual offer of Palestinian nationality to "Lebanese" Palestinians (although the Lebanese state might then annul refugee residence rights). In the second case, the present situation of limited Palestinian national struggle could continue, though the Lebanese state might act independently of a Middle East settlement to reduce the size and concentrations of the refugee community. In the third case, with repatriation of "Lebanese" Palestinians prohibited, towteen (settlement) would be forced on Palestinians against their will and that of their Lebanese hosts. Lebanese nationality might then be offered to a limited number. The rest of the Palestinian refugee population would remain a disadvantaged and fragmented "nation-class," subject to many kinds of pressures to migrate.

NOTES

1. Estimates of the number of refugees entering Lebanon in 1948 range between 110,000 and 130,000—around one-twelfth of all 1948 Palestinian refugees. This number (which represented one Palestinian for every ten Lebanese) was larger in proportion to Lebanon's size and economic capacity than in any other of the host countries; Jordan contained more Palestinians only when it annexed the West Bank.

2. G. Tueni, author interview, 24 May 1991.

3. S. Natour, *The Legal Status of the Palestinians in Lebanon* (in Arabic, unpublished photocopy, no date), p. 12.

4. S. Natour, *The Legal Status of the Palestinians in Lebanon,* pp. 4–5.

5. For example, Shawki Fakhoury, Ministerial Committee for Palestinian Affairs, in an interview in *L'Orient/Le Jour,* 29 September 1992.

6. S. al-Hout, author interview, 3 May 1991.

7. Reported in *L'Orient/Le Jour*, 2 October 1992.

8. *L'Orient/Le Jour*, 21 September 1992.

9. *L'Orient/Le Jour*, 29 September 1992.

10. A sampling of protests is recorded in *L'Orient/Le Jour* (1992): Maronite Deputy Boutros Harb (5 September), Minister of Interior Sami al-Khatib (9 September), the Supreme Islamic Shi'ite Council (23 September), Salim el-Hoss, a former prime minister (25 September); and Ambassador Shammas in the UN (3 October).

11. It is said that when Lebanon's three "heads of state" (Hrawi, Husseini and Karameh) visited President Bush in September 1991, Bush asked them how many Palestinians there are in Lebanon. An embarrassed silence followed. No census has been conducted in Lebanon since 1932.

12. The question of the number and residence status of the Palestinians is complicated. First, not all UNWRA registered refugees are Palestinians; second, not all Palestinians are registered with UNWRA. Of those not registered, there are two categories: "legal," those who have residence permits, estimated at 20,000; and "illegal," without residence permits, an unknown number. An unknown number of Palestinians have taken on Lebanese citizenship.

13. Official camps destroyed by war: Nabatieh (destroyed in 1974); Dubaya, Jisr al-Basha, and Tel al-Za'atar (1976). Unofficial camps: Karantina (1976); Daouq (Sabra) and the area around Shatila (1985).

14. The return of all persons displaced by war, Lebanese and Palestinians, was part of the Ta'if Accord (12 October 1989). At the time of writing, this process had not begun, and evictions had been frozen, but the head of the Office of Displaced Persons, Elie Hobeiqa, had announced that as soon as return begins "all non-Lebanese will have to leave [occupied buildings] immediately." *Al-Safir*, 8 October 1992.

15. Interview in *Al-Safir*, 5 October 1992.

16. *Al-Safir*, 14 August 1992.

17. As of March 1992, UNWRA had 2,312 local employees; not all are Palestinian.

18. UNICEF, *Preliminary Results of the 1992 Surveys on Literacy and Vocational Training*. Also includes child health and school enrollment.

19. UNWRA stopped basic rations in 1984 except to hardship cases and during bouts of fighting. Recently free children's meals and free school stationery have been stopped, and help with hospitalization was sharply reduced.

20. "Special hardship cases" receive monthly rations, some children's clothing, blankets, building indemnities if in camps, and aid with self-help projects.

21. The survey was conducted by two local NGOs, Popular Aid for Relief and Development, and the Vocational and Social Development Association.

22. UNWRA, December 1991.

23. A recent partial survey found the incidence of diarrhea and acute respiratory infection in children under five years to be higher in displacement centers than in the camps (UNICEF, *Preliminary Results of the 1992 Surveys*).

24. UNWRA provides twenty-five general, thirteen specialist, and eight dental clinics, six laboratories, and consultants for diabetes and hypertension.

25. Palestinian Red Crescent Society, *PRCS Medical Services: Past, Present and Future*. Beirut, 1992.

26. UNWRA's 1991 Health Report cites a "noticeable increase in mental disorders."

27. Survey conducted by NPA and UNWRA.

28. For example: crafts training (NPA, Mar Elias); community-based rehabilitation centers for children (UNWRA, Nahr al-Bared camp, a second planned in Bourj al-Barajneh); and integration of mentally handicapped children in kindergartens run by the Kanafani Cultural Foundation.

29. While researching this chapter I heard of a woman going to all the offices in Mar Elias camp trying to raise LL 6,000,000 ($2,400) to recover her newborn baby from a hospital where it was being held in default of payment after needing incubation.

30. The number of UNWRA schools and students was actually less in 1991 (seventy-seven schools, 33,090 students) than in 1980–1981 (eighty-seven schools, 36,860 students). Most UNWRA schools work on the double shift system, and essential facilities (such as electricity) are often lacking, but the agency has recently set up schools near displacement centers and is said to be making efforts to improve its standards and program.

31. UNICEF, *Preliminary Results of the 1992 Surveys.* This study found a 16.1 percent success rate in the brevet examination (last preparatory class) for 1991. The highest rate was in the North (34 percent), the lowest in the South (5.7 percent).

32. In 1991, the fees of private Beirut secondary schools averaged $550, not including extra expenses (*Les Palestiniens du Liban et l'education: la crise des annees 80* [unpublished report, Beirut, 1991]). It should be noted that the PLO provides low-cost secondary schools in Tripoli, Sidon and Barr Elias (Bekaa), but not in Beirut.

33. Some independent local associations: In'ash al-Mukhayem (embroidery production, kindergartens); the Ghassan Kanafani Cultural Foundation (kindergartens, teacher training); Najdeh Association (embroidery production, vocational training, kindergartens); Beit Atfal al-Sumood (aid and social care for orphans in needy families); the Vocational and Social Development Association (technical/vocational training); Popular Aid for Relief and Development (medical, hygienic, and transport services for the displaced); the Arab Resource Center for Popular Arts (craft training).

7

Israel's Foreign Policy Objectives in Lebanon: A Historical Overview

Don Peretz

Israel's foreign policy makers have always been divided over their objectives in Lebanon. These divisions reflect the larger goals of Israeli foreign policy, ranging from modest to grandiose: from seeking normal good neighborly relationships, to striving for extension of Israel's frontier northward (or at least making Lebanon a satellite, much as Syria has done over the past decade and a half). Israeli objectives in Lebanon have centered on four principal themes: (1) security of Israel's northern border; (2) alliances with the Maronite community; (3) Israel's relations with Syria; and (4) Lebanon's water resources, especially from the Litani River. This chapter will focus on the first three themes, addressing the water issue only in relation to the establishment of the Israeli border (1923). Detailed discussion of Israel's interest in Lebanese water sources appears elsewhere in this volume.[1] The present discussion provides a historical overview of the changing focus and differing degrees of Zionist/Israeli interest in Lebanon.

Prior to Israel's establishment in 1948, Zionist leaders were keen to ensure the physical and economic security of their future state, and to cultivate local alliances that would be useful in countering local opposition to Israel's creation. Lebanon's resources and people, especially the Maronite Christians, were attractive in this regard. Events during this early period played an important role in shaping later Israeli perceptions of Lebanon and the Lebanese from both a security and an alliance perspective.

Following the first Arab-Israeli war in 1948, Lebanon proved to be one of Israel's quieter neighbors, and was not, therefore, a primary concern of Israeli foreign policy. This situation changed, however, after the second wave of Palestinian refugees and (more important) fighters settled in Lebanon during the late 1960s and early 1970s. As the Lebanese-Israeli border became increasingly turbulent, Lebanon gained renewed prominence in Israel's foreign policy; South Lebanon became a target for Israeli military strikes countering Palestinian activity in Lebanon and elsewhere.

After 1975, and the outbreak of civil war in Lebanon (and the consequent destabilization of the state, fragmentation of the nation, and Syrian intervention), Israel's foreign policy objectives toward Lebanon became more aggressive and intrusive, culminating in the massive 1982 invasion. The grandiose goals of this invasion soon faded, however, as the dangerous Lebanese quagmire caused Israel's decisionmakers to reevaluate their perceptions of Lebanon (formed in the pre-1948 period) and to moderate their foreign policy goals considerably, although not to the point of withdrawing Israel's presence or ceasing cross-border raids.

RESOURCES, BORDERS, AND FRIENDS: PRE-1948

Lebanon was a target of early Zionist foreign policy long before the Jewish state was established in 1948. During and after World War I, when Zionist leaders were seeking to establish a territorial base for the Jewish homeland in the Middle East, the borders of Palestine were not yet defined. Because Zionist leaders hoped that part, if not all, of the Palestine region would eventually be designated as the Jewish homeland, they were eager to influence the demarcation of Palestine's borders.

In 1919, at the Paris Peace Conference, Zionist leaders submitted a memorandum requesting that Palestine's northern border run from the Mediterranean coast south of Sidon, northeast across the Litani River to Mount Hermon in Syria. The principal justification was to include the Litani River and its headwaters within Palestine, as one of the water sources necessary for the development of the future Jewish homeland.[2] Zionist leader Chaim Weizmann argued in a letter to Lord Curzon that the Litani was urgently needed to supplement Palestine's limited water resources. Weizmann observed that "the irrigation of Upper Galilee and the power necessary for even a limited industrial life must come from the Litani. . . . If Palestine were cut off from the Litani, Upper Jordan and Yarmuk, she could not be economically independent."[3]

France, Lebanon's mandatory guardian, insisted that the Litani remain entirely within Lebanon. In March 1923, an agreement between France and Britain fixed the border between Palestine and Lebanon, a border that retains international recognition until today.[4] Despite general acceptance of this border, many Zionist and (later) Israeli leaders continued to regard the Litani as the country's "natural" northern frontier.

Throughout most years of the mandate and during the first two decades of Israel's history, its border with Lebanon was the least troublesome from a security perspective. Although the 1923 border bisected an area that had been a single economic unit during Ottoman times, the resulting dislocations were compensated for through mandatory agreements that legalized traditional cross-frontier movements. Prior to Israel's establishment in 1948, individuals were given free access to properties severed by the border and many laborers were permitted to cross from Lebanon into Palestine.[5]

Nevertheless, Palestine's northern border was not without incident. For example, during the Arab revolt from 1936 to 1939, Arab nationalist guerrilla forces used South Lebanon as a base to attack northern Palestine. Neither the French nor the Lebanese government were willing to crack down on the guerrillas for fear of arousing Arab nationalist sentiments. The French, having had to cope with a nationalist uprising in Syria, were unwilling to interfere; the Lebanese government decided to ignore the problem. The British response, on the other hand, was to orchestrate "unofficial" raids against Arab villages in Lebanon using a newly organized force of Jewish commandos. Many of these commandos would later become commanders in the Israeli Army; their experiences in Lebanon in the 1930s significantly shaped their later attitudes and perceptions about the strategic importance of the Lebanese border.

Unable to halt the cross-border attacks, the British mandatory government contracted Solel Boneh, an affiliate of the Histadrut,[6] to construct a barrier along Palestine's borders with Lebanon, Syria, and Transjordan. This barrier, called Tegart's Wall, was intended to fend off cross-border incursions into Palestine by guerrilla forces, but was hardly a success. Not only did it fail to prevent cross-border incursions, it "stirred up the wrath of villagers on both sides of the frontier because it erected for the first time an artificial barrier to the trade, both legal and contraband, which has gone on between adjacent villages from time immemorial."[7]

Following the Arab revolt of the late 1930s, the security situation in northern Palestine returned to normal. The incursions, however, had greatly intensified Zionist apprehensions concerning the security of this area, especially because Jewish settlers in the north were greatly outnumbered by indigenous Arabs who were long accustomed to free cross-border movement (in fact, many Arab families had branches on both sides of the frontier). Indeed, these apprehensions were to provide incentive for Israeli forces to remove the Arab inhabitants from northern frontier villages during the first Arab-Israel war in 1948.

During World War II, when Vichy authorities took over the French mandatory government in Beirut, the British officially closed the Lebanon-Palestine border. Intent on overthrowing the Vichy government, the British organized Operation Exporter, an attack on Lebanon that included a battalion of Jewish commandos. The attack succeeded in ending Vichy rule in Syria and Lebanon by July 1941. Moreover, it was extremely valuable to Israel's future military leaders, giving them extensive insight into the military geography of South Lebanon; if South Lebanon was not to be included within Palestine's (later Israel's) frontiers, they concluded, then it would be useful, if not necessary, to garrison the region with friendly Lebanese forces to prevent cross-border incursions.

After World War II, the Lebanese-Palestinian border again became a point of confrontation as Arab guerrillas attacked Jewish settlements and British forces in Palestine. Lebanon did not, however, play a major military role in the first Arab-Israeli war. Although Lebanese forces crossed the border into a sector of Palestine designated as part of the Jewish state on 15 May 1948 (Israel's first day of independence), they were eventually driven out. When exploratory talks were initiated with Lebanon in January 1949, Israel withdrew from four villages it occupied; it was unwilling, however, to give up other areas considered strategic near the Syrian-Lebanese border. Not until Syria agreed to negotiate, two months later, was Israel willing to conclude an agreement with Lebanon. Ever since, Israel's relations with Syria have been a determining factor in relations with Lebanon.[8]

The 1949 Armistice Agreement confirmed the Palestine-Lebanon border as the demarcation line between the two countries and called for demilitarized zones on both sides in which neither country was to maintain more than 1,500 troops.[9] Although the agreement required the removal of large concentrations of conventional forces from the border, Israel's security position had been strengthened by Arab refugee flight and by the Israeli Army's removal of Arabs from several border villages. Furthermore, a number of new Jewish settlements, which doubled as paramilitary bases, were established along the frontier.

Zionist (and later Israeli) leaders sought more than just secure borders with Lebanon; they also looked north for potential allies. Contacts with the Lebanese Christian community began during the mandatory era, when Zionist leaders developed relationships with Maronite leaders who supported the establishment of a Jewish state.[10] These relationships shaped early Zionist and later Israeli perceptions of Lebanon. Many saw Lebanon as a largely Christian enclave in the midst of a hostile Islamic Arab heartland.

As a result, Israeli leaders have long considered Lebanon the weakest link in Arab nationalist efforts against the Jewish state. They often attempted to manipulate divisions within Lebanese society to their own advantage, hoping that through diplomatic efforts Lebanese Christians, (particularly the Maronite community) could be, if not allied, at least neutralized in Israeli confrontations with Arab nationalism. The rationale underlying this policy was that through close contacts with such groups (who might themselves be wary of pan-Arab movements) Israel could fragment the Arab/Islamic world, weaken it, and thus substantially diminish the power of Arab nationalist opposition to the Jewish state. Through alliances with other foes of pan-Arabism, Israel could break out of its isolation in the Middle East.

In 1937, David Ben Gurion (later to become Israel's first prime minister) observed that "Lebanon is the natural ally of the Jews of the land of Israel. . . ." Closeness between Palestine and Lebanon, he believed, would "give us the possibility to expand—with the agreement and benediction of our neighbours who need us."[11] Ben Gurion argued that because of Lebanon's "totally different heritage and culture from the rest of the [Arab] League," Muslims could not dominate its policies. Establishment of a Christian state, therefore, would be a natural step: "It has historic roots and it will find support from large forces in the Christian world, Catholic and Protestant alike." However, "without our initiative and our energetic help it will not come about. . . . This is now the CENTRAL TASK or at least ONE of the central tasks of our foreign policy. . . . We will not be forgiven if we miss this historic opportunity. . . ."[12]

Not all Israeli leaders were as enthusiastic about the possibilities of altering Lebanon's borders and enlisting its Christian population in the cause of Israel. As Foreign Minister Moshe Sharett wrote in his diary, ". . . This is an empty dream. . . . The Maronites are split. Those who favour Christian separatism are weak and will not dare do a thing. . . . If we begin to agitate and push we will get entangled in an affair that will bring us only disgrace. . . ."[13] Sharett pointed out that the Christians were no longer a majority in Lebanon, and that many non-Maronites wanted no part of a Maronite-dominated state. There was serious danger that such schemes would "throw Lebanon's Moslems into the arms of Syria. . . ." Moreover, he noted, even many Maronites cast their lot with Arab nationalism. He feared that, by engaging in such maneuvering, Israel would cause itself uncalculated damage vis-à-vis the Arab states and Western powers alike.

Sharett failed to dissuade Ben Gurion of the folly of his scheme.[14] Later, Ben Gurion's protegé, Moshe Dayan, recommended "buying" a Lebanese officer who would declare himself "savior of the Maronite population. Then the Israeli army would enter Lebanon, occupy the necessary territory and set up a Christian regime allied to Israel and everything would turn out just fine."[15]

Sharett lamented the military's "simply appalling lack of seriousness" in its "whole approach to neighbouring countries, especially to the more complex questions of Lebanon's internal and external situation." Sharett's warnings went unheeded at the time and later—to much greater folly—in 1982. Indeed, Prime Minister Menachem Begin was to defend Israel's 1982 invasion of Lebanon by marshaling Ben Gurion's early legacy.[16]

SECURITY OF THE NORTHERN BORDER AND THE PALESTINIAN "PROBLEM": 1950s–1973

By the 1950s, Israeli policymakers had greatly moderated their objectives in Lebanon. They recognized that Lebanon's domestic considerations prevented its leaders from separating themselves from the rest of the Arab world by signing a separate peace treaty with Israel. Moreover, the Israeli-Lebanese border, no longer disputed, had received general international recognition. In the first part of this period, Israel's border with Lebanon was its calmest frontier.

While Lebanon aligned itself with the rest of the Arab world in international fora dealing with the Arab-Israeli conflict, it did not threaten Israel's security or vital national interests. Despite the influx to Lebanon of tens of thousands of Palestine refugees during the 1948 war, they were not yet a threat to northern Israel. The two countries were able to police and to curtail greatly cross-border incursions and smuggling by means of the Israel-Lebanon Mixed Armistice Commission (MAC).[17]

By the mid-1960s, however, the border began to prove troublesome when the first Palestinian guerrilla factions emerged and mobilized. An initial *fedayeen* attack from Lebanon occurred in June 1965, followed by gradual escalation of cross-border commando incursions. Tensions were exacerbated during the 1967 Arab-Israeli war when Israel decided to abrogate the authority of the UN Truce Supervision Organization and its four MACs including the one with Lebanon.[18]

Following the ejection of Palestinian commando factions from Jordan during 1970–1971 and relocation of many in South Lebanon, the region became a major target of Israeli commando and air attacks; Israel's anti-fedayeen activity shifted from its frontier with Jordan to South Lebanon. In May 1970, the Israeli Army conducted its first large-scale sweep of the region, which was followed by similar incursions in 1972 (setting a precedent for the major attack of 1978).

Militarily, Palestinian commando attacks during the early 1970s were limited in scope, "not particularly effective and had a very limited impact on northern Israel."[19] Indeed, Israeli "retaliatory" policy was directed more at curtailing terrorist attacks against Israelis outside the region than at retaliating for incursions into northern Israel.

By 1974 the situation in northern Israel changed. Fedayeen strikes from South Lebanon became increasingly frequent, causing larger numbers of Israeli casualties. In addition to military strikes, Israel responded by constructing a security fence twelve feet high, with electronic warning devices, along the border; a dirt track was laid on the Israeli side to detect infiltrators.

CIVIL WAR IN LEBANON: 1975–1985

Several factors converged in 1975 to focus Israel's attention on the Lebanese frontier. The Israeli public were demanding action against the fedayeen attacks. Within Lebanon, outbreak of the civil war greatly diminished what little authority the government had been able to assert in the South. With the entrance of Syrian forces into Lebanon, Israeli authorities established an unofficial "red line" along the Litani River, south of which they would not tolerate Syrian military presence.[20] It appeared that spheres of influence were beginning to emerge with the area south of the Litani falling inside an Israeli zone.

When Palestinian fedayeen temporarily moved north to participate in battles around Beirut, Prime Minister Yitzhak Rabin initiated a "pacification" program for South Lebanon. Its three components, announced by Defense Minister Shimon Peres in July 1976, were: humanitarian relief for Lebanese residents in southern villages, expulsion of all non-Lebanese military forces from the area, and establishment of a pro-Israeli South Lebanese militia to help keep out the fedayeen. Services, including water supply, medical care, and cross-border trade, were made available in the hope that Lebanese border villages would become outposts of anti-fedayeen collaboration.[21]

By the end of 1976, Israel had organized a Lebanese militia under Major Sa'd Haddad (of the disintegrated Lebanese Army) to replace its own patrols. This militia, later renamed the South Lebanese Army (SLA), was armed, clothed, fed, and trained by Israel, and Israeli officers were attached to it as advisers. Haddad's force was to act north of the border as an early warning system, alerting Israeli forces to the presence of Palestinian commandos.

When the fedayeen returned to the South, severe fighting erupted between Haddad's militia, the Palestinians, and Lebanese leftist forces. Because of the external sponsorship involved, the fighting became a war by proxy between Israel and Syria, fought with Lebanese players on Lebanese soil.

When Prime Minister Menachem Begin and his right-wing Likud Party assumed office in June 1977, he proclaimed that Haddad's militia was necessary to save the Christians of South Lebanon from "genocide." Israel, he asserted, would "never abandon the Christian minority across the border."[22] Begin's statement signaled a new shift in policy: a return to the earlier program of capitalizing on Lebanon's sectarian differences through Israeli support for establishing sectarian enclaves in the country. Initially Begin's government continued the rather cautious policies of its Labor predecessor, including support for Major Haddad's militia and continued attacks on Palestinian bases in Lebanon. In March 1978, however, Israel launched a major incursion into Lebanon, Operation Stone of Wisdom, following a fedayeen attack on an Israeli bus south of Haifa.[23] This invasion, which resulted in Israel's temporary occupation of the South up to the Litani River, was the beginning of a new phase in relations between Israel and Lebanon: South Lebanon leaped to the forefront of international attention, resulting in establishment of a new United Nations peacekeeping force

(UNIFIL), and Lebanon became a question of prime significance in Begin's foreign policy.[24]

After the 1981 election that returned Likud to power, Ariel Sharon became minister of defense with authority to carry out his broad-ranging scheme to extend Israel's influence in the region. Policy toward Lebanon was only a small part of Sharon's "Grand Design" for the Middle East. His strategy encompassed relations with Egypt, Syria, Jordan and the Palestinians, and involved: annexation of the Golan Heights in December 1981; further integration, if not outright annexation of the West Bank and Gaza; promotion of the "Jordan is Palestine" concept as a solution for the Palestinian problem; removal of the Palestinian threat from South Lebanon; and elimination of the PLO as a significant military and diplomatic actor. The latter two goals incurred grave consequences for Lebanon, especially given that the PLO's entire operation was headquartered in Lebanon's capital city, Beirut.[25]

The Lebanese phase of Sharon's grand design was based on a number of premises: "that a large-scale operation in southern Lebanon was unavoidable, that Israel could afford to act only once on a large scale, that the problem in the South could not be solved without solving the wider Lebanese crisis, that a solution to that crisis was possible, and that it could be the key to a significant change in the politics of the whole region."[26] The operation entailed advancing on Beirut to create a new strategic situation, totally destroying PLO operations in Lebanon, forcing Syria to leave the country, and placing the Lebanese Front under Bashir Gemayel in charge of the government.

High-level contacts between Israeli government officials and the Maronite community started in 1976 (before Begin became prime minister), between Yitzhak Rabin and the Chamoun, Frangieh, and Gemayel families. When Sharon took over Israel's security and diplomatic planning, relations with the various Maronite leaders were both more frequent and more open. The idea was broached to link Bashir Gemayel's election as president with a large-scale Israeli operation that would reach as far north as Beirut. Sharon obviously considered the Lebanese Front to be an integral partner in an anti-PLO (pro-Israel) alliance, and in his "big plan" for Lebanon.

In the debate among Israelis leading up to the 1982 invasion, Operation Peace for Galilee, Prime Minister Rabin and Mordechai Gur (former chief of staff) argued against a large-scale invasion. They were less strenuously opposed, however, to a limited border incursion that would give Israel control of a "security zone" on the Lebanese side of the border. Even several members of Begin's cabinet had reservations about a large-scale invasion; they would later charge that Sharon deceived the government by concealing the broad outlines of his "big plan."[27]

The invasion proved to be a far more complicated and difficult military venture than Sharon and his military chief of staff, Eitan, had envisaged. More problematic than the military complications, however, were the political ramifications. Although the initial operation received support from most Israeli political factions and was tacitly accepted as a necessary requisite for Israel's security by top officials in the U.S. government, Peace for Galilee appeared to get out of hand when Sharon sent Israeli forces north of the Litani to the outskirts of Beirut. By the summer of 1982, the Lebanese invasion had become the first war to arouse extensive public opposition in Israel. The number of soldiers and officers opposed to the war was larger than ever before; even members of the high command were critical. Public opposition reached an all-time high following the massacre of Palestinians in the Sabra and Shatila refugee camps: hundreds of thousands of Israelis demonstrated against the government.

Israel's siege of Beirut also severely strained its relations with the United States. Although U.S. and Israeli objectives in Lebanon originally coincided, the siege and Sharon's conduct of the war drove a wedge between the two countries. U.S. officials were apprehensive about Sharon's heavy-handed tactics, fearing that they would destabilize not only Lebanon, but the entire Middle East.

In the negotiations leading to the abortive May 1983 peace treaty between Israel and Lebanon, Sharon continued to pursue parts of his original strategy by attempting to convert Lebanon into a quasi-satellite under Israeli military control. Israel's security demands included: establishment of three Israeli-operated early warning installations in various parts of Lebanon; integration of the Israeli-manipulated Haddad militia into the Lebanese Army; and withdrawal of Israeli troops according to an Israeli schedule contingent on withdrawal of all other foreign forces. Diplomatic demands included normalization of relations between the two countries and establishment of an Israeli liaison office in Beirut.[28] Although a compromise agreement was signed in May 1983, it was rejected by the Lebanese Parliament soon after, leaving the status of relations between Israel and Lebanon in limbo.

Israeli public pressure forced subsequent governments to curtail greatly their control of Lebanon south of Beirut. During the 1984 election, both leading parties (Labor and Likud) recognized the growing public impatience with the occupation and promised to withdraw. The Labor-Likud coalition government (formed in 1984) withdrew Israeli forces from all but a fifteen-mile-wide "security zone" by 1985.

One of the most alarming unforeseen results of Israel's 1982 invasion was its effect on Lebanon's Shi'ite community. The invasion ignited Shi'ite hostility, and helped to galvanize the following of the newly emergent, Iranian-backed Hizballah movement. Hizballah became the most radical actor in the Lebanese imbroglio, and the most insistent on total withdrawal of Israeli forces from *all* Lebanon, backing their demands with persistent guerrilla attacks in Israel's self-declared "security zone."

ISRAEL'S "SECURITY ZONE"
AND CONFLICT WITH HIZBALLAH: POST-1985

Although Israel recognizes its international border with Lebanon, it clearly perceives the region south of the Litani as vital to its security. Israel will not tolerate the presence of any other non-Lebanese (i.e., Syrian or Palestinian) or unfriendly (i.e., Hizballah) forces in this area.

Since 1985, Israel has maintained control of its self-declared "security zone" by way of its proxy, the SLA. Periodically, Israeli military units have struck at hostile forces north of the zone and attacks by the Israeli Air Force have continued against Palestinian and Shi'ite bases. Relations between Israel and Hizballah have continued to be inflamed, subjecting South Lebanon to ongoing attacks and counterattacks. For example, in July 1989, Israeli-Hizballah relations dangerously deteriorated when Israeli forces abducted Sheikh Abdul Karim Obeid, a pivotal figure in Hizballah. In 1991, when Israel released several hundred Shi'ite prisoners as part of a prisoner exchange agreement, Sheikh Obeid remained in Israeli hands as hostage for a missing Israeli airman (who was captured in 1986 and is believed to be held by militant Shi'ites).[29]

Since departure of the Israeli Army during 1985, it appears that the "red line" established during the 1970s was reestablished, if not on the map, then in Israeli consciousness. Nearly all principal Israeli political groups, certainly Labor and Likud, recognize the "security zone" and the "red line." Within Likud and among the parties to its right, there are those who still believe in Sharon's "Grand Design" for the Middle East and "big plan" for Lebanon. Many still maintain contacts with Israel's former allies in the Lebanese Forces, still envisage the possibility of gaining access to the Litani waters, and still believe that the PLO presence and Syrian influence in Lebanon can be excised. These aspirations, however, are held by a small, but politically influential, group of militant nationalists.

The bilateral negotiations initiated at Madrid in October 1991 as part of the new Middle East peace effort stalled during the first year. With the formation of a new Labor coalition led by Prime Minister Yitzhak Rabin in 1992, however, prospects for breaking the stalemate improved. The Labor Party platform stated that Israel desired a peace treaty with Lebanon "on the basis of the existing boundary" and that it had "no interest in Lebanese land or Lebanese waters. . . . Israel will respect an independent and peaceful Lebanon." On the other hand, these conditions were qualified by insistence on maintaining "the security zones by means of local forces with the backing of the IDF [Israeli Defense Forces] as long as necessary to preserve security and check hostile acts. . . ."[30] Hence, Israel has continued its noncompliance with Resolution 425.

While many Labor Party members acknowledge that much Israeli policy in Lebanon has been a mistake, those who control the security apparatus insist that Israel cannot leave until a strong Lebanese government, not subject to Syrian control, is formed, and until the Lebanese Army proves itself capable of securing Lebanese territory. Like its predecessor, the Rabin government perceives the Lebanese government and most of the area under its control as a Syrian satellite rather than an independent entity. Failure to achieve progress in the negotiations with Lebanon is blamed on Syria; the Ta'if Accord and the governments formed after it are looked on with great mistrust because of the large role assigned to Damascus in implementing the accord.

Mainstream Israeli observers perceive future relations with Lebanon in the larger context of Middle East politics. If other foreign forces withdraw from Lebanon (meaning the Syrian Army and Palestinian commandos) then Israel too, they assert, will be willing to renegotiate its position in South Lebanon. If stability returns to the country and Lebanese security forces regain control of areas vital to Israel, negotiations will be greatly facilitated, they believe. As for the question of the Litani, they think that it should be placed on the larger agenda of Middle East regional economic development. Eventually some form of regional cooperation must be devised to cope with the water shortage that faces not only Israel, but most of its neighbors.

In the meantime, what confidence-building measures are feasible? If the new Lebanese government succeeds in establishing its authority throughout the country including the South, and proceeds to disarm the remaining "resistance" groups, the raison d'être for Israel's occupation will be eliminated. Israel, for its part, could adopt a more forthcoming attitude toward UNIFIL, demonstrating greater cooperation with the UN force. Of course, Israel's greatest contribution toward improving relations with Lebanon would be to adopt a more compromising position toward Syria in the Golan Heights controversy and toward the Palestinians in the West Bank and Gaza Strip. At this point in time, Israel's relations with Lebanon are really a function of its relations with other parties to the Arab-Israeli conflict. The principal issues in any conflict between the two countries have little if anything to do with claims that Lebanon or Israel have against each other, but are in large measure the result of Israel's relations with Syria and the Palestinians.[31]

NOTES

1. See the chapter by Amery and Kubursi.
2. See "The Zionist Organization's Memorandum to the Supreme Council at

the Peace Conference, 3 Feb. 1919," in David H. Miller, *My Diary at the Conference of Paris* vol. 5 (New York: Appeal Printing Co., 1924).

3. Cited in Frederic C. Hof, *Galilee Divided: The Israel-Lebanon Frontier, 1916–1948* (Boulder: Westview, 1984), pp. 11, 13.

4. See "Agreement Between His Majesty's Government and the French Government Respecting the Boundary Line Between Syria and Palestine from the Mediterranean to El Hamme," *Treaty Series No. 13* (1923).

5. According to some observers, Lebanese authorities deliberately neglected development of Lebanon's southernmost regions because they expected that Israel would sooner or later acquire control of the region. For further discussion see the chapters by Charif and by Amery and Kubursi in this volume.

6. The Histradrut, established in 1920 by the Jewish Labor Movement, is Israel's largest labor union federation.

7. *The Times* (London), 26 July 1938, p. 11, cited in Hof, *Galilee Divided,* p. 47.

8. Kenneth Bilby, *New York Herald Tribune,* 25 April 1949, cited in George Kirk, *Survey of International Affairs, The Middle East 1945–1950* (London: Oxford, 1954), pp. 288–289, 295.

9. "Israeli-Lebanese General Armistice Agreement 1949," Ras En Nakoura, 23 March 1949, in Lebanese Center for Documentation and Research (CEDRE), *Lebanese Israeli Negotiations: Chronology, Bibliography, Maps,* pp. 259–263.

10. For example, a number of Lebanese archbishops, as well as former President Emile Eddé, supported the establishment of a Jewish state in Palestine. In 1936, the Maronite Patriarch articulated this support before the Peel Commission. Likewise, leaders of the Maronite Church testified at the 1946 United Nations Special Committee on Palestine (UNSCOP) in favor of a Jewish state. See Itamar Rabinovich, *The War for Lebanon, 1970–1983* (Ithaca & London: Cornell University Press, 1984), pp 104, 225.

11. Jonathan Randal, *The Tragedy of Lebanon: Christian Warlords, Israeli Adventurers and American Bunglers* (London: Chatto & Windus, The Horgath Press, 1983), pp. 188, 190.

12. Randal, *Tragedy of Lebanon,* pp. 190–191.

13. Randal, *Tragedy of Lebanon,* pp. 192–194.

14. Indeed later, in 1955, Ben Gurion proposed to exploit tensions between Syria and Iraq as an opportunity for Israeli intervention in Lebanon, and wondered whether Lebanese Druze and Shi'ites might be persuaded to join the Lebanese destabilization plan.

15. Randal, *Tragedy of Lebanon,* pp. 192–193.

16. Begin stated that Ben Gurion had planned to divide Lebanon by setting up a Christian state north of the Litani River. The difference, claimed Begin, was that he was open in his policy objectives whereas Ben Gurion had resorted to subterfuge. See Simha Flapan, *The Birth of Israel: Myths and Realities* (London: Croom Helm, 1987), p. 5.

17. As part of the 1949 armistice agreements among Israel and Egypt, Lebanon, Syria, and Jordan, a mixed armistice commission was established in each agreement to include Israeli, Arab, and third-party representatives.

18. If, as some analysts contend, Israel's goal was to annex South Lebanon, June 1967 would have been an opportune time. The real intent underlying Israel's cancellation of the armistice agreement with Lebanon, however, was to achieve legal consistency; according to the agreements, no single one could be canceled without cancellation of the other three. In order for Israel to cancel its agreements with Egypt, Syria, and Jordan, therefore, it had to also end its agreement with Lebanon.

19. Hof, *Galilee Divided*, p. 74.

20. The 1976 "red line" understanding between Israel and Syria (in which the United States played broker), was an attempt by the two countries to avoid direct confrontation in Lebanon.

21. Part of the humanitarian relief program called for employing "safe" (mostly Maronite) Lebanese in Israel. Thus, the "Good Fence Policy" was based on the philosophy developed during the Mandate years: to make Lebanese friends, in the hope that they would aid in the fight against Israel's enemies in Lebanon and the wider Arab world. Ben Gurion's dream (as discussed earlier), however, did not reemerge fully until the Likud government assumed office in 1977.

22. Hof, *Galilee Divided*, p. 81.

23. According to the military correspondent of the *Jerusalem Post*, the attack was initiated to "break the tightening terrorist stranglehold around the Christian enclaves in the central and northern sectors of southern Lebanon." See Hirsh Goodman, *Jerusalem Post (International Edition)*, March 21, 1978, p. 7.

24. Although international pressure forced Israel to withdraw, it maintained an active presence in a self-declared "security zone" along the border, which was placed under the command of Haddad's militia.

25. Sharon clearly linked Israel's inability to control Palestinians in the West Bank and Gaza with the continued existence of the PLO. When Sharon's specific schemes to pacify West Bank Palestinians failed (and prompted a "mini-intifada" at the time), Sharon blamed the PLO and vowed to destroy the organization. Indeed, prior to the 1982 invasion, Sharon told the U.S. ambassador to Israel that the envisaged operation in Lebanon would help solve the problem of the West Bank and Gaza by eliminating PLO influence in the occupied territories (*New York Times*, 28 May 1985).

26. Rabinovich, *War for Lebanon*, pp. 132–133.

27. Rabinovich, *War for Lebanon*, p. 123.

28. For discussion of the tripartite United States, Israel, and Lebanon negotiations leading to the proposed treaty, see Efraim Inbar, "Great Power Mediation: The USA and the May 1983 Israeli-Lebanese Agreement," *Journal of Peace Research* vol. 28 no. 1 (1 Feb. 1991), pp. 71–84.

29. Violent attacks in the South continued to escalate throughout 1992 and into 1993. In February 1992, Israeli-Hizballah exchanges increased dramatically following the Israeli assassination of the Hizballah leader Sheikh Abbas Musawi. In the fall of 1992, Hizballah assaults on the SLA set off a series of rocket and artillery duels along the border, accompanied by Israeli air strikes into Lebanon. The latter actions prompted Hizballah to mount a rocket attack into Israel proper. Israel responded with its biggest deployment of forces and artillery along the border and in the "security zone" since 1985, and with intensive bombardments north of the zone. *Editor's update:* In July 1993, following Hizballah attacks on the SLA zone, Israel launched its fiercest military onslaught on South Lebanon since 1982. Upon commencement of Israeli airstrikes, Hizballah launched Katyusha rockets into northern Israel. For seven days, Israel bombarded 100 Lebanese villages leaving 132 dead and 500 wounded. Approximately 350,000 civilians fled the area. On 31 July, the U.S. secretary of state brokered a cease-fire that stopped the bombing. Israel's declared purpose for the attack, Operation Accountability, was to create a massive exodus from the South to "put pressure on the Lebanese government" to rein in Hizballah. Following the cease-fire, Lebanese Army units deployed alongside certain UNIFIL positions in the South, although the Lebanese government declared that it could not oppose acts of resistance against Israeli targets in occupied Lebanese territory. In August, Hizballah continued its attacks in the southern, occupied zone, and Israel recommenced (more limited) airstrikes in retaliation.

30. See "The Labor Party Platform on Foreign Affairs & Security—1988," in Efraim Inbar, *War & Peace in Israeli Politics: Labor Party Position on National Security* (Boulder: Lynne Rienner, 1991).

31. It is notable, in this regard, that Israeli Prime Minister Rabin pointed to Syrian responsibility for the violent escalation with Hizballah in South Lebanon during October and November 1992; he suggested that Syria was encouraging (and not restraining) Hizballah actions. See Peretz Kidron, "Israel and Lebanon: Commitment to Stay," *Middle East International* (20 November 1992), p. 7.

8

Determinants and Characteristics of Syrian Policy in Lebanon

As'ad Abukhalil

Foreign intervention in Lebanese affairs is not a new phenomenon. Lebanese factions and leaders, aware of the powerful domestic advantages that could be won through alliances with external powers, have been urging various external actors to intervene on their behalf since before the country's creation. Likewise, external powers have had their own reasons and interests for cultivating client relationships with Lebanese partners. Indeed, foreign support of Lebanese sects and factions was not uncommon in the nineteenth century when European powers, competing for footholds in the Ottoman Empire, "sponsored" various sectarian groupings throughout the Middle East.[1]

Lebanon's independence, based on the 1943 National Pact, did little to halt foreign intervention.[2] The uniqueness of Lebanon's political system, along with the country's relative freedoms (absent in other Arab states) attracted a variety of states and their intelligence services. As a result, Lebanon became a center of regional and international intrigue. Meanwhile, Lebanese organizations and actors, anxious to enhance their positions within the delicately balanced political system, continued to seek foreign patrons. The war's eruption in 1975 only enhanced outside eagerness to intervene in the fighting, an eagerness that was welcomed by Lebanese factions who were seeking foreign sponsors to serve their narrow agendas.

Despite this long history of foreign intervention,[3] the present-day level of influence (i.e., Syrian) in Lebanon is, in many ways, unprecedented. Given the size, scope, and potential duration of Syrian involvement in post-Ta'if Lebanon, the motives behind this involvement need to be understood. As a small step in this direction, this chapter outlines some of the major determinants and characteristics of Syrian policy in Lebanon. Although it does not review the history of Syria's relations with Lebanese political actors, a few introductory observations are warranted on Lebanese attitudes toward foreign intervention in general and, in particular, toward Syrian intervention.

The fact that numerous external players have intervened in the tragic Lebanese game has nurtured a tendency among many Lebanese to belittle the indigenous causes of the war, reinforcing a myth that the Lebanese, themselves, are not responsible for the war, but are its innocent victims. This myth takes various forms and multiple ideological guises, but is typically expressed as a conspiracy theory that explains the war as an orchestrated act of aggression against Lebanon by foreign powers. (Of course, the identity of the external power[s] responsible for Lebanon's demise changes according to the political orientations of the various Lebanese factions.)

Conspiracy theories only obfuscate the realities of Lebanon's war and, more important, deny the domestic factors that encouraged foreign intervention. In many ways, the multiplicity of external actors gave Lebanese leaders more options, enlarging their room for political maneuver. It was for this reason that conspiracy theories became so prevalent and popular. Various Lebanese players devised and marshaled these theories with great political expediency, either to legitimize the intervention of an external power (when it was politically advantageous) or to protest against an external intervention (when it was politically disadvantageous). In this way, popular political attitudes toward external forces were filtered through the myths and political preferences of Lebanese warring factions. As a faction's alliances shifted, so too did its myths and political attitudes.

Although detailed analysis of the Lebanese factions' shifting perceptions of and relations with external players is beyond the bounds of this chapter,[4] a brief overview of the attitudes held by Lebanese right- and left-wing coalitions with respect to Syrian intervention follows.

Lebanon's ultranationalist, Maronite-led, conservative establishment subscribes to (and promulgates) the myth that prior to the arrival of the PLO and Syrian forces in Lebanon, the country enjoyed absolute sovereignty and independence (*watan mutlaq al-siyadah*). Their coalition's declared purpose, therefore, has always been expressed in terms of "restoring" Lebanon's sovereignty and independence. Restoration of Lebanon's sovereignty was portrayed as the necessary precondition to end the war, and the primary national goal.[5]

Thus, the ultranationalist opposition to Syrian intervention (which, notably did not emerge until 1978) and to PLO activities, was ostensibly directed at returning the decisionmaking process to Lebanese hands. Underlying the rhetorical insistence upon full restoration of Lebanon's sovereignty however, is the unspoken belief that Lebanon's problems are entirely the result of foreign interference.

The problem, of course, is that this belief is not shared by all Lebanese.

Moreover, this "sovereignty first" perspective confounds understanding of the Lebanese conflict in at least two regards. First, it ignores the fact that many Lebanese do not believe that Lebanon enjoyed absolute sovereignty prior to the arrival of the Palestinians. Second, by attributing Lebanon's troubles to outside interference, it dismisses the genuine domestic grievances articulated by many Lebanese. In so doing, this view serves to glorify the structures and conditions of prewar Lebanon to a degree that is not shared by most of Lebanon's Muslims as well as other non-Muslim critics of the political system. Nevertheless, ultranationalist Maronite leaders have consistently attributed mounting domestic public opposition to Arab (or Soviet) designs against the Lebanese national interest.

Likewise, elements of Lebanon's leftist/Muslim coalition developed a similarly narrow, self-serving perspective on external intervention. They, too, objected to foreign interference only when it was militarily and politically supportive of the other side. For example, whereas the leftist/Muslim coalition opposed Syria's intervention in 1976 (when Syria did so on behalf of the Lebanese Forces, and against the Lebanese National Movement, LNM), they reversed this stance from 1977 onwards—supporting Syria's role under the slogan of preserving the Arabism of Lebanon. This political definition of Lebanon's identity seems to be the product of the narrow interests of militias and leaders, as well as of sectarian experiences and agendas.

In brief, it is fair to say that the attitudes of the various Lebanese factions toward Syrian military presence in Lebanon have undergone dramatic changes according to the shifting positions of Lebanese militias and other organizations and linked to the changing role of Syria itself.[6]

SYRIA'S POLICY TOWARD LEBANON: THREE EXPLANATORY PARADIGMS

No scholarly consensus presently exists concerning the nature of the Syrian decisionmaking process under Hafez al-Asad. In secretive, autocratic regimes like that of Syria, one cannot be certain about the procedures of rule and the specifics of the exercise of power. One can formulate some kind of perspective, however, by studying Asad's tenure, and by a careful, critical reading of Syria's official political literature. Of course, the political literature of any oppressive regime is of limited face value to the researcher because public statements are often made to rationalize policies to the people. For example, if one were to rely on the Syrian constitution, one would conclude that Syria is a functioning democracy.

Scholars use various paradigms to explain the determinants of Syria's foreign policy decisionmaking process. The paradigm of choice for most, if not all, Israeli scholars, and for some U.S. scholars, is the Greater Syria paradigm. The term "Greater Syria" refers to the idea that Syria, Lebanon, Palestine, and Jordan constitute one geographical, cultural, and political entity and that all borders between them should be eliminated. Analysts who employ the Greater Syria paradigm believe that all Syrian actions and foreign policy orientations emanate from a deep desire to create Greater Syria. This perspective is often used by politicians, journalists, and scholars to explain all actions and policies of the Syrian government and to underline the notion that Hafez al-Asad harbors expansionist aims.[7]

Aside from its political convenience in Israel and the West, this paradigm seems to attribute irrational motivation to Syrian political behavior. To assume that Hafez al-Asad is motivated by a secret aim to create Greater Syria, is to believe that Asad is an ideologue at heart, with little or no appreciation of the political environment in which he operates. This assumption, however, contradicts the view held by most experts on Syria (including Asad's critics) that Asad is more intelligent than many leaders in the region. After his many years in power, characterized by ruthlessness and large-scale use of force against opponents, it is unlikely that he is oblivious to the tremendous political and military obstacles that render the creation of a Greater Syria far-fetched at this point in history.

Even the Lebanese members of the Syrian Socialist National Party (SSNP)—the party that founded and championed the Greater Syria notion—have relinquished this dream, and appear to have refocused their energies on Lebanese domestic politics. Similarly, pro-Syrian Baathists in Lebanon no longer call for unity with Syria. The idea is just not taken seriously anymore; its appeal in the 1940s, 1950s, and 1960s was based on repercussions of the Zionist success in Palestine, at a time when the region's newly created political entities were seen as creations of colonialism.

Having said this, however, it is true that Syrian political literature is filled with references to the closeness of the Syrian, Lebanese, and Palestinian people, but this rhetoric is simply a propaganda technique (aimed at parading the "Arab unity" credentials of the Syrian regime, which is founded on Baathist ideology).[8] To accept this rhetoric at face value is to ignore a number of critical facts. First, Asad's rise in the ranks of the Baath Party occurred at a time when there was intense rivalry between the Baath and the SSNP; it is unlikely that Asad became a convert to the SSNP cause (as some analysts, like Daniel Pipes, argue). Second, the SSNP in Lebanon today has two branches—one loyal to Syria, the other to Yasir Arafat and Libya. Third, the SSNP is not Syria's only client in Lebanon. Few of the major or minor remnants of the LNM are truly independent of the Syrian regime (with the exception of the pro-Iraqi Baath and the Murabitun, a Sunni militia).

Even though the former advocates of Greater Syria have now abandoned it as a practical objective, many scholars and analysts still marshal this perspective to explain Syrian motivations and foreign policy behavior. This explanation, however, is more political than analytical. Such observers use the Greater Syria paradigm to dismiss Syrian opposition to Israel's occupation of Palestine as nothing more than an irredentist, expansionist dream in the head of Hafez al-Asad. As such, the paradigm serves the political agendas of all those who benefit from having Syria cast as an irrational and irredentist actor in the Middle East.

A second paradigm used to explain Syrian policy can be referred to as the *raison d'état* approach. This perspective assumes that the interests of Syria as a country coincide with those of the Syrian regime—that Hafez al-Asad is motivated more by concern for the welfare of the Syrian people and the integrity of Syrian national territory than by concern for the preservation of his own narrowly based regime. The best example of this approach can be found in the writings of Patrick Seale.[9] Seale's analysis suggests that Asad's policies are primarily shaped by Syrian national interests, not by petty calculations aimed at facilitating the imposition (and preservation) of Asad's rule at all costs.

It is true that sometimes the interests of a regime can coincide with the interests of the state or nation. Syria's decision to go to war in October 1973 was, many Syrians would argue, in the interests of both the regime and the state. In analyzing the narrow basis of the Alawite-dominated regime, Hanna Batatu makes this observation: "While some of Asad's policies—for example, his grants of land in the plain of al-Ghab to peasants from the Alawi Mountain—have been at least partly affected by his Alawi background, broader considerations have been at the basis of other actions taken by his regime."[10]

Ultimately, a regime's primary interest revolves around the preservation of the elite in power. The raison d'état approach obscures this primary thrust of Asad's policies, which has consistently been directed at maintaining his grip on power in Syria.

The third paradigm, the one favored by this writer, is *raison du régime*. This approach considers Syrian foreign policy orientations to be determined by the interests of the regime in power (Asad's Alawite-dominated Baathist party), thereby focusing analysis on the origins of the ruling elite and the reasons behind its dominance. The raison du régime perspective highlights the undemocratic background of the Syrian regime, and the resulting strategies that Asad must employ to maintain himself in power without electoral legitimacy: Asad's undemocratic regime, in its quest to generate some semblance of political legitimacy, tries to justify its actions publicly in ways that conform to the public mood of the Syrian population. Often, this requires the regime to rationalize its deeds and policies ideologically, by employing rhetoric drawn from Islam and from pan-Arab nationalism (the latter due to the Baathist background of the men in power).

There is ample evidence supporting the idea that raison du régime underpins much of Asad's decisionmaking. For example, the regime's violent campaigns against its domestic opponents (the Muslim Brotherhood, a Sunni fundamentalist movement) in the late 1970s and early 1980s illustrate just how far the regime would go for purposes of pure self-interest and self-preservation. Only an apologist for the Syrian regime could argue that the violent crushing of the Hama rebellion in 1982 was necessitated by the interests of the Syrian people.[11]

This raison du régime perspective can explain Syrian actions and policies without being beguiled by the regime's propaganda. It requires critical and skeptical analysis of the claims and arguments made by the regime. This approach, in fact, can be used to explain the foreign and domestic policies of most Arab states (even though these regimes also rationalize their policies by equating their own political interests with national interests). A regime may pursue policies harmful to its own interests, but this is usually the result of political miscalculation; pursuit of certain policies under the rubric of raison du régime does not always result in the interests of the regime being served. For example, the domestic and foreign policies of Sadat were intended to further the cause of his regime domestically although they later cost him his life.

Just as analysts disagree on Syrian motivations and intentions toward Lebanon, so too do the various Lebanese political forces. Those Lebanese who serve Syrian political interests in Lebanon view (or claim to view) Syrian policies as a function of the national interests of Lebanon, Syria, and the Arab nation simultaneously. Syria's enemies, however, view its policies as detrimental to Lebanese and Syrian national interests.[12] It is difficult, of course, to assess accurately the sincerity of any political player. One cannot know whether Syria's friends and foes are sincere in their declarations, just as one cannot determine whether Asad really believes that the interest of his regime coincides with the national interest of Syria.[13] For this reason, it is perhaps useful to consider the general characteristics that have marked Syrian actions in Lebanon.

CHARACTERISTICS OF SYRIAN POLICY IN LEBANON

Rewarding of Clients and Punishing of Foes

This maxim is a major pillar of Syrian policy in Lebanon, and explains some of the shortsightedness of Syrian policies. So insistent is the Syrian regime on rewarding clients, that it often tramples sectarian sensibilities in the process. Elie Hobeiqa, for example, who was ousted from the chairmanship of the Lebanese Forces in 1986, was given a ministerial position in the Lebanese cabinet (during the post-Ta'if appointments) by virtue of his strong Syrian backing. This move, however, alienated important Maronite sectors, even those who considered Hobeiqa to be representative of their viewpoints. Syrian support for Hobeiqa was seen as an act of provocation—an attempt by the Syrian regime to impose its Lebanese client as a legitimate sectarian representative.

Syria's longstanding policy of rewarding its clients and punishing its foes has, at times, intensified sectarian frictions in the country. This is because Syria's attitude toward the various Lebanese sects was sometimes shaped by the desire to impose its political will, rather than by a nuanced understanding of the intricate political dynamics within each of the sects. For example, Syria's unhappy relationship with Bashir Gemayel was due in part to Bashir's antagonistic policies toward Syria, but also to Syria's support for Suleiman Frangieh. Syria, considering Frangieh to be representative of the Maronite community, wanted him to be the sole Maronite leader, and opposed his competitors (i.e., Bashir). Syria's support for Frangieh was based not on love for the man, but on his consistently pro-Syrian stance (at least since 1976).[14]

The limitations of Syria's dependency on cultivated clients is evidenced by the fact that following Israel's 1982 invasion, there was widespread support for Bashir Gemayel, even among some former Syrian clients in the Lebanese Parliament.

Likewise, Syria's policy to punish its foes also proved limiting: It precluded Syria from cultivating relationships with some of the genuine representatives of the sectarian communities. For example, in the early 1990s, the Phalange Party under George Sa'ade decided to reverse its previous position regarding Syria by attempting to restore ties with Damascus. Syria, however, was not to be wooed. It ignored Sa'ade's numerous appeals in 1992 to cancel or postpone the scheduled Lebanese elections, which were opposed by the majority of Christians (as later evidenced by the very insignificant Christian participation in the three electoral rounds). Syria's insistence on holding elections (despite the successful Christian boycott) underlines its disregard for Lebanese public opinion when it conflicts with Syrian policy orientations.

Syria's eagerness to reward its traditional friends and loyalists is readily observable in the composition of the members of the first post-Ta'if cabinet. Among those rewarded, for example, were Hobeiqa and SSNP members (among the Christians), and Abdallah al-Amin (among the Shi'ites). Al-Amin's good fortune is particularly illustrative. He was given a precious Shi'ite cabinet seat, despite the fact that he lacks a Shi'ite power base and was an unknown in South Lebanon only a few years ago. He is, however, the head of the pro-Syrian Baath Party. Amin's appointment, along with those of pro-Syrian SSNP members, reflect a classical Syrian clumsiness in Lebanon: Immediate Syrian gains and interests are pursued with complete disregard for the dynamics within the Lebanese confessional communities.

To be sure, Syria scored successes in Lebanon, but these were accomplished not so much by shrewd calculation, as by the miscalculations of Lebanese factional leaders and the heavy deployment of the Syrian Army. As noted, Syria's policy of rewarding its clients has not always been successful. Some clients proved to be fickle. Others, like those that Syria imposed as leaders in Lebanon, were discredited in their own communities; their political—and in some cases physical—survival is a function of the continuation of Syrian military dominance in Lebanon. Syria's clumsy "friend or foe" policy will leave it with a very narrow basis of support once the Syrian Army leaves Lebanon.

Mantig Al-Ouwwah *(The Logic of Force)*

Throughout Asad's reign, Syria has demonstrated its willingness to use massive military force to pursue political objectives in Lebanon, with little regard for Lebanese and Palestinian lives.[15] The 1976 military deployment allowed Syria to pursue its objectives in Lebanon, even when these conflicted with the objectives of major Lebanese and Palestinian players. This "logic of force"[16] approach did not develop because of an irrational Syrian love of violence; rather, it was shaped by the military and intelligence apparatus of Asad's regime, which has wielded crucial influence in Damascus since the 1970 coup d'état.

Asad's willingness to use force (whether against the PLO-LNM coalition in 1976, or against the Lebanese Forces after 1978) gave Syria an advantage when dealing with Lebanese substate groups. Before the war, the Syrian government was unable to impose its will on the Lebanese government, and had to resort instead to restrained, classical forms of punishment such as border closures (for example, in 1973, to protest the Lebanese Army crackdown against PLO forces). Moreover, prior to 1975, pro-Syrian groups had little appeal in Lebanon, although there were always some Lebanese parties and organizations that took advantage of Syrian military and (meagre) financial sponsorship to further their interests.

Before the war, the multiplicity of external actors in Lebanon helped to reduce the heavy-handedness of any single player. Furthermore, external actors were deterred from intervening in Lebanon because of the possibility that such actions might prompt a rival external actor to also intervene. After 1975, and especially after the mid-1980 U.S. debacle in Lebanon, only Syria and Israel maintained deep interest in Lebanon and continued to intervene militarily.[17] Overall, the efficacy of Syria's use of force to pursue political gains was enhanced by the changing political situation.

Syria's use of force in Lebanon was directed less against Israel, and more against its Lebanese and Palestinian foes (as will be explained below). Notably, Israel tolerated Syrian intervention when it was directed against the PLO and its Lebanese allies. (Of course, when Syria later reversed its course and intervened against Israel's Lebanese allies, Israel then opposed Syrian interference.) Similarly, Syria has also demonstrated a tolerance of Israeli military actions in Lebanon. Indeed, it is clear that Syrian policy has consistently sought to avoid a military confrontation with Israel in Lebanon.[18]

The logic of force policy did not always benefit Syrian interests in Lebanon. Often it contributed to the hardening of Syrian opposition groups in Lebanon. For example, the crackdown against Bashir Gemayel's forces after 1978 only bolstered his leadership within the Christian camp. Similarly, the use of force, albeit by proxy, against the Palestinians during the 1985–1988 War of the Camps dealt a severe blow to Syria's efforts to create an alternative to Arafat's leadership of the PLO. The bombardment of Palestinian camps by Syrian allies contributed directly to the elimination of the pro-Syrian Abu Musa group as a political factor in Palestinian politics.

Control of the PLO

Control of the PLO (especially before 1982) was a major feature of Syrian policy in Lebanon. The Syrian regime has always feared a PLO free hand in Lebanon which, in Syrian eyes, could prompt Israel to intervene. The regime was at pains, over the years, to prevent Lebanese and Palestinian groups from dragging it into an unwanted military confrontation with Israel. Asad was also concerned that the rising influence of the PLO in Lebanese politics would eventually threaten the security of his own regime. Asad feared that a PLO-LNM victory might threaten Syria's control over the Lebanese agenda vis-à-vis the Arab-Israeli conflict, and could result in the emergence of a new, powerful, and radical Arab neighbor. Asad's Alawite-dominated regime could not afford to be flanked by two radical Arab states (the other being Iraq) that would, no doubt, challenge the authenticity of Syria's pro-Palestinian credentials. Syria's military intervention in 1976, therefore, was prompted by the desire to perpetuate its power and maximize its influence, and not, as some analysts suggest, to "preserve Lebanon's unity, pluralistic community, and independence."[19] It is important to note, however, that the disintegration of Lebanon into sectarian enclaves was also highly undesirable from the Syrian regime's point of view, given its own sectarian sensitivities (that is, the Alawite minority's control over the Syrian state apparatus).

Prevention of a Decisive Victory by Any Militia

Throughout the war, Syrian policy in Lebanon consistently sought to prevent a decisive victory by any of the Lebanese combatants. By not allowing one party or faction to control Lebanon, Syria upheld its own political and military prominence.

This objective was the key factor in Syrian condemnation of LNM leader Kamal Jumblatt, when he wanted to continue the battle against the Lebanese Forces, relying on PLO support. Syria could not accept a complete defeat of the East Beirut–based militias, because this would leave Lebanon squarely in the hands of the LNM side. A radical, left-wing regime in Lebanon, as already discussed, would have boosted PLO influence, undermined Syrian control over the Lebanese-Israeli issue, and might have caused serious domestic problems for the Syrian regime. Alternatively, a victory by the Lebanese Forces was also unacceptable. This situation would have weakened Syria's strategic posture by giving Israel a major role in Lebanese politics (as occurred following the Israeli invasion of 1982). An LF victory would also have created a critical domestic problem for the Syrian regime, which was always conscious of Sunnite sensibilities.[20]

Thus, Syria allowed conflicts to take place between militias (and, some would argue, even encouraged certain hostilities) in order to play one party off against the other. Syria would not, however, allow a Lebanese domestic conflict to rage beyond control, unless it served Syrian political interests. For example, it is arguable that the internecine conflicts in West Beirut between the various militias in 1987 served the interests of the Syrian regime because they fostered popular support for the return of the Syrian Army to West Beirut.

The Priority of Syrian Regional Alliances

Just as the Syrian regime would not allow the Palestinians and their allies to drag it into unwanted confrontation with Israel, so too would it prevent events or parties in Lebanon from determining the nature of its regional alliances. Syria's alliance with Iran never led Syria to grant Iran an unrestricted and unrestrained role in Lebanese affairs; it did, however, facilitate Iranian entry onto the Lebanese scene, which the Iranian regime eagerly exploited. Similarly, Syria has tolerated a Saudi role in Lebanon, but only when it conformed with Syria's designs and policies. The appointment of Rafiq Hariri as prime minister should be understood within this context of Syria's political parameters. On the other hand, Syria has consistently refused to allow Iraq to play any role at all in Lebanon.

The Iranian revolution and the Iran-Iraq war posed serious threats to Syrian aims in Lebanon because Iraq's Lebanese clients (especially before 1982) were engaged in campaigns against Iranian interests. The rise of the Iranian-backed Hizballah movement in the wake of the Israeli invasion also posed a challenge for the Syrian regime: Syria had to balance its desire to maintain its Iranian regional alliance with its determination to prevent any one party in Lebanon from gaining the upper hand. The various clashes involving Hizballah (especially in 1987) could have resulted in a crackdown against all Hizballah cells in Lebanon, had it not been for the Syrian desire to avoid a rupture in its relations with Iran. Damascus only tolerated Hizballah's rise to prominence in Lebanon because the organization's sponsor was Iran. Later, Hizballah became a bargaining chip for Syria, useful in the Syrian-U.S. and Syrian-Israeli peace talks.

PERSPECTIVE

The study of Syria's policies and actions reveals that regime's obsession with its position and control in Lebanon, not with ideological dreams. The ideological motivations of Arab regimes are often exaggerated in the West because their rhetorical declarations are taken too seriously. There is no evidence that Syria wants to annex Lebanon, as the proponents of the Greater Syria theory allege. Clearly, the regime in Damascus can benefit from its control of Lebanon without resorting to annexation. In fact, Syrian foreign policy is not all that ideological, as evidenced by Syria's agreement to participate in the 1991 Arab-Israeli peace talks according to the conditions set down by Israel's Likud government. Syria's reversal on its position with respect to the talks was determined by Asad's pragmatic reevaluation of Syria's regional role in a changing international environment.[21] The collapse of the Soviet bloc deprived Syria of its primary international patron: Syria would no longer be able to exploit Soviet-U.S. rivalry for its own regional advantage. Moreover, the Gulf War allowed Syria to join a U.S.-sponsored coalition that included governments Syria had once dismissed as reactionary (e.g., Saudi Arabia).

The Lebanese elections of 1992 also left Syria with an important advantage in Lebanon. To be sure, some successful candidates (the Sunni and Shi'ite fundamentalists in particular) were not to Syria's liking, but the general flavor of the elected parliament is clearly to Syria's political advantage. Even the fundamentalists can be co-opted by virtue of Syrian military and political influence in Lebanon. The newly "elected" parliament might lack the credibility that former Lebanese parliaments had, but it will play the role of cementing juridically the Lebanese-Syrian alliance that was a centerpiece of the Ta'if Accord. Finally, as long as Syria maintains its troops in Lebanon, and as long as the world remains indifferent, no regional or international rivals will be capable of threatening Syrian political dominance in Lebanon in the foreseeable future.

NOTES

1. For further discussion see the chapters by Salem and Ayoub in this volume.

2. In theory, the National Pact, which was based on the understanding that Lebanon's communities (especially the Maronites and Sunnis) would refrain from pursuing independent external alliances, should have ended or at least contained domestic encouragement of foreign intervention.

3. Sometimes, the external actors balanced each other off. For example, in the 1950s and 1960s, the Egyptian and U.S. governments enjoyed great influence in Lebanon. Egypt's ability to dominate the country, however, was undermined by virtue of U.S. influence and alliances with local Lebanese forces. At other times, external actors helped their Lebanese clients gain the upper hand. After 1976, for example, the Lebanese Forces tried to benefit from Israeli interest in Lebanon, a strategy that delivered a short-lived success following Israel's 1982 invasion, and the election of Bashir Gemayel. The Israeli option is now discredited, especially after the 1982–1983 "war of the mountain" in which Israel aided both protagonists (i.e., the Druze and the Maronite fighters). Moreover, the successful guerrilla campaign against Israeli forces in South Lebanon in the wake of the 1982 invasion changed Israeli public perceptions of the Lebanese question. The Israeli public and government became unwilling to intervene heavily in Lebanon on the side of the right-wing militias (as in the past) although the Israeli government still claims the right to bomb Palestinian and Lebanese targets deep inside Lebanese territory, and still occupies its self-declared "security zone."

4. For a more detailed discussion see As'ad Abukhalil, "Arab Intervention in the Lebanese Civil War: Lebanese Perceptions and Realities," *The Beirut Review* vol. 1 no. 2 (Fall 1991).

5. For example, in a memorandum presented to the Lebanese president in 1975, the Maronite League and the Lebanese Monastic Orders deemed all other considerations meaningless (see "*Mudhakkirat al-ruhbaniyyat al-lubnaniyyah wa-l-rabitah al-maruniyyah ila-r-ra'is Sulayman Frangiyyah,*" *Al-Amal,* 15 October 1975). Similarly, in the vow (*al-'Ahd*) of the Front of Freedom and Man (the predecessor of the Lebanese Front) Sharbil al-Qassis stressed that "the Lebanese alone are the ones who determine their destiny, that they alone preserve sovereignty" (see the text in *Al-Nahar,* 15 February 1976). More recently, General Michel Aoun rationalized his War of Liberation against his many enemies, by employing sovereignty slogans (suggesting that the war was aimed at securing Lebanon's sovereignty and independence). In February 1990, Aoun presented the Lebanese people with a bizarre choice between the Ta'if Accord and *al-siyadah* (sovereignty). In his own mind, and in the minds of his followers, Aoun represented sovereignty (see the text of his speech in *Al-Nahar,* 3 February 1990).

6. Salem's chapter in this volume contains an overview of the various Lebanese perspectives toward Syria today.

7. For two works that employ the Greater Syria paradigm, see Moshe Ma'oz, *Asad: The Sphinx of Damascus: A Political Biography* (New York: Weidenfeld & Nicholson, 1988); and Daniel Pipes, *Greater Syria: The History of an Ambition* (New York: Oxford University Press, 1990).

8. Baath parties rule in both Syria and Iraq. Baathist doctrine supports pan-Arab nationalism and socialism.

9. Patrick Seale, *Asad of Syria: The Struggle for the Middle East* (Berkeley: University of California Press, 1989).

10. Hanna Batatu, "Some Observations on the Social Roots of Syria's Ruling Military Group and the Causes for Its Dominance," *The Middle East Journal* vol. 35 no. 3 (Summer 1981), pp. 332–333.

11. Patrick Seale attempts to explain Asad's brutal bombardment of Hama using the raison d'état paradigm, arguing that the rise of Muslim fundamentalists

posed a serious security threat for the state. Robert Fisk, on the other hand, clearly details the incident from a regime-protection point of view; see *Pity the Nation* (London: Andre Deutsch Limited, 1992).

12. Some critics of Syrian policy in Lebanon have argued that Syria's involvement in Lebanon weakened its regional position and distracted it from the central Arab-Israeli arena.

13. It is of note, however, that the sincerity question is not, as often implied in Western writings, peculiar to Arab politics. The sincerity of all politicians can be questioned.

14. Another example involves Syria's decision to support Musa al-Sadr in 1976, promoting him as the spokesman of Lebanon's Shi'ites, even though he was discredited at the time and his militia could not attract mass Shi'ite support (which was solidly behind the PLO-LNM coalition).

15. Israeli policy in Lebanon has followed the same callous logic, although Israeli objectives were usually diametrically opposed to those of Syria.

16. This term is borrowed from a book by this title authored by Sheikh Muhammad Husayn Fadlallah.

17. In the 1980s and early 1990s, both Iraq and Iran intervened indirectly in Lebanon through their sponsorship of various Lebanese militias. Iraq demonstrated an interest in Lebanese affairs shortly after the end of the Iran-Iraq war, but this focus was short-lived (mainly because Saddam was planning his invasion of Kuwait). Iran continues to maintain interest in Lebanon, fueled by the increase of Shi'ite political power and the emergence of its client, Hizballah. While Iran does not enjoy the national and geographical advantages of Syria vis-à-vis Lebanon, Hizballah's success in the 1992 elections may intensify Iranian interest in Lebanese affairs.

18. This approach is a function of Asad's strategic thinking on the Arab-Israeli question, that is, Syria will choose the time and place of the military confrontation with Israel.

19. See Mahmud Faksh, "Syria's Role and Objectives in Lebanon," *Mediterranean Quarterly* vol. 3 no. 2 (Spring 1992), p. 82.

20. The regime's Sunnite sensibilities were not to determine the course of Syrian policy and practice, as the 1982 bombardment of Hama exemplifies.

21. Of course, the ideological declarations of the Syrian regime over the years can now be used to undermine its position in the talks.

9

Lebanon's U.S. Connection in the New World Order

Michael C. Hudson

Emerging shakily from a decade and a half of civil war, the Lebanese face two fundamental and daunting tasks: restoring political legitimacy at home through reconciliation and structural reform, and establishing a supportive external environment that will promote both security and reconstruction. Of the two, the first is perhaps the most important and the most difficult, but the second is formidable as well. What follows is an attempt to sort out some of the opportunities and obstacles that face Lebanese policymakers as they contemplate their country's place in the so-called "new world order" of the post–Cold War and post–Gulf War period.

LEBANON'S GEOPOLITICAL UNITY

Like Lebanon itself, any analysis of Lebanon's international situation in the 1990s is fraught with contradictions and ambiguities. From a global, long-term perspective, the country's future is bright. The United States dominates the Middle East as never before in the new post–Cold War and post–Gulf War world. Insofar as the United States supports a united and independent Lebanon, therefore, the Lebanese would seem to have good reason to be optimistic, but from a regional, short-term standpoint, the picture is murkier. Notwithstanding a formal and supportive policy position, Washington is hampering Lebanon's reconstruction by its "friendly sanctions"—a set of measures that greatly inhibit Lebanese-U.S. economic and cultural links. Moreover, Washington's unique relationship with Israel and its cultivation of Syria are, at best, a mixed blessing for Lebanon. In theory, the United States possesses the leverage to influence both of Lebanon's powerful and not-so-benign neighbors, but in practice it indulges Israel's occupation of Lebanese territory along the international frontier and Syria's continuing presence in much of the rest of the country.

Throughout its brief history as an independent state, Lebanon has always been internally weak and thus unusually dependent upon external patrons. For historical and sociological reasons, Lebanese stability and prosperity have required patrons both at the international and regional levels. In the so-called "new world order," the U.S. connection should theoretically serve as the keystone of support for the post–civil war "new republic." At the same time, Beirut needs some kind of regional support—the kind of support that is durable (not hostage to inter-Arab or Arab-Israeli tensions) and not predatory. During the First Republic (1943–1975) accommodations were reached on both levels, but they were not stable.

During the Cold War, external patronage of Lebanon passed from France to the United States (as leader of the West). In return for U.S. and Western support, Lebanon provided a useful locale for finance, commerce, regional diplomacy, intelligence gathering, and cultural interaction. Lebanese politicians offered moderation in regional politics, a nonthreatening stance toward Israel, and a pro-Western stand in the Cold War. Lebanon's assets may not have propelled it into the category of vital interest for the United States, but they certainly were convenient. This convenience function should not be underestimated, but it should not be exaggerated either. For the United States, Lebanon was a convenience that could be done without, as the civil war period showed. When the United States became directly involved in 1982, in the name of vital interest, and suffered death, injury, and hostage-taking as a result, many Americans wondered whether Lebanon was worth the costs. If the Clinton administration is wary about supporting the new Lebanese republic and renewing a U.S. presence, it is due in part to our having been previously oversold on Lebanon's importance.

Regional patronage involved a more complex relationship with multiple and competing ideologies and states; while not altogether successful, Lebanese leaders nevertheless found a way of accommodating Arab nationalism and Lebanese particularity, and playing off the rivalries of Hashemites, Saudis, Egyptians, and Baathists of different stripes. For many years there was a modus vivendi in place with Israel, broken finally when the Palestinians emerged as a significant force, utilizing the political space and resources they had managed to create for themselves in Lebanese society. In exchange for being more or less left alone by its more powerful neighbors, Lebanon could offer itself to the region as a convenience, serving a function similar to the one it provided to the United States and the West. During the 1950s and 1960s, Lebanon made itself useful as a regional center for finances, services, culture, communications, and, of course, tourism. Lebanon also served a political function—as the "Hyde Park Corner" of Arab politics. This was not altogether appreciated by regimes that saw opposition movements using Lebanon to undermine their power; the other side of that coin, however, often found the same regimes using Lebanon as an ideological or intelligence staging area to project their influence into the domains of their adversaries. Lebanon was a major theater for the battle of words in the "Arab Cold War" between the "nationalist progressives" and the "Western lackeys."

Although these tacit bargains, which provided a stable linkage between Lebanon and its international and regional protectors, collapsed for a time during the 1958 crisis, on the whole Lebanon's politicians established a fairly secure niche of convenience for the country until the beginning of the civil war in 1975. Given the tensions and turbulence in Lebanon's geopolitical environment, this was no small accomplishment. The question now is whether, after the prolonged catastrophe of civil war, Lebanon can establish stable new relations with key external powers that will promote its own internal healing and external security.

PROBLEMS IN THE
LEBANON-U.S. RELATIONSHIP

It does not require exceptional perspicacity to discern that the United States is the key external actor in shaping Lebanon's future. The United States was always important in this respect, but it is uniquely so in the new global environment. Not only does the United States possess enormous direct and indirect influence over the investment resources needed for Lebanon's reconstruction, it also exerts more leverage in the Arab and Middle East state system by virtue of its leverage over the largest and most powerful countries in the region, as well as the smallest. Without an alternative superpower to turn to for backing, regimes and movements in the region have powerful incentives to cooperate with the United States rather than oppose it. In the region, only Iran seems prepared to mount a serious challenge, yet it probably does not have the capability to sustain one; since the crippling of Iraq there is no major Arab state that can seriously oppose Washington.

Whether U.S. dominance is good for Lebanon will largely depend on the evolution of U.S. policy. If the United States adopts a neo-imperialist role and seeks to intervene heavy-handedly in the domestic affairs of Third World countries and to impose its idea of order, the consequences could be negative. In the Middle East, for example, a U.S. crusade against Islamism coupled with continued indulgence of Israeli expansionism would compromise ruling elites in politically sensitive societies such as Lebanon's. Assuming, however, that the United States pursues a more liberal, prudent, and sophisticated course, the main objective for Lebanese leaders would seem to be, first, how to get the attention of the United States, and, second, how to fashion a new, mutually attractive "bargain" in the "new world order."

This task may not be as easy as many Lebanese and Americans (and Lebanese-Americans)—cognizant of the historical and cultural ties between the two countries—would like to think. A look at the practical state of U.S.-Lebanese relations in the early 1990s reveals the nature of the problem and belies the roseate tone of official utterances on the subject. It shows just how much damage was done in the 1980s by the bombings of the U.S. embassy, the destruction of the Marine barracks with 241 dead, the hijacking of civilian aircraft, and the prolonged hostage crisis. In 1985, President Ronald Reagan banned all air transportation to and from Lebanon and suspended the rights of two Lebanese carriers, Middle East Airlines and Trans-Mediterranean Airways, to operate to the U.S.[1] Although slightly modified in 1992 by President George Bush, this prohibition, according to an official on the Lebanon desk in the State Department, is the main stumbling block for private business investing in Lebanon today, and the U.S. government is not considering lifting these restrictions in the immediate future.[2]

In 1987, Secretary of State George Shultz, acting under an Executive Order permitting the invalidation of passports to countries "where imminent danger exists to the public health and physical safety of United States' travellers," pronounced that U.S. citizens in Lebanon were in immediate peril and that U.S. passports would not be valid for travel to, in, or through Lebanon. The State Department declared that "the measure was taken to convince American citizens of the seriousness of the danger, especially apparent after the latest wave of kidnapping in West Beirut, and of the limited ability of the U.S. government to protect its citizens in Lebanon."[3] This ban has been extended annually since its inception. In a 13 January 1993 warning, the department stated: "The situation in Lebanon is so dangerous that no U.S. citizen can be considered safe from terrorist acts. While all the remaining hostages have been released, the organizations which abducted them continue to operate within the country."[4] Representatives of two interested citizens' groups, the American Task Force for Lebanon and the American-Arab Anti-Discrimination Committee, stated in interviews that they did not think the U.S. government had any intention of lifting the ban in the near future.[5] However, in January 1993 the U.S. government did remove Lebanon from the list of countries whose citizens might be eligible for temporary protected status in the United States because of danger to their personal safety in their home country; the attorney general stated that the U.S. embassy in Beirut had reported that the security situation for Lebanese citizens was steadily improving.[6] This announcement was greeted with mixed feelings by Lebanese, some of whom had engaged in activities opposing Syria's presence in Lebanon and feared persecution not by militias but by the Lebanese government itself.

Even after the conclusion of the Ta'if Accord in 1989 (of which the United States was a silent but important backer) U.S. aid to Lebanon remained minuscule. Total allocations did rise somewhat, from $22 million in fiscal year 1989 to $28 million in FY 1990 and 1991, but they fell to $24 million in FY 1992. None of this aid, incidentally, was allocated to the Government of Lebanon, but rather to U.S. and international institutions and private voluntary organizations.[7] Administration proposals to provide $400,000 from international military education funds to help upgrade the Lebanese Army were blocked in Congress by Senator Jesse Helms, because "we cannot pretend that anyone but Hafez al-Asad is making the decisions in Beirut. And I refuse to agree to handing over even one cent of U.S. tax-payer funds to that man and his minions."[8]

The civil war has taken a heavy toll on what had been a harmonious and mutually beneficial relationship between Lebanon and the United States. That relationship, in its cultural dimension, long precedes the actual establishment of the independent Republic of Lebanon in 1943, going back to the establishment of American Protestant missionary activities in the 1820s and the Syrian Protestant College (later the American University of Beirut) in 1864.[9] In 1942, the United States appointed a Diplomatic Agent and Consul General, George Wadsworth, in newly (and nominally) independent Lebanon; Wadsworth supported the British minister, Maj. Gen. Edward Spears, in helping make Lebanon's independence a reality against last-ditch French resistance in November 1943.[10] Thus began a happy relationship. Although not of great intrinsic importance, Lebanon was a useful listening post and staging point when Washington began to design its postwar strategy to secure Arabian oil (and its owners), protect the new state of Israel, and deny influence to its emerging Soviet rival. Commenting on a 1948 U.S. intelligence report, Irene Gendzier has observed: "It was evident that Washington officials had a high estimate of Lebanon . . . as a home port of an ideological sort. The unconditionally pro-Western optic of Lebanon's political elite was a source of consolation in a region that was apprehended with caution if not anxiety."[11]

By the middle of the 1950s these anxieties had crystallized into outright alarm. The rise of Arab nationalism, the emergence of Gamal Abdul Nasser in Egypt, the Soviet-bloc arms sales to Syria and Egypt, and growing Arab-Israeli friction culminating in the 1956 Sinai-Suez war, dealt setbacks to all three U.S. "vital interests" in the region. In 1958, when Egypt and Syria joined to form Nasser's United Arab Republic, Arab nationalist populism soared in Lebanon, exacerbating the growing internal cleavage between President Camille Chamoun's fervently pro-Western government and a powerful coalition of disgruntled notables and young reformists and ideologues.

Having been the only Arab leader to accept the Eisenhower Doctrine in 1957, Chamoun had positioned himself well to receive U.S. protection as

Lebanon slipped into civil war. After several desperate pleas he finally obtained a U.S. military intervention. The intervention, however, was triggered by the nationalist coup in Iraq, not the Lebanese president's predicament, and it led not to Chamoun's survival but his replacement by the commander of the Lebanese Army, General Fouad Shehab. It was the fear of international communism, masquerading as Arab nationalism, that alarmed Washington; it feared that other pro-Western dominos would fall unless strong actions were taken. Lebanon might have been a small domino but it shared a border with Israel and also sheltered many U.S. commercial, cultural, and governmental establishments.

The U.S. intervention in 1958 was bloodless, short, and successful—in glaring contrast to the debacle of 1982–1984.[12] The threat to Lebanon's independence and pro-Western orientation was parried, and the country was to enjoy another decade and a half of comparative stability. Being a convenience for a great power had paid off.

After 1975, however, Lebanon became increasingly inconvenient. The outbreak of civil war, pitting Phalangists against Palestinians, the extremism of both conservative Christian and radical Muslim and left-wing forces, exposed the economic inequalities as well as the sectarian divisions embedded in Lebanese society. L. Dean Brown, a special envoy from Washington (the first of several) tried unsuccessfully to negotiate a settlement in 1976 and appears to have given Syria encouragement to settle matters in its own way. A large number of Lebanese notables, including former president Suleiman Frangieh, were convinced that Secretary of State Henry Kissinger wanted to solve the Arab-Israeli problem by giving South Lebanon to the Palestinians. While there is no corroborating evidence for this view, it is clear that Kissinger's diplomacy in the aftermath of the 1973 Arab-Israeli war ignored the Palestinian dimension of the regional conflict as well as the spread of Palestinian power and militancy in Lebanon, and thus it probably contributed to the country's collapse. Within Lebanon, Muslims and Arab nationalists (along with Palestinians) reviled the United States for its support of Israel while many Christians bitterly criticized the United States for abandoning them.

The darkest period of U.S.-Lebanese relations began in 1982, when Secretary of State Alexander Haig apparently gave an "amber light" to Israel's defense minister, Ariel Sharon, to launch a massive punitive raid into South Lebanon. The United States and indeed some Israeli leaders appear to have been surprised by Sharon's march all the way to Beirut. It is possible that U.S. policymakers believed that larger security interests could be served by this bloody adventure: the physical liquidation of the PLO and the installation of a pro-Israel government in Beirut. Such outcomes, from the Reagan administration's perspective, would have significantly set back Soviet and Syrian influence in the region, forced the Palestinians into accepting a "Jordanian option" solution to the Arab-Israeli conflict, removed Lebanon as a breeding ground for radical, anti-Western political movements, and enhanced Israel's security. In retrospect, it is clear that U.S. policymakers misunderstood both the Lebanese and regional situation. As Israeli forces advanced toward Beirut, rolling back Palestinian irregulars and Syrian forces, Washington dispatched veteran troubleshooter Philip Habib to negotiate a cease-fire.[13] After Habib thought he had done so, he assured Syrian president Asad to that effect. However, when Israel reneged—and continued to advance—Asad felt betrayed. U.S. credibility with the Syrians was seriously damaged—a matter that would lead to major setbacks for the United States later on. Then, with Israeli forces besieging West Beirut, Habib did succeed in negotiating the evacuation of PLO forces. Under his plan, a multinational force, including U.S. Marines, would move in to ensure the protection of the large civilian Palestinian refugee population from subsequent harm by Lebanese Christian militias. Thinking the job finished, the multinational forces withdrew after only sixteen days. It was then that matters spun out of control.

The assassination of President-elect Bashir Gemayel on 14 September 1982 led in quick succession to Israel's occupation of West Beirut (again, contravening a commitment made to Habib) and to the infamous massacre of Palestinians in the Sabra and Shatila refugee camps by Christian militiamen. Back came the multinational forces, but their new mission was ill-defined. Lebanon's new president, Amine Gemayel, proved unequal to the task of stabilizing and reuniting the country, even though the United States strongly backed his efforts. Reflecting its deep-rooted pro-Israel tilt, the U.S. government brokered the peace treaty of 17 May 1983 between Israel and Lebanon. Under the terms of that agreement, the southern third of the country would be a "security zone" in which Lebanese troop deployments or overflights would require Israeli approval. The Israeli-supported South Lebanon militia would be incorporated into the Lebanese Army. Lebanon's treaties with Arab countries not in conformity with the May 17th Agreement would be nullified; military transfers from other Arab countries would be curbed, as would anti-Israeli political activity or publishing. The new Lebanese government, having come to power under the shadow of Israeli tanks, considered this to be the best deal obtainable—convinced perhaps by the United States.

However, the new secretary of state, George Shultz, failed to calculate Syria's response, underestimating the extent to which Damascus had recovered from its military and political losses suffered the previous summer.[14] He also did not sufficiently appreciate the militancy and capability of Lebanese Shi'ite Islamist organizations, which were being strengthened by Syria and Iran. Syrian intelligence was probably behind the assassination of Bashir Gemayel. Moreover, the suicide car bomb that destroyed most of the U.S. embassy on 18 April 1983 was probably orchestrated by a group called Islamic Jihad. As the United States beefed up its component in the multinational force, its forces found themselves increasingly drawn into the ongoing battles between the Lebanese government, on the one hand, and Druze and Shi'ite militias, on the other. By providing military training to the Lebanese Army and assisting in spotting artillery strikes against the Druze and Shi'ite elements, the Americans came to be seen as partisans of Gemayel's regime and the Lebanese Christian militias—in short, as just another militia themselves.

Matters went from bad to worse. On 23 October 1983, 241 sleeping Marines were killed when a large truck, laden with explosives, crashed into their compound at Beirut International Airport.[15] French troops in the multinational force suffered a similar attack. Within four months, the president of the American University of Beirut was murdered, Druze and Shi'ite militias drove the Lebanese Army out of West Beirut, the Marines "redeployed" to naval warships offshore, a U.S. fighter aircraft was shot down by Syrian artillery, the battleship New Jersey bombarded the Chouf mountains with its 16-inch guns, and Lebanon abrogated its May 17th Agreement with Israel. As Islamist groups began taking U.S. and European hostages, Lebanon's onetime patron withdrew, wounded and humiliated, its influence at a low ebb. Lebanon, for its part, continued to fester. Unprotected by the West and vulnerable to intrusive, ambitious neighbors, Lebanon had never been less in control of its affairs; never had its geopolitical environment been so toxic.

That environment began to change at the end of the 1980s. Israel was forced to withdraw from almost all of Lebanon. The Palestinians launched their intifada and positioned themselves for diplomatic negotiations. The long war between Iraq and Iran ended in limited defeat for Iran. The disintegration of the Soviet Union deprived Syria of its superpower alternative to the United States. This was the context in which a new initiative on Lebanon got under way, organized through the Arab League and led by Saudi Arabia, Morocco, and Algeria. After long efforts, quietly supported by the United States, the Saudis convened what remained of the 1972 Lebanese Chamber of Deputies in the city of Ta'if in 1989 and produced a formula that would lead to the reestablishment of a more or less legitimate government. As silent but indispensable partners to the Ta'if process, Washington and Damascus moved to establish themselves as external "protectors" of the new Lebanese republic.

PROSPECTS

Lebanon and the United States both held national elections in 1992, and the governments that emerged each took promising steps toward developing a new and mutually advantageous relationship. In Lebanon, a new and long-overdue parliament approved a government led by the millionaire business-man Rafiq Hariri, whose reputation and good connections with Saudi

Arabia and the United States inspired some needed credibility both at home and abroad. Despite the continuing Syrian presence and low voter turnouts in Christian areas, Lebanon's political processes appeared to have been somewhat normalized. Security forces continued to extend the authority of the state into South Lebanon, the southern suburbs of Beirut, and the Maronite mountain. The main militias, ostensibly disarmed (except for Hizballah), were now participating in normal politics; and even Hizballah contested and won several seats in the new parliament. With the freeing of the last U.S. hostages, internal security was getting back to normal.

During the presidential election campaign in the United States, candidate Bill Clinton appeared to endorse the anti-Syrian position urged on him by the Council of Lebanese American Organizations, a group dominated by conservative Maronites, many of whom remained devoted to General Michel Aoun. Once elected, however, President Clinton lost little time in dispatching his secretary of state, Warren Christopher, on a Middle East fact-finding tour during which he made a surprise visit to Beirut. "My visit to Beirut today was the first by a secretary of state of the United States in a decade. It symbolizes our commitment toward the Lebanese Government," he declared on 22 February 1993.[16] In testimony before a congressional committee on 8 March, the secretary specifically referred to Lebanon when summarizing the objectives of his recent trip. Lebanese diplomats in Washington expressed cautious optimism that some of the U.S. restrictions toward Lebanon, such as the prohibition on Middle East Airlines landing rights, might be eased. In Congress, Senator Helms reconsidered his blockage of international military education training funds for Lebanon. Although the new administration initially showed little inclination to ease the travel ban or authorize direct economic assistance to the Lebanese government, it appeared prepared to offer indirect support, as indicated by the World Bank's $175 million emergency loan for Lebanon signed in March 1993. This was perhaps the crucial opening to activate a $3.7 billion multilateral pooled loan over five years to underwrite Lebanon's reconstruction.[17]

Encouraging as these signs are, they do not necessarily signify that Lebanon is out of the woods. Lebanon remains to a large extent hostage to an uncertain regional geopolitical situation. Syria, for better or worse, is Lebanon's regional patron, but its role is not altogether beneficent. It continues to resist U.S. pressures for its redeployment to the Bekaa Valley as envisaged in the Ta'if Accord. While the United States would like the Syrians to pull back, it is reluctant to press them hard at a time when it is trying to encourage Syrian flexibility in dealing with the Israelis. Privately, Lebanese officials express hope that a Syrian-Israeli phased agreement over the Golan Heights might eventually be extended to include the Israeli "security zone" in adjacent South Lebanon.

The situation was not eased—indeed, it was worsened—by the dramatic agreement between Israel and the PLO in September 1993 on a "declaration of principles" to end their long conflict. By neglecting to mention the 400,000 Palestinian refugees in Lebanon, the declaration dismayed Lebanese across the political spectrum. Lebanese leaders were forced to mirror Syria's unhappiness with the Israeli-PLO Agreement, which seemed to put a freeze on the other dimensions of the Arab-Israeli conflict. Since Syria's presence and influence in Lebanon is taken as a pretext for Israel to remain in South Lebanon, there is still a vicious circle that needs to be broken.

Matters are further complicated by ideological ferment in the region. During its civil war, Lebanon experienced both Christian and Muslim extremism. The Ta'if process was intended to restore the centrists—if not secularists, at least more tolerant in their religious commitments. The most militant currents among the Maronites have been at least temporarily weakened. On the other hand, among the Shi'ites, the Hizballah movement is still permitted a license, as it were, for armed struggle against Israel. Ideological moderation within Hizballah led to its downplaying earlier calls for an Islamic republic in Lebanon and its successful participation in the 1992 parliamentary elections. Both developments seemed to indicate a readiness to accept the new Lebanon of the Ta'if Accord. Nevertheless, Islamist currents throughout the region show no sign of diminishing, and Islamism places Palestine and Jerusalem among its highest priority concerns. Collapse of the Arab-Israeli negotiations, therefore, would almost certainly exacerbate the problem of South Lebanon and perpetuate Lebanon's internal problems.

If Lebanon is to cope successfully with the ideological and security issues that are likely to fuel continuing instability in the Middle East in the years ahead, it will need to reinvent itself. As a weak state resting precariously on a divided society, it will need to cultivate external patrons, one of which will have to be the United States. It is to be hoped that U.S. Middle East policy will be sufficiently liberal, sophisticated, and balanced so as not to delegitimize regimes with which it is friendly. A vital task for Lebanon's policymakers will be to demonstrate Lebanon's importance to Washington, as well as to key Arab and Middle Eastern capitals. In the pre–civil war period, Lebanon's importance lay in the conveniences it offered. During the civil war Lebanon's significance rested on its inconvenience—indeed, on its capacity to destabilize the whole region. During those dark years, the distinguished journalist Ghassan Tueni, Lebanon's UN representative, sought to enlist Western help for his country by warning that if Lebanon is sick, the whole Middle East will catch pneumonia. Proxy battleground for Israelis and Palestinians, hotbed of religious militancy, haven for "terrorists," springboard for Iranian, Iraqi, Syrian, and other ambitions, Lebanon could marshal only its nuisance value to enlist outside help. This was not a very effective strategy. Now, in the post-Ta'if, post–Cold War, post–Gulf

War era, Lebanon has an opportunity to reinvent itself in a positive manner, as a small state worthy of outside support and protection.

By tradition and sociological necessity, Lebanon's political vocation must be liberal. It needs to reestablish itself as a forum of political and cultural expression for the Arab world, and a model for civil society elsewhere in the region. As neighboring economies liberalize and integrate themselves, Lebanon can supply the services that will be required for such development. It can function as a meeting ground for the dialogue between the Arab-Islamic world and the West, not a dumping ground for other people's problems. Its diversity—a necessity—can become a virtue. To the extent that it can serve these functions, Lebanon will be able to demonstrate to the United States and its regional neighbors that it is an asset—not a strategic asset as much as a moral and developmental asset—in the region, and between the region and the international community. Only internal reconciliation, reform, and leadership will make such a reinvention possible. The key, then, to a successful foreign and security policy lies in Lebanon's domestic arena.

NOTES

1. Presidential Determination no. 85–14; Federal Register vol. 50 no. 152. S1835, 7 August 1985.

2. Interview, 2 March 1992; name of the official withheld at his request.

3. Interpreter Releases, 2 February 1987, p. 150.

4. Travel warning issued by the State Department Bureau of Consular Affairs, 13 January 1993.

5. Interviews with Mr. Deeb Keamy, American Task Force on Lebanon, and Mr. Greg Nojeim, American-Arab Anti-Discrimination Committee, 3 March 1993.

6. Federal Register vol. 58 no. 24. 7582, 8 February 1993. Notwithstanding its own assessments of improved security and the pressure of Lebanese-U.S. groups, the United States continued to maintain the ban. At a press conference in December 1993, the incoming ambassador to Lebanon, Mark Hambley, denied that the United States was using the ban to pressure the Lebanese government to disarm the Hizballah militia, but he insisted that "elements within Hizballah and some other organizations" were threatening to American citizens: "That is the reason that we feel compelled to maintain this ban regarding travel to Lebanon." *Mideast Mirror,* 2 December 1993.

7. *U.S. Overseas Loans and Grants Assistance from International Organizations* (Washington, D.C.: U.S. Agency for International Development, 1993), p. 16.

8. Senator Jesse Helms, letter to a constituent dated 7 May 1992.

9. See James A. Field, Jr., *America and the Mediterranean World* (Princeton: Princeton University Press, 1969), pp. 92–103; Bayard Dodge, *The American University of Beirut: A Brief History* (Beirut: Khayat's, 1958).

10. Stephen H. Longrigg, *Syria and Lebanon Under French Mandate* (London: Oxford University Press, 1958), pp. 323–333; Major General Sir Edward Spears, *Fulfilment of a Mission: Syria and Lebanon, 1941–1944* (London: Seeley, Service and Cooper Ltd., 1977), chs. 17–21 and passim.

11. Irene L. Gendzier, "The Declassified Lebanon 1948–1958: Elements of Continuity and Contrast in US Policy Toward Lebanon," in Halim Barakat (ed.), *Toward a Viable Lebanon* (Washington: Georgetown University Center for Contemporary Arab Studies, 1988), p. 192.

12. The best overview of the 1958 crisis and U.S. intervention is Fahim I. Qubain, *Crisis in Lebanon* (Washington: The Middle East Institute, 1958); see also Charles W. Thayer, *Diplomat* (New York: Harper, 1959), chs. 1–3.

13. An excellent account of Habib's mission is by a Georgetown University senior, Kevin Hopkins, "Philip C. Habib: Presidential Emissary to the Middle East," Institute for the Study of Diplomacy, Georgetown University, 1992, 69 pp. Hopkins's study is based in part on an interview with Ambassador Habib shortly before his death.

14. A critique of the Reagan administration's policy may be found in Michael C. Hudson, "The United States' Involvement in Lebanon," in Halim Barakat (ed.), *Toward a Viable Lebanon,* pp. 210–231.

15. U.S. Department of Defense, Commission on Beirut International Airport Terrorist Act, 23 October 1983 (unpublished), pp. 2–15 and passim.

16. *Middle East Intelligence Report,* 24 February 1993, quoting *Radio Lebanon* of 22 February 1993.

17. During the summer of 1993, after a massive Israeli retaliatory bombardment in South Lebanon, the United States approved $1.85 million in spare parts and authorized the future sale of "lethal" military equipment for the Lebanese Army. The United States also began providing small amounts of aid directly to the Lebanese government, despite some congressional objections that it would only help Syria.

Part 3

·

Toward
Socioeconomic Stability

10

Regional Development and Integration

Hassan Charif

Lebanon's instability was perhaps more a problem of region than of religion. The uneven socioeconomic development of Lebanon's various regions was one of the most destructive factors contributing to the outbreak of war in 1975. Prior to the war, Lebanon's geography and society were weakly knit together. As a result, disparities in regional development played a significant role in Lebanon's destabilization. In the war's aftermath, it is vital that plans for the country's long-term reconstruction, restabilization, and rehabilitation redress this source of instability. Priority must be given to the equitable development and integration of all regions inside Lebanon. If Lebanon is to become a stable homeland acceptable to all its citizens, this regional reunification must be conceptual and ideological as well as economic and political.

THE SITUATION BEFORE 1975

Lebanon's present-day boundaries were forged in 1920 by the French mandatory power, which appended the city of Beirut to Mount Lebanon along with outlying regions to the north, south, and east (the "annexed provinces"). Prior to 1920, the economic and social life of these annexed provinces was based on balanced relations with the surrounding Ottoman provinces of Syria and Palestine, as well as Mount Lebanon and Beirut. The annexed provinces, however, had generally developed stronger economic and social ties with the Syrian and Palestinian provinces than with Mount Lebanon. This preference was largely due to certain restrictions created by Mount Lebanon's special administrative status within the Ottoman

Empire, (as well as the intermittent bloody confrontations there) and to the geographical proximity of Syria and Palestine.

After the 1920 borders were drawn, most ruling circles in Lebanon continued—conceptually, politically, and economically—to consider these provinces as "annexed," that is, not as integral parts of the country. As a result, the leaders of the new Lebanon failed to promote overall integration of the country, and provided no suitable social and economic structures capable of substituting for the annexed provinces' diminishing ties to Syria and Palestine. Rather, the country's political, socioeconomic, and geographic life became centered in and around Beirut, which was looked upon as the capital of Mount Lebanon. This excessive centralization of activity meant the developmental needs of Lebanon's outlying areas were basically neglected.

The strong pre-1975 centralization of economic, social, and political activities in Beirut and Mount Lebanon has been described at length in various studies. For example, Ahmed Sbaiti notes:

> The physical and social infrastructure required to set the machinery of economic activity in motion was in place in Beirut and Mount Lebanon. . . . A survey of sectorial development reveals that Beirut and its environs [i.e., Mount Lebanon] had the best developed facilities—by local standards—for transport (port, airport, roads, mass transit, etc.), telecommunications, electricity, industry, hospitals and private schools and universities. . . .[1]

And, as another study indicates:

> By 1975, Beirut was the locus of three-fourths of the country's banking activities, and two thirds of its industrial activities and foreign trade. Air transport, communications, university education and the central government were also centered in Beirut. One of the major imbalances of pre-war Lebanon was the predominance and primacy of greater Beirut. In 1975, Beirut accounted for more than half of Lebanon's population, over two thirds of economic activity, two thirds of overall employment, the entire state administration, and all of the country's higher education.[2]

This prewar centralization, in combination with the transformation of agricultural production in the countryside, played a major role in prompting the migration of thousands of farming families to urban slum areas around Beirut (collectively known as the Belt of Misery).

Like most developing countries, the Lebanese countryside supported traditional subsistence agriculture. During the prewar years, however, agricultural production was slowly transformed, as more profitable commercial crops (i.e., fruits, poultry, and tobacco) replaced traditional subsistence ones. As city dwellers came to dominate the ownership and operation of this commercial agriculture, only a few rural farming families were able to weather the transformation and remain on the land. Most small peasant farmers, driven into bankruptcy, began to drift toward Beirut in the hope of finding economic opportunities. Most ended up in the Belt of Misery, an impoverished hotbed of discontent.

The situation in South Lebanon was particularly desperate. Massive military bombardments by Israel only added to the area's economic neglect and misery, while various other forms of violent disruptions (many related to the Palestinian presence) resulted in most of the area being placed under martial law.[3] In addition, Israeli claims on the South's water resources delayed most irrigation plans, thereby contributing to the continued under-development of the area and, in turn, to the intensification of rural migration toward Beirut's urban slums.[4]

Although many factors contributed to the pronounced centralization of socioeconomic and political activities in and around Beirut, primary among these was the conceptual tunnel vision of Lebanon's leaders and elites who tended to overlook the fact that the annexed provinces were an integral part of the country. Evidence of this neglect was (and is) clearly reflected in the "official" version of Lebanon's national history, circulated by the state, taught in schools, and reiterated by the major mass media. A reading of this national history suggests that the annexed provinces barely existed; in it, the historic cities of Tripoli, Tyre, and Sidon—larger and economically more active than Beirut until early in this century—appear only inter-mittently and sporadically, as an accident of some relations with the Mountain.

Inhabitants of Lebanon's annexed provinces resented (and continue to resent) the center's conceptual and practical dismissal of their importance and relevance to the country. Their sense of alienation was integral to the struggle over the identity of Lebanon and its "Arab realities." Insistence on Lebanon's Arabness was not just an ideological matter for inhabitants of the annexed provinces; it reflected their need to be integrated organically, to be given a rightful place in the historic, political, and socioeconomic realities and activities of the country.

DEVELOPMENTS DURING THE WAR YEARS

While the devastation of the civil war cannot be exaggerated, it is important to note two significant side effects: the relative repopulation of the country-side, and the growth and development of regional urban centers. These two trends were prompted by a number of factors, including continuous military strife, forced displacement of population, intensive fighting in Beirut that forced many people to flee the city, and recurrent, militia-imposed restrictions on movement of goods and people. Combined, these factors also prevented many Lebanese from accessing important services and institutions concentrated in Beirut. Regional urban centers gradually mobilized local resources to respond to increasing local needs and developed their own facilities, services, institutions, and infrastructure to fill the gap created by the absence of central authority and its agencies. The result was a de facto decentralization of social and economic activity and of public administration and services.

The Political and Conceptual Framework

Lebanon's warring militias were less interested in gaining control over each other's territories than in conserving and consolidating their de facto local power and autonomy in newly created sectarian enclaves where each purported to defend its sect.[5] Thus, while all factions paid lip service to the unity of Lebanon's land, people, and institutions, each was building local structures as substitutes for vanishing central authority. This led to the establishment of many quasi-autonomous cantons, each with its own local administration, services, and economic structure.

Along with the de facto establishment of autonomous regional administration, most political and sectarian groups pressed for restructuring the obsolete Lebanon, which was based on the 1943 National Pact. They demanded decentralization and a greater regional say in management of resources and economic and social activities, as well as in the central government. These new aspirations, along with growing practical needs, facilitated development of local administrative and political structures (e.g., "People's Committees," "civic" or "autonomous" administrations) as well as services and infrastructure.

Although today few Lebanese seek establishment of autonomous cantons segregated by sect, the war demonstrated the necessity and feasibility of decentralizing public administration as well as political, social, and economic activities. It is noteworthy that the 1989 Ta'if Accord specifically calls for this decentralization.

The Changing Demography

Repeated rounds of fighting and destruction in and around Beirut forced thousands of people to seek refuge in remote rural regions, many returning to their original villages and towns after losing their houses and sources of income due to almost complete stoppage of economic activities and services in the center. By 1990, the population of greater Beirut had declined to one-half of its 1975 level.[6]

Moreover, sectarian violence against civilians forceably displaced thousands of people from heterogeneous into factionally more homogeneous regions.[7] By 1990, the total number of displaced Lebanese was more than 1.2 million, about 30 percent of the total population.[8] Many displaced people sought safe haven in rural areas, where reasonable earnings could be gained by returning to subsistence agriculture. This trend continued throughout the war, producing what may be called a reverse rural migration. Many villages, townships, and regional urban centers witnessed massive increases in population, but also noticeable increases in agricultural production.

The people of South Lebanon were particular victims of the war. Thousands took part in agonizing mass movements to and fro between the Belt of Misery and their native villages, fleeing either renewed fighting in Beirut or massive shelling and destruction by Israeli forces in the South. Their repeated uprootings cost them most of their belongings, yet their plight was ignored by both the vanishing central authority and preoccupied local warlords.[9] The few communities that escaped this trauma had to accommodate many displaced and destitute people.

Infrastructure and Services

Due to paralysis of central authority and services, local groups gradually developed their own public administration and infrastructure to handle growing local needs. Alongside these local political, administrative, and paramilitary structures, many regions witnessed the development of infrastructure and services. For example:

- access to external trade through legal or illegal ports;
- municipal services such as water, electricity, and garbage collection to complement, replace, or supervise those of the central government agencies;
- education committees to assist and supervise private and public schools as well as higher educational facilities;[10]
- medical services (including public clinics, emergency services, first aid organizations, and civil defense groups).

Many regional urban centers also enjoyed a construction boom in office buildings, shopping centers, residential buildings, private schools, and hospitals.

Economic Activities

A remarkable aspect of the wartime regional revival was a flourishing economic development, resulting from decentralization or establishment of businesses, including banks, insurance companies, exchange counters, service agencies, shopping centers, branches of Beirut-based companies, and industries (especially construction) in rural areas.

Revival of Traditional Subsistence Agriculture

Although no reliable statistical data exist, it is evident that subsistence agricultural production enjoyed a relatively successful revival brought about by the return of thousands of peasants and farmworkers. The lack of alternative sources of income, along with skyrocketing inflation, compelled many of these war returnees to sustain themselves by way of subsistence agriculture, particularly in the fertile lands of the South.

Other Relevant Activities

An interesting trend (not necessarily related to the war) was the return of a few wealthy former emigrants to their home towns or villages. Many invested generously in real estate, construction, and (to a lesser extent) agriculture. This trend, along with generous remittances from expatriates to their families, helped to create many new jobs and to sustain the growing local economic activities in rural areas.

In sum, the prewar centralization of political and socioeconomic activities was neither justifiable nor unavoidable. With proper planning and a minimal allocation of effort and resources, Lebanon's destabilizing regional imbalances can be eliminated; furthermore, regional urban centers might relieve much of the congestion in and around Beirut.

INTEGRATION WITH EQUITY

The prewar years are testament to the evils of excessive centralization and concentration of activities. The war years demonstrated the possibility and feasibility of flourishing regional development, in the absence of a domineering center. Consequently, reconstruction of Lebanon's political, social, and economic structures must take account of the changes wrought by the war, particularly the rising confidence of social, political, and economic groups in the regions outside of Beirut and Mount Lebanon. Accordingly, the needs and aspirations of these rural regions must be respected when reconstituting Lebanese society, so as to avoid the return to excessive and destabilizing prewar centralization.

Political and administrative decentralization during the war years was excessive; in fact, it was sometimes detrimental. The economic and social decentralization, however, yielded some very positive fruits, with only minor side effects that can easily be eliminated once Lebanon regains political and economic stability.

The Conceptual Framework

As already noted, Lebanon's traditional ruling elites regarded the country as a mere extension of Mount Lebanon and Beirut. The war's aftermath presents an opportunity to correct this narrow vision, and to develop a vision of Lebanon that includes all of its regions on equal terms. Such a vision, however, must be ideologically and conceptually adopted by the new state elite and administration, and must then be translated into concrete action. A promising move in this direction would involve rewriting Lebanon's "official" history to incorporate the cultural, economic, and political contributions of all of its regions (e.g., the rich historical traditions of literature and culture in Jabal Amil, Tripoli, and Sidon).

Decentralization of Infrastructure and Services

To sustain the healthy aspects of decentralization gained during the war years, concerted efforts are required to ensure that the reconstruction process does not focus solely on Beirut at the expense of the regions. Revival of Beirut is important, but it must maintain the development and prosperity of regional urban centers. Coordinated action by the central government, its agencies, local groups, and the private sector should include the following steps:

- construction of national and local transport networks linking the regional urban centers to each other and to Beirut;
- development of national communications networks (phone, fax, mail) that ensure regional access to the center;
- countrywide rehabilitation and development of basic services and infrastructure, especially in regional areas where basic services were previously scarce;
- development of ports outside of Beirut (i.e., in Tripoli and Sidon);[11]
- decentralization of the public administration, with proper delegation to regional offices.

In relation to this last point, a comprehensive study must be conducted to assess the feasibility of decentralizing or redistributing public services, agencies, and institutions, including those related to health, education, energy production, and civic affairs.

Equitable Distribution of Economic Activities

During the war years, the diminishing role of the economic center demonstrated the feasibility of a multipolar economic system in Lebanon. Regional urban centers were able to respond successfully to the challenge, providing reasonable opportunities for entrepreneurs who dared, or were compelled, to venture into operation away from the destruction in Beirut. It is necessary to sustain and encourage this trend by providing the requisites for continued regional operation. The central authorities can and must play an important role—directly or through incentives—to avoid the recentralization of activities. Among the incentives that may encourage the development of the private sector in Lebanon's regional areas are:

- assigning regional industrial zones, and equipping them with adequate infrastructure;
- establishing free zones away from the center, particularly around regional ports or inland border points;
- providing financial facilities to productive ventures (e.g., local branches of industrial and agricultural investment banks, easy loans, extended credit, tax exemptions, priority in state purchases);
- encouraging and facilitating the establishment of private facilities and services, such as hotels, restaurants, business centers;[12]
- providing incentives for residency in regional urban centers, such as housing loans, educational grants, improved schools and entertainment facilities, adequate medical services;
- reviving and encouraging industrial trade fairs (e.g., reactivating the Tripoli fairgrounds).

Agriculture and Regional Development

As noted earlier, war-induced reverse urban migration led to a relatively successful revival of subsistence agriculture. It is important to study this phenomenon and exert serious effort to sustain it, now that peace and job opportunities may reverse the trend again, luring small farmers and laborers back to the empty promises of Beirut. Again, a major factor that might encourage Lebanon's rural population to remain would be the sustained development and prosperity of regional urban centers. More specific steps, however, may be required. These include providing subsidies to small farmers, fair priority distribution of cash crops quotas (e.g., tobacco in the South), organizing production and consumption cooperatives, setting up mechanisms for easy access to local and export markets, providing agricultural guidance and services, establishing research centers to stimulate development of improved crops and pesticides, enhancing irrigation projects, and organizing rural production fairs and crop festivals.

South Lebanon, in particular, requires special attention given the continued Israeli presence and ongoing military disruptions, both of which may compel many people to drift back to Beirut. The South's main crops (tobacco, citrus fruits, olives) should be given special incentives, such as access to export markets, and increased quotas. Above all, the central government and the international community must exert pressure on Israel to ensure its military withdrawal from the area, or at least to reduce its indiscriminate punitive bombing of villages.

TOWARD A NEW LEBANON:
SOME TANGIBLE RECOMMENDATIONS

This chapter has highlighted a number of measures that would encourage the equitable socioeconomic integration of a more stable and prosperous Lebanon. The central authorities, however, have made no serious effort with respect to the country's regional development and decentralization, despite the Ta'if Accord's provisions in this regard. To date, plans for Lebanon's reconstruction suggest that revival of the center is taking priority over the prosperity and development of regional urban centers. It may be fitting, therefore, to end with some concrete recommendations for the central authorities and those members of the international community concerned about Lebanon's unity, stability, and prosperity.

Recommendations to Lebanon's Central Authorities

Political reforms must be worked out to prepare the ground for regional integration and development. Two specific requirements of these reforms are:

1. Decentralization of state machinery, public administration, and institutions, either by locating various departments equitably throughout the regions, or by establishing local branches. This process should include the development of proper laws and decrees to secure sharing of political power and decisionmaking between the center and the regions.
2. Development of plans for Lebanon's reconstruction, rehabilitation, and socioeconomic development that integrate all Lebanon's regions on equal terms. The state has a responsibility to ensure the fair allocation of all available public resources throughout the country.

The central authorities also have a responsibility to take immediate action to foster rapprochement among the Lebanese—to give them a stake in Lebanon's future. Initiatives in this regard should include:

1. Developing, producing, and disseminating mass media programs that increase public awareness of the whole of Lebanon in terms of its geography, population, regional cultural traditions, and the similarity among its various regions and regional groups. These could take the form of radio and video programs, films, and articles in journals, magazines, booklets, and brochures.
2. Adopting measures to induce the reactivation of professional soci-

eties and unions, with encouragement to conduct their duties in all regions, and to undertake social activities that bring together members across factional and regional lines.

3. Reactivating interregional cultural and benevolent societies (educational, medical care, social assistance, child and old age care, etc.) with incentives to establish such societies where needed.

4. Organizing and supporting cooperative and competitive activities (such as sporting, cultural, and musical events) between different age groups of various regions. An important measure would be the organization of interregional tours, particularly for the younger generation who were isolated in factional and regional enclaves for fifteen years, and possess little knowledge of the rest of their country.

Recommendations for International Assistance Groups

Reconciliation and reconstruction are monumental tasks, beyond the intrinsic capabilities of Lebanon's available human and financial resources. International assistance is vital and could play an important role in the equitable redevelopment of the country, helping to reduce destabilizing discrepancies between the center and the regions. Specific areas for constructive action by the international community include:

1. Providing reconstruction assistance that treats Lebanon's infrastructure as a whole, but pays special attention to the needs of rural regions;

2. Undertaking reconstruction and development projects in rural areas and regional urban centers, particularly in the most devastated areas (i.e., the South);

3. Offering joint venture incentives that encourage business development outside of Beirut (e.g., priority in investment loans or grants, purchase of products, technical assistance);

4. Providing assistance to benevolent and nonprofit institutions and agencies in rural areas, such as technical schools, child care agencies and orphanages, handicapped rehabilitation agencies, and women's training groups;

5. Organizing tours that venture beyond Beirut to include regional festivals and activities;

6. Providing technical assistance to regional agricultural projects;

7. Organizing special programs in countries with affluent citizens of Lebanese descent, such as "visits home" that include tours of various Lebanese regions. In this way, participants may be prompted to invest in their towns and villages of origin.

CONCLUSION

Reconstructing Lebanon, as this chapter has indicated, is an enormous, long-term task for the Lebanese, and for others concerned about the country's future. If future stability is to be assured, the goal must not be to reinvent the old Lebanon, which contained within it the seeds of destruction. Rather, the task is to build a new Lebanon that integrates all Lebanese equally, regardless of region, religion, or culture. This task is made more arduous by fifteen years of hostilities and fear. The new central authorities may be steering Lebanon's political life into safer, pacific waters. There are, however, some discouraging signs. The government's apparent preoccupation with the reconstruction of Beirut arouses dismay in the regions. Administrative centralization and corruption remind many observers of prewar practices that fueled the revolts and hostilities that erupted so many years ago. It is hoped that these liabilities—still limited—will be corrected effectively and soon. The central authorities must regain the confidence and loyalties of the Lebanese people through concrete action that demonstrates serious commitment to helping *all* of Lebanon emerge from the ashes and develop toward a better, more stable, and unified future.

NOTES

1. Paper presented by Ahmed Sbaiti at CIIPS second workshop on Lebanon, *Socioeconomic Reconstruction: Current Conditions and Future Needs* (Ottawa, December 1990).

2. American Task Force for Lebanon, *Working Paper* (Washington: ATFL, 1991). Background paper prepared for a conference held in Washington, D.C., in June 1991. Hereafter referred to as ATFL, *Working Paper.*

3. See chapters in this volume by Brynen, Sayigh, and Peretz.

4. Prior to the war, displaced southerners formed over 70 percent of the population of Beirut's Belt of Misery. See Hassan Charif, *The South of Lebanon* (Belmont, Mass.: Association of Arab-American University Graduates, 1978) and the chapter by Amery and Kubursi in this volume.

5. See the chapter by Corm in this volume.

6. ATFL, *Working Paper,* 1991.

7. See the chapter by Corm in this volume.

8. ATFL, *Working Paper,* 1991.

9. Charif, *The South of Lebanon.*

10. Of particular note is the development of provincial branches of the Lebanese University.

11. By 1975 the heavy port traffic at Beirut meant that dozens of ships often waited several weeks for access. Alternative ports, serviced by adequate road networks and transportation facilities, would help reduce the costly congestion at Beirut and would stimulate the economic development of other regional urban centers.

12. Government support may be direct (through decrees and incentives) or indirect (the result of public support facilities such as regional tourist and information centers, regional trade promotions, fairs, festivals, and conferences).

11

Reflections on Lebanon's Reconstruction

Ahmed A. Sbaiti

Lebanon has emerged from sixteen years of war all but devastated. Its economy, once called "miraculous," is in shambles, its currency's purchasing power eroded,[1] its public administration virtually disintegrated, its physical infrastructure practically destroyed. A quarter of the population is displaced, living in substandard housing, while another quarter—mostly professionals and skilled workers—have left the country (many never to return); unemployment holds at around 40 percent.

In the wake of the Ta'if Accord, and the Lebanese government's relative success in establishing security in most of the country (except for the South), plans are being developed for the formidable task of reconstruction. This is not the first time that such plans have been drawn. In 1977, after the Two-Year War (1975–1976), the Lebanese government thought that reconstruction was possible and proceeded accordingly to create the Council for Development and Reconstruction (CDR), making it the focus of the reconstruction effort. Again in 1983, following the Israeli invasion, the same motivation encouraged the government to renew the CDR's mandate. However, in both cases (and for a number of reasons) the CDR was unable to effect substantial progress on the reconstruction front.

This chapter offers reflections on the requisites for Lebanon's reconstruction effort in the 1990s. It outlines the basic characteristics of Lebanon's prewar economy and surveys the various (major) reconstruction plans that followed in war's wake. Drawing on this initial overview, it highlights some of the major issues facing Lebanon's current reconstruction effort and identifies areas for action by outside players interested in assisting Lebanon's resurrection.

If there is one lesson to be drawn from Lebanon's prewar socioeconomic profile, and the wartime attempts at reconstruction, it is this:

Reconstruction is not just a matter of rebuilding destroyed physical infrastructure; rebuilding for the long term means looking at Lebanon in its totality—from its prewar socioeconomic and regional imbalances (which must be redressed) to the destruction and changes wrought by the war. Just as Lebanon's devastation has been all-encompassing, so too must be the reconstruction process. The magnitude and scope of this task would tax the resources of any country. It will be all the more difficult for one just emerging from fifteen years of chaos and devastation.

LEBANON'S ECONOMIC EXPERIENCE: 1950–1975

Lebanon's "miraculous" economy maintained steady growth from independence through to the beginning of the 1975 war. This growth was skewed, however, since it was virtually devoid of social content; the economy was almost totally owned and run by the private sector with negligible governmental control. Even before the war erupted, Lebanon needed to correct the income and other social inequalities that resulted from its economic boom after 1950.

Lebanon's prewar free market system was characterized by ardent laissez-faireism fostered by the government's 1946 decision to remove restrictions on international transactions (and on the movement of capital and persons) and the gradual unification of exchange rates. Estimates show that the economy grew by an average of 7 percent per year during the 1950s, and at a slightly slower rate throughout the 1960s and early 1970s.[2] This growth was manifest in three major areas: balance of payments surpluses, more or less stable exchange rates and prices, and good employment levels. These attributes promoted tremendous confidence in the Lebanese economy, attracting foreign capital and encouraging domestic investment.

Lebanon's economic success was also enhanced by regional factors. The creation of the state of Israel in 1948 and the subsequent embargo placed on it by Arab states meant that traffic normally using the port of Haifa was rerouted to Beirut.[3] Given the lack of other adequate alternative port facilities in the region, Beirut became a regional focus, and Lebanon's land and sea transport sectors developed (and thrived) accordingly. Lebanon also profited from the political turmoil and controlled economic environments characteristic of the other Arab states during the 1950s and 1960s. Lebanon's relative political stability and open economic system attracted a massive movement of both capital and trained people from the surrounding states. Also by the late 1960s, the Arab states in the Gulf—oil-rich, but service-poor—found themselves in great need of Lebanon's well-developed service sector. Lebanon became their service center for transportation, education, health, banking, contracting, and tourism. Combined, these attributes encouraged numerous major multinational and international businesses to locate their Middle Eastern headquarters in Beirut.

Lebanon's economic experience resulted in an economic base that was responsive to ever changing markets in the country and region. This base was composed of a weak agricultural sector, a small but growing industrial sector, and a dominant services sector whose collective share of the gross domestic product (GDP) averaged 80 percent over the years.[4]

Consequently, in terms of price stability, employment levels, and balance of payments surpluses, Lebanon's prewar economic performance was nothing short of miraculous. However, its long-term success was marred from the outset by four socioeconomic inadequacies: (1) a lack of government economic and social policies and planning; (2) centralization of economic activities in Beirut and Mount Lebanon (to the neglect of other regions in Lebanon); (3) uneven development among and within Lebanon's regions; and (4) the dominance of the trade and service sector over other more productive sectors (for example, the agricultural sector, the growth of which would have developed three-fifths of the country).[5]

The lucrativeness of the Lebanese economy was due largely to the impressive success of Lebanon's private sector. However, private sector dominance, fostered by the government's ardent "hands off" policy, was not without costs. The government's policy willfully limited public sector participation in economic development, restricting its role to building the physical infrastructure necessary for private sector economic activity. This "hands off" policy also limited the scope for successive Lebanese governments to decide the rate and pattern of economic development, leaving the country rife with socioeconomic and regional imbalances.[6]

The lack of improvements targeting social needs was manifest in the public sector's meager stature and inadequate spending on social infrastructure. Health services, education, housing, sanitation, electricity, and water all suffered—especially in rural areas. Government-funded infrastructure projects were restricted in scale and location, limited to supporting existing private economic activities (i.e., in the region of Beirut and Mount Lebanon, often to the exclusion, and at the expense, of the outlying regions to the south, east, and north). Even in the highly developed areas in and around Beirut, services that should have been provided, or at least regulated, by the public sector were controlled by private sector enterprises. This meant that essential services, such as education, were offered as commodities to be sold on the open market. This pattern of inadequate development of public spending on social services continued during the war years. Between 1977 and 1987, 89 percent of all public expenditure was spent on infrastructure compared to 11 percent spent on social infrastructure.

Hassan Charif's chapter (in this volume) discusses Lebanon's regional inequalities and the country's political, social, and economic centralization. Suffice to note in summary that Lebanon's prewar economic development was characterized by the virtual absence of government policies for the planning, execution, and supervision of the private sector, and for the maintenance and control of economic growth.[7] By its willful decision not to develop policies for the balanced economic development of the country, the government unwittingly planted the seeds of future, long-term instability.

THE WAR AND ITS WAKE:
DAMAGES AND RECONSTRUCTION EFFORTS

When the war started in 1975, fighting would start and stop intermittently, sometimes with weeks or months separating outbreaks of hostility. Battles were generally "roving," erupting in one area while the rest of the country remained calm, then stopping, only to flare up elsewhere. In this way, over time, destruction encompassed the entire country.

The destruction tended to follow a pattern: the service facilities (hotels, restaurants, banks) were damaged or destroyed first, followed by the physical infrastructure (ports, airport, electricity lines, telecommunications). Eventually, substitute services were set up (e.g., illegal ports, leased telecommunications lines from Cyprus). These private substitutions drained the public coffers by appropriating the government's services-based revenues (and thereby further eroding government authority).[8] Throughout the war period, many reconstruction projects were started, and some even completed, only to be destroyed again in renewed fighting.[9]

Creation of the Council for Development and Reconstruction

In January 1977, after the Two-Year War (1975–1976), the Lebanese government created the Council for Development and Reconstruction (CDR) to establish a general framework for the reconstruction effort, channel external funds, and coordinate expenditures. The CDR, responsible directly to the council of ministers, was granted unprecedented powers for a Lebanese government unit.[10] Its wide-ranging responsibilities reflected the government's commitment to the task of reconstruction and its awareness of the limited capacity that existed within the administration to plan, program, and implement reconstruction activities.

In 1978, CDR commissioned experts to assess the damage and issued its first reconstruction project document, detailing both the damage and corresponding reconstruction and developmental costs for each economic sector. Total cost estimates were $7.5 billion (1978 prices), of which $4.75 billion were to be spent by the public sector and $2.75 billion by the private sector.

In developing this project, CDR articulated certain guidelines, some of which acknowledged the need to alleviate Lebanon's prewar socioeconomic inequities. These principles are still relevant to Lebanon's new reconstruction efforts in the 1990s:

1. The public sector would provide a framework for conducting economic activities and establishing general infrastructure, but principal economic activities would continue to originate in the private sector.
2. Private initiative would be encouraged and private sector economic activities supported both directly and indirectly (by the government).
3. Three sets of issues were paramount: meeting the basic needs of the populace, achieving regional balance in the reconstruction process, and improving living and working conditions in rural areas.
4. Reconstruction activities were to be coordinated within a long-term perspective of national development.
5. Reconstruction would be based largely on external loans and grants, with the government providing 20–25 percent of total expenditures in counterpart funds.

The 1978 project was an action agenda expected to take eight years to implement (1978–1985). Although law and order were not fully restored to all parts of the country, CDR decided that reconstruction efforts could not wait, and proceeded accordingly.[11] At first, it appeared that the political and security situation was conducive to reconstruction. The public administration, although inefficient, was still intact, a stock of well-designed projects was waiting for implementation, and outside donors were friendly and interested. Many projects were started: rehabilitation of roads, power, water, industry, telecommunications, Beirut's port and airport, schools and hospitals; in addition, there were studies on waste management, new hospital construction, technical and vocational schools, and other works. Some projects were completed; others, for a variety of reasons, were not. Overall, the effort was hampered by cyclical warfare (1978, 1981, and 1982) and by civil disorder.

In retrospect, however, the 1978 plan was more a shopping list of projects than a coordinated plan derived from an interactive analysis of Lebanon's social, economic, political, administrative, and human resource problems. Thus, it reflected a mentality prevalent in Lebanese government circles: "Let's rebuild what was destroyed in the past two years and things will be fine after that." The essential difference between a sector's reconstruction needs and its development needs remained obscure; CDR guidelines (no. 3 and no. 4, above) were never heeded. The 1978 plan did, however, greatly enlarge the scope of public sector involvement in the reconstruction process.

CDR's 1983 Reconstruction Project

In June 1982, Israel launched its second invasion of Lebanon, causing a huge setback for the country's political, social, and economic well-being. Nevertheless, by December 1983 CDR had prepared yet another reconstruction project that addressed the fresh damage resulting from the invasion (including damage to just-completed reconstruction projects), as well as the damage that had occurred between 1978 and 1982. The total cost estimates for the 1983 project were $15 billion, to be spent over nine years.[12]

The 1983 project followed the 1978 guidelines and had similar characteristics except that its damage assessments and corresponding reconstruction costs were based on estimates, because no systematic surveys were conducted. However, the 1983 project differed from its predecessor in other important ways: (1) support for the private sector was scaled down from 29 percent of public expenditures to 4.5 percent (because the public sector was responsible for repairing the post-1977 massive damage to infrastructure); and (2) CDR itself was restructured along functional lines into five departments (programs, projects, finance, legal, and administration) designed to streamline project preparation, financing, and implementation. Regrettably, resumption of cyclical warfare after 6 February 1984 prevented the 1983 project and reorganization from taking effect.

The World Bank's 1983 Reconstruction Program

In November 1982, the World Bank sent a mission to Lebanon to help the government plan its reconstruction effort. The mission developed a reconstruction program (to commence in 1983) that defined "urgent" works to be completed by 1985, and other, "nonurgent," works to be started thereafter. The World Bank's three-year program is noteworthy because, although based on CDR estimates, it differed considerably from the CDR program, especially in its identification of priority projects in economic and social infrastructure, where the CDR program was substantially deficient.[13] Perhaps most important was the World Bank's emphasis on the need to move away from an ad hoc approach to reconstruction. The formulation of institutional and policy frameworks to guide reconstruction and development of each economic sector was considered just as important as physical rebuilding. This key policy element was almost entirely absent from both CDR projects (1977 and 1983).[14]

Efforts from 1983 to 1987

In 1983, hopes were high that war in Lebanon had been laid to rest forever, but these hopes soon proved false, as renewed fighting added yet more destruction and prevented implementation of the World Bank plan. Undeterred, the CDR opted to execute its own project. However, the reconstruction effort faced formidable challenges.

The ongoing violence and political instability engendered a sense of despair among many Lebanese, such that by 1985, Lebanon's brain drain commenced in earnest, with the mass emigration of skilled workers and professionals. Post-1985 chaos (in combination with the "war system") caused government paralysis, greatly reducing the capacity of the public sector to function. Lebanon's financial crisis deepened as a result of skyrocketing inflation rates, a greatly depreciated Lebanese pound, and expanded government spending ($800 million on weaponry in 1983/84). This forced the government to freeze public capital investments by line ministries. Accordingly, the CDR emerged as the principal capital investment agency,[15] and its attention was diverted from reconstruction to supporting the maintenance and operation of public facilities—tasks normally undertaken by the line ministries.

Runaway inflation further hampered the reconstruction process by prompting price reviews for contracts already let. This led to higher contract values (in Lebanese pounds), such that by 1986, new budgetary advances from the government to the CDR were insufficient to cover cost increases for projects under way. Many projects had to be rescheduled, scaled down, or suspended altogether. All of these elements contributed to the increasing erraticism of fund allocations, and the eventual drying up of external funding sources.

Although the CDR prepared three annual investment programs,[16] many projects started after 1983 remained unfinished, delayed by deteriorating political, economic, and administrative circumstances.[17]

From Paralysis to Revival: Post-1987

The government's lingering paralysis (from late 1985 until 1988) and its subsequent split into two rival cabinets (from September 1988 until October 1990) brought the civil administration to near standstill.

However, following the 1989 signing of the Ta'if Accord, the government revived the CDR and gave it responsibility for preparing (with the help of local and international consultants) a national recovery plan and a reconstruction program. A two-phase plan was suggested involving a three- to five-year Emergency Recovery Program (ERP) to address the immediate needs of the population (costing an estimated $3.9 billion) and a longer-term reconstruction cum development plan lasting beyond the year 2000 (to cost an estimated $15 billion). In addition, plans were drawn up for rebuilding Beirut's central business district and other commercial centers, a task estimated to require fifteen years and cost $6.7 billion.

The ERP targets economic sectors directly affecting the livelihood of most Lebanese, such as water, sewerage, sanitation, electricity, health, housing, education, transport, and telecommunications. The medium-range plan proposes to continue these essential programs while beginning to rebuild other sectors of the economy, such as agriculture, industry, and tourism. The long-term plan is expected to address developmental aspects of all sectors.[18]

The Lebanese government is expected to shoulder a good share of the work, especially in ERP's first phases—to set the whole process in motion. The public sector is expected to be involved in (1) emergency repairs and rehabilitation to remove infrastructure bottlenecks and restore productivity; (2) implementation of economic stabilization measures to facilitate repatriation of private capital (needed to finance medium- and long-term investments); (3) programs to correct socioeconomic imbalances and alleviate poverty; and (4) programs to rebuild the institutional capacity of public agencies, with emphasis on economic infrastructure. The private sector is expected to take on the remaining reconstruction tasks and to reinvigorate the economy.

THINKING RECONSTRUCTIVELY:
PAST LESSONS, CURRENT ISSUES

A plethora of issues must be resolved before and during the reconstruction process. Some of these have been around (unresolved) since Lebanon's independence; others emerged (or became evident) during the war and past attempts at reconstruction. Below are some of the key issues facing those in charge of Lebanon's reconstruction effort in the 1990s.

CDR's Post-Ta'if Role: Some Problems

CDR is, in effect, a super-ministry, given its far-reaching and all-encompassing powers. The circumstances that led to CDR's broad mandate over reconstruction have not dissipated. Both the scale of reconstruction needs and the public sector's diminished capacity (resulting from many years of war) demand that a specialized agency spearhead the reconstruction effort. CDR has the necessary flexibility to adjust to rapidly changing conditions and to respond swiftly to perceived needs.

However, as mentioned earlier, the war caused CDR's activities to be increasingly diverted into routine implementation functions (although CDR's mandate specifically limits its implementation role to projects with special problems). Thus, instead of revitalizing the bureaucracy and strengthening the line ministries, CDR began to replace these ministries altogether. This was a task for which CDR was neither created nor prepared.

Now that CDR is once again charged with Lebanon's reconstruction, there needs to be a clear delineation of roles. The line ministries and agencies should resume primary responsibility for project implementation, even though they will continue to function merely as executing agencies under CDR supervision. CDR, therefore, will still shoulder the bulk of responsibility for reconstruction. Unfortunately, CDR's mandate is fraught with many potential problems:

1. Current CDR staff is neither sufficient for, nor technically capable of, carrying out this multitask mandate. Moreover it is virtually impossible to find qualified Lebanese willing to accept CDR's low wages (even though they are perhaps the highest in the civil service). Aware of this problem, the World Bank has suggested the augmentation of CDR staff with a project management unit (PMU), which would be staffed by a consulting firm (or consortium of firms). While the PMU director would report directly to the president of CDR, all other team members would work in existing CDR divisions, performing specific functions and providing on-the-job training. This may double or triple the size of CDR staff, creating new problems relating to limited space and funds as well as the need for increased internal coordination.

2. Presently, the line ministries are only shells. Some ministries no longer have operational premises. The World Bank has suggested adding a sector implementation unit (SIU) to each ministry and government agency. The SIU would be composed of a team of recruited consultants (as in the PMU), and would act as "owner" of the project to be implemented, providing assistance to the ministry in project operation and maintenance following implementation. The SIU's proposed far-reaching powers would, in effect, place implementation of Lebanon's reconstruction mostly in the hands of non-Lebanese.

3. To avoid overlapping responsibilities and ensure coordination, the World Bank proposed that CDR establish a technical coordination committee (TCC) with representatives from CDR and each SIU. Given the size of its staff, CDR would likely be represented by PMU; thus, TCC would also be staffed mostly by non-Lebanese.

The issue of PMUs and SIUs reveals one of postwar Lebanon's most troubling afflictions: the lack of trainable (let alone trained) manpower. During the many years of war, many professional and skilled Lebanese left the country, never to return. Those who stayed had neither training opportunities nor the chance to use their skills. In addition, Lebanon's educational system, once considered the best in the Middle East (if one had money) has all but collapsed. By 1992, many high school graduates could barely read. Most of those qualified for university studies face financial problems. If Lebanon is ever to recover, it requires—now—a massive, long-term undertaking of manpower resource development at the national level. Efforts are under way to redress this situation somewhat; a number of Arab funding agencies are supporting a two-year training program for civil servants sponsored by the American University of Beirut. While this effort in itself is not enough, it points the way for further efforts.

Finally, if CDR is to be able to execute reconstruction plans, the government must provide some 20–25 percent of the costs in the form of local money. The long-term sustainability of reconstruction will be threatened if the government is unable to provide the local counterpart costs on time.[19] The government must ensure that the required funds are available when needed. Finally, funding institutions will want their loan agreements ratified by the proper authorities to become effective for disbursement purposes. Therefore, a procedure for rapid ratification of loan agreements should be put in place.

Other Issues

The above discussion has highlighted some of the technical issues that could become bottlenecks in the reconstruction process. There are many other potential stumbling blocks. For example, although CDR's 1978 guidelines for reconstruction still remain valid today, it is not clear that they have ever been effectively operationalized in plans. Clear policy directives are still required on the following issues:

Economic growth and public welfare: delineation of roles for public and private sectors. In order to ensure Lebanon's long-term stability, economic growth should be balanced with some measure of social content, either through public expenditures or through government policies and regulations protecting the public interest.

Economic efficiency and privatization. While the government should provide the framework for reconstruction, support for private sector economic activities should be maintained and increased—including private sector involvement in the operation and maintenance, if not outright ownership, of key facilities. The issue of privatization of certain activities and assets is now hotly debated. Some analysts consider privatization the only way to rationalize certain economic sectors (such as telecommunications). Others, however, fearing monopolization, support the creation of public sector companies under private management. Still others prefer gradual privatization, to enable public assets to reach a certain level prior to privatization. Whatever the final solution, government policies and controls are required to ensure that key services (such as water, sewerage, sanitation, electricity, and telecommunications) are available to all citizens of Lebanon. Otherwise, privatization could result in depriving many Lebanese people of those services. In this respect, hands-off economic policies are harmful.

Reconstruction and development. Reconstruction plans should assign high priority to equitable development all over Lebanon. The government should develop policies to reduce the huge income discrepancies among regions, and to foster development of employment opportunities, services, and better living conditions in Lebanon's rural and other neglected areas. Policies should also encourage development of the economy's productive sectors (rather than focusing solely on services and trade).

Decentralization. The government should decentralize administrative tasks and procedures and delegate them to local authorities in each region. Incentives should also be provided to encourage decentralization of economic activities.

Dynamics of the reconstruction process. As reconstruction will extend beyond the 1990s, plans drawn up today or next year must be capable of modification, as conditions and circumstances (both indigenous and exogenous) change. The entire reconstruction process—planning, implementation, financing, management—must be dynamic enough to respond to change.

Future of the economy. The current weakness of the economy not only limits its absorptive capacity (hence limiting the speed and magnitude of annual expenditure on reconstruction) but also limits the country's ability to provide counterpart funding for donor monies (for both reconstruction and debt service). A scheme to strengthen the economy should have top priority. The Lebanese must decide on what course to plot for the long-term reconstruction of their economy: Should it be rebuilt to remain service dominated, or should the productive sectors (agriculture and industry) be promoted, and to what extent? (See the paragraph on reconstruction and development.)

The Lebanese people and their government face the daunting task of developing satisfactory solutions to all of these issues (among others). To do so, however, they need help and support from the outside, as the final section details.

CONCLUDING REMARKS: POST-TA'IF RECONSTRUCTION

Reflections on Lebanon's past clearly indicate that Lebanon's future recovery will happen only if the reconstruction process is tackled in toto.

Lebanon's problems are far too interrelated to adopt a piecemeal or ad hoc approach to recovery.

Lebanon's reconstruction will involve a careful, extremely complex, demanding, and multifaceted process. The country is devastated; thus, everything is a priority. On the other hand, every need must vigorously compete with every other for the scarce financial and human resources that are (or will be) available. Furthermore, the elements of reconstruction are not only competing, but could be contradictory.[20] Plans to fix one problem inevitably affect others, meaning no single task can be addressed in isolation.

Developing a plan for Lebanon's reconstruction will be like developing a highly complex system comprising political, economic, financial, institutional, human, and administrative subsystems—each in need of attention, all in dynamic interaction.[21] The government, therefore, must balance the projected benefits of reconstruction programs against their potential costs, especially those that increase or prolong the suffering of the Lebanese people.

Because of the complexities and potential pitfalls of Lebanon's reconstruction, the country needs comprehensive help from outside—from foreign governments and aid agencies, international and Arab funding institutions, United Nations agencies, prominent world figures, and Lebanese abroad.

Undoubtedly, these outside players will have competing objectives, agendas, and timetables. Because the size of the effort required is immense, coordination among all the donors as well as between the donors and the various government ministries and agencies could well become a nightmarish task. It is proposed, therefore that a specialized office be opened—the *Office of Coordination of International Assistance to Lebanon.* This office (based in Lebanon) would act as a liaison among donors and between donors and the Lebanese authorities. Such an office could be empowered to make certain decisions on behalf of the donors, thereby shortening decisionmaking time and speeding the reconstruction process. Ideally, it would be funded by donors and would remain in place at least for the duration of the Emergency Recovery Program (three to five years).

Overall, outside assistance should be directed toward supporting the Lebanese government in its design and implementation of development and reconstruction programs. Specifically, Lebanon needs outside assistance in the following areas: *training,* to enable the Lebanese to manage, operate, and maintain projects; *public administration and management,* to help develop and implement comprehensive reforms of government institutions and agencies—including their structures, procedures, manpower, and work habits; *fiscal reform,* especially in the areas of revenue generation, private sector financing, and creation of capital markets; and *resource mobilization,* especially in devising programs to encourage expatriate Lebanese to participate in the reconstruction effort. In addition, Lebanon would benefit from international advice, or round-table conferences, that openly debate some of the key issues the country must address. For example, learning of other countries' experiences with privatization would be most helpful. As the chapter by Charif details, Lebanon would benefit from international assistance that targeted the development of Lebanon's regions.

Of course, Lebanon's resuscitation also requires financial help from outside. Unfortunately, the reconstruction of Lebanon is taking place in the midst of a worldwide recession, and at a time when the attention of the world community is diverted to many other world issues. In spite of this, the outlook for Lebanon is only gray, not black.

Even though Lebanon's needs are immense, the resources required for the ERP's next three years are manageable—some $2.1 billion. Another $1.8–$2 billion will be needed in years four and five.[22] The Lebanese government is expected to underwrite 20–25 percent of these costs, meaning that some $600 million annually will be required from outside donors—an amount not impossible to raise. Already, there is some $1.2 billion from the outside world in varying degrees of commitment.[23] In addition, a number of important international, regional, and Arab funding institutions are deeply committed to assisting Lebanon's recovery.

My optimism is not to imply that the funding effort will be simple or easy, because it will not be. Rather, my point is that securing funding, difficult as it may be, is a simple task compared with that of resolving the many issues highlighted in this chapter. Rebuilding Lebanon for the long term does not require money so much as comprehensive policies and programs that balance reconstruction with development, and economic recovery with some measure of public benefit—for all Lebanese.

NOTES

1. From 1990–1992, the value of Lebanon's currency weakened almost daily in relation to foreign currencies. Following the formation of the 1992 cabinet, the currency appeared to stabilize, although it remains to be seen whether this stability will continue in the long term.

2. Samir Makdisi, *Financial Policy and Economic Growth: The Lebanese Experience* (New York: Columbia University Press, 1979), p. 3. See also Kamal Hamdan "Les Libanais face à la crise économique et sociale: étendue et limites des processus d'adaptation," *Revue Maghreb-Machrek* no. 125 (1989).

3. Lebanon's economy also reaped substantial benefits from the Palestinian presence, especially after 1970.

4. Makdisi, *Financial Policy,* 1979.

5. For further discussion of Lebanon's prewar socioeconomic imbalances, see the chapter by Charif in this volume.

6. See Makdisi, *Financial Policy,* 1979.

7. Specific consequences of government nonplanning included: (1) an inade-

quate, state-run educational system (with no national policies) existing next to a high-standard, but expensive and elitist, private school system (the state-run system, at best, provided a mediocre education); (2) an unevenly distributed and improperly maintained social services system for health, water supply, sewerage, electricity, and transit; (3) a highly overpriced housing sector; (4) a declining agricultural sector due to rural-urban migration (among many other reasons); and (5) an overly dominant services sector.

8. For detailed discussion, see the chapter by Corm in this volume.

9. For a detailed analysis of sectoral damage as well as reconstruction needs and costs, see A. Sbaiti, "Reconstruction and Development of Lebanon's Economic Sectors: 1991 and Beyond" (presented at CIIPS workshop in December 1990).

10. CDR was responsible for overall planning, programming, and budgeting; coordination of proposals and allocations between sectors for priority projects; procurement and mobilization of funds; payments to suppliers and contractors; disbursements of loans and grants; facilitating project implementation by line ministries; implementation of "special" projects (at the request of the Council of Ministers); and overall program monitoring.

11. CDR initiated the process based on a number of lofty (if unrealitic) premises related to the guidelines already listed above: (1) the government would provide incentives to encourage decentralization of economic activity (away from Beirut); (2) taxation would be made more equitable to yield greater revenue; (3) measures would be taken to counteract inflation during reconstruction; (4) CDR would monitor and oversee the process, submitting periodic reports to the Council of Ministers; and (5) reconstruction would aim at strengthening the operational and administrative capabilities of the responsible government units.

12. Sbaiti, "Reconstruction and Development of Lebanon's Economic Sectors."

13. For example, the World Bank project allocated fewer funds to housing, waste management, and private sector support than the CDR's 1983 project, and more funds to education, telecommunications, electricity, health, and the development of Beirut's central district.

14. World Bank, "Lebanon Reconstruction Assessment Report," Report no. 4434-LE (April 1983), p. 25.

15. CDR's share of total public sector investments rose from 19 percent in 1979 to 25 percent in 1980–1982, to 47 percent in 1985, and to 53 percent in 1986.

16. CDR's annual investment programs amounted to $630 million in 1983, $950 million in 1984–1985, and $282 million in 1987.

17. For example, some 112 contracts (worth $600 million) were signed for road rehabilitation between 1978 and 1987. As of 31 January 1989, only 43 percent of these were close to completion. During the same period, some 695 schools were under repair or rehabilitation; of these, only 28 percent were more than 90 percent complete.

18. The ERP plans were reviewed by Arab and international funding institutions (including the Arab Fund for Economic and Social Development [AFESD] based in Kuwait, the World Bank, the Kuwait Fund, the Arab Fund, the Abu Dhabi Fund, the Saudi Fund, the Islamic Bank, and the OPEC Fund) prior to an international donors meeting (1993) to solicit funds and assistance in kind from the world community.

19. A condition for continued outside finance, especially from funding institutions such as the World Bank and AFESD, is that the country remain current on repayments of loans and interest.

20. For example, certain measures required to create the needed economic

environment for reconstruction could, if not properly managed and monitored, wreak havoc with other requisites for reconstruction. Reconstruction will require huge expenditures. If expenditures exceed the economy's absorptive capacity, however, they could push inflation to soaring new heights.

21. Systems control and optimization provide a useful model in this regard. See J. W. Forrester, *Principles of Systems* (Cambridge, Mass: Wright Allen Press, 1969).

22. Thereafter, it is assumed (perhaps too optimistically) that the economy will no longer be as dependent on outside help.

23. This pool of donors does not include the Lebanese abroad, whose collective fortune is estimated at some $40 billion. These expatriate funds could be tapped by year four, when, it is hoped, the country will have proven itself to the outside world—prompting investor confidence, including that of its skeptical expatriates.

12

The Litani River:
The Case Against
Interbasin Transfer

Hussein A. Amery & Atif A. Kubursi

Water is a relatively scarce commodity in Lebanon, especially in the provinces of the Bekaa and the South, which are almost solely dependent on the Litani River and its tributaries. These rural provinces, constituting over 60 percent of Lebanon's area, share a number of critical attributes. They are the country's principal agricultural regions, but are also its least developed and most impoverished. They are also the provinces in which the largest concentration of Lebanon's Shi'ites reside. In many ways, the welfare of these rural areas was largely ignored—falling outside the political and economic mainstream—in the Lebanon of the First Republic (1943–1989).

THE SOCIOECONOMIC AND POLITICAL SETTING

The Lebanon that emerged after 1943 was based on a confessional society and economy underpinned by an extensive intersection of interests between Maronite bureaucrats and Sunni trading families. The bureaucrats were primarily interested in developing and securing a stable source of public finance that, given the conditions and structures of the Lebanese economy at the time, could only be based on custom duties and foreign imports. Much of this activity was primarily controlled by a handful of powerful Sunni trading families in the coastal cities of Beirut, Tripoli, and Sidon. These traders considered it to be in their best interest to have a government that restricted itself to building an efficient social infrastructure and maintaining a policy environment favorable to free trade.

This intersection of interests manifested itself politically in the 1943 National Pact. It also manifested itself, in a less obvious but still significant manner, by way of an implicit economic social contract that provided the political accord with a strong economic base. Under the terms of this implicit contract, the public sector invested heavily in building an extensive infrastructure of trade routes, ports, airports, warehouses, and communication networks, while restricting any of its activities that might promote competing commodity producing sectors (in agriculture and manufacturing) or regions that could undermine the dominance and free flow of imports. The contract also fostered a probusiness policy environment with minimal government interference, including bank secrecy laws, a free foreign exchange market, and no income or profit taxes. Other sects and regions were virtually cut out of this "condominium" and the prosperity it engendered.

Lebanon's current economic predicament is rooted in the unmanaged, mercurial successes it experienced from the 1950s to the mid-1970s and, in a less obvious way, in the confessional structure of the society and economy. The civil war brought about a massive destruction of infrastructure and productive capital, profuse losses in human capital, and substantial displacement of the population. It also brought an end to the implicit social contract of 1943.

The Lebanese today face the challenge of not only reconstructing their economy but also reconstituting their society and polity. Although the task is daunting, it also provides an opportunity to correct some of the destabilizing flaws of Lebanon's First Republic. There is a need for a new social contract. This new contract must be based on a more balanced economy, in which commodity-producing sectors moderate the lopsided services-biased production structure of the First Republic, and in which the disenfranchised regions and communities in Lebanon are represented more equitably and integrated into the mainstream of the society and economy.

If Lebanon is to consolidate its unity and stability, it is essential, as this chapter argues, that the government invest in the development of South Lebanon, to uplift the socioeconomic status of the residents of this neglected area. This vitally required development demands the effective and comprehensive exploitation of the resources of the Litani River. However, this proposition is not as simple as one might think, for although the Litani flows entirely within Lebanon's territory, its resources are thought to be coveted by Lebanon's powerful neighbor to the south.

Israeli interest in augmenting its water supply has become, at the beginning of the 1990s, a compelling issue. Today, Israel is utilizing all of its renewable water resources, and the gap between its water supply and demand is widening. As Table 12.1 shows, Israel is expected to have an annual water deficit of approximately 550 million cubic meters (mcm) by the year 2000. Other forecasts place that shortfall as high as 800 mcm.[1] Because water is basically a nontradable resource, Israel's looming water crisis can only be solved through domestic readjustment (i.e., restructuring its economy) or through an increased supply. The latter solution necessarily would involve Israel's neighbors. The fact that Israel has become dependent on the water resources of the West Bank raises questions concerning Israel's future designs on the water-rich Arab territories that it occupies, including the West Bank, Golan Heights, and southern Lebanon.

Table 12.1 Profiles of Water and Economic Conditions in Lebanon and Israel (water in mcm/year)

	Lebanon	Israel
Jordan River		
Flow generated	130	730[a]
Withdrawn	0	600
Litani River		
Flow generated	920	0
Withdrawn	440	0
Water consumption[b]		
Domestic	151	446
Industrial	75	124
Agricultural	950	1179
Present water resources		
Water available	4980	1950
Water withdrawn/supplied	950	1930
Projected water demand (year 2000)		
Water demand	4451	2500
Surplus/shortfall of water	+529	−550
Economic sectors, as percent of GDP		
Service	71%	32%
Industry	21	58
Agriculture	8	10
Percent of labor force (1985–1990) in		
Service	58%	62%
Industry	27	32
Agriculture	14	6

Sources: U.S. Army Corps of Engineers, *Water in the Sand: A Survey of Middle East Water Issues* (Washington, D.C., June 1991); World Resources Institute, *World Resources 1992–93* (New York: Oxford University Press, 1992); Food and Agriculture Organization, *Production Year Book* 46 (1992); Arab Centre for the Study of Arid Zones and Dry Lands (ACSAD), *The Condition of Water Resources in the Arab World* (in Arabic) (Damascus: ACSAD, 1991); J. Khuri and A. Droubi, *Water Resources in the Arab Region* (Damascus: ACSAD, 1990).

    Notes: a. Includes runoff from the West Bank and Golan Heights.
        b. These data are from 1990 for Lebanon, and from 1987 for Israel.

The hydrostrategic significance of South Lebanon is rarely considered as a factor underlying Israel's continued occupation of the "security zone." This issue, however, is worthy of some attention.

In the hostile and uncooperative environment of the Middle East, the issue of water takes on a whole new dimension, especially given the resource's scarcity and strong association with economic development. For example, it has been argued that Israel's initiation of the 1967 war was motivated in part by its lack of resources, especially water.[2] Indeed, approximately 35 percent of Israel's water consumption today originates in the various Arab territories it occupied as a result of that war. Israel did not commence its overt presence on Lebanese soil until 1978, when it proclaimed a "security zone" in South Lebanon for "security" reasons. Although hard evidence is lacking, there is growing speculation concerning the real motives behind Israel's continued presence in southern Lebanon up to the western bend of the Litani River (Map 12.1). These speculations are buttressed by knowledge of Israel's historical interest in the Litani, as well as its growing water crisis.

THE LITANI AND EARLY ZIONIST PLANS:
A HISTORICAL REVIEW

A central objective of the early Zionists was the establishment of a Jewish "national home" in Palestine. Another important objective was to root the Jewish immigrants in the new land (hence the Zionists' ideological commitment to agricultural production). The focus on farming yielded further advantages, which included securing the territorial integrity of the country through rooted occupation of peripheral areas, guaranteeing the new country's self-sufficiency in food, and expanding the carrying capacity of the land to sustain additional immigrants.[3] In hot, semiarid Palestine, however, farming required water, and lots of it.

Aware of water scarcity and its intrinsic threat to their future homeland, Zionist leaders in Europe actively lobbied the French and the British governments between 1916 and 1948 to adjust the northern and northeastern borders of Palestine to include the whole catchment of the Jordan River and a large part of that of the Litani River. Chaim Weizmann, head of the World Zionist Organization (WZO), articulated WZO's demands in letters he sent to various British government officials. In one such letter to British Prime Minister David Lloyd George, Weizmann argued that Lebanon being a "well watered" region, the water resources of the Litani River were "valueless to the territory north of the proposed frontiers [i.e., Lebanon]. They can be used beneficially in the country much further south." Weizmann affirmed WZO's conviction that "the [Bekaa] Valley of the Litani, for a distance of 25 miles above the bend" in the river was essential to the future of the Jewish "national home" (see Map 12.1).[4]

The WZO desired that Israel's eastern borders be drawn a few kilometers east of the Jordan River, and thus include its major tributary, the Yarmouk River. On 30 October 1920, Weizmann wrote to Britain's

**Map 12.1 The Hydrological Significance of Israel's Self-declared "Security Zone"
in South Lebanon**

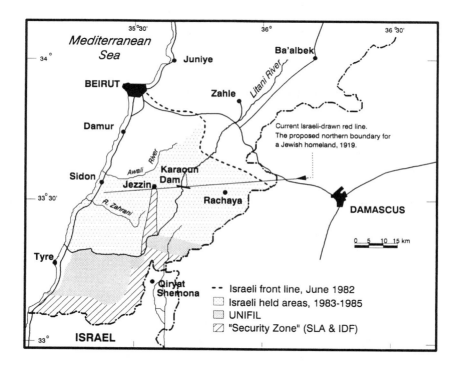

Map legend:
- -- Israeli front line, June 1982
- Israeli held areas, 1983-1985
- UNIFIL
- "Security Zone" (SLA & IDF)

Current Israeli-drawn red line.
The proposed northern boundary for
a Jewish homeland, 1919.

foreign secretary, Lord Curzon, stating that "if Palestine were cut off from the Litany, Upper Jordan and Yarmouk (rivers), to say nothing of the western shore of the [sea of] Galilee, she could not be economically independent. And a poor and impoverished Palestine would be of no advantage to any power."[5]

Zionist demands, however, were not met when the British Mandate determined the boundaries of Palestine to include only those areas that, today, are called Israel, the West Bank, and Gaza Strip.[6]

Although WZO failed in its hydrological demands, the issue was shelved but not forgotten. The Zionists refocused their efforts on their main objective, namely the creation of their state. During the war that accompanied Israel's declaration of independence in 1948, Israel occupied a stretch of southern Lebanon up to the Litani River, but later withdrew, albeit incompletely.[7]

ISRAEL AND THE LITANI: 1948–1982

Having access to the Litani River was on Israeli government officials' minds early in the state's formative years. In 1953, when regional tensions erupted over the use of the Jordan River, the United States dispatched Eric Johnston to the region with a plan for water sharing. The Johnston Plan called for the establishment of a Jordan Water Authority composed of Israel, Jordan, and Syria, which would manage these countries' joint exploitation of the river. It was thought that such cooperation would facilitate the irrigation of larger tracts of land and thereby speed up the process of absorption and resettlement of Palestinian refugees. The Johnston Plan was based on the principle that water must be used within the river basin.[8]

This principle did not completely mesh with Israel's determination to develop its full agricultural potential. Israel's response to the Johnston Plan, therefore, was a plan of its own—the 1954 Cotton Plan—that suggested the diversion of one-half of the Litani River's annual flow (400 mcm) into the Jordan River (for Israel's benefit).[9] It is worth noting that the Cotton Plan went further than any previous water-sharing proposal, in that it prepared the engineering schemes necessary to accomplish the diversion. Israel's demand to include the Litani River in the Johnston Plan of 1954 was, according to Berger, based on its contention that "there could not be a fully effective regional plan which did not use the Litani River."[10] Johnston countered Israel's demands by stating that the United States had no grounds for requesting Lebanon to share the resources of the Litani—a wholly Lebanese river—with nonriparian states. Ultimately, the increasing political and military uncertainty throughout the region caused Israel to hesitate and then back down from any coercive acquisition of Lebanese territory near the Litani.

The diaries of Moshe Sharett, prime minister of Israel in the mid-1950s, reveal that David Ben Gurion (the first prime minister of Israel) and Moshe Dayan (Israel's chief of staff and later defense minister) were strong advocates of an Israeli occupation of southern Lebanon up to the Litani River. Sharett quotes Dayan as saying in 1954, "All that is needed is to find an [Lebanese] officer, even at the rank of captain, to win him over or buy his co-operation so as to declare himself the saviour of the [Christian] Maronite population. Then the IDF [Israeli Defense Forces] will enter Lebanon, occupy the relevant territory and form a Christian government in alliance with Israel. The territory south of the Litani will be annexed to Israel and everything will fall into place."[11]

In the wake of the 1967 war and Israel's territorial gains at the expense of three of its four neighboring Arab states, Moshe Dayan reiterated his longstanding view that Israel had achieved "provisionally satisfying frontiers, with the exception of those with Lebanon."[12]

Dayan's blueprint for Lebanon was ultimately implemented in 1978, when Israel created its so-called "security zone" in southern Lebanon. This territory was officially placed under the control of Sa'd Haddad, a Christian and a major in the Lebanese Army who, in 1979, declared a Christian Maronite state in southern Lebanon.[13] Haddad then headed an Israeli financed, trained, and equipped Lebanese militia (later renamed South Lebanese Army or SLA). Until today, the SLA, together with the Israeli Defense Forces (IDF), controls a strip of southern Lebanon up to the western bend of the Litani River (see Map 12.1).

Israel was not faced by an imminent crisis of water scarcity when it occupied the West Bank and the Golan Heights in 1967, or when it occupied southern Lebanon in 1978. The declared objective of all three actions was Israel's security and peace. Recall, however, that today more than 35 percent of Israel's water consumption originates from territories captured in 1967. One can infer that, past strategic considerations aside, a likely future-oriented objective of Israel's occupation of the West Bank is economic, water being the major attraction.[14]

With this West Bank precedent as a backdrop, Israel's historic interest in the Litani and its conduct in southern Lebanon during the 1970s and 1980s worries Lebanese officials who view Israel's presence in southern Lebanon as one intended to secure access to the Litani water. Israel's actions have hardly been reassuring in this regard. Shortly after it established the "security zone," the Israeli Army prohibited well drilling in that area of South Lebanon. After the invasion of 1982, Israeli army engineers carried out seismic soundings and surveys near the Litani's western bend; these were likely done to determine the optimum place for a diversion tunnel. Moreover, they "seized all the hydrographic charts and technical documents relating to the Litani and its installations."[15] Through its occupation, Israel also controlled most or all of the waters from the Hasbani and

Wazzani rivers (tributaries of the Jordan), which rise in Lebanon; over the years, there have also been reports of water siphoning from the Litani into the Jordan River basin.[16] The distance from the Litani's western bend to the nearest tributary of the Jordan River is less than 10 kilometers (see Map 12.1). The Litani's proximity makes its waters easily divertible into the Jordan River system through underground canals or pipelines. The Jordan River, which empties into Lake Tiberias, supplies Israel with about one-third of its water needs.

No one can yet categorically conclude that the Litani waters are being diverted, because Israeli forces have cordoned off large tracts of land near the crucial western bend of the river, preventing researchers, journalists, and observers from approaching the area.[17] However, in 1984, J. K. Cooley asserted that

> A watchful American military observer claims to have seen Israelis burying pipes deep in a hillside near Marj'Uyn after the Israeli invasion of 1978, indicating that the Israelis might be secretly siphoning water underground from the Marj Plain in southern Lebanon into Israel, without affecting the measured flow of the Litani. Such a diversion would tap the extensive underground aquifer which is fed by seepage from both the Litani and the Hasbani rivers and by underground streams from the Mount Hermon region.[18]

More recently, an overt water diversion case was reported:

> In the late 1970s and early 1980s, Lebanese officials reported that small tributaries of the Hasbani River were being diverted to Israel near the northern town of Metulla. Independent water analysts stated that after the 1982 invasion, Israel engaged in a much more serious diversion of Lebanese waters by attaching stopcocks at a pumping station on the Litani river. The stopcocks were designed to switch at least part of the flow— which is generated entirely within Lebanon—to Israel via a specially constructed pipeline.[19]

If Israel indeed harbors ambitions to "share" in Lebanon's Litani resources, these ambitions will be difficult for the Lebanese state to prevent. The post–civil war Lebanese government is weak, its control over the South is marginal, and Israel has a distinct advantage given its occupation by proxy of the strategically placed (for water diversion) "security zone." Israel could pursue its desire to tap the Litani either through a unilateral water diversion scheme (which appears to be the situation now), or through bilateral negotiations where Israel would use the "security zone" as a bargaining chip to reach a water "sharing" agreement with Lebanon.[20]

Some analysts see the latter possibility—a water-sharing arrangement reached in the context of an overall settlement to the Arab-Israeli conflict— as a viable and promising path to peace. With respect to Lebanon, contemporary Israeli proponents of interbasin transfers acknowledge that a scheme proposing to export Lebanese water to Israel would encounter significant public outcry, especially in the South. They argue, however, that the potential benefits accruing to the Lebanese as a result of such a scheme would soon stifle public protest, since "payment for the water and the potential for greater supply of electricity than Lebanon could produce on its own [because the flow into Lake Tiberias generates greater electricity output than the flow into the Mediterranean] would be significant incentives for the Lebanese."[21]

Commenting on Israel's occupation of southern Lebanon, R. J. Rowley observed that for Israel the lure of the Litani is twofold: the river offers both water quantity and quality.[22] Israel's surface and subsurface water sources have come under significant stress due both to scarcity and high demand; this stress has precipitated a deterioration of water quality. For example, the salinity level in Lake Tiberias (Sea of Galilee), a major source of water in Israel, is over 250 ppm. This level of salinity is too high for some of Israel's principal crops (e.g., citrus fruit trees). The water of the Litani River, with a salinity level of 20 ppm, has the potential to dilute the salinity of Lake Tiberias. Some observers are convinced that "it is purity that makes the Litani very attractive to the Israelis."[23]

Another attractive feature of the Litani is the relative ease with which it could be diverted into the Israeli water system. The Litani River's annual flow is estimated at 920 mcm,[24] of which an estimated 480 mcm flow past the Khardali Bridge near the Israeli-occupied area by the western bend of the Litani. Before the river empties into the Mediterranean, approximately 125 mcm of its water is used in the Kasmieh irrigation project. One estimate of the volume that Israel could potentially divert—if it secured sustained access to the Litani—stands at approximately 800 mcm per year.[25] However, this volume would only be attainable if Israel were to reoccupy the Karaoun Dam (which it occupied between 1982 and 1985) and to tap southern Lebanon's subterranean springs as well as the Wazzani water potential (see Map 12.1).[26]

Israel's growing water needs are creating a compelling atmosphere in which Lebanon may well be convinced or coerced in the name of cooperation and peace to accept the idea of an interbasin transfer of water. Israel's strategic occupation of the South maximizes its potential for securing access to the Litani—either covertly or overtly. The other side of the cooperation or transferring coin, however, is an unstable Lebanon that is deprived of the capacity to develop its own resources.

When Lebanon's domestic focus was on economic growth through trade and on regions populated by the dominant traditional groups of the National Pact, the issue of the Litani was not so pressing. Today, however, as Lebanon emerges from war its quest for stability and security is necessarily linked to development of its regions and to demarginalization of its formerly neglected citizens (i.e., those based in rural areas, especially the South). As the remainder of this chapter will argue, these two requisites for Lebanon's future stability can only be achieved with complete and effective control and exploitation of the Litani River and the revitalization of the complete Litani River Project.

SOUTHERN DEVELOPMENT AND THE LITANI: IS THERE ANOTHER OPTION?

In 1959, 49 percent of the Lebanese labor force was engaged in agricultural activities, a proportion that contracted rapidly, reaching 19 percent in 1970 and 12 percent in the mid-1970s.[27] The contribution of agriculture to gross national product fell from 20 percent in 1950 to 9 percent in 1974. This dramatic transformation was due in part to labor-substituting technologies introduced at a considerable rate throughout the 1960s and at an even greater rate during the 1970s. By 1975, the result of this upheaval in human terms was that some 40 percent of Lebanon's rural population had left the land, many attracted by empty promises of economic opportunity in Beirut. Within fifteen years, tens of thousands of Lebanese families lost their rural livelihood. Most of these farmers were Shi'ite; as their livelihood waned, so did their national allegiance.

In the introduction to this chapter we argue that Lebanon's confessional system of government created observable dichotomies in development. This argument is supported by the analysis of Samih Farsoun, who, after reviewing a number of socioeconomic studies and data sets from the 1970s, reached two conclusions:

> The first is that considerable demographic, social and economic differentiation exists between the populations of the two religions and among the Islamic sects, but not among the Christians. The intra-Muslim variation is large, with the Shi'ite placing in the lowest socioeconomic status of the six major sects of Lebanon. The second clear cut conclusion is that Muslims in general are substantially more disadvantaged in socioeconomic terms than Christians.[28]

The Shi'ite population, largely concentrated in South Lebanon, has suffered both neglect from the Lebanese government and frequent Israeli bombardments (beginning in the late 1960s). With neither their economic nor physical safety guaranteed, the residents of southern Lebanon became resentful and distrustful of the Lebanese government.

In the early 1970s, the Shi'ite community violently protested a plan to divert the Litani River to quench the thirst of the rapidly expanding city of Beirut. In 1973, Imam Musa al-Sadr, the leader of the Shi'ite community, demanded among other things a firm commitment from the government to develop the South and Bekaa; he was "particularly emphatic about using the resources of the Litani River to greater advantage."[29] To back his demand, al-Sadr threatened the collective resignation of all Shi'ite ministers from the cabinet.

Fifteen years of war did not remedy Lebanon's regional development problems—especially those related to water. Of Lebanon's 1,810 villages and cities, 1,479 are supplied with water and 254 are not (seventy-seven settlements were abandoned or destroyed).[30] The most recent (1984) statistics reveal that 25 percent of Lebanon's population does not have adequate access to sanitary facilities. Six percent of the deprived live in urban areas, 82 percent in rural areas, the majority of these living in the most impoverished areas of the South and Bekaa.[31] It is fair to argue that development and improvement of infrastructure in these neglected areas will augment the demand for water and access accordingly (see Figures 12.1 and 12.2).

Lebanon's water needs have been projected to exceed its supply by the year 2020 (Table 12.2). The projected increases are based on (1) population growth, and (2) the fact that today less than 30 percent of Lebanon's arable land is irrigated, thus consuming only 20 percent of the country's total renewable water resources. The share of this sector of water would certainly accelerate once the Litani Project is completed.

Table 12.2 Anticipated Demand for Water in Lebanon, 1985–2030 (mcm/year)

	1985	2000	2010	2020	2030
Domestic	151	280	419	585	755
Industrial	75	185	335	527	755
Agricultural	900	3986	4160	4513	4883
Total water demand	1126	4451	4914	5625	6393
Total available	4980	4980	4980	4980	4980

Sources: J. Khouri and A. Droubi, *Water Resources in the Arab Region* (Damascus: Arab Centre for the Study of Arid Zones and Dry Lands, 1990) and ACSAD, *The Condition of Water Resources in the Arab World* (in Arabic) (Damascus: ACSAD, 1991).
Note: Projections are based on current rates of population growth.

It is axiomatic that the development (and restabilization) of southern Lebanon will depend upon effective exploitation of the Litani River, the largest in the country. South Lebanon has 19.3 percent of the country's total land area and about 15 percent of its population; 99 percent of its settlements (411 out of a total of 415 villages and cities) have fewer than 5,000 residents, and 69 percent of all residents are classified as rural.[32] Most of the socioeconomic demands of South Lebanon's residents can best

Figure 12.1 Sectoral Water Withdrawal, 1989

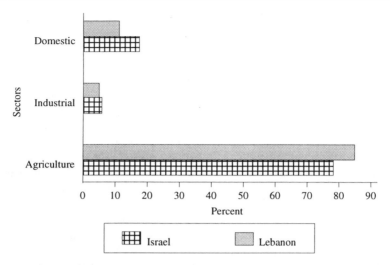

Source: Based on data from World Resources Institute, *World Resources 1992–93* (New York: Oxford University Press, 1992).

Figure 12.2 Irrigated Land as Percentage of Arable Land, 1970–1989

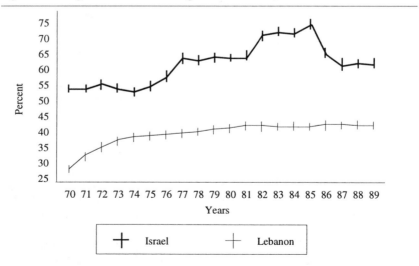

Sources: World Resources Institute, *World Resources 1992–93* (New York: Oxford University Press, 1992) and Food and Agriculture Organization, *FAO Production Year Book* 44 (1990).

be addressed by using the Litani River's water to irrigate this fertile but arid area and to electrify the region. A mere 11 percent of the South's arable area is presently irrigated.

The Litani Project of the 1950s involved an irrigation and electrical generating scheme whose main purpose was to improve farmlands and villages and to raise the standard of living in the South and Bekaa. Most of the work for the Bekaa had been completed by the early 1970s. The scheme to irrigate the South, however, became stalled following the eruption of war; Israel's 1978 invasion and subsequent creation of a "security zone" ended any hope of progress.

The Litani River Project, or some version of it, must be completed if reborn Lebanon is to survive beyond infancy. Irrigation generally provides farmers with relative economic stability and increases their net incomes. It also helps to sustain domestic demand for locally produced goods, thereby saving the country valuable foreign exchange. While much of South Lebanon has electricity service, power supplies are too limited to meet the rapidly expanding population's growing demands. Electrification provides the opportunity to link irrigated agriculture to industrialization. Irrigation typically boosts agricultural output. Processing agricultural products locally creates (better) jobs and increases the income of the area as well as the country. Boosting the region's hydroelectrical output, therefore, is essential for increasing the standard of living of southern Lebanese residents, and is an integral part of the infrastructure necessary for the area's industrial development.

Industrial development of southern Lebanon is consistent with capturing the country's emerging comparative advantage in water-intensive agriculture. The industrialization of this output is quite opportune now that the exchange rate is undervalued, the confessional accord no longer favors an overvalued Lebanese pound, South Lebanon is teeming with cheap labor, and the domestic market is reviving.

CONCLUSION

If a Third Republic is to be born, Lebanon must redress the uneven regional development that occurred under the narrow social accord of 1943. The new social contract must be based on a broad alliance of sects, classes, and political orientations; benefits must accrue—and be perceived to accrue—to all members of the cooperative alliance. From this perspective, the development of southern Lebanon is a critical and vital priority. The Litani River is the cornerstone of this strategy.

Israel, however, appears to harbor a different agenda for the Litani waters. We have suggested that Israel's territorial occupations of Arab land—including Lebanon's—are affected (perhaps driven) by hydrological

imperatives. Israeli planning is influenced by water resources in the occupied territories; Israel's reliance on them will grow with the country's
water deficit. We have also suggested that the situation in southern
Lebanon is coming to resemble that of the West Bank and Golan after the
1967 war: an Israeli occupation, followed by an enforced status quo, followed by a move to tap the territory's resources.

Contrary to Israeli claims that Lebanon is "wasting" its water, the
Lebanese government has been utilizing over 40 percent of the river's
annual flow and is developing further irrigation and hydroelectrical generation plans for South Lebanon and the Bekaa. Given the government's
socioeconomic obligation toward its long-neglected southern population,
an interbasin transfer from the Litani into the Jordan River system would
be detrimental to Lebanon's internal stability. As Lebanon struggles to
rebuild its society and economy, full exploitation of the Litani River basin
has become a strategic imperative—a developmental priority with the
potential to balance and moderate the social and economic tensions likely
to emerge in the new Lebanon.

NOTES

1. T. Naff and R. C. Matson, *Water in The Middle East: Conflict or
Cooperation* (Boulder, Colo.: Westview Press, 1984).
2. Atif Kubursi, *The Economic Consequences of The Camp David
Agreement* (Beirut: Institute of Palestine Studies, 1981); J. Stauffer "Arab Water in
Israeli Calculations: The Benefits of War and the Costs of Peace," in A. M. Farid
and H. Sirriyeh (eds.), *Israel and The Arab Water* (London: Ithaca Press, 1985) pp.
75–83; H. A. Amery, *Scarcity-Induced Conflict: The Lebanese-Israeli Conflict
Over Water* (Masters thesis, Wilfrid Laurier University, 1987).
3. All of the early Zionist agricultural goals have largely been achieved, but
at a substantial cost to the economy and to neighboring riparian states. Farming in
Israel is heavily subsidized, as is the cost of water for irrigation, yet government
agronomists estimate that less than one-half of Israel's irrigated agriculture is economically productive and a fraction of its agricultural production is economically
viable (after all the subsidies have been accounted for). In spite of severe pressure
on the country's water capacity, agricultural interests still prevail. Attempts to real-
locate water permanently from agriculture to domestic or industrial use have been
mostly unsuccessful. For details, see J.R. Stauffer, "Arab Water in Israeli
Calculations," pp. 75–83; H. Kamm, "Israel Farming Success Drains It of Water,"
New York Times, 21 April 1991; and J. R. Stauffer, "The Lure of the Litani," *Middle
East International,* 30 July 1982, pp. 13–14.
4. M. W. Weisgal (ed.), *The Letters and Papers of Chaim Weizmann,* vol. 9
(Jerusalem: Israel University Press, 1977), p. 267.
5. F. C. Hof, *Galilee Divided: The Israel-Lebanon Frontier, 1916–1984*
(Boulder, Colo.: Westview Press, 1985), pp. 11–13.
6. Many plans for sharing and managing water were advanced to deal with
the meager resources. Unlike numerous others, the 1944 Lowdermilk Plan and the
1948 Hays Plan (based on regional cooperation) regarded the Litani River as part of

the Jordan River system and suggested that one-half of its flow be used by Israel.

7. In fact, from 1948 to 1975, Israel slowly expanded to annex, de facto, pieces of Lebanon's territory. These totaled 169,763 dunums by the end of 1975. See E. Hagopian, "Lebanon and the Arab Question," in E. Hagopian and E. Farsoun (eds.), *South Lebanon,* Special Report no. 2 (Association of Arab-American University Graduates, 1978); and E. Berger, *The Covenant and the Sword: Arab-Israeli Relations 1948–56* (London and Toronto: Routledge and Kegan Paul, 1965).

8. E. Berger, *The Covenant and The Sword,* pp. 139–140; J. K. Cooley, "The War Over Water," *Foreign Policy* vol. 54 (Spring 1984), pp. 3–26.

9. T. Naff and R. C. Matson, *Water in the Middle East,* and E. Hagopian, "Lebanon and the Arab Question."

10. E. Berger, *The Covenant and the Sword,* pp. 139–140.

11. Itmar Rabinovich, *The War for Lebanon, 1970–1983* (London: Cornell University Press, 1984), p. 163.

12. F. C. Hof, *Galilee Divided,* p. 36.

13. Liva Rokach, *Israel's Sacred Terrorism: A Study Based On Moshe Sharett's Personal Diary* (Belmont, Mass.: Association of Arab-American University Graduates, 1985); F. C. Hof, *Galilee Divided.*

14. A. Kubursi, *The Economic Consequences of the Camp David Agreements.*

15. J. K. Cooley, "The War Over Water," p. 22.

16. J. K. Cooley, "The War Over Water," p. 22; M. Abu Fadil and D. Harrison, "Arab-Israeli Negotiations: That Was Not the Idea," *The Middle East* (March 1992), pp. 21–27; A. P. Gemayel, "A Peace Based on Justice Not Weaponry" (in Arabic), *Al-Hayat* (30 October 1992), p. 17.

17. *Al-Nahar,* 3 March 1990.

18. J. K. Cooley, "The War Over Water," pp. 22–23.

19. T. Collelo, *Lebanon: A Country Study,* 3d ed. (Washington: Library of Congress, 1989), p. 117.

20. H. A. Amery and A. A. Kubursi, "Le Litani clé de la renaissance économique et de la stabilité politique du Liban," *Ecodecision* (September, 1992), pp. 55–57; H. A. Amery, *Scarcity-Induced Conflict.*

21. Elisha Kally, *Options for Solving the Palestinian Water Problem in the Context of Regional Peace,* Working Paper no. 19, The Harry Truman Research Institute for the Advancement of Peace (Jerusalem: Israel-Palestinian Peace Research Project, Winter 1991–1992); see also J. Schwarz, *Israel Water Sector Study: Past Achievements, Current Problems and Future Options* (World Bank, October 1990).

22. R. J. Rowley, *Israel into Palestine* (London: Mansell Publishers, 1984), pp. 145–146.

23. T. Naff and R. C. Matson, *Water in the Middle East,* p. 65.

24. It should be acknowledged that estimates for the Litani's annual flow range from 650 mcm to 980 mcm. The figure adopted here is based on recent research by the U.S. Army Corps of Engineers (1991).

25. The 800 mcm figure is contested. The former director general of the Litani Water Authority in Lebanon asserts that 400 mcm per year can be diverted to Israel from the Litani at the river's western bend. Others put this figure at 100 mcm per year. The figures vary according to the area from which the diversion will take place.

26. A. Baalbaki and F. A. Mahfouth, *The Agricultural Sector in Lebanon: The Significant Changes During the Civil War* (in Arabic) (Beirut: Dar al-Farabi, 1985). See also *Al-Nahar,* 24 March 1986.

27. See two chapters in H. Barakat (ed.), *Toward a Viable Lebanon:* Albert H. Hourani, "Visions of Lebanon," pp. 3–14, and Samih K. Farsoun, "E Pluribus Plura or E Pluribus Unum? Cultural Pluralism and Social Class in Lebanon," pp. 99–132.

28. Samih K. Farsoun, "E Pluribus Plura or E Pluribus Unum?" pp. 123–124.

29. M. Goria, *Sovereignty and Leadership in Lebanon 1943–1976* (London: Ithaca Press, 1985), p. 163.

30. *Al -Nahar,* 5 August 1985.

31. Vander Leeden et al., *The Water Encyclopedia* (Chelsea, Mich.: Lewis Publishers, 1990).

32. *Statistical Abstracts of the Ministry of General Planning* (Beirut: Department of Central Statistics, 1972).

13

The Economic Reconstruction of Lebanon: War, Peace, and Modernization

Nasser H. Saidi

OBJECTIVES OF ECONOMIC RECONSTRUCTION

It is now four years since the historic signing of the 1989 Ta'if Accord. During the past three years the state of violent confrontation between the various Lebanese factions and parties has ended, bringing welcome respite to Lebanon's beleaguered population. The task now is to rebuild.

Rebuilding, Lebanon will confront intricate and multidimensional issues—social, political, psychological, and economic. Rebuilding, Lebanon must resolve not only the fundamental problems that led to conflict and war, but also those that have emerged as consequences of war. Lebanon must also look to the future—it must plan and provide the structures necessary for growth and development in the twenty-first century. The war has left agonizing scars: The country's physical infrastructure as well as its organizational and human resources have been destroyed, impaired, damaged, or, as in the case of skilled labor, migrated abroad. Despite the magnitude and complexity of the task, the ultimate objective is clear: construct a solid, stable foundation on which to erect an open, free, and democratic society.

This chapter focuses primarily on the economic aspects of Lebanon's resuscitation. This focus does not reflect my professional bias as an economist. Rather, it reflects my conviction—based on my reading of the experiences of other wartorn countries[1]—that economic recovery and growth can act as the single most important unifying force in restoring Lebanon's battered national fabric. Constitutional, legislative, administrative, and social reforms are the essential foundations for reconstruction. Indeed, it is crucial that such reforms be widely accepted and understood to provide permanent safeguards to Lebanon's stability. It is the economic dimension, however,

195

that must provide the means to implement reforms: economic resources must be mobilized if social and other reforms are to succeed. Furthermore, the expectation that war's end will yield economic recovery and greater wealth is, itself, an incentive to guard the peace. The expected peace dividend must outweigh any potential gain from further conflict.

These requirements provide guidelines for economic policy during reconstruction. First, Lebanon's physical and organizational infrastructure must be designed to accommodate the looming realities of the twenty-first century. We cannot and should not try to rebuild the past. In particular, our infrastructure planning must take into account (1) the geographical redistribution of population, new population centers, and other demographic transformations (e.g., changes in family structure, increased participation of women in the labor force) wrought by the war; (2) the implications of a continuing opening and liberalization of the Syrian economy (providing both opportunities and challenges for the Lebanese economy); and (3) the consequences of peace between the Arab countries and Israel for regional trade and development.

Second, economic efficiency must be balanced with an equitable distribution of public resources across regions. In the prewar period, large disparities in the level of real income and development emerged between Lebanon's various regions (especially between rural and urban areas), and was accompanied by a maldistribution of income across individuals and communities.[2] These disparities helped protract the conflict and delayed its resolution. (The war augmented and reinforced existing disparities.) The prewar and war periods also show an unbalanced distribution of government expenditures across regions—particularly with respect to infrastructure investment. This imbalance exacerbated disparities and inequalities, as well as perceptions of discrimination. A national reconstruction program should strive to reduce these disparities and attend to the needs of previously neglected areas.

Third, property rights must be protected. The post-1975 breakdown in law and order led to widespread violation of both civil and property rights (i.e., the rights of individuals, business, institutions, and the state to use and dispose of resources freely). In particular, the ability of the state and public sector to collect taxes and other sources of revenue was severely impaired. The result was a recourse to taxation through inflation (with all the inherent negative socioeconomic consequences). The violation of property rights had other important consequences: (1) the diversion of scarce resources to private means of protection and enforcement, and (2) a disincentive to invest, resulting in a reduction of capital expenditures. Because the reconstruction process is mainly dependent on generating a substantial and sustained increase in investment spending, the protection and enforcement of property rights is crucial. The risk of investing in Lebanon is directly linked to the issue of property rights; unless property rights are effectively protected, neither domestic nor foreign sources of capital will have the incentive to invest. This implies a functioning legal and judicial system and the enforcement of law and order, and, in turn, requires state investment in the courts, the police, and internal security forces as well as the penal system.

Fourth, an economic policy regime favorable to the development of the private sector must be maintained. (This implies a competitive market economy, a primary role for the private sector, free international capital mobility, and floating exchange rates.) As outlined below, the bulk of investment spending for reconstruction must originate in the private sector (domestic and external). To attract these resources, the main role of the public sector will be to provide infrastructure (public utilities and services, security, and the legal framework), financial and monetary stability (to increase productivity in the private sector), and incentives for increased investment (such as low levels of taxation).

FOUR CORNERSTONES OF RECONSTRUCTION STRATEGY

Any reconstruction strategy must rest on providing a credible, long-term framework for political stability. Lebanon's historical experience has demonstrated repeatedly that political instability generates economic instability, and that temporary solutions lack credibility and cannot lead to a renewal of economic growth. The Ta'if Accord proposed an initial framework for restoring Lebanon's stability based on greater power sharing among Lebanon's communities (by way of limited constitutional and political reform). However, the accord also confirmed the system's confessional and sectarian characteristics.[3] This was a "mini-max" solution: the maximum set of reforms acceptable to one side, the minimum required by the other. While the accord was an important step in ending the conflict, it must be radically reviewed if it is to provide an effective framework for creating an open and democratic society. To be credible, political reform must be perceived—across the political spectrum—as embodying a long-term permanent solution, capable of being implemented. Consequently, if Lebanon is to emerge as a modern state ready for the twenty-first century, its foundations must be secured upon the four primary building blocks that follow:

Political reform and modernization. A secular, democratic system, with a bill of rights and obligations that defines a citizen's rights and obligations regardless of his religion, race, or other inherited characteristics must be created. Only a democratic system is capable of accommodating demographic and social change without leading to conflict. Lebanon's current regime thwarts change: Power is monopolized by those who have no incentive to promote change and who benefit most from maintenance of the status quo ante. Indeed, Lebanon's previous and present political regime reinforces the existence of noncompeting groups because individuals cannot compete across the sectarian divide.

Fundamentally, economic freedom must be accompanied by political freedom: both are reflections and facets of individual freedom. In Lebanon, citizens compete without communal distinction in private sector markets for goods and labor, but are not free to choose or to compete in the political arena, in the public sector's labor market, or in the market for votes. Is it possible to promote an economic system based on competition and laissez-faire while maintaining a political system based on controls and constraints that prevent political competition between individuals and groups? No. Eventually, constraints on individual freedom in the political domain will translate into constraints on economic freedom and an eventual breakdown of the system.

We must actively reform our political system to ensure competition in both the political and economic domains, and to provide constitutional safeguards that protect the rights of minorities.[4] In particular, parliamentary representation must be made free of sectarian or community constraints. Here the choice is between immediate or gradual reform. An immediate abolition of "political confessionalism" would require widespread acceptance or consensus for change. In the war's aftermath, such a consensus may not be forthcoming; abrupt reform, therefore, may be neither feasible nor advisable. If a gradualist approach is preferred, then a program for political reform should be prepared and announced.[5]

An international agreement to act as a counterpart of the Ta'if Accord. Given Lebanon's recent history of war and instability, certain international guarantees could prove crucial to reestablishing Lebanon's international credibility as a trading partner and regional business center, and reviving investor confidence through the reduction of investment risk. It appears unlikely that foreign investment and aid will be forthcoming until an agreement for the withdrawal of foreign armed forces is implemented. Foreign investors and grantors need assurance that funds will be invested as agreed and will not be misappropriated, destroyed, or captured, and that the debt servicing capacity of the country will not be impaired due to the presence of foreign armed forces (be they friendly or hostile).

This proposed international agreement, therefore, should encompass two essential elements of Lebanon's recovery. First, it should uphold Lebanon's independence, territorial integrity, and sovereignty within internationally recognized borders, and confirm the various UN resolutions calling for Israel's unconditional withdrawal from South Lebanon and the Bekaa. Although the agreement would be signed by Lebanon's neighbors and the major powers, its enforcement would require a reinforcement of the Lebanese Army, possibly supplemented on an interim basis by an international armed force (a UNIFIL empowered to use force?). Second, the agreement should be supported by an international loan and aid package to assist in rebuilding Lebanon's destroyed infrastructure and to help boost investor confidence. Investor confidence is vital, given that Lebanon's reconstruction depends on its ability to attract external funding (expected to cover two-thirds of all necessary capital expenditures).

Economic reconstruction. The economic program for reconstruction should define four elements: (1) a government strategy for the reconstruction process and a comprehensive, consistent set of economic policies;[6] (2) a set of sector priorities with respect to infrastructure and basic services (e.g., power, communications, water, and sewerage);[7] (3) the respective roles of government and the private sector during various stages of reconstruction—in particular, any potential privatizations should be planned and their financial consequences for the government's budget programmed; (4) an economic stabilization package, as well as macroeconomic policy objectives (i.e., monetary, exchange rate, and fiscal policies). Given the current fiscal crisis it is important to control and limit budget deficits, and to give the private sector better access to credit markets.[8]

Institute and promote regional economic development and equitable distribution of public resources. In particular, the reconstruction process and infrastructure spending should aim to repair the damage in regions that suffered disproportionately during the war (e.g., parts of Jabal Lubnan and the South) and to implement a priority program to provide infrastructure and public services in Lebanon's neglected areas (according to demand, as well as existing and future demographic patterns).[9]

RECONSTRUCTION REQUIREMENTS

Sixteen years of civil war and numerous Israeli invasions have produced substantial physical and human devastation. Over 150,000 people (about 5 percent of the resident population) were killed during the period 1975–1990; more than 300,000 where maimed, injured, or disabled.[10] Although no comprehensive, definitive survey of damage and destruction has been undertaken, partial evidence points to extensive damage across all sectors, with destruction of physical capital well in excess of U.S.$15 billion.[11] Basic infrastructure—roads, ports, communications, power, water, and waste management facilities—is in particularly bad shape, having suffered both war destruction and prolonged neglect (i.e., lack of investment and maintenance).

Table 13.1 indicates the magnitude of resources required for reconstruction.[12] It contains very rough estimates of required investment spending and other magnitudes for two reconstruction scenarios over a ten-year period starting in 1993.

Table 13.1 Reconstruction Scenarios, 1993–2002

Variables	Scenario 1	Scenario 2
Cumulative GDP (U.S.$ billion)	174	145
GDP growth rate (percentage, average)	17%	14%
Cumulative investment (U.S.$ billion)	37	26
Investment percentage of GDP (average)	26%	25%
government investment (U.S.$ billion)	7	3
percentage of total investment (average)	19%	11%
Normal government spending (U.S.$ billion)	26	22
Private investment (U.S.$ billion)	30	23
External finance (U.S.$ billion)	24	20
percentage of GDP (average)	14%	14%
percentage of total investment (average)	66%	78%

The important aspect of the table is that it provides orders of magnitude and indicates the relative importance of the private sector, as compared to the limited role of the public sector. It also suggests a number of useful observations concerning Lebanon's economic reconstruction requirements:

1. To regain prewar real income growth rates will require that high capital expenditures—in excess of U.S.$25 billion—and a high investment ratio—in excess of 25 percent of GDP—be sustained over a decade.
2. Given normal government spending and tax collection, there is limited scope for government investment spending. Therefore, the bulk of government investment spending should be concentrated in the early years and should target capital expenditures that are directly productive and that increase the private sector's production possibilities.
3. Resources arising from the flow of annual domestic saving will be able to contribute only about one-third of total investment requirements. Lebanon's reconstruction will, therefore, depend on external resources and foreign investment (both private and public) for the bulk of capital expenditures.

Box 13.1 Reconstruction Scenarios: Assumptions and Principles

The scenarios in Table 13.1 assume that the objective is to regain the prewar growth paths of real income and consumption over a given period. Clearly, the absorptive capacity of the economy and the ability of government to manage reconstruction are limited. Adjustment incurs substantial costs; hence, it is not optimal to attempt to reach the prewar real income path rapidly. I assume the projected growth rate of real output to be a weighted average of the gap between actual output and potential output and of the long-term potential growth rate of real output.[a] The simulations imply a gradual return, over twenty to twenty-five years, to the prewar path of real income: it takes more than one generation to rebuild and to regain the long-term potential level of real income.

Investment requirements are directly related to the projected output path through a "flexible accelerator" model of investment. Given the existing capital stock, an increase in real activity raises the expected rate of return to net investment, and, as a result, increases the rate of capital expenditures. Further, other things remaining constant, the lower the existing capital stock, the higher the marginal product of capital and the higher the expected rate of return to net investment, leading to higher capital expenditures. Hence the "flexible accelerator" model of investment implies that because of war-related destruction of capital, there will be above normal rates of return to investment, generating above normal investment rates.[b]

Normal government spending and government investment are projected on the following basis: (1) the size of the public sector will eventually return to the prewar pattern, so that normal spending will not exceed 15 percent to 18 percent of GDP, and (2) the government has to satisfy an intertemporal budget constraint: given the existing level of public debt outstanding, the present value of total government expenditures cannot exceed the present value of the tax and nontax revenue the government is able to collect. Alternatively, given government spending plans for normal and reconstruction activities, and given expected tax and nontax collections, the maximum amount of the public debt cannot exceed the difference between the present value of revenue and the present value of government spending. Public debt outstanding is limited by the government's ability to collect tax and nontax revenue currently and in the future, a measure of the government's fiscal capacity.[c] In turn, revenue is directly linked to the level of output and real activity. In particular, all other things equal, higher income growth rates allow a higher level of debt and higher government spending financed by larger tax revenues.

The scenarios are based on a number of important principles assumed to govern fiscal policy and public finance over the reconstruction period, including: (1) it is not optimal to raise taxes to finance the temporary costs of reconstruction; (2) it is optimal to borrow or issue debt both domestically and abroad to finance reconstruction and infrastructure projects (the government will be able to service and potentially able to repay debt at later dates when aggregate income and government revenues are higher); (3) taxation should be used to cover normal government spending, that is, the normal ratio (up to 18 percent) of expenditure to GDP. It is also assumed that tax administration has been reformed and that the tax collection rate has returned to normal, pre–civil war patterns.

(continued on next page)

Box 13.1 continued

Notes: a. Let $Y^*(t)$, $Y(t)$ denote the log of the potential and actual level of output, respectively, and let T represent the trend growth rate of real output; then the output path is generated by: $Y(t) - Y(t-1) = v[Y^*(t) - Y(t-1)] + (1-v) T$, where v is the rate of adjustment parameter. Note that as the output gap $[Y^*(t) - Y(t-1)]$ is reduced, the growth rate converges to the trend growth rate of 5.9 percent per annum. Clearly, the lower the costs of adjustment, the larger the value of the adjustment parameter.

b. The model utilized to generate projected investment requirements is of the form: $I(t) = a + bY(t) + cK(t-1)$ a, $b > 0$, $c < 0$ where I is the rate of investment, Y is the level of real output, and K denotes the capital stock.

c. The projections are based on the assumption that tax and nontax revenue collection revert to the normal, prewar patterns of revenue collection. Nontax revenues include income from property, fines, fees, and charges, including those arising from crude oil pipeline transit fees. Pre-1975, these nontax revenues contributed between 18 to 24 percent of total receipts; they could represent an important source of revenue in the future.

RETURN MIGRATION AND
THE FINANCING OF RECONSTRUCTION

Lebanon's reconstruction requires substantial resources—especially from external sources. However, Lebanon is seeking more than financial support alone. The country's reconstruction also requires the skills of its former residents, now located abroad (estimated at 750,000 people).[13]

The return of Lebanon's human resources will prove critical to the success of the reconstruction process. First, returnees contribute directly to the labor supply and to total output. Second, they bring with them important skills and technical know-how (acquired abroad) that they can transfer to the local labor force thereby raising local productivity and capacity to adapt to technical progress.[14] Third, they possess professional skills that could make important contributions to managing reconstruction (e.g., technical knowledge and the know-how to plan, organize, and implement projects).

Although the demand for returning expatriate labor is high, the supply side is problematic. For most expatriate Lebanese, return to Lebanon is an investment decision: the total income prospects of return are compared against the prospects of remaining abroad.[15] Total income includes direct earned income (of self and family members), the value of amenities (hotels, educational and leisure centers, hospitals, and the like), as well as nonmonetary factors such as availability of public facilities and services (education, health, parks, museums, and the like). It also includes perceived future economic prospects for their children.

The decision to return is based, therefore, on an intricate set of perceptions concerning (1) availability of political, physical, social, and legal infrastructure, (2) social amenities and housing, (3) long-term positive economic prospects, and (4) expectations of low income taxes. Reversing Lebanon's brain drain requires that returnees perceive a permanent change in the country. Their decisions are based on the expectation of long-term, credible change in the above mentioned factors and of the country's commitment to reform. Temporary measures or policy changes that do not involve long-term commitments will be insufficient to attract emigrant professionals and skilled laborers.

Likewise, the decisions made by potential foreign investors (both public and private) are guided by their perceptions of Lebanon's potential benefits and risks. Attracting private capital (including direct investment) requires the expectation of long-term political, macroeconomic, and financial stability to reduce the perceived risk of investment. In principle, investment in Lebanon will yield above normal (after tax) returns. Moreover, opportunities abound in most sectors and across a broad range of activities, especially in real estate development (including the major project of rebuilding downtown Beirut), tourism, banking, trade, financial services, and all activities related to reconstruction of infrastructure.

To attract foreign private capital (and ensure that it is channeled into productive investments) Lebanon needs to strengthen its banking system and develop its financial and capital markets. Both debt and equity markets require development. In particular, there is potential for a successful revival of the Beirut stock exchange, which, in theory, could have a capitalization of between U.S.$ 2 billion to $2.5 billion.[16]

Attracting official capital resources—such as loans, grants, aid, or by way of a Lebanon Reconstruction and Development Fund (LRDF), envisaged by the Ta'if Accord—requires a credible reconstruction strategy and a national financial program. Given the government's limited fiscal capacity, it is important to control the buildup of external public debt to ensure that it be effectively serviced. A number of recommendations can be noted in this context:

- Resources should be channeled to productive investments that generate a competitive rate of return and compensate for underlying risk; they should not be directed at raising consumption.
- Funding should be on a project specific and not a general purpose basis. Moreover, project funding should be based on feasibility studies or cost-benefit analysis, and projects should aim to be self-financing over time.[17]

• Because accountability is crucial to reassuring external funding sources, externally funded projects should—whenever feasible—be undertaken by lenders/donors, possibly on a turnkey basis. This would assist in reducing potential bribery, corruption, and diversion of funds.

• To access foreign financial resources—in particular from Lebanese abroad—Lebanon should consider launching Lebanon Reconstruction and Development Bonds (LRDBs), long-term (ten to fifteen year) bonds denominated in foreign currencies. These bonds could provide long-term funding suitable for financing infrastructure and long gestation projects (e.g., power stations, ports, roads). Indeed, the LRDF could launch such bonds. Governments wishing to assist Lebanon could provide guarantees or tax exemptions on such bonds, substantially reducing financing costs.[18]

• The LRDF could act as a major channel for international aid and loans. It could also provide incentives to private capital by sponsoring the creation of private investment and venture capital funds (and participating in their funding). Such investment funds could take equity stakes or invest in the debt issued by new or existing enterprises. They could also be attractive to foreign investors who do not have sufficient information to invest directly, and who are looking for a means to diversify investment risk.

• The LRDF could also play a major investment banking role in a potential privatization program for public sector entities and utilities. For example, it could provide initial resources and funding to rehabilitate these enterprises prior to privatization, and could prepare them for an initial public offering.

STRUCTURAL REFORMS FOR MODERNIZATION AND RECONSTRUCTION

A successful economic reconstruction program demands that the authorities implement a number of economic policy changes and structural reforms. I focus, briefly, on a number of the more critical areas for reform.[19] Clearly, most of the reforms proposed below could only be implemented by a government that is credible, committed to reform, and able to generate domestic and international support. It must also be capable of pursuing economic policies that are unlikely to be reversed over time.

Fiscal Reform

The war devastated the government's capacity to administer and control its expenditures and revenues. In turn, this breakdown in the fiscal system led to growing budget deficits, an explosion of the public debt, and a resort to monetary finance.[20] The result was an acceleration of price and wage inflation that approached hyperinflation during 1985–1990. It is critical for the success of the reconstruction process that the government secure a steady stream of revenue. This requires comprehensive overhaul and reform of the tax and budget systems (presently based on an outdated, pre–World War II French code). The major objectives of fiscal reform should be to:

Provide tax and nontax revenues to cover the permanent component of government expenditures. In the pre-1975 period, total government expenditures varied between 13 percent and 15 percent of GDP, reflecting the government's role in the economy. Given the increase in permanent government spending during reconstruction, and the increased expenditure necessary to maintain the higher stock of infrastructure capital, the size of government is bound to rise. The fiscal system should be designed so that the yield from tax and nontax revenues amounts to between 18 percent and 20 percent of GDP on the average (taking into account the effects of normal fluctuations in economic activity on revenues).

Reduce dependence on indirect taxes (custom duties and the like). Indirect taxes are regressive and adversely affect the poorer strata of the population.

Introduce a modern system of personal and corporate income taxation and maintain low income tax rates. Income tax rates should be in the range of 10 percent to 20 percent. To create a modern tax collection system, the government must invest in the infrastructure of tax administration, as well as impose and enforce strict penalties for tax evasion.

Introduce market prices for public sector services (power, water, transport, and communications). The revenue collections systems for these amenities also require reform.

Reform the budget process. A unified budget that regroups the central government, commissions, agencies, and autonomous bodies should be introduced along with a regular audit process, to ensure accountability and control graft and corruption.

Index the tax system for the effects of inflation. A large number of taxes and revenues from concessions and government-owned properties are set according to a specific basis and have not been adjusted for inflation. These should be changed to an ad valorem basis. Similarly, the tax system should be designed to eliminate the effects of bracket creep. With earned income rising because of inflation, people have been moved into higher tax brackets.[21]

Privatization

Presently, the public sector's physical capacity and overall efficiency in providing services and utilities is either severely impaired or nonexistent. Privatization of a number of government-owned activities could help to resolve existing problems. Services such as communications, power, and transport are potential candidates for privatization. However, there are a number of meanings and possible means for "privatization."[22] In Lebanon's case, the major issues tend to revolve around the following questions:

• How do we avoid turning a public monopoly into a private, uncontrolled monopoly that could impose higher prices and, possibly, lower quality service? In many cases, the problem is one of management efficiency rather than public ownership. Implementing private sector management practices may be the solution, rather than a sale or transfer of assets.
• Given the small size of the Lebanese economy, how do we guard against production inefficiency stemming from the less than optimal size of production and distribution facilities? The optimization of facility size may eliminate competition by precluding the possibility of several (or many) private sector suppliers.
• What valuation should be placed on assets destined for sale to the private sector? In some cases the enterprises are loss making (e.g., electricity), and the private sector might require a subsidy to take over the enterprise!

There are also sociopolitical considerations. As a consequence of war and the absence of security, various groups and militias took over government functions, enterprises, and activities. By restoring public enterprises (and their services) as part of the reconstruction process, the government will demonstrate its will and ability to reunite the country and restore confidence in national institutions. Privatization could be considered at a later stage once essential services and utilities have been restored. Lastly, and above all, Lebanon needs to create a legal, regulatory, and institutional framework for privatization to set common standards across the entire Lebanese territory and possibly to subsidize certain regions or areas.

Housing Policy and Rent Control

A substantial part of Lebanon's stock of residential and office buildings has been damaged or destroyed. In addition, the war caused large displacements of the population (both voluntary and forced). As a result, a substantial disequilibrium exists between the total demand and supply of housing, and in its distribution across regions. Restoring the stock of business and residential buildings, and supplying new buildings, is therefore an urgent priority.

In addition to the destruction and damage, the combination of high inflation rates since 1985 (averaging over 80 percent a year) with past and existing rent control legislation has (1) generated substantial price distortions by lowering the relative price of property services compared to market price levels, (2) led to substantial wealth redistribution away from property owners and, more important, (3) dramatically cut the market value of rented property, and (4) led to shortages of rental property.

As a consequence, rent controls act as a tax: they lower personal and labor mobility, reduce the supply of new residential and business space, and remove incentives to restore existing housing stocks. Importantly, rent controls lower the value of property as collateral in the credit market, adversely affecting bank balance sheets and impeding efficient credit market operations.

To rectify these problems, plans for large-scale housing projects are now under consideration. However, the housing problem is largely the consequence of market distortions caused by government policy and parliamentary legislation. Had rent controls not been enforced, and had rental rates been allowed to increase with the market prices during 1986–1990, the market for housing would not be in disequilibrium today. Past government intervention and political expediency are the source of the housing problem.[23]

Rapid and complete removal of rent controls is critical to the reconstruction process. New construction should not be subject to controls; existing property should be freed. Removing these controls means that rental rates will rise and wealth will be redistributed back in favor of property owners. Therefore, some measures may be warranted to offset the capital loss to lower income persons. A solution here would be to impose a capital gains tax (a housing tax), to absorb a substantial percentage of the increase in rental rates. The proceeds of the special housing tax would be used to fund or subsidize low-cost housing either through a special program or through the Banque de l'Habitat. The eligible portion of the affected population—the poor and lower income strata—could borrow capital for housing investments at preferential conditions. Hence, the basic policy measure would be to accompany rent deregulation with appropriate incentives aimed at increasing the supply of low to medium cost housing.

Banking and Monetary Reform

The banking system must play an important financial intermediary role during reconstruction in order to channel domestic saving and international capital into efficient investments. The existing system, however, is riddled with problems. In addition to war-related administration regression and asset impairment, it suffers from capital inadequacy arising from insufficient provisions against past and potential loan losses, and the reduced market value of property held as security. A number of reforms and policy changes are therefore required to resuscitate the financial system:

Mergers. The central bank has encouraged and enforced mergers to absorb smaller and higher risk banks. Acceleration of this process would strengthen the financial soundness of the banking system. In particular, any further rescue operations of ailing banks should be stopped; it is better that they fail than become a burden on taxpayers.

Banking sector equity. Within the near future, Lebanese banks should move to increase equity resources and the capital-to-risk asset ratio in line with the Basel Accord. This process should be accompanied by tighter banking supervision and control as well as closer regulatory coordination with external banking authorities.

Central bank independence. Over the past decade the central bank has been reduced to the role of government financier, with an increasing proportion of budget deficits being financed through money creation. It is therefore imperative to make the central bank independent of the treasury and government. Monetary policy should aim to control inflation through control of money growth. The central bank should not become a reconstruction or development bank.

Management of international reserves. Lebanon holds substantial international reserves, valued in excess of U.S.$4.5 billion (as of end-1992), about two-thirds in gold—more than 9 million ounces.[24] In the 1980s, Parliament passed legislation, ostensibly to prevent a squandering or *mainmise* of reserves under the Gemayel administration, that prohibited the central bank from transactions in its gold holdings, effectively freezing the holdings. This legislation should be rescinded, as this constraint on management of reserves is both costly and inefficient. Gold only generates a return or yield when there is a sustained upward movement in the price. This, however, is likely to occur only in international inflationary circumstances (e.g., as in the late 1960s and 1970s) and is unlikely in the near future. Gold holdings should be managed as part of an international portfolio structured to earn a return comparable, if possible, to the return that could be earned through alternative forms of investment such as deposits and bonds. In particular, I would advocate: (1) gradual conversion of Lebanon's gold holdings—in cooperation with major central banks—into a bond portfolio invested in government bonds issued by major countries (the United States, Canada, Italy, Germany, Switzerland, Japan, France, and United Kingdom); (2) creation of a competent, trustworthy bond portfolio management commission within the central bank that includes external representatives and advisers;

and (3) if judged necessary, application of existing legislative restrictions to the bond holdings.

Had the above policy been in operation since 1986 with proceeds of gold sales invested in a diversified international government bond portfolio, the value of the bond holdings would now exceed U.S.$6 billion (as compared to the gold's current market of about U.S.$3 billion).[25] At current yields on international government bonds, annual earnings would be in excess of U.S.$250 million. The government cannot afford to forgo such income; it could potentially cover a substantial portion of the budget deficit, estimated at about U.S.$900 million in the past two years.

Development of Lebanon's capital markets. Developing Lebanon's capital markets is integral to a financing program for funding reconstruction.[26] Lebanon needs to develop its debt and equity markets to provide the financial instruments suitable for medium- and long-term investment. The availability of well-functioning capital markets will greatly facilitate the process of attracting foreign private capital.

The rudiments of a market for investing in and trading government debt are present. The size of the domestic public debt, which in 1993 exceeded U.S.$2 billion, is likely to grow substantially during reconstruction. The institutional, legal, regulatory, and technical framework should be elaborated to enable transactions in debt likely to be issued by private corporations and by public utilities (power, ports, water, transport, and communications) to finance capital projects.

The development of the Beirut stock market could yield a promising source of capital. There are several sources of growth for this market. First, there are the shares in the downtown Beirut real estate development company (Solidere) with a capitalization that could be about U.S.$1.5 billion. In addition, there are potential equity issues from the cement and other industries, banking, hotels, and tourism as well as from the potential privatization of public utilities. The total initial size of the market could be about U.S.$2.5 billion, which is comparable in size to other emerging stock markets. Second, if the process of economic liberalization continues in Syria, it is likely to be accompanied by a privatization of Syrian industry and commerce. Those companies, as well as Lebanese-Syrian joint venture companies, could be listed on the Beirut stock exchange, expanding its scope and the possibility of risk diversification.

LEBANON'S DEVELOPMENT IN REGIONAL CONTEXT

As Lebanon moves into a reconstruction phase after sixteen years of war, it must reconsider its regional role. Three strategic elements should be taken into consideration: (1) Saudi Arabia and the Gulf countries have developed direct financial and trade links with the West; (2) Syria is in the process of a major liberalization and privatization of its economy; and (3) peace negotiations are under way between the Arab states and Israel. Each of these developments suggests implications for the future of Lebanon and its economy.

First, Lebanon's economy cannot rely solely on its traditional banking and financial services. It should develop more specialized financial services, exploiting its comparative advantage in human resources. Indeed, under appropriate conditions, Beirut could become a regional capital market providing capital market related services, channeling funds, and serving as a trading link for emerging stock markets in Jordan, Kuwait, Saudi Arabia, and Syria.

Second, the Lebanese and Syrian economies are, to a large extent, complementary. As Syria opens up, there should be substantial scope for a mutually beneficial increase in trade of goods and services. Prospects also exist for increased specialization in each of the economies. For example, (1) Syria's raw agricultural output could be an input for the development of an agro-industrial and food processing capability in the Bekaa and North Lebanon; (2) Syrian crude oil could be processed in Lebanon's refineries and its gas used in power stations feeding both Syria and Lebanon; and (3) Syria could draw on Lebanon's experience in realizing its own underdeveloped tourism potential.

Third, as prospects for peace in the region improve, there is scope for a multinational trade, aid, and development package whose purpose would be to (1) provide adjustment assistance in the transition away from economic systems dominated by military and defense requirements, (2) support liberalization of the Syrian and other economies in the region toward competitive market systems, and (3) fund regional projects in a number of areas—transport, communications, water, and power resources—that would promote and enhance peace. Lebanon can and should play a pivotal role in designing and identifying the objectives of such a regional plan.

NOTES

1. See the discussion in Part 1 of Jack Hirshleifer, *Economic Behaviour in Adversity* (Chicago: University of Chicago Press, 1987). Literature on the economic aspects of civil—as opposed to international or regional—conflict is limited.

2. It is estimated that prior to 1975 the top 20 percent of the population received 55 percent of total income, while the bottom 20 percent received only 4 percent. The war increased poverty and led to greater inequalities in income distribution.

3. For analysis of the Ta'if Accord, see the chapter by Maila in this volume and his more detailed analysis in *Les Cahiers de l'Orient* nos. 14–17 (1992).

4. Some of these ideas in this and the preceding paragraph are developed in Nasser Saidi, "A Programme for Economic and Political Freedom in Lebanon" (unpublished, Beirut, 1993).

5. A specific policy proposal for a gradualist approach to electoral reform could be as follows: (1) allow up to one-fourth or one-third of the seats in the next parliamentary election to be open to all candidates, without sectarian or other restrictions. Increase the proportions in subsequent elections, thereby creating an open system within twelve to sixteen years (an acceptable horizon for such matters); (2) institute a bicameral system and a senate (as envisaged in the Ta'if Accord) to protect the rights of minorities. See also the chapter by el-Hoss in this volume.

6. In particular, the strategy should set out the sources of the financing program for reconstruction such that the potential inflationary consequences of increased government expenditures are limited.

7. The Bechtel Dar Al-Handasah report *Recovery Planning for the Reconstruction and Development of Lebanon* (Beirut, December 1991) sets out the elements of a priority rehabilitation program.

8. For further discussion of the elements of an economic stabilization package see Nasser Saidi, "The Role of Capital Markets in Lebanon's Reconstruction," *Journal of Economic Research* vol. 2 no. 1 (Beirut, 1993).

9. One possibility is to create regional development funds in which the level of funding is related to regional income per head and its deviation from the national average.

10. See N. Saidi, "Economic Consequences of the War in Lebanon," Banque du Liban, *Bulletin Trimestriel* nos. 28–30 (1987).

11. For a comprehensive discussion see Ahmed Sbaiti, *Reconstruction and Development Needs of Lebanon's Economic Sectors: 1991 and Beyond,* presentation at CIIPS Workshop no. 2 (Ottawa, December 1990); the World Bank's 1983 Mission Report; and the 1991 Bechtel-Dar Al-Handasah report which identifies a priority program with sector funding requirements totaling $4.4 billion (1991 prices) spread over five years and 126 projects.

12. Note that the table identifies investment requirements to regain the prewar growth path of real income; that is, it assumes the economy will catch up (over a twenty-five year period) to the level of income that would have prevailed in the absence of war. Clearly, the capital expenditures are substantially more than those required for reconstruction. See Nasser Saidi, *War, Reconstruction and the Public Debt* (Beirut: Banque du Liban, June 1984) for discussion of the methodology and underlying macroeconomic constraints and relationships.

13. See the papers by N. Khalaf, "Manpower Movement and the Lebanese Conflict," in Banque du Liban, *Bulletin Trimestriel* no. 11 (1981), pp. 4–12, and "Manpower Requirements of Lebanon's Reconstruction Plan," Banque du Liban, *Bulletin Trimestriel* no. 12 (1982), pp. 4–16.

14. For discussion of these "complementarity effects," see Nasser Saidi, "The Role of Capital Markets."

15. See discussion in Nasser Saidi, "Lebanon 1988: Potential and Conditions for Reconstruction, Return Migration and Capital Flows," and papers by J. Faddoul and H. Bsat in *L'économie Libanaise face aux défis* no. 3 (Beirut: Rassemblement des Dirigeants et Chefs d'Entreprises Libanais, 1989).

16. For discussion on developing the debt and equity markets, see N. Saidi, "The Role of Capital Markets."

17. A good example is Beirut International Airport (BIA). Assuming that BIA is an independent authority, it could issue long-term bonds to finance the rehabilita-

tion and expansion of its facilities. Its debt could be serviced from user charges (e.g., passenger taxes), landing fees, and the sale and/or rental of duty-free concessions. Similar financing techniques could be used for the ports and a number of public utilities. With respect to certain other infrastructural projects and purely public goods, the government should clearly identify the sources of debt service and repayment.

18. Providing an exemption of interest income or capital gains from foreign taxation can lead to an annual saving of up to 3 to 4 percent in debt service, depending on the level of interest and tax rates. Israel has used this device very effectively in its sale of Israel development bonds to Jews in the United States. The foreign bonds issued by Israel have a tax status similar to that of tax exempt local municipal bonds.

19. Note that we are addressing reforms of an economic nature as compared to organizational, administrative, or other reforms equally crucial to the country's modernization. Also, a number of other positive economic measures that do not require radical policy changes could be implemented, such as (a) seeking preferential trade status with the EEC and the Gulf Co-operation Council, and (b) developing free trade zones.

20. I discuss the sources and consequences of budget deficits and their financing in N. Saidi, "Deficits, Inflation and Depreciation: Lebanon's Experience, 1964–1988," in Nadim Shehadi (ed.), *Politics and the Economy in Lebanon* (London: Centre for Lebanese Studies and The Centre of Near and Middle Eastern Studies, 1989), and in "Government Spending and Taxes: Anatomy of a Crisis 1964–1982," Banque du Liban, *Bulletin Trimestriel* no. 23 (1984), pp. 5–11.

21. This has aggravated unequal distribution of after-tax income. For example, employees and salaried individuals have faced tax rates of up to 40 percent on incomes equivalent to $500 per month. A related distortion has been increased tax avoidance through the payment of bonuses and other forms of nontaxable income.

22. See R. Hemming and A. Mansoor, "Privatization and Public Enterprises," IMF Occasional Paper no. 56 (January 1988) and Said el-Nagger (ed.), "Privatization and Structural Adjustment in the Arab Countries," paper presented at a seminar held by the United Arab Emirates in Abu Dhabi, 5–7 December 1988.

23. Beneficiaries of rent controls have created lobbies and pressure groups to maintain these controls, meaning that politicians can now use the leverage they possess in controlling rents to their own advantage in the political marketplace.

24. This ratio, one of the highest for any country, is not justified given the absence of any yield on the holdings.

25. See N. Saidi, "Management of International Reserves: A Portfolio Approach and Gold Conversion Proposal" (unpublished, Beirut, 1993).

26. See N. Saidi, "The Role of Capital Markets."

Part 4

·

Toward
Sociopolitical Stability

14

The War System: Militia Hegemony and Reestablishment of the State

Georges Corm

For more than fifteen years, Lebanese society was prey to a system of totalitarian terror perpetrated by armed militias. The militias shared common goals: divide Lebanon's traditionally consensual civil society along sectarian lines and paralyze the Lebanese state. This fundamental fact was often overlooked, however, because analysts tended to portray local aspects of the fighting as a spontaneous, quasi-biological struggle between elements of the population labeled "Christian" and "Muslim." Observers tended to focus on the "Christian" or "Muslim" declarations of militia chieftains, rarely examining the totalitarian foundations of militia activities, despite an abundance of evidence.

I have elsewhere described how the totalitarian militia system emerged and became firmly entrenched.[1] I shall briefly summarize these events, before discussing the factors that have impeded the clear understanding of the militia phenomenon. Only a clear grasp of the problem will enable us to struggle effectively against its continuance in one guise or another.

MODERN HISTORICAL PRECEDENTS IN THE REGION

The disintegration of the Ottoman Empire prompted the emergence of armed militias that radically transformed Middle Eastern society by sowing violence and discord. These militias emerged because of interference by foreign powers in the affairs of the declining Ottoman Empire. Outside

A previous version of this chapter was printed in *Maghreb-Machrek* no. 131, January–March 1991 (Paris: la Documentation Française) as "Liban: le 'système' milices" by Georges Corm.

powers poured arms, financial support, and training into the hands of local elites who were rising up against the institutions of the established authority. Both the Armenian militias and the Haganah (the armed wing of the Zionist movement) provide examples of this phenomenon. As is well known, the French, British, and Russian armies proved incapable of protecting their Armenian clients, and the entire Armenian community in Turkey was violently eradicated. The case of the Haganah, however, was more "successful." The British, Russians, and Americans increased their financial and military support, working diligently toward the establishment of the state of Israel. The result was the uprooting of most of the Palestinian community from most of its ancestral homeland.

Indeed, in the space of fifty years, large stretches of the former Ottoman Empire were completely transformed, with radical shifts in population and mode of government. Armed militias founded on ethnic or religious loyalties claimed the right to establish national states and protect particular ethnic or religious groups. In so doing, they brought about radical demographic, social, and political changes.

This historical backdrop is crucial to understanding the role of militias in Lebanon, especially because a considerable number of Armenians and a large number of Palestinians sought refuge in Lebanon. By 1967, the Palestinians in Lebanon had begun to form armed militias with the dual aim of reconquering the lost Palestinian lands and protecting the Palestinian population in Lebanon against attacks by the Israeli Army and certain Lebanese militias. Lebanese militias began to emerge in the early 1970s and were hostile to an armed Palestinian presence in their country.

It is important to note that large-scale military operations in Lebanon did not begin on 13 April 1975 (a date often erroneously taken as the beginning of the war), but on 28 December 1968, when Israel mounted a raid on the Beirut International Airport, destroying Lebanon's entire fleet of civilian airliners.[2] After that date, Israeli armed incursions into Lebanon became common occurrences. One could recall, for instance, the assassination of three Palestinian leaders in Beirut by an Israeli Army commando in the spring of 1973. It is in the framework of this severe destabilization of the Lebanese state that the militias emerged and flourished.

CHARACTERISTICS OF THE MILITIA SYSTEM

Building a Material and Military Base

The first concern of the militias was to build a material base which would enable them to finance their drive for domination.

Looting and confiscation of private property. Actions of this type were numerous and incessant. The most famous was the pillaging of the port of

Beirut in 1976 by the Phalange militia (estimated to have caused between U.S.$1 billion and $2 billion in damage). Another example is the looting of the downtown and market areas (also estimated at U.S.$1 billion to $2 billion) by agreement between two supposedly enemy forces: the Phalange and a militia coalition known at the time as the "Palestino-progressive." Looting, theft, and confiscation of property after 1975 probably totaled another U.S.$1 billion to $2 billion. In total, the various militias seized approximately U.S.$5 billion to $7 billion.

Militia tolls and taxes. The militias demanded outright ransoms from industrialists, merchants, or wealthy investors (easily totaling U.S.$500 million since 1975). Other fund-raising schemes included taxes on exports and imports and on the movement of people through illegal ports established by the militias (and not subject to any state control); restaurant taxes; tolls on the passage of goods from one militia-controlled zone to another; and taxes on gasoline and flour.[3]

Destruction of the banking sector and speculation on the Lebanese pound. In the wake of the 1982 Israeli invasion, the Phalangist party came to power and continued the large-scale looting of Lebanon, albeit on a more sophisticated level. The Phalange undertook actions that appeared to be bent on destroying the banking sector and causing the collapse of the Lebanese pound—for profit, of course. Banks headed by people within or close to the Phalange began to fail, e.g., in 1982–1983, First Phoenician Bank and Capital Trust Bank. These two newly founded banks held considerable reserves, and it is likely that funds were embezzled on a massive scale to benefit the party (700 million and 350 million Lebanese pounds respectively, worth more than U.S.$250 million at the time). Between 1982 and 1988, a confidant of Amine Gemayel (the Phalangist president of Lebanon) ran Intra Investment Co., a holding company largely government controlled. Intra served as a conduit for embezzled capital and eventually collapsed, along with its main banking outlets, Banque al-Macherk and Banque de Participation et de Placements (in Paris and Geneva). Apparently, all major Lebanese militias took some share of the profits generated by collapsing banks or the plunging exchange rate of the Lebanese pound. Indeed, the pound began its precipitous decline after the Phalangists replaced the directors of the central bank and the Commission de Controle des Banques in 1985. These militia profits were generated at the expense of innocent Lebanese depositors and citizens.

Drugs, toxic wastes, contraband dealings with neighboring countries, thefts from foreign humanitarian assistance, piracies at sea. Although no precise data are available, these activities are so notorious in Lebanon that they are virtually impossible to deny. The cultivation of drugs has increased dramatically in the Bekaa Valley, where the Syrian Army has been installed since 1976. The militias clearly play an important role in transporting and refining drugs, as indicated, for example, by the dismantling in 1989 in France of a drug trafficking ring linked to one of the large Lebanese militias. Annual revenues from the drug trade are estimated to be in the U.S.$700 million to $1 billion range. It is impossible to determine what share of these funds is disbursed among the various interested parties in Lebanon.

Arms appropriated from the Lebanese Army. After 1975, the militias seized great quantities of arms from the Lebanese Army arsenals. Despite militia seizures, the government continued to replenish its stocks, usually paying in cash, as was the case in 1982–1983 when Lebanon purchased U.S. arms valued at U.S.$1 billion.

*   *   *

It is estimated that through all activities of the kind listed above, the large militias procured an average of U.S.$1 billion per year, for a total of some $15 billion over a fifteen-year period. These financial resources were employed to pay fighting units and administrative employees of the parties, create personal fortunes for the main militia chieftains (much of which is deposited in banks outside the country), and invest in various industrial, commercial, real estate, and banking enterprises.

Militia coffers were also filled with both cash and armaments by outside powers. Indeed, the militias often functioned as clients through which regional powers could exert their influence. The so-called Christian militias received assistance from Israel, probably from Saudi Arabia, Jordan, and Egypt, and, between 1987–1990, from Iraq (to counter Syrian influence in Lebanon). The so-called Muslim militias were basically assisted by the PLO, Libya, and Iran (which primarily supported Hizballah, with some support to Amal). After 1982, the budget of the Iranian embassy in Lebanon surpassed U.S.$100 million per year in order to pay militiamen recruited by Hizballah. A rough estimate of all foreign assistance is double that of the amounts raised locally.

Thus, over a fifteen-year period, Lebanese militias accrued some U.S.$30 billion to $40 billion in armaments, supplies, and money from domestic and foreign sources. In return, they inflicted U.S.$20 billion to $30 billion of destruction on public and private property through intentional, blind shelling of civilian targets. Militia actions produced social and economic devastation for the communities that they claimed to represent and protect: tens of thousands of Lebanese became impoverished, displaced, or exiled. The social, political, and economic composition of every Lebanese community changed drastically from what it was in 1975.

Types of Violence and the Creation of Community Ghettos

Generally, armed factions in a civil war employ violence, in which the civilian population suffers cruelly, in order to dominate the entire territory, eliminate opposing factions, and reconstitute a functioning state as quickly as possible. In the case of Lebanon, this pattern clearly does not apply.

Apart from the spring of 1976, when the Lebanese National Movement attempted to invade the territory dominated by the so-called conservative Christian militias, the violence practiced by the militias since 13 April 1975 clearly shows that their aims were threefold: to paralyze the state and the army; to divide Lebanon into sectarian ghettos; and to terrorize the population by treating Lebanese not on the basis of their individual views (e.g., pro- or anti-Palestinian, pro- or anti-reform) but on the basis of the community to which they are ascribed.

With the exception of the fighting in the spring of 1976 and in the Shouf and the South organized by the Israeli Army in 1982–1983 and 1984–1985, the militias very quickly acknowledged one another and their respective communal territories.[4] It was the civilian population that spontaneously refused to accept the division of Lebanon into communal ghettos, and desired continued freedom of movement. The militias, in order to prevent Lebanese civilians from venturing outside their communal ghettos and the protective cover of "their" militia, inflicted unspeakable violence on innocents. In fact, most casualties in the conflict were civilians who were not aligned with any particular militia or ideology. These people were victimized by the following means:

- *sniping,* used to prevent movement from an area dominated by one particular militia to others, or at least making such movement extremely dangerous. The number of people killed or wounded by snipers is estimated at about 20,000.
- *kidnapping* of civilians without any political affiliation (carried out by militias or groups protected by the militias). These kidnappings were perpetrated on a religious basis whenever citizens entered areas deemed to belong to a religious community not their own. The number of people who were kidnapped and who disappeared without a trace or whose mutilated bodies have been recovered is estimated at about 15,000.
- *blind shelling* of civilian apartment buildings in areas dominated by other militias. These shellings were aimed at ordinary, nonpoliticized citizens in order to demonstrate that they, too, faced anonymous danger at any time from other religious communities. The number of these victims is estimated at some 80,000.

In all three cases, people were not victimized by armed factions that hoped to dominate the entire country but rather by a system that directed violence against the communal identities of the Lebanese. The reasons for this focus were twofold, (1) to bind Lebanese of a particular religious faith to the militia that claimed to represent and defend their community against other sectarian groups; and (2) to cleanse minority groups from certain areas in the large cities, as well as from communally mixed towns and rural regions.[5] When religiously motivated kidnappings were not sufficient, militias resorted to mass expulsions (e.g., the incidents in Ras al-Nabaa, Karantina, Damour, and the Shouf, to name but a few).[6]

Sectarian demarcation lines were established throughout the country by the spring of 1976 and were never changed thereafter, although at times they were temporarily dismantled when regional events produced attempts to reconstitute a central government under the influence of one or another of the regional powers (e.g., Syria in 1977 and Israel in 1982).

This is not the place to examine the militias' roles in the policies of one or another of the regional powers. It is important to note, however, that all the militias behaved in similar fashion, as if they were genuine partners in crime against the civilian populations that they allegedly were protecting and defending. Their combined actions culminated in the suppression of all liberty, especially the freedom to think and express oneself in terms other than defending the identity of one's own community.

Systematic Elimination of Freedom of Expression

Freedom of expression was eliminated at a different rate in different areas of Lebanon during the war. Public muzzling depended on the region and the extent of internal divisions within the particular militia. The Phalangist drive for domination, and the active support it received from certain regional and international powers, led very quickly to the suppression of freedom of expression in the so-called "Christian" areas. This control was imposed allegedly to preserve "Christian society" and maintain its cultural differences from "Islamic society." Control was effected by the following means:

- *assassinations* and then *expulsions* of politicized citizens belonging to the parties of the Lebanese National Movement, especially its leading Christian members who lived in areas dominated by the Phalange;
- *brutal attacks* on any Christian political faction that did not align itself with the positions taken by the head of the party or of the militia (e.g., Ehden, Safra, etc.);
- *prohibition* of the sale of newspapers that expressed opposing views;
- *development of militia-run press organs* to voice their political lines.

The diversity of political forces and policies in the so-called Muslim camp, including Palestinians and Syrians, hampered the development of a legitimating political code that was as coherent as that of the Christians. However, each of the three large "Muslim" militias (the Druze PSP, Shi'ite Amal and Hizballah) developed its own media. After 1982, the rising power of Hizballah reinforced the trend to totalitarianism (in particular through the assassination of neo-Marxist, and therefore secular, intellectuals) with the purpose of rendering all political expression in the so-called Muslim areas "Islamic." Thus, an authoritarian form of political expression was created parallel to that established in the so-called Christian areas.

The Lebanese media were completely transformed by militia activities. State-controlled media, which had a monopoly on radio and television until 1975, were completely supplanted by militia outlets. The two or three independent newspapers that managed to survive practiced severe self-censorship in order to avoid militia reprisals for any article that openly criticized either the militias or their regional sponsors. When several Lebanese journalists were assassinated, the media took the message to heart, as is perfectly understandable.[7] The sole purpose of the militia-owned and militia-controlled press was to justify their policies, legitimize their criminal activities (by which they pursued their policies), and transfer the blame to other armed factions or their regional sponsors.

When foreign newspapers continued to arrive in Lebanon at all, their price was prohibitive for ordinary citizens. In any case, the foreign press never discussed the fact that militia totalitarianism violated basic human rights. Instead, it tended to view the emergence of the militia system as a logical and natural consequence of what it considered to be a civil war between Christians and Muslims, both of whom had some legitimate claims. This perspective obscured the international community's understanding of the criminal nature of militia activities.

In addition, the militias were very active overseas, producing informational pamphlets, making political contacts, and raising funds, as well as infiltrating and monitoring expatriate Lebanese communities. All activities of Lebanese emigres were closely watched, and intimidation or diversion techniques were employed whenever dissident opinions began to gain ground.

Disregard for the State and Religious Institutions

The militias aimed from the very outset to paralyze the state, not to seize it. The destruction and looting of state property and resources clearly demonstrate that the ultimate purpose of the militias was to dismember state and country. One should note, however, the energetic and ingenious efforts of civil servants on all levels to keep the wheels of government turning, despite militia pressure. Members of the Lebanese Army also struggled valiantly to uphold their institution, despite constant attempts by the militia system to dismember it (in order to organize battalions on a confessional basis, thereby making them militia affiliates). The militias did succeed in paralyzing the army through blackmail and assassination of Lebanese parliamentarians and other leading political personalities. Moreover, the so-called presidential elections of 1976, 1982, and 1989 were parodies: When regional and other powers chose to intervene directly in elections, they hid behind militia groups (which would often carry out the regional will) or engaged their powerful propaganda machines to justify outside interference.

Even religious institutions were not spared. Respected religious leaders who sought to end militia rule (and the accompanying regional struggle for power within Lebanon), were simply assassinated. Sheikh Sobhi el-Saleh, Mufti Hassan Khaled, and Bishop Khoreiche all suffered this fate. Other religious authorities received militia threats that were meant to silence them. Some religious leaders, however, both Christian and Muslim, actually encouraged the militias by openly advocating violence instead of democratic dialogue in parliament.

THE IMPOSSIBILITY OF RESISTING MILITIA RULE

At first glance, there seems to have been an appalling conspiracy of silence protecting the criminal gangs born of the militia system. At a time when international public opinion, media, and human rights organizations were denouncing oppression ever more vigorously everywhere in the world, the cloak of silence surrounding Lebanese militias' totalitarian oppression of those they claimed to protect appears very strange, even incomprehensible. In fact, far from suffering the condemnation of the international and Arab communities, the militia chieftains have been continually rewarded, either by accession to the presidency itself (in 1982) or with ministerial positions in various governments of so-called national reconciliation, which only enabled them further to dismantle the state and enrich themselves.

There are a number of factors, both inside and outside Lebanon, that explain why so few voices denounced the militias' activities and their leaders. Because these factors overlap, they are difficult to categorize, but we shall commence with the simplest before addressing the more involved phenomena related to international and Arab public opinion.

1. *Fear for physical safety.* For most Lebanese, fear of violent physical punishment deterred open denunciation of militia activities. In addition to assassination attempts against independent political leaders, numerous ordinary citizens were attacked, molested, or abducted for criticizing one

militia chieftain or another. Even militia members who refused to carry out particularly repugnant orders were often summarily executed.

Nevertheless, the Lebanese engaged in numerous acts of nonviolent resistance to militia rule. Courageous individuals continued to move from one region of the country to another and to hold demonstrations for peace and for the dismantling of demarcation lines.[8] The importance of these forms of patriotism and popular resistance still have not been duly recognized, especially because so many people died or disappeared as a result.

2. *Outbursts of communal hysteria.* The fears of citizens who had been herded into ghettos and subjected to daily communal violence and brainwashing by militia-run media helps to explain the occasional outbursts of general communal hysteria after 1975. These outbursts were always stimulated by outside events or intervention (e.g., Israel and its purported "defense" of the Christian minority; Iran, following the rise of the Ayatollah Khomeini and its development of a privileged relationship with the Lebanese Shi'ite community; right-wing parties in France and their sympathy for the "Christians," fueled by the myth of a firm friendship reaching back to the Crusades; "Christian" fear of the Palestinians and Syrians; "Shi'ite" rejection of the Palestinians, etc.). Some of the most extreme outbursts of communal hysteria, directly provoked by the Israelis, occurred in the Shouf in 1983 and in the area of Sidon in 1985.[9]

These bouts of hysteria obviously helped reinforce the idea that the militias truly represented their communities, especially in the eyes of international opinion. Within Lebanon itself, however, the hysteria was very short-lived. As soon as the violence subsided, opinion within the various communities tended to revert to the view that the militias involved were only acting as the agents of regional powers and that their massacres and forced displacement of populations were catastrophic for the community or communities involved. Fear, however, always muzzled a clear, direct statement of these convictions.

In order for anyone to speak out without undue risk, it was necessary to blame either outside forces or sectarianism in general. Direct censure of those responsible locally was impossible. The only criticism permitted by the militia system was that which suited it, namely criticism of an entire community and its leaders (denunciation of "the Muslims" in the case of Christians and of "the Christians" in the case of Muslims). The joint responsibility of the warlords for their destruction of the state as well as their other numerous crimes could never be established and vigorously denounced. For this reason, the numerous protest movements that arose throughout the war years—such as trade union strikes, marches, meetings of civilian associations against war or in support of human rights—never directly attacked the militia chieftains. These public protests were always in favor of peace and national reconciliation or against the withdrawal of the state. To venture any further than these general slogans was to endanger the personal security of those involved.

3. *The psychological refusal to recognize the rise of totalitarianism in Lebanese society.* The Lebanese were afraid to recognize militia violence for what it really was: totalitarian violence aimed at destroying the very foundations of Lebanese society. By clinging to the theory of a struggle for power between "Christians" and "Muslims," the Lebanese paradoxically preserved a glimmer of hope that an internal settlement could be arranged that would permit a return to normalcy. There was also perhaps an element of psychological defense at work in order to make it possible to carry on. This phenomenon was reinforced by the fact that in a microsociety such as Lebanon, where there is little distance between political leaders and common citizens, and where many families had at least one member who sought adventure and fortune in the militias, it was difficult to admit that a previously consensual and democratic society had given birth to such ruthless, totalitarian monsters. We should recall in this regard the extent to which conspiracy theories and blaming fifth columns helped the Lebanese turn a blind eye to the emerging totalitarian violence.

It is not surprising that hopes were high that new political arrangements (ranging from the 1976 Constitutional Document to the 1989 Ta'if Accord) could stop the violence that was considered to be the accidental result of poor political practices on the national level, or of the "Christian" monopoly on power. The appointment of militia chieftains (under the influence of one or another of the regional powers) to implement these new political arrangements was based on the illusion that Lebanon's explosion was essentially a civil war between Muslims and Christians in which the militias were the legitimate defenders of one cause or another. In this way, hope was kept alive that a consensual state could be reestablished on the basis of a civil society that transcended the various sectarian communities.

Most Lebanese also refused to accept the fact that the realities in the Middle East had changed many years earlier. Dictatorial Arab regimes had greatly increased their respective strengths and aspirations to become great regional powers, and Israel had become determined to stamp out a Lebanese political regime based on Islamic-Christian consensus and to deny the Palestinians their most fundamental rights.[10] Only the militia chieftains, and certain intellectuals close to them, understood this altered regional environment. The chieftains decided that to play a significant regional role, it would be necessary to dismantle the state and establish communal ghettos that the militias would protect, with help from their respective regional sponsors.

The Phalangist party consistently took this tack right from the start. Despite an international consensus in 1982 that sanctioned Phalange control of the state, the party continued to encourage sectarian violence and the division of the country into communal ghettos dominated by militias.

The Lebanese National Movement (LNM), which began as a broad intersectarian movement calling for deconfessionalization, also degenerated into sectarian practices. It suffered greatly from the tragic assassination in 1977 of its leader, Kamal Jumblatt, who had realized only too late the dangers of destabilizing the state and of an alliance with the Palestinian militias.[11] In 1978, the transsectarian nature of the LNM was further eroded with the disappearance of Imam Musa al-Sadr, who was attempting to revive the traditional consensus system in Lebanon. In the end, the LNM became nothing more than a contradictory alliance of "Islamic" militias controlling communal subghettos with the assistance of Iran and Syria. The ensuing internal struggles claimed thousands of victims, not to mention the ferocious battles between the so-called "Shi'ite" Amal militia and various Palestinian militias from 1985 to 1988, and the savage intrasectarian skirmishes between Amal and Hizballah beginning in 1988, which caused more than 2,000 civilian casualties.

This atmosphere of communal terror muzzled independent citizens and eventually caused them to internalize this fear as a result of the violence described above. This internalization of fear of the "other" paved the way for the ascendancy of the politically authoritarian views of intellectuals associated with various militias.

The militias succeeded in attracting to their causes moderate intellectuals who provided the public with conciliatory scenarios that cast the militias as indispensable elements to any reconciliation. According to these intellectuals, it would not be possible to return to a unified country based on a broad social consensus without recognition of the militias' role and of the service they had performed by upholding the cause of each allegedly persecuted or oppressed community—causes supposedly at the core of this civil war.

4. *International public opinion.* Perhaps because of the threats, the attitudes held by the Lebanese public are understandable. Foreign public opinion, however, is more difficult to fathom.

The international press reached a zenith of intellectual laziness in the case of Lebanon. Despite the immense complexity of the situation and brutal outside interference, the international press complacently accepted the split between "Christians" and "Muslims" as the sole explanation of the conflict.[12] This simplistic perspective justified all the violence, while the criminal aspect of the attacks on the civilian population was never mentioned, or only very selectively. The prevailing view cast the Lebanese as being locked in an innate, quasi-biological struggle between Christians and Muslims, with each militia only doing its best to defend "its" community against the savage attacks of others.

The bias in many influential quarters in the West that favored the Christians often clouded the issue, preventing an appreciation of the fate visited on the entire Lebanese population. Although the Phalangist party held only five seats in Parliament in 1975, it was immediately deemed the legitimate representative of all Lebanese Christians; this in turn indirectly legitimized the acts of violence committed by the Phalangist militia. The voices of leading Christian politicians who opposed Phalangist domination were largely ignored by the mainstream press and international media. Thus, Raymond Eddé, despite his great personal popularity as a leader of the "Maronites," could not get a hearing in his place of exile in Paris, even though France has long been the main source of international news about Lebanon. Television, radio, and newspapers always preferred to interview the authorized representatives of the militias, rather than anyone independent of them.

The views disseminated internationally were therefore those of the "Christian" and "Muslim" militias. Even academic analysis tended to reflect this bias, or at least increasingly accepted the idea that the militias were the legitimate organs of their religious communities, and that these communities were the sole sociopolitical reality in Lebanon. Thus, despite all the evidence to the contrary,[13] the complexities of the conflict were reduced to a simple war between Christians and Muslims. This simplification, although convenient, helped to mask and legitimize the interference of regional and international powers in Lebanon, especially when this interference was requested by one or another of the militias. It also justified the inaction of other powers, and their failure to condemn the warring factions in Lebanon, which were allegedly incapable of working out a mutually acceptable means of restoring the peace.

With international opinion adopting this attitude, the matter was quickly settled: No one bears moral responsibility—let alone any legal liability—for the tens of thousands of dead, disappeared, and disabled, or for the massive devastation and theft. "The Lebanese" as an abstract group or classification were collectively to blame for their division and misfortunes. The catastrophe they endured was their own fault.

For fifteen years there was a blank check for violence, and in the unrelenting horror that followed, everything was allowed. The 150,000 who died were seen as the victims of an abstract, quasi-biological fate which befell the Lebanese, and not the victims of flesh and blood militia chieftains who continue to claim with impunity that they are indispensable champions of national reconciliation, even as they continue to dismantle the state and murder indiscriminately.

As the above discussion suggests, Lebanese inability to resist militia domination resulted not only from fear for physical safety but also from profound psychological influences rooted in factors both inside Lebanon and on the international stage. There were many barriers to any denunciation—even a moral denunciation—of the militias and their crimes, despite the fact that their activities are indeed crimes against humanity.

From the point of view of group psychology, the Lebanese today fulfill the basic definition of an oppressed people, that is, they tend to consider themselves collectively responsible for what has happened, and thereby absolve the totalitarian butchers of their crimes. The prattle about the collective responsibility of *all* Lebanese serves only to excuse those Lebanese who made a profession of indiscriminate sectarian violence against unarmed civilians from answering for their crimes. The Lebanese habit of internalizing fear of militia chieftains combines with a truncated understanding and analysis of the conflict to perpetuate a belief in the abstract, collective responsibility of the "Muslims" or the "Christians." The result is paralysis of all political action aimed at identifying those actually responsible for the violence and developing the means necessary to neutralize or even punish them.

CONCLUSION: REBUILDING THE STATE

For the Lebanese state to firmly reestablish itself and shelter the complex Lebanese society in an open and democratic fashion, the logic of the militias must be effectively repudiated; that is, we must overcome the obfuscation and distorted language that cast the conflict as nothing more than a civil war between Christians and Muslims.

At the present time, there is great danger that nothing substantial will change and all that will be built is a shadow of a state under foreign domination, with outside powers deeming themselves directly or indirectly to be the guarantors and arbiters of the new arrangement between the communities. In this sense, the Ta'if Accord represents little more than a return to the logic of the Protocol of 1861 and the regime of the *Mutassarrifiyya*.[14] Lebanon is moving backward after a period of unprecedented social, economic, and demographic upheaval.

The Ta'if Accord fails to draw lessons from the previous, unsuccessful attempts to resolve the conflict, and retains the view that an interethnic struggle is the root of the problem. Ta'if purports to dilute the influence of militia chieftains by admitting them into the parliament (initially by the thoroughly undemocratic process of cabinet appointments) and by redistributing powers within the communities. Lebanon is required to maintain "privileged relations" with Syria, while no precise, concrete deadline or procedure for the withdrawal of Syrian troops has been established. The notion of a "government of national reconciliation" remains a key element in the accord, thus perpetuating and legitimizing the presence of the warmongers and their foreign sponsors in the highest councils of government. Unlike the Protocol of 1861, which gave birth to the regime of the Mutassarrifiyya, no great international power has been appointed guarantor of the accord. Hardly anything is left of the Lebanese state; it remains at the mercy of its two powerful neighbors, Syria and Israel (and is also subject to Iranian influence), which have torn it apart ever since the so-called "red line" agreement was formulated in 1976 under the aegis of the United States.[15]

The crude, brutal realism of the Ta'if Accord (which rewards the champions of communal violence) is supposedly offset by its encouragement of so-called "idealistic" and "utopian" aspirations, that is, its provision for the eventual elimination of the sectarian political system. If such a state is to be built, it must be grounded on certain fundamental principles. However utopian these principles may appear, they embody the only possible realism:

1. Violence committed against unarmed, apolitical civilians on the basis of their communal affiliation or geographic location is a crime. The state, which has the sole monopoly on violence and which must guarantee individual liberty and the integrity of society, cannot remain indifferent to such crimes, lest it lose its own credibility.

2. The communal identity of leaders in no way qualifies them to administer the state. An effective administration requires institutions that function in accordance with clear, nondiscriminatory principles and that are equipped with specific constitutional mechanisms for preventing a person, or group of persons, from violating these principles, whether in the name of any religious community or secular ideology of any kind.

There are numerous countries in which amends for massacres and forced population displacements have never been made (or made only partially). There always remains in these societies, however, a hidden unease, a latent instability, and the legitimacy of the governing authorities is fragile. This unease can only be eliminated by establishing effective institutions of representative democracy and a strong, legitimate army at the service of democratic authority. These two elements are critical to reinstilling citizens' confidence and helping them recover their dignity as fully functioning human beings. Only in this way will Lebanon be able to quell the political forces that have inflicted horrific violence upon the Lebanese psyche since 1975.

NOTES

1. See in particular "Mythes et réalités du conflit libanais," *Cosmopolitique* 6 (March 1989) (English version in *Third World Affairs,* 1988) and *Géopolitique du Conflit Libanais* (Paris: La Découverte, 1986).

2. Israel's attack was in retaliation for a Palestinian guerrilla attack on an El Al jet at Athens airport.

3. For this see "Liban: l'argent des milices" in *Les cahiers de l'Orient* 2nd quarter no. 10 (1988).

4. The mixed population areas in the Shouf region and around the city of Sidon did not suffer any forced displacements from 1975 to 1982. During Israel's occupation of Lebanon (in 1982–1983 in the Shouf and in 1985 in the South), it took over responsibility for the safety of the civilian population. However, Israel allowed the Lebanese Forces' militia freely to enter these regions (where it had not previously been present) and to commit numerous sectarian atrocities. The militias that had dominated these regions since 1975 responded with no less hideous reprisals. The Israeli Army refused to allow battalions of the Lebanese Army or of the Multinational Force stationed in Beirut to enter the area and put a stop to this militia-led bloodbath, while turning a blind eye to the entry of militia arms and reinforcements. Stunning massacres and forced population displacements occurred in September 1983 and again in October 1985 when the Israeli Army, during its troop withdrawals, refused any coordination with the Lebanese Army.

5. On Black Saturday (December 1975), the Phalangist militia undertook to kill all Muslims found in the central business district of Beirut under its control, in reprisal for the assassination of three "Christian" civilians. At least 200 people were murdered. One of the Phalangist executioners recounted the slaughter in ingenuous but revolting fashion in a sensational book, for which this henchman of the militia system was rewarded with an appearance on the famous French television program "Apostrophes," hosted by B. Pivot. See J. Saadé, *Victime et bourreau* (Paris: Calmann Levy, 1989). In the same "literary" vein, see P. Meney, *Même les tueurs ont une mère* (Paris: La Table Ronde, 1986) in which a man who had fought in various militias gives a matter-of-fact account of his activities.

6. Discussion of the fighting and expulsions that caused the population transfers from these areas can be found in Robert Fisk, *Pity the Nation: Lebanon at War* (London: Andre Deutsch, 1990).

7. Discussion of the pressures exerted against both domestic and foreign journalists in Lebanon can be found in Fisk, *Pity the Nation.*

8. See Corm, "Mythes et réalités."

9. See note no. 3 in this chapter.

10. Israeli documents show that various Israeli governments devised plans to destabilize Lebanon as far back as 1950. See my *Géopolitique du conflit Libanais; Le Monde Diplomatique* (September 1982) reproduces extracts from these documents.

11. This is clearly evident in the collection of his final thoughts, confided to a French journalist and published under the title *Pour le Liban* (Paris: Stock, 1978).

12. See N. Beyhum, "Crise sociale et production de nouveaux acteurs dans le conflit libanais" in P. Salta and G. Corm (eds.), *L'avenir du Liban dans le context régional et international* (Paris: Editions E.D.I., 1990).

13. Examples of contrary evidence include the conflicts between the Syrian Army and the Lebanese National Movement in 1976, the Amal militia and the Palestinians in 1985–1987, the Syrian Army and the Palestinians in 1983–1985, Amal and Hizballah militias in northern Lebanon in 1986–1990, the intra-Christian struggles in 1978, 1980, 1986, 1988, and 1990, and Israel's invasions in 1978 and 1982.

14. The 1861 protocol resulted in Mount Lebanon's political and administrative reorganization as a Mutassarrifiyya (an administrative territory with special standing in the Ottoman Empire). For two decades prior to 1861, a clash of contradictory interests between France and England in the region pitted the leaders of the local Maronite and Druze communities against each other, leading, at times, to

bloody confrontation. The protocol reflected an understanding among the great powers of the time (France, England, Austria, Prussia, Russia, and the Ottoman Empire) that made Lebanon essentially a European ward. During this time, the basic foundations of Lebanon's modern confessional system were put in place. See Georges Corm, *Contribution à l'étude des sociétés multiconfessionnelles* (Paris: LGDJ, 1971).

15. The "red line" agreement, orchestrated by the United States, was an understanding that permitted the Syrian Army official entry into Lebanon as far south as the Litani River—with Israeli acquiescence—in order to end Palestinian-Lebanese confrontations and exercise control over the PLO armed movements. In return, the Israeli Army was authorized to intervene in all territory south of the Litani. For discussion on the U.S. role in this agreement, see my study "Liban: Crise endogène ou crise régionale?" in *Mahgreb Machrek* 122 (October–December 1989).

15

Religious Identity and Citizenship: An Overview of Perspectives

Raghid el-Solh

In developing societies such as Lebanon, religious identity and citizenship often entwine in dynamic relationship. The interplay of religion and citizenship with respect to Lebanese politics and, consequently, to armed conflict, has received much attention, but has generated more questions than comprehensive answers. The major questions tend to be variations of the following: What is the nature of the relationship between religious identity and citizenship in Lebanon? Do religious loyalties supersede those of the citizen to society and the state? Did the intensity of religious identification originate from within Lebanese society? Did it occur because of internal social, political, and economic dynamics? Was it a product of external intervention, or of both domestic and external factors? Finally, how durable is the present relationship between religious identity and citizenship in Lebanon, and what impact will this have on the future of the country? Not surprisingly, the proposed answers represent markedly different viewpoints. This chapter presents a brief overview of these major perspectives, all of which reveal something about peace and conflict in Lebanon.

RELIGIOUS IDENTITY AND CITIZENSHIP: COMPETING OR COMPATIBLE LOYALTIES?

It has sometimes appeared, especially during times of war, that the Lebanese sense of citizenship was determined by religious affiliation—that Lebanese religious sentiments and commitments superseded loyalty to the country. This appearance has prompted some analysts to describe Lebanon as a confederation of sects rather than a nation. On the other hand, one must ponder the extent to which war itself has influenced and shaped appear-

231

ances. Lebanon has not always been at war. If the analytical focus shifts to Lebanon's times of peace and prosperity, the relationship between citizenship and religious identity appears in a different light. The new focus suggests that both loyalties could exist as distinct phenomena; the Lebanese may feel differing levels of affiliation to the various elements of their composite social structure (e.g., family, tribe, sect, party).

This peacetime perspective does not consider alternate social loyalties to be—by definition—opposed or contradictory to national loyalty or patriotism. Thus, a Lebanese could be a member of a religious community, could join a political party, or support a football club, while placing his commitment to the country above the loyalty to these groups. In other words, Lebanese society is not unique or phenomenal with respect to religion and citizenship. How, then, do advocates of this perspective explain sectarian fighting in Lebanon? They do so by disputing a unidimensional explanation of the conflict—Lebanon's wars were not *caused* by religious sentiments alone, rather they erupted by way of multidimensional factors, involving a complex interplay of social, political, economic, cultural, and sectarian factors.

Thus, while some analysts consider the Lebanese war to be a primordial fight among religious communities, others perceive it to be an overlapping struggle among social classes, political parties and leaders, external forces, as well as religious communities. The latter group cautions that although religion may have appeared as a significant factor at certain points during the fighting, it should not become the sole analytical focus, lest it mask the relevance of other factors and actors on the Lebanese battlefield.

SECTARIANISM IN LEBANON:
REAL OR ARTIFICIAL, ORGANIC OR ACQUIRED?

The debate on the nature of the relationship between citizenship and religious identity usually spills over into the historical arena. Efforts are directed toward identifying the origin of this relationship, in the hope of discovering whether Lebanese loyalties and sentiments are real or artificial, organic or acquired. Here too, analysts do not agree. One school of thought prefers to ascribe a paramount role to external forces, especially Western powers, in the preservation, intensification, and manipulation of religious feelings among the Lebanese. This perspective cites the imposition of the *millet* system by the Ottomans (in which each religious denomination was organized under its own ecclesiastical authorities), the *règlement organique* by the European powers, and the 1926 Constitution by the French mandatory authorities; these were devices through which foreign powers maintained, intensified, and manipulated religious sentiments and loyalties in

Lebanon (for their own purposes).[1] Some analysts from within this perspective blame external forces for the eruption of fighting in 1975.

By contrast, other analysts underline the role of domestic forces and causes in sharpening religious sentiments and loyalties, arguing that Lebanese factions, propelled by these sentiments and loyalties, "have permanently and consistently attempted to manipulate foreign forces in their fight against their [domestic] adversary."[2] A variant of this perspective highlights the role of the Maronites and the Sunnis, who, in "confessional condominium," consecrated or even produced the 1943 arrangement of the confessional system.

A third view attributes the flare-up of confessional animosity to a complex interplay of domestic and external factors, although the relationship between these factors is not constant (nor do analysts within this perspective agree on the specific contours of the interplay). Hence, sometimes the interests of domestic and external actors (such as the Lebanese ruling elite, certain Lebanese sects, or foreign powers) coalesce, prompting them to conspire in joint exploitation of the Lebanese. At other times, these actors function independently to produce the same effect. In the end, therefore, the Lebanese ruling elite, or even counterelite,[3] is accorded considerable blame for Lebanon's troubles. By exacerbating confessional differences among the Lebanese (to reinforce their respective popular power bases) Lebanese leaders rendered Lebanon incapable of protecting itself against the foreign exploiters of its fragile social-cum-confessional policies.

DURABILITY OF THE RELATIONSHIP
AND PRESCRIPTIONS FOR FUTURE STABILITY

There are two main approaches to the issue concerning the durability of the relationship between religious identity and citizenship in Lebanon. The first generally accepts the validity of the assumption that Lebanese society comprises distinct communal groups. This approach, therefore, favors continuation or refinement of the confessional system. The second flatly rejects the organic reality of Lebanon's sectarian troubles, and considers that Lebanon's ills would best be cured through some form of deconfessionalization of the system. Within each of these broad approaches, many different schools and perspectives abound.

Continuation/Refinement of the Confessional System

According to the adherents of this school, the confessional system is neither an ephemeral folly nor a mischievous arrangement. The system embodies Lebanon's deep-rooted social realities, guaranteeing the country's independence and ensuring the peoples' freedom. From this basic assumption derive several different perspectives concerning viable options for Lebanon's stable political organization. These options fall into two main two categories: pluralistic multiconfessionalism and monoconfessionalism.

The pluralistic multiconfessional option. This option favors the maintenance of Lebanon's confessionally based political system, with (perhaps) some rebalancing of the confessional quotas. According to Michel Chiha, the leading proponent of the multiconfessional option in the 1960s, Lebanon is a country "of partnered sectarian minorities." Lebanese democracy, however, differs from ideal democracy: Whereas the latter entails a parliamentary system that represents individuals, the former espouses a system that represents Lebanon's sectarian minorities (as groups).[4] Samir Khalaf, in his often quoted 1968 paper, "Primordial Ties and Politics in Lebanon," found advantages in the sectarian system: "Rather than making unrealistic attempts to abolish confessionalism and in doing so run the risk of fomenting sectarian factionalism," he argues, "a less drastic and more effective remedy would be to upgrade the democratic structure within the framework of confessionalism. There is certainly ample room for extensive administrative reform without amending Article 95 of the constitution."[5]

Proconfessionalist perspectives are challenged by those who do not accept the basic underlying assumption (i.e., the organic reality of Lebanon's sects). The challengers argue that Lebanon's confessionalism is neither as deep-seated nor as all-prevailing as assumed. For example, the counterargument goes, intrasectarian fighting graphically indicates that religious sentiments do not monopolize the loyalty of the Lebanese. Moreover, many studies and surveys have shown that, even at the climax of Lebanon's "confessional war," sentiments unrelated to confessional allegiances were more widespread among the Lebanese than confessional feelings.

A second argument against the confessional system is couched in utilitarian terms. While it is wrong to exaggerate its pitfalls, it is equally wrong to overlook its failures. A perilous failure of the confessional system, according to its critics, was the gradual enfeeblement of the Lebanese Army. The institution began to weaken because of a government policy that insisted on striking a balance between Christian and Muslim recruits (to ensure a continuous flow of candidates from both sects). However, considerably fewer Christians than Muslims were willing to join the army. The reasons for this disparity were economic and social; young men in Christian communities were more likely to find better opportunities in government service or in private business than those in Muslim communities. A career in the armed forces, therefore, was not as appealing to Christians, and was reflected by the lack of Christian recruits. To maintain the government-decreed confessional "balance," the army commander had to keep the number of troops at a minimum, despite the large pool of Muslim recruits waiting to join. The entire situation degenerated into a farce when Muslims, desperate for army jobs, began to pay money to Christian counterparts to join the army, so that their mutual applications would be approved. A Christian entering military service in this manner usually resigned or opted out, leaving the Muslim recruit happily occupying his military job.

The overall outcome of this policy was to keep the Lebanese Army relatively weak, especially in relation to the looming geopolitical difficulties resulting from the creation of Israel and the beginning of the Arab-Israeli conflict (which logically would require a strengthening of the Lebanese Army).

A third argument against the confessional political system considers that the system was the product of specific historical conditions. These conditions, however, have ceased to exist. For example, one argument contends that Lebanon's confessional arrangements for power sharing embodied a democratic parity because they reflected the relative demographic importance of Muslims and Christians (at the time of independence). Demographic change has shattered this parity, it is argued, such that maintenance of the same sectarian quotas is unrealistic. Reality dictates some manner of system revision or replacement.

The monoconfessional option. Some players on the Lebanese scene believe in the organic reality of Lebanon's sects, but consider the country's power-sharing formula (based on the National Pact) to be a conspiracy against the peoples of Lebanon. According to advocates of this theory, the Lebanon of the National Pact should be killed, banished, and then resurrected anew. These actors, who advocate some variation of a monoconfessional option for Lebanon, fall into two groups.

The first group advocates the replacement of Lebanon's multiconfessional, pluralistic formula with a confessional hegemony: that is, political power would become openly and unabashedly the preserve of a single religious community. Fadi Fraim, leader of the Lebanese Forces for a short period in the early 1980s, lamented the formula of "no victor, no vanquished," because it implicitly sanctioned reconciliation and power sharing among the religious communities. Fraim asserted that there was a victor—the Maronite community, led by the Lebanese Forces—that should therefore be entitled to control the new Lebanon.

Ironically, Hussein Moussawi, leader of Islamic Amal, agreed with Fadi Fraim that one religious community should administer Lebanon, although he disagreed as to the identity of the victorious community. Moussawi obviously meant the Muslim community, which, he stated, would ultimately apply the Sharia but allow the Christians to "live in all the security they enjoyed in the Islamic state at the time of the Prophet

Mohammad and after."[6] His vision for Lebanon, in other words, was the *dhimmi* system.

Fraim and Moussawi were offering either to "Maronize" or "Islamize" Lebanon, respectively. Either scheme would entail relegating the nondominant religious community to second-class citizenship. This aim could have been achieved either through diplomacy (by convincing members of the other sects to accept the offered status) or through coercion and intimidation. It would have been very unlikely that either Muslims or Christians (as groups) would have willingly settled for second-class citizenship through words alone. Yet, imposing monoconfessional hegemony through force was impossible given that no actor on the Lebanese scene (not even the Syrians) was ever in control of all Lebanon's territory. Although unrealistic, these calls and schemes for monoconfessionalization did incur a consequence: they encouraged secessionist thoughts among Lebanese of all sects. Indeed, secessionist principles characterize the second group of monoconfessionalists.

The second group (like the first) believes that the heterogeneous nature of Lebanese society was artificial, unstable, and wrong. This group, perceiving other religions and sects to be a threat, tends to demonize them. They believe that the best solution to Lebanon's ills would be "confessional cleansing," such that the state and society would belong exclusively to one sect. The second group (unlike the first) advocates confessional secession—the division of Lebanon into independent confessionally pure ministates. This was the gist of the memorandum presented by the Order of Lebanese Monks and the Maronite Association to the French envoy M. Couve de Murville, who visited Lebanon on a peace mission in 1975. The only solution, according to the two Maronite groups, was "a return to the formula of old, independent and neutral Lebanon, with the guarantee of the superpowers" (that is, the *Mutassarrifiyya*). They agreed that "when Lebanon loses Sidon, Tripoli and part of Bekaa and Akkar . . . then humanitarian Lebanon will gain tremendously."[7] In a similar, but more clandestine, manner, Sheikh Said Sha'ban, head of the Islamic Unification Movement since 1983, established a quasi-Islamic republic in Tripoli and encouraged the Christians of his "principality" to migrate elsewhere.

The Deconfessionalist Approach

Other analysts and observers who are well versed in the discrepancies and failures of Lebanon's sectarian system call for Lebanon's deconfessionalization. Deconfessionalist proponents concur that institutionalization of confessionalism inhibited the emancipation of the Lebanese. The system prohibited elevation of the Lebanese to the level of free citizens, thereby stultifying the country's transformation from a conglomeration of sects and confessions into a coherent national body. Deconfessionalists generally tolerate the presence of religious sentiments and loyalties in society. However, they abhor the intrusion of these loyalties into every field of human and social transaction in Lebanon. The deconfessionalists may be divided into two broad groups: the secularists and the democrats.[8]

The secularists. Secularists call for Lebanon's comprehensive secularization, a process that, according to Roger Scrunton, entails two aspects:

> The first involves the gradual disappearance of religious thought, feeling and imagery from the understanding of the worldly things, so that religion either ceases to exist or else is confined to an abstract worship of the transcendental. . . . The objective aspect of secularization consists in the process whereby religious offices, institutions and ceremonies are extruded from public life, in education, lawmaking, administration and government.[9]

In line with this thinking Ina'm Raad, a leader of the Syrian National Party, called for "the separation of religion from the state, abolishing the barriers between the state, abolishing the barriers between the different sects and denominations, and banning the clergy from interference in national, political and judicial affairs."[10] According to Raad, this reform would free Lebanese citizens from the fetters and constraints inhibiting their full participation in public life. Moreover, as procommunist Lebanese historian Masoud Dahir has argued, this separation would also rid Lebanon of the crises and wars that have befallen it since independence.[11]

The issue of secularization, in both its objective and subjective forms, is presently a matter of extensive debate engaging various ideologies and political tendencies in the Arab world. The fundamentalists, especially of the Islamic variety, sit in stark opposition to secularization. Islamic fundamentalists reject the division between the city of Man and the city of God, since they believe that Islam encompasses both. They regard secularism as an attempt to suppress religion rather than as an endeavor to separate it from the state; secularism is part and parcel of a Western crusade to destroy the *umma* and to subjugate the Muslims. Its bearers in the Arab world, therefore, are (in the words of the fundamentalist writer Zuhair Sulayman), "the sick and the agents of foreign powers."[12]

By contrast, nonfundamentalists in the Arab world discuss objective secularism in more subtle tones. For example, some, like well-known secularist Sadiq Jalal al-Azm, argue that secularization in the region is not a new phenomenon—it is a process that started at the beginning of the century. Although religious fundamentalists of the Arab world have attempted to arrest and reverse the secularization process, they have either failed, or have succeeded only in slowing its development (except, perhaps, in Sudan).

Prosecularists also distinguish between those brands of secularism that aspire to free the individual, enabling him to be master of his faith, and those that do not. For example, communism, Kemalism, and fascism were all secularist ideologies and movements but none demonstrated a concern for individual liberty or for the concept of citizenship (except, perhaps, in very remote, abstract, and utopian forms). Kemalism, which influenced Arab political thought considerably, suppressed both religious institutions and individual freedoms, including that of choosing one's personal dress.

In August 1922, for example, Kemalist authoritarianism revealed itself when Ataturk proposed that the powers of the sultanate and caliphate be terminated. Much to Ataturk's dissatisfaction, his proposal appeared to meet with strong opposition in the national assembly. He proceeded to quash the dissent with the following threat:

> The question under discussion is not whether or not we should leave the Sultanate and sovereignty to the nation. That is already an accomplished fact—the question is merely how to give expression to it. This will happen in any case. If those gathered here, the Assembly and everyone else, could look at this question in a natural way, I think they would agree. Even if they do not, the truth will still find expression, but some heads may have to roll in the process.[13]

Much like their ideological ancestors, communist movements in the Arab world, along with most revolutionary nationalist movements (Arab, Syrian, local), were secularist but not necessarily democratic. Rather, the regimes produced by these movements have, for the most part, attempted to marginalize, neutralize, or even suppress religious institutions and practices. They have done so not to defend individual or civil liberties, but, usually, to defend the interests of the ruling elite.

Finally, some secularists of the Arab world, such as Iyad al-Qattan, director of the Royal Cultural Center in Jordan, suggest that in Arab societies an alliance exists between the state and religious institutions.[14] Therefore, just as secularization in Western societies focused on ending the alliance between state and church (thereby divesting the ruling elite of its sacred status) so too must the Arab world go through the same process of secularization if democracy is to be achieved (that is, the establishment of the rule of the people, by the people, and for the people). It is difficult to contend, however, that the clerical class in Iraq, Syria, Tunisia, Algeria, Libya (to name the most obvious) is the ally of the ruling elite in those countries. It is perhaps more accurate to conceive of the clerical class as either part of the state machinery used to disseminate the ruling elite's ideology, or as an opposition force challenging the ruling class. Moreover, legitimation of the ruling elites rests more on national than religious principles. The regimes in Iraq, Syria, and Libya (as well as Nasser's Egypt) ground their legitimacy in Arab nationalist ideology. The legitimacy of the

Tunisian and Algerian regimes is based on the legacy of anticolonial struggles. The quest for modernization is also part of the legitimating ideology.

One could argue, therefore, that the forces of secularism and democracy are not necessarily the same, and that there may be a difference between secularist and democratic agendas. For while the secularist considers separation of the state from religious institutions to be the central and primary objective, the democrat is obliged to consider different priorities.

The democrats. Lebanese democrats acknowledge the intervention of the Lebanese clergy (in their many persuasions) in the political and social arenas. They do not, however, consider this intervention to be the major obstacle preventing the development of a coherent concept of citizenship among Lebanese. The democrats, therefore, envisage a less radical form of deconfessionalization than the pure secularists. They advocate the renewal and reform of Lebanon's politically pluralistic multiparty system.

Democrats consider Lebanon to be confronted by a host of varied challenges—some come from within, but many emanate from external and regional variables. One such challenge is the monoconfessional movements discussed above. These internal exclusionist movements are made more dangerous because of external patronage of this idea. For example, following the Israeli intervention in Lebanon, Israel tried to foster a monoconfessional system that would have acted as a vehicle for Israeli interests in Lebanon. This policy would have produced a system of apartheid, nullifying any potential for developing a sense of citizenship among Lebanese. The Israeli challenge has not completely receded. Israel still holds part of Lebanon's territory and intends to use it to pressure the Lebanese to accommodate Israeli interests and plans. On the other extreme, Lebanese democrats are confronted by the intervention of Iran, whose ultimate (stated) aim is to transform the Lebanese state into a theocracy with a monoconfessional system of government.

Last, Lebanese democrats are confronted with the challenges of Syria's intervention in Lebanon. The Syrian ruling elite has been considerably more successful than any other external actor in pursuing its objectives in Lebanon. The democrats may find this challenge to be the most significant. The obvious aim of the Syrian ruling elite is to maximize its influence in Lebanon, and consequently to reshape the Lebanese political system along principles of government applied in Syria, that is, a single party regime with a highly centralized government.

Confessionalists and secularists might find merit in one or more variations of this single party scheme. However, all such schemes are difficult for Lebanese democrats to accept. They are incompatible with the need to emancipate the citizens of Lebanon, and they would not encourage development of suprasectarian loyalty to the country (and its legitimate institutions).

As this survey has suggested, many different regional forces are interested in promoting exclusionist sectarian tendencies among the Lebanese. To diffuse these regional pressures and influences, Lebanese democrats will have to forge a broad domestic alliance, cutting across religious barriers, social classes, and different professions. In this alliance, a certain section of the clergy could play a positive role; this is not unusual for the clerical class in the Arab world.

By way of conclusion, one observation: Should Lebanese democrats succeed in fostering this broad alliance, and in guiding it along reformist lines, they could well provide the cohesion and leadership required to enhance the Lebanese national spirit, to develop a coherent concept of citizenship in the country, and, thereby, to extricate Lebanon from its present, tenuous condition.

NOTES

1. See, for example, the chapter by Ayoub in this volume.
2. William Pfaff, *International Herald Tribune,* 15 April 1989.
3. For clarification see chapter by Faris in this volume.
4. Michel Chiha, *Lubnan fi shakhsiyyatihi wa hudurihi* (Lebanon in Its Character and Presence) (Beirut: al-nadwa al-lubnaniyya, 1962), pp. 38, 43.
5. Samir Khalaf, "Primordial Ties and Politics in Lebanon," *Middle East Studies* vol. 4 (1968), pp. 243–269.
6. *The Middle East* (October, 1963), p. 23.
7. *Al-Safir,* 22 December 1975.
8. For a variation on the secularization argument, see the chapter by Khairallah in this volume; for a democratic version, see the chapter by el-Hoss in this volume.
9. Roger Scrunton, *A Dictionary of Political Thought* (London: Pan Books, 1962), p. 240.
10. *Al-nadi al-thaqafi al-arabi, al-qiwa al-styasiyya fi lubnan* (The Arab Cultural Club, The Political Forces in Lebanon) (Beirut: Dar at-taliah, 1970), p. 381.
11. Masoud Dahir, *Lubnan: al-isitqlal, al-mithaq, wal-sigha* (Lebanon: The Independence, the Pact and the Formula) (Beirut: Mahad al-inma al-arabi, 1977), p. 381.
12. Zuhair Sulayman, *Al-almaniyya marad mumit, at-tawhid* (Beirut, October 1987).
13. Bernard Lewis, *The Emergence of Modern Turkey* (London: Oxford University Press, 1967), p. 258.
14. *Al-Mouaten* no. 5 (April 1992), pp. 14–15.

16

Lebanon Between Religious Faith and Political Ideology

—————— · ——————

Mahmoud Ayoub

Alas for the nation in which sects abound, but in which religion is little found.

These prophetic words, uttered by Lebanon's beloved poet Khalil Jibran decades before the fifteen-year war, still accurately describe the country's sad plight today. Like most countries in the Arab East, Lebanon is a mosaic of ethnic and religious communities. Despite much good will and nationalistic fervor, however, its communities have been unable to form a nation bound by a single history and common destiny. Lebanon's past history, present reality, and social structure are overlaid with a host of conflicting historical, national, religious, and political myths that mean different things to different people. The following few pages attempt a brief analysis of Lebanon's past in order to place the present in perspective and to look at its future candidly and realistically. This analysis focuses on just one of Lebanon's communities—the Maronite Christians—because it is illustrative of the main argument of this chapter, that is: Lebanon's difficulties did not result from the inability of different religious communities to live together. Religious differences per se were not, and are not, the problem. Intercommunal tensions were more the byproduct of the manipulation of communal identity and loyalties to serve the ideological, political, and geopolitical ends of various internal players and external powers—especially the colonial powers.

Lebanon's internal differences have been perpetuated and accentuated by longstanding myths. One myth that most Lebanese have come to accept is that Lebanon, as it exists today, has always been a country or distinct sociopolitical entity. This is assumed not only by religious and political groups (for self-serving purposes), but even by respectable academics.[1]

Several other historical and ideological misconceptions follow from this myth. The first is that Lebanon is part of the Arab East in geography only, that historically and religiously it is a unique country belonging to the West and subscribing to similar secular values. A second misconception is that Lebanon has always possessed a Christian history and character. In order for this unique Lebanon to be totally severed from the history of the region, a Phoenician past was invented from which Lebanon moved (magically it seems, ignoring more than a millennium of intervening history) to a Christian and Western identity. These misconceptions have led most Lebanese, regardless of their religious or sectarian affiliations, to nourish a false pride in this fictitious past—their invented national identity—and to imagine themselves superior to other peoples of the region.

The accuracy of these perspectives, however, is not upheld by the available historical record. From the seventh until the present century, Mount Lebanon (and later the Lebanese Republic) served as a haven for several distinct religious communities and tribal entities, as well as political groups and individuals fleeing various forms of persecution and conflict. Chief among these were the Maronite Christian, Druze, and Shi'ite Muslim communities. It has been at least circumstantially argued that the Maronite and Druze communities migrated as tribes from southern Arabia, first to the Orontes River valley in northern Syria and then to Mount Lebanon during the seventh and eleventh centuries.[2] The ancestors of the Shi'ites of Jabal Amil in South Lebanon and those of the Baalbek region likewise migrated from the Yemen, possibly before Islam. Thus, the Maronites, Druze, and Shi'ites most likely migrated from the same general area of Arabia, each settling in a distinct region of Mount Lebanon. All three communities, then, may have had a common origin, although each developed its own internal history which determined its historical relationship to the other two communities and the rest of the region.

The early history of the Maronite community is obscure and highly controversial. Of special significance (to this chapter) is the Maronites' gradual turn toward Rome, eventually to become a Uniate Catholic church around 1180 (preserving the Syriac liturgy and Eastern rite). From that time onward, the majority of the Maronite community tended to ally itself with the West. For example, many Maronites assisted the Crusaders in their effort to "liberate" the Holy Land from the Muslims,[3] and in 1510, Pope Leo X issued a papal bull commending the Maronites as a faithful Catholic Christian community planted among "infidels" (Muslims), "schismatics" (Greek Orthodox), and "heretics" (Jacobites and other non-Catholic Christian sects): "a rose among thorns."[4]

However, Maronite interest in cultivating close relations with the Roman church, and subsequently with France, was primarily motivated by the geopolitical exigencies of the struggle among European and Muslim powers for control of the Middle East—not by religious or cultural loyalties. Thus, when Constantinople became the capital of Muslim power, the Maronite patriarch wrote to the pope requesting that he be considered a "Frank"—a European—and as such an ordinary member of the pope's Latin parish.[5] The patriarch was not speaking for himself alone, but for his community. Although religious loyalty was, no doubt, a factor, his request was more than mere Christian zeal; it was a call for protection and patronage.

The Maronites reaped economic and educational benefits from their Western religious and political patrons. In the long term, however, the price for these benefits has been too dear. First, the Maronites' effort to be assimilated into (rather than just allied with) Latin Christianity and Western culture increasingly obscured their identity as a community with its own rich religious and ethnic heritage. Franciscan and later Jesuit missionaries transformed the Eastern character of the Maronite church. Embodied in this transformation was a long process of acculturation, aided by French schools and other educational and cultural missions established among the Maronites by the seventeenth century.

Maronite clerics invented not only a Catholic history for their community, but also a European lineage. They erroneously asserted that, from its inception, the Maronite church had been Catholic in faith and in communion with Rome. Moreover, popular tradition continues to consider John Marun, the second founder of the Maronite church in the seventh century, to have had a Frankish mother, a Carolingian princess. It apparently does not matter that the Carolingian dynasty appeared a century later.[6] It also does not matter that John Marun's nephew, Ibrahim, led the Maronites from the Orontes valley to Mount Lebanon to escape bloody conflict with Byzantine Christians—not to avoid Muslim persecution.

Prior to their alliance with the West, the Maronites had always taken their Arab origins for granted. In one district of Syria, for example, there were Maronites who identified themselves as belonging either to the Qaysi or Yemeni tribes (as did other migrant tribes to the area). From the beginning of their known history, the Maronites were a tribally based community and a distinct sect within Eastern Christianity.[7]

Maronite history is important because it has played a decisive role in the political, economic, social, and religious life of Lebanon both before and after the creation of the Lebanese Republic. Moreover, Maronite history holds a profound lesson for all religious communities in the Middle East, namely that it is possible for a wide diversity of religious and ethnic communities to exist side by side in social and religious harmony. Maronite history demonstrated that intercommunal coexistence was possible when the different communities respected one another as communities of faith ready to accommodate and to work together toward common goals and mutual benefits. This was not an ideal dream, but a reality that characterized intercommunal relations in the Lebanon region for a considerable time when, under stable Ottoman rule, an active silk trade brought communities together to share in a common prosperity despite their religious diversity. It was during this period, from the sixteenth to the mid-nineteenth century, that a number of Maronite families came into prominence as landlords. (These Maronite families continue to enjoy a certain prestige in the social and political life of their community and of the country as a whole.)

The Ottomans appear to have recognized the special communal structure of the region, particularly Mount Lebanon. Thus, at least during the early stages of their rule, they dealt with the Maronites not as a religious group (*millet*), but as a tribal community, often according it favorable treatment. Indeed, even prior to the Ottoman Empire (circa the ninth century) through to the eighteenth century, the Maronites lived in Mount Lebanon virtually free from persecution or any significant pressures from Muslims. During this time they also displayed a remarkable ability to accommodate themselves to changing circumstances. It must therefore be asked: What are the root causes of the present disharmony and mistrust that have torn the country apart and that greatly impede the likelihood of future cooperation and coexistence?

In my view, the causes are many—including both external and internal factors—but certainly the interference of the West in the religious, political, and cultural life of the Maronite community played an important role. Of course, this interference was not limited to the Maronites or even to other Christian groups. It often included non-Christian communities, particularly during the late nineteenth and early twentieth centuries when European colonial powers, competing for strategic footholds in the Middle East, further entrenched the principle of divide and rule in the region.

European interference served to accentuate religious differences and to encourage narrow sectarian loyalties, thereby seriously disrupting the communal life of Mount Lebanon and the adjacent coastal region. European interference ushered in a new era of social and religious discord in the history of Lebanon and the rest of the Middle East.[8] The consequences for the Maronites were particularly tragic because of the community's constant vacillation between Eastern and Western national and cultural loyalties— between Arab Eastern Christian and Western French Catholic. The resulting tension and its bloody ramifications, however, had little to do with any particular religious doctrine or creed; rather it resulted from narrow political considerations.

As Ottoman power waned and European influence increased in the region, European powers adopted the Christians of Syria-Lebanon and Palestine as clients, placing the Christians under their direct protection. Indeed, French protection of the Maronites began even earlier than this. From the seventeenth century onward, France employed all possible means to keep the Maronite community within its sphere of influence. It also sought to foment trouble among religious minorities in Mount Lebanon and the adjacent (Syrian) regions.[9]

Some Arab Christians—particularly the Maronites, many of whom were educated in the West or in Western institutions established in Mount Lebanon by the Catholic church or by France—were employed as consuls and vice consuls representing their European patrons. That is, they represented foreign powers in their own country. This unnatural political alliance, regardless of arguments in its favor, cut the Maronite community off from the rest of the local communities and set it on a collision course with Ottoman, as well as local Muslim and Druze, authorities. Indeed, it is fair to say that French protection of the Christians in Syria-Lebanon and the pressure France exerted on the Ottoman state to grant special privileges to the European powers on the pretext of protecting Christian minorities contributed substantially to the eruption of civil strife in 1,860 between the Druze and Maronites in which thousands of innocent people perished. French intervention to protect the Christians in 1860 led directly (in 1861) to the special *Mutassarrifiyya* status of Mount Lebanon (as an administrative unit under the exclusive jurisdiction of an Ottoman Christian governor, approved and backed by a protective consortium of European powers) which basically allowed for Western rule by proxy. The Mutassarrifiyya was reorganized as a more-or-less confessional state (resembling, in many respects, the Lebanese Republic after its independence in 1943). The Mutassarrifiyya was not, as some have argued, a good experience in multiethnic and multireligious living.[10] Rather, it was a prelude to the emergence of confessional states in the Middle East dominated by religious, sectarian, and civil strife.

The Western idea of sponsoring the creation of small, confessional states in the Middle East reaches back to the mid-nineteenth century. In this regard, it is important to observe the confluence of French and British imperialistic interests and activities in the region. In addition to their creation of a Christian state for the Maronites, they also created a confessional homeland for the Jews. Although unsuccessful, France also tried to create an Alawite ministate in Syria. These policies greatly contributed to destruction of the social mosaic of Middle Eastern society, and to the all-too-familiar state of conflict that has plagued the area for over a century. During those times of trouble, the Ottoman state tried to curtail the colonial ambitions of Britain and France in North Africa and the Levant, especially in Syria-Lebanon, but was unsuccessful.

Although France's direct colonial interests ended with Lebanon's independence in 1943, Lebanon remained essentially a sectarian entity dependent—culturally, politically, and even spiritually—on the West, particularly France. As a result, a principal cause of Lebanon's social and religious discord and resultant socioeconomic misery was its inability to transform itself from a colonial entity into an independent state.

Despite the proliferation of sectarian-related conflict in the Middle East, it is fair to argue that, historically, the peoples of the Middle East have been communal and pluralistic, rather than ideological, individualistic, or nationalistic. In the public realm, each community has striven to preserve its religious autonomy rather than its faith or theological doctrine. The latter issues have been the concern of each community internally, not of society as a whole. Likewise, Lebanese society has been communal rather than sectarian. To be sure, its communities are distinguished by religious and sectarian affiliation rather than by ethnic and linguistic identity, but this is because Lebanese society is, generally speaking, ethnically, culturally, and linguistically homogeneous. Sociocultural disequilibrium, where it exists, is due to economic and educational disparities, and to fabricated ethnic myths, rather than to religious affiliation. Lebanon's communal reality is rooted in the country's history and social structure. Day-to-day social relations within this communal framework have been based on common courtesy. In the context of this culture of courtesy it is bad manners to inquire even casually about a person's religious beliefs, as a popular adage denotes: "To each his religion, and may God help him to live by it."

The political system that Lebanon has adopted since its independence reflects a more recent sectarian reality. The system collapsed in 1975 not because it was sectarian, but because it no longer could serve a society experiencing rapid demographic change. In fact, the confessional proportions on which the system was constructed had never actually existed in the Greater Lebanon of the modern republic. This is because the 1920 annexation of the coastal and anti-Lebanon regions to the province of Mount Lebanon incorporated a large Sunni Muslim element, which meant a new demographic structure. In this new and enlarged Lebanon, the Maronites were no longer an absolute majority. Rather, they became simply one of the many religious minorities in postcolonial Lebanon.[11]

Another issue that aggravated Lebanon's already fragmented society was the local emergence of Western-style nationalist movements and Western-inspired political/religious parties formed on the basis of ideology. These parties constituted politicoreligious sects, embodying the same type of fanaticism and bigotry that they accused their sectarian opponents of harboring. Thus, through its educational, technological, and ideological institutions, the West contributed further to the breakdown of the social, cultural, and religious mosaic of Middle Eastern and particularly Lebanese society. Of course, no one can or should deny the benefits these institutions brought to the Middle East. The bitter irony, however, is that the country that benefited most from these institutions has paid the highest price for their benefits.

This chapter has suggested that the principal cause of Lebanon's social and religious ills was the country's inability to transcend its past and transform itself from a colonial entity into an independent, modern state. Although all Lebanese now agree on the need for change, they disagree on its exact nature and extent. The question that greatly occupies the Lebanese intelligentsia both inside and outside Lebanon is: "What are the options?" Unfortunately, answers to this question often are framed by groups that present their own religious or political ideology as the only panacea for all the country's ills. Many of these ideologies are completely insensitive to Lebanon's cultural and religious traditions, advocating a total break with the past and the immediate transformation of Lebanon from an Eastern homeland to a Western state.

The options offered by both religious and political ideologies may be reduced to four. The first proposes to make Lebanon either a Muslim or a Christian state whose minorities would either be kept as second-class citizens or transported to another Christian or Muslim country. This option has been espoused by both Christian and Muslim extremists, but is not really taken seriously. (It has even been denied by its proponents.)

A second option proposes to retain the sectarian political system with some minor modifications to reflect current social and demographic realities.[12] This option seems to be, at least for the present, a viable one. For this reason it provided the basic framework for the Ta'if Accord.

A third option proposes eradication of religion from public life and adoption of secularism or secular democracy.[13] This option can assume a vehement aversion to religion when it is advocated by political ideologues. Although a number of Arab states in the region have attempted to pursue this course—adopting secular democracy as a state ideology—the results so far have not been encouraging. Even Turkey has not proven a model for this option, where a small class of Western-educated intellectuals and public servants sits atop a deeply religious population. All attempts to stifle popular piety in Turkey have failed.

A final option proposes abolition of political sectarianism but preservation of religion as a social and spiritual framework operative in the lives of the various religious communities. In my view, this option is the wisest and most realistic option. It, alone, seriously recognizes the significance of the cultural and spiritual heritage of the Middle East, of which Lebanon is an integral part. It also affirms the universally desired goal of achieving a culturally and spiritually pluralistic world.

To abolish political sectarianism means to administer the state on the basis of the common good, not on the basis of sectarian affiliation or narrow sectarian interest. It means that public servants should be chosen on the basis of their qualifications, not on the basis of their sectarian affiliation. This, of course, requires that educational, social, and economic opportunities be available to all citizens without regard to sectarian affiliation, gender, or any other considerations.

To be realized, this ideal needs faith, patience, and, most of all, the freedom of every person to choose her or his way of finding the truth. This was the ideal preached by the ancient prophets of the Middle East—Moses, Jesus, and Mohammad. The Middle East gave the world an enduring universal civilization in Judaism, Christianity, and Islam; should it now renounce its greatest gift?

NOTES

1. This seems to be the assumption of Samir Khalaf in his interesting essay, "Ties That Bind: Sectarian Loyalties and the Restoration of Pluralism in Lebanon," *The Beirut Review* vol. 1 no. 1 (Spring 1991), pp. 32–61. It is even more apparent in G. C. Anawati, "The Roman Catholic Church and Churches in Communion with Rome," in A. J. Arberry (ed.), *Religion in the Middle East* vol. 1 (Cambridge University Press, 1969), pp. 354–356.

2. See Kamal Salibi, "Tribal Origins of the Religious Sects in the Arab East," in Halim Barakat (ed.), *Toward a Viable Lebanon* (London: Croom Helm, 1988), pp. 19–20 and 25–26, and Kamal Salibi, *A House of Many Mansions* (Los Angeles: University of California Press, 1990). The author bases his argument on an interesting interpretation of the names of the two communities.

3. The Maronite community did not uniformly embrace the West. As Kamal Salibi details, many Maronites refused to turn Uniate in 1180, which led to intracommunal war. There were also many Maronites who opposed the Crusaders, and who occasionally sided with the Muslims against them (see *House of Many Mansions*, pp. 87–98).

4. Salibi, *House of Many Mansions*, p. 72. The phrase "a rose among thorns" is from the Song of Solomon (2:2).

5. Salibi, *House of Many Mansions*, p. 76.

6. Salibi, *House of Many Mansions*, pp. 82–84.

7. Salibi, *House of Many Mansions*, p. 90.

8. See the chapter by Corm in this volume.

9. This is significant because in 1926 these adjacent regions were annexed to Mount Lebanon, when France created the Maronite-dominated state of Greater Lebanon.

10. See Samir Khalaf, "Ties that Bind."

11. Currently the country has seventeen Christian and Muslim sects, all of which must be represented in its fragile sectarian political system.

12. This appears again to be the view of Samir Khalaf in "Ties that Bind," where the "ties" are confessional loyalties.

13. This is the view of Daoud Khairallah, who is less radical than some in that he sees a social and spiritual role for religion and prefers secular democracy to secularism. See Khairallah's chapter in this volume.

17

Prospective Change in Lebanon

——————— · ———————

Salim el-Hoss

THE REQUISITES OF SOUND TRANSITION

The end of war should underline the need to build a state of peace—one that can consolidate the foundations of stability and set the country on a steady course of orderly evolution and progress. Unless the right kind of state is built, with all the proper systems and institutions, the country's exit from violent crisis may not mean an end to the nightmares of Lebanon, but rather a shift from one kind of nightmare to another.

Reconstruction

The country's future health can be assured only if the present menacing problems of convalescence are properly resolved. It would be ironic, to say the least, to think of long-term plans to build the appropriate institutional fabric of a healthy state when the immediate outlook of that state is effectively at stake, threatened by the grave consequences of a long, devastating conflict.

Lebanon emerged from its ravaging crisis with a great deal of its basic infrastructure all but destroyed. Even its capital city, Beirut, the once-bustling business and services center of the Middle East, is now disastrously short of electric power, water supply, telecommunication facilities, housing, and office space. The government's budget is handicapped by a large, chronic deficit, and the economy is afflicted with rampant inflation.

A previous version of this chapter, prepared for CIIPS final workshop (November 1991), was printed in *The Beirut Review* no. 3 (Spring 1992), pp. 3–16.

People's living conditions have deteriorated to critical and, for many, below-subsistence levels.

So serious has the impact of these problems been on life in Lebanon that any undue delays in grappling with them are apt to have at least three far-reaching effects: (1) stalling the reactivation of the economy, thereby aggravating the plight of a large segment of the Lebanese population; (2) tarnishing the image of legitimate authority and eventually undermining its credibility as the anchor of all hopes to extricate the country from the onerous legacy of war; and (3) impelling more Lebanese to quit their country, thereby further draining society of valuable resources for recovery and growth.

The launching of the long-anticipated International Fund for the Reconstruction of Lebanon, approved by the Baghdad Arab Summit of 1990, is expected to serve as the springboard for a wide-ranging reconstruction program for Lebanon. Although its capital allotment ($2 billion) does not appear sufficient to cope with Lebanon's vast reconstruction requirements, it is adequate for the purpose on two counts.

First, the mere establishment of the fund, with the various big industrial powers alongside the Arab Gulf countries subscribing to its capital, is an act of faith in the future of Lebanon; it should stimulate supplementary private and institutional investment capital flows. Second, the fund is more than merely a source of direct investment in Lebanon; it is a catalyst. Its inherent credibility and prospective technical capabilities should prove instrumental in attracting large amounts of project financing from international institutions, special funds in industrial and oil-producing countries, and even private organizations and individuals, including Lebanese emigrants. No wonder we view the fund as an essential contributing factor for a sound transition to a healthy future.

Liberation of the South

Another major challenge to a sound transition is the continued occupation of a vital portion of southern Lebanon by Israel. Unless and until the state regains full sovereignty over all Lebanese territory, including the occupied South, prospects for a healthy state of affairs will continue to suffer from the debilitating and destabilizing repercussions of a gaping wound. Lebanon's best prospect to achieve this objective lies with prompt implementation of UN Security Council Resolution 425 of 1978, which calls for immediate and unconditional withdrawal of Israeli troops from Lebanese territory. (In his original 1990 text, Salim el-Hoss also discussed Lebanon's need for parliamentary elections in order to relegitimize the government in the people's eyes. At that time, he noted, conditions in the country were causing skeptics to question the "government's ability to ensure . . . a democratic election process." However, he added, "even a less than perfect performance would be better than no election at all." El-Hoss reconfirmed this position in the fall of 1992, following the Lebanese elections [personal interview].—*Ed.*)

PROGNOSIS AND REMEDIES

There has been no single prognosis of Lebanon's crisis, which was associated with a nearly total collapse of the state and its major institutions. Any such prognosis, however, is bound to lead eventually to a recognition that the country's salvation can only be achieved through building the right kind of state. In other words, plans for the desired state should deal with the ills that have been identified with the defunct state of the pre-Ta'if era. The desired state should, in a nutshell, have the attributes of a strong, just, non-sectarian, administratively decentralized, and democratic system of authority.

The conflict has been portrayed by one line of thinking—albeit simplistically—as a clash between two distinct syndromes gripping the two major communities in Lebanon: that of fear on the predominantly Christian side and that of injustice on the predominantly Muslim side. The Christian community, as a large yet dwindling minority, particularly in a regional context, was allegedly worried about its identity, status in society, freedoms, and more concretely its position in the political spectrum of the country. The Muslim community, having supposedly achieved a numerical demographic edge in Lebanon, complained of a built-in political and administrative bias against it within the system; hence the political schism bedeviling Lebanese society in the pre-Ta'if era.

It was widely felt at an early stage of the crisis that what the country lacked most was a powerful and fair-minded central authority. It is likely that under the reign of a powerful central authority there would have been no chance for any sense of fear to take root, and under the reign of a fair-minded government there would have been no chance for any sense of injustice to prevail; hence the emphasis on the need for a strong army on one side, and the call for more equitable power sharing in the political system on the other. The clash between these two postures generated a great deal of friction and ill feeling.

With time the gulf between the two postures led representatives from both religious communities to entrench themselves behind more sophisticated platforms. While some called for political decentralization of the state, others called for political deconfessionalization of the system.

The call for decentralization was too often embodied in plans to federalize Lebanon into highly autonomous geographic entities, so drawn as to have distinct sectarian colorings. Certain plans betrayed the intentions of their authors to break up the country eventually into virtually independent entities, or at least so the opposing factions suspected. The call for full political deconfessionalization of the system, on the other hand, was only too often interpreted by its opponents as a disguised drive to preserve the sectarian system while shifting the reins of hegemony in the system from one sectarian hand to the other. The advocates of political deconfessionalism had on their side the full weight of argument for equality among citizens as one of the basic human rights to be honored in any civilized society. Their rejection of discrimination in the system along religious or sectarian lines was plausible and uncontestable. Their adversaries countered at times, however, with a disarming challenge; they called for full secularization, which would require the Muslims to abandon some of their religious tenets relating to marriage and inheritance. The net result of these political duels was deadlock.

The one platform to which there could be no articulate opposition was the call for democracy. Nevertheless, different conceptions of democratic practice have too often been voiced.

One is tempted to claim that in Lebanon there have been plenty of freedoms but very little democracy. Democracy may be conceived as the constitutional, legal, and institutional framework for the exercise of freedoms in a society. Abundant as have been the freedoms afforded by the system in Lebanon, democracy seems to have been lacking. Pragmatically, at least three phenomena stand in evidence of this fact, namely the absence of equal opportunity, the system's failure to exhibit the kind of resilience characteristic of democracy, and the near complete absence of political accountability.

Sectarianism, inasmuch as it reflects a negation of equal opportunity among individuals in society, has been antithetical to democracy. The rigidity of the sectarian formula practiced in the various realms of public life, at all levels of the political system as well as in the civil service, the military establishment, and, until 1990, the justice department has been a barrier to equal opportunity. Thus, regardless of one's worth or qualifications, personal or professional, unless one is of a particular sectarian affiliation, one stands no chance of attaining any particular post. This sectarian discrimination has been instrumental in breeding disenchantment and frustration among individuals, and radicalization in the ranks of underprivileged groups. In addition, it has inflicted untold damage on the efficiency of the various branches of government through its negative impact on personnel loyalty, morale, and motivation. To some extent, it may even explain the fragility of the Lebanese Army when faced with any communal trouble.

The system's patent lack of resilience was another phenomenon testifying to the dearth of democracy in Lebanon. Significantly missing in the system was a built-in mechanism of checks and balances that a true democracy must include. Unlike Western democracies, where the advent of a problem would evoke some corrective or remedial mechanism—such as a governmental or legislative action, a call for parliamentary elections, a change of government, a cabinet reshuffle, a referendum, a purge in an administration, or the like—emergent problems in Lebanon tended to fester and grow, at times to the point of a full-fledged national crisis. The strongest evidence of the lack of sufficient resilience in the system, which also calls into question the very democracy of that system, is the devastating fifteen-year crisis that broke out in 1975.

It is indeed indicative that in almost five decades of independence, between 1943 and 1990, not a single organic constitutional amendment was ratified. The only two amendments registered were procedural and momentary: one in 1948 to allow for the otherwise unconstitutional reelection of President Bishara al-Khoury for a second term, and the second in 1976 to allow for President Elias Sarkis's early election (which, it was hoped, would help expedite the end of internal hostilities and terminate the fledgling national crisis). The results in both cases were short-lived.

Democracy is intrinsically identifiable with public accountability, under which responsibility is inextricably associated with authority. In Lebanon, this has obviously not been the case. Since its independence in 1943, the country has been beset by frequent crises. Seldom has there been an occasion when a leader or notable politician has had to pay for gross negligence or dereliction of his duties (no matter how bloody the result). In a more genuine democracy, lesser political aberrations than the crises that marred Lebanon's recent history would have damaged or ended the careers of leading politicians. Instead, in Lebanon's political game, as a saying goes, "none are accountable for a mishap; all claim credit for redressing it."

THE TA'IF POLITICAL REFORMS: LEBANON'S "SECOND REPUBLIC"

The Ta'if Accord introduced some significant constitutional reforms to the system, thus signaling the onset of a new political era, and hence of the so-called Second Republic. The new republic is largely a modified version of the old; similarities between the two are indeed unmistakable. The new regime is, as was the old, predicated on sectarian foundations with the three top posts in the political hierarchy reserved for the three major religious communities: the president is to be a Maronite Christian, the speaker of parliament a Shi'ite Muslim, and the prime minister a Sunni Muslim.

Although the prerogatives of the president of the republic have been somewhat reduced—the executive authority having been shifted to the council of ministers as a collegial body—the president is left with enough power to ensure a primary and pivotal position for the Maronite community in the system. As head of state, he is regarded as overall custodian of the country's unity, independence, territorial integrity, and constitution. He may preside over all council of ministers meetings that he chooses to attend, and has the right to raise emergency matters not listed on the council's agenda. He does not, however, have the right to vote. He is president of the Higher Defense Council. He is the final cosignatory, after the prime minister, to all decrees and has the prerogative to return decrees for reconsideration by the council of ministers within a specified period of time. It is his responsibility to name a prime minister at the conclusion of parliamentary consultations, the results of which are deemed binding. He agrees with the designated prime minister over the cabinet and cosigns with him the decree proclaiming the formation of any new cabinet. By agreement with the prime minister, he may negotiate treaties with foreign countries, which subsequently must be approved by the council of ministers and, under specific conditions, by the parliament.

The prime minister, as head of a greatly reinforced council of ministers, has emerged from the Ta'if Accord with an enhanced stature; so have the ministers as members of the council. The speaker of parliament's position has also been bolstered, since his term of office was made to coincide with a full term of Parliament. Formerly he was elected on a yearly basis.

In Parliament, the balance between Christians and Muslims, formerly observed in a six-to-five ratio, has been revised in order to assure equal representation for the two communities. Slightly revised rules of sectarian distribution have been prescribed for the civil service, but in fact sectarianism has not been abandoned in the administration.

The veritable hallmark of the so-called Second Republic is reflected in the article of the constitution that vests executive authority in the council of ministers. Formerly it was vested in the person of the president of the republic, which he had to exercise in collaboration with the ministers concerned, each in his particular realm.

Obviously the Ta'if Accord has not eradicated confessionalism from the system. It has only revised its practice, avowedly with a view to achieving a fairer power-sharing formula. Whether it has, in fact, achieved this remains a matter of controversy.

As a sectarian, and therefore discriminatory, regime, the Second Republic does not embody the aspirations of enlightened Lebanese, nor does it represent an inherently stable formula. The balance it prescribes is apt to be upset by any demographic change that might take place over time. Besides, it does not address the basic grievances associated with the pre-Ta'if political environment. It has not allayed one community's fears, nor has it eradicated another community's sense of injustice. It has not provided for more effective accountability at the political or administrative levels; hence, it does not appear to have provided for a greater measure of democracy.

The Ta'if Accord has, however, articulated well-conceived general principles for devolution of power. In addition to emphasizing explicitly the need to develop a strong central authority and to preserve the greatest intercommunal mix in any administrative reorganization of the country, the accord provides for a greater measure of decentralization by delegating further administrative authority to the provinces and districts. This decentralization is hoped to bring government services closer to the reach of citizens in the various districts. The accord also calls for expanded administrative decentralization at the level of smaller geographic units (*qada'* and town) so as not to endanger the unity of the state. Furthermore, it calls for unified national development planning that also takes account of the different needs of the various regions.

A PROFILE OF THE DESIRED STATE

The profile of the desired Lebanese state will not be the view of one person alone, but rather will emerge by way of democratic interaction among various alternative plans or visions. The following profile is my own view of a desired image for Lebanon's "Third Republic." It should be underlined that any such projection cannot grow out of a void and should not constitute a break with the past or with the evolutionary change unleashed in Ta'if. In fact, the seeds of such envisioned change are to some extent embedded in the folds of the Second Republic.

1. The projected regime will have to be a democratic one. One may go as far as to say that if the system is indeed made adequately democratic, then nothing else should specifically be sought by way of reform; all further reforms would be generated by the democratic process, and would therefore be acceptable (stemming from the democratic interaction of the people's free will).

Because a perfectly sound democratic process is not conceivably attainable under the prevailing circumstances in Lebanon, it follows that ensuring the basic rules of the democratic game is a necessary, but not sufficient, condition for democratic political change. Experience has too often shown that unless the basic conditions of a democratic environment abound in the fabric of a society, a sudden and massive injection of democratic practices into that society may foster opposite forces that ultimately undermine democracy. In Lebanon these opposite forces have emerged due to such phenomena as sectarianism, regionalism, and political feudalism or traditionalism. These phenomena are endemic to the country's body politic, and have hampered the inculcation of democratic values when confronting issues and problems. Poverty and lack of proper education within a relatively large sector of society, and frequent exposure to foreign interferences, are additional contributing factors. Consequently, it would not be sufficient to project the imposition of the conventional rules of the democratic game as a sole objective. Certain additional checks and balances or safeguards will have to be introduced through the basic parameters of the system. Among these the following may be contemplated:

a. Enactment of an election law proclaiming the whole of Lebanon as a single electoral district, thus making it possible for the electorate to break loose from the straightjacket of sectarianism, regionalism, traditionalism, and political feudalism.

b. Promotion of party politics. Among the means to be considered for achieving this goal would be to restrict the prerogative of nominating candidates for parliamentary elections to authorized political parties. In order to preclude undue proliferation of parties, certain regulations may be considered, such as requiring authorized parties to have a minimum membership, or to have representation in various districts of the country; requiring any party that does not win a certain minimum percentage of the ballot in any round of elections to be eliminated from future rounds; or a combination of such or other pertinent regulations.

c. Imposition of a regulation that proclaims cabinet membership and parliamentary membership to be mutually exclusive. This would effectively preclude anyone from assuming a post in cabinet and a seat in Parliament simultaneously. Experience in Lebanon has shown that the possibility of a member of parliament assuming a cabinet portfolio has been a factor in enhancing the influence that the executive authority wields among the deputies, and has consequently weakened Parliament's ability to counterbalance the executive. Accountability, therefore, which is germane to sound democratic practice, was impaired. Consequently, separation of the two responsibilities may help to bolster the accountability of government to Parliament.

d. Creation of a more distinctly presidential regime. All tested power-sharing formulas within the executive authority, more particularly between the president of the republic and the prime minister, have thus far left a great deal to be desired. The president, as in France, should have broad, well-defined powers, for which he should be held responsible. He should be elected by direct public ballot, with no regard to his religious identity. His mandate should be relatively short, say for four years, and possibly, as in the U.S. case, renewable only once. As in France, he would be accountable practically to the public at reelection time and, in the interim, vis-à-vis the Parliament, through holding the cabinet constantly liable to a vote of no confidence. The president's accountability in this sense may be further enhanced if he is allowed a change of cabinet for only a limited number of times during a single term, beyond which he would have to step down or face public ballot again.

e. Adoption of the referendum mechanism to decide major issues. It should be possible to hold referendums at both national and local levels, depending on the nature of the issue.

2. The system should be politically secularized. This could be achieved by abolishing sectarianism at the administrative, judiciary, and military levels. Of course, deconfessionalization cannot be accomplished solely by legislation. A nonsectarian electoral law would help, as would a well-conceived antidiscrimination policy. Within the media, this policy should be based on an agreed upon, nonsectarian orientation; within the military, factionally mixed battalions and brigades should be promoted and exposed to the right kind of instruction and indoctrination; within the educational system, all schools should be required to adopt uniform textbooks, at least for history and civics.

The Ta'if Accord contained a provision calling for the formation of a high-ranking committee, including the president of the republic, the prime minister, the speaker of parliament, and others, whose task would be to lay down plans and programs for the eradication of confessionalism, and to follow up on their implementation.

The abolition of sectarianism will likely have to be pursued gradually, in different phases. The first phase may involve making all of Lebanon a single electoral district, and electing a certain percentage of the total membership of Parliament without regard to religious affiliation. This percentage may be gradually expanded as sectarian tensions taper off. When the percentage of nonsectarian representation reaches a certain level, it may be appropriate to start a bicameral system, with a senate established on the basis of equitable sectarian balance. Its task would be limited to ratifying major legislation, such as constitutional amendments and the like. This would help allay the fears of minorities.

3. The administrative division of the country should be carried out along the well-conceived principles laid down in the Ta'if Accord: a strong central authority; expanded authority for governors (*muhafiz*) and mayors (*qa'immaqam*); enhanced presence of various government departments in the districts, so as to make the government services and facilities more readily accessible to all; a revamped administrative landscape of the country to ensure the maximum intercommunal blend in every district, preserving the reality of coexistence and the unity of land, people, and institutions; and adoption of an even greater degree of administrative decentralization for the smaller administrative units (e.g., the qada' and smaller entities) with locally elected councils. This decentralization approach should be coupled with comprehensive socioeconomic development planning for the regions.

4. The powers and prerogatives of the supervisory agencies of the

public service (civil service, general inspection, and accounting court) should be enhanced and insulated from the strains and stresses of politics. This would help to shield the government machinery against any possible exposure to or allegations of corruption, nepotism, favoritism, and all undue political pressures.

Regardless of what may be said about prospects for the future, the Lebanese are now cognizant of the fact that the road to a better future can only be a democratic one. The future being a dynamic process of continuous change and evolution, the Lebanese have learned to look to democracy not only as a means to a better end, but also as an end in itself.

18

Secular Democracy: A Viable Alternative to the Confessional System

Daoud L. Khairallah

One of the most important differences between modern and traditional societies resides in their attitudes toward change. Successful modern societies are able to evaluate and modify even deeply rooted beliefs, values, and practices when these conflict with new scientific discoveries, the dictates of reason or, most of all, the collective impulse to survive and grow. In such societies, progress or change for the better is itself a dominant member of the pantheon of social values. Traditional societies, however, carry immense resistance to change. In Lebanon, resistance to changing the confessional system borders on the suicidal.

This chapter attempts to demonstrate that Lebanon's perennial problem, the confessional system, perpetuates the society's resistance to change, and is the root cause of its numerous ills. It argues that the Ta'if Accord has not been, and cannot be, a solution. Only the full-fledged adoption of secular democracy can lead Lebanon out of its self-destructive paralysis, toward a united, fully sovereign, and forward-moving statehood. Only secular democracy can provide a guarantee against the recurrence of fratricide.

Throughout the discussion, I critique the most salient arguments that favor the maintenance of Lebanon's confessionalism in one guise or another and that are against (or shy away from) a fully secular democratic system. This critique is largely confined, however, to the arguments and views expressed during the four workshops sponsored by the Canadian Institute for International Peace and Security (which best represent the general discourse on this subject).

CHARACTERISTICS OF
LEBANON'S CONFESSIONAL SYSTEM

If Lebanon is to stand against the internal and external forces that threaten its sovereignty, it has no more compelling need than unity among its people. No obstacle to national unity and social integration has proven more formidable than the confessional system. The disintegrative effect of this system has manifested itself in every aspect of Lebanese political life. Confessionalism is the root cause of the Lebanese problem.

The confessional system has two main distinguishing features: (1) political rights and entitlements are allocated to individuals according to their confessional affiliation, and (2) personal status laws,[1] and institutions through which these laws are applied, are under the exclusive control of the religious authorities of Lebanon's seventeen officially recognized sects. The application of the personal status laws and the exercise of political entitlements are intimately related. Together they form the breeding ground for a confessional culture that prevents social and political integration, and undermines any true democratic experience.

Under the prevailing system an individual's political entitlements, as well as his rights and obligations with respect to inheritance and personal status, are decided from birth. The mold that casts his social identity is pre-determined. It cements the individual to his sect. Through his family and sectarian upbringing, the individual inherits all the historic experience, generated fears, and biases harbored by the sect. The aspirations of the sect become the goals of its members. If achievement of such goals is thwarted, the culprit is not the state, but another sect or group of sects. Political life is perceived as a zero sum game in which the gains of one sect mean losses for others. Instead of representing the united national will, the state is merely a fragile shell for containing the struggle among sects. In a very practical sense, the sects in the prevailing system have become agents of disintegration and obstacles to national unity.

The confessional system permeates every aspect of Lebanese political life. It has been either a major cause of, or a serious impediment to solving, almost every significant problem that Lebanon has faced throughout its modern history. Examples abound; a few are listed below.

Undeniably, foreign intervention has been one of the most important factors in the Lebanese calamity since it began to unfold some eighteen years ago. Successful intervening powers, whether by invitation from internal sectarian groups or through manipulation of sectarian sentiments, have historically supported one sect against another. For the purposes of this chapter, it is not necessary to elaborate further on the relationship between intervening foreign powers and the various militias and sectarian leaderships during the last eighteen years.

The sectarian culture has prevented the emergence of a common

Lebanese identity and a shared national interest. Even the notion that Lebanese are Arabs (and thus share a common destiny or interest with neighboring Arab peoples) has been bitterly contested along sectarian lines, with serious political consequences. Thus, when regional developments or foreign challenges require a united national stand, Lebanon cannot muster the national will to act. Dissonant sectarian perceptions of the national interest frustrate the expression of a united national will at every turn.

Intersectarian struggle has also rendered ineffective every state institution necessary for social cohesion and political unity. When fighting broke out among the various sectarian militias, the government was unable to restore law and order. The army and police force—the very institutions entrusted with upholding law, order, and the security of the state—disintegrated and scattered under the shattering pressure of confessional leadership and loyalties.

No significant system change, however badly needed, can take place if it is likely to affect the precarious balance among the sects. Lebanon has alienated itself from scientific approaches to solving problems. Not only is a general population census taboo (the last was conducted in 1932), but any serious study (say, of a labor or social security problem involving surveys and statistical work) is also strongly opposed lest it show a change in the presumed demographic proportions of the sects.

Certainly, some aspects of the Lebanese crisis, such as the inequitable distribution of wealth, are not necessarily a direct product of the confessional system. Nevertheless, the popular diagnosis of such problems is often spelled out in sectarian terms. The opinion that the haves belong to an exploiting sect and the have-nots to an exploited sect is readily accepted by members of certain sects, regardless of its inaccuracy and distortion. As effective measures to solve such problems become entangled in sectarian jargon, inequities are left unresolved—perpetuated and protected by the pervasiveness of a rigid confessional system.

This system has continuously hindered any effective application of the rule of law, the most important manifestation of democracy. Lebanon's armed confessional militias, which destroyed the authority and institutions of the state over a period of sixteen years, are but a dramatic expression of the confessional leadership's determination to defend its narrow interests or expand its entitlements. Interference from confessional leaders to frustrate proper administration of justice has been notorious since the early days of independence. Currently, notwithstanding the cessation of hostilities and establishment of a government in which the confessional leadership is represented, this same leadership is preventing the government from exercising its basic duties, such as enabling displaced peoples (amounting to one-fifth of the total population and contributing substantially to the housing crisis) to regain their homes and properties.

When a causal relationship is so evident between the confessional system and all important manifestations of the Lebanese problem, how can we escape the conclusion that abolition of the confessional system is essential to an effective solution?

CONFESSIONALISM UNDER THE TA'IF ACCORD

The Ta'if Accord has been widely hailed as a great landmark on the way toward solving Lebanon's problems.[2] It is curious that regional and international powers have expressed far more enthusiasm for this accord than the Lebanese themselves (including the leaders of the confessional establishment).[3] Although Ta'if has been credited with stopping the bloodshed and restoring state authority, nothing could be further from the truth.

For a full year following the accord's birth (1989), encompassing election of a new president and appointment of a new government, not a single militiaman was disarmed, not an inch of Lebanese territory was liberated, and nowhere on Lebanese soil was the effective sovereignty of the state reestablished. In fact, the country endured greater destruction and bloodshed during that year than in any other.

Whatever semblance of normalcy, stability, or recovery Lebanon enjoys at present is a direct consequence of Syria's determination (in a suitable international environment). It cannot be attributed to the spirit of reconciliation among Lebanese that the Ta'if Accord is presumed to have produced. Ta'if's failure to end the bloodshed and restore the authority of the state is amply proven by the de facto recognition given to Syria—by Lebanese and foreign authorities—as the underwriter of stability in Lebanon.

The Ta'if Accord's failure is hardly surprising, since it lacked any basis for uniting the country and integrating its shattered society. Rather, it was an attempt to rejuvenate the very system that caused the disintegration of the country in the first place. Ironically, leaders with neither the ability nor the incentive to rebuild what they had destroyed were charged with restoring the state and its institutions. It was only logical that the needs that could not be tackled by the Ta'if-generated government would be met by an outside force (Syria), with an inevitable loss of part of the country's sovereignty.

Some proponents of the accord do not see it as an end solution, but as the road to Lebanon's Third Republic, because, although it maintains the basic elements of the confessional system, it provides for eventual deconfessionalization.[4] This is a lame excuse for a defective solution to a problem that caused so many years of war, and a misleading exaggeration of the likelihood that Ta'if will serve as a vehicle for eventual deconfessionalization.

While proclaiming political deconfessionalization as a national objective, Ta'if entrusts the achievement of this goal to the confessional establishment. It charges Parliament—"which is elected on equal sharing by Muslims and Christians"—to form a "national commission headed by the president . . . [with] . . . political, intellectual and societal personalities in addition to the head of parliament and prime minister."[5] The commission must present its recommendations for deconfessionalization to the president and the council of ministers, but the accord provides no guidelines for this commission and sets no time limit on its work, nor does it specify whether the recommendations will be binding on Parliament or the council of ministers, the two institutions most representative of the confessional establishment.

The full extent of the accord's commitment to deconfessionalization boils down to this: It gives the confessional establishment an unguided, nonbinding, open-ended mandate to abolish itself. Moreover, should a serious threat to the system materialize, the accord comes to the rescue in very precise and binding terms; should "parliament enact an election law which is not based on religious affiliation records," then, "concurrent with the election of the first parliament on a national rather than confessional basis, a senate will be created wherein all spiritual families will be represented."[6] The senate would have authority on matters of major importance. Furthermore, in order to guarantee the preservation of confessional culture and prevent separation between religion and state (which is one of the pillars of modern democratic rule and would logically be at the heart of deconfessionalization) the Ta'if Accord gives top religious authorities the right to petition the constitutional council in matters of personal status law, freedom of religious belief and practice, and freedom of religious education.[7] Thus, the very document purported to provide a framework for abolishing confessionalism elevates laws that are at the heart of confessional culture to the level of constitutionally protected rights. Indeed, it bestows upon religious authorities privileges that are denied ordinary citizens with respect to any right under the constitution.

Thus, the Ta'if Accord perpetuates the confessional system and the Lebanese problem. It is there to promote the interest of the confessional leadership, not curtail it. Any of its provisions likely to dilute confessional and feudal influence will be violated, as events during the 1992 parliamentary elections revealed.[8] All appearances of stability—from partial disarmament of the confessional militias to the parliamentary elections—will last only so long as Syria's will and incentive to play sponsor and underwriter endure. The most deplorable shortcoming of this presumed agreement among Lebanese is its failure to produce vitally needed national unity. Lebanon remains shattered, its government so discredited that it is not a credible participant even in decisions affecting its destiny, let alone its sovereignty and territorial integrity.

SECULAR DEMOCRACY: A VIABLE ALTERNATIVE

An alterative political system must be found if Lebanon is to survive and flourish as an independent country. It is clear what such a system must do: transcend the barriers that separate Lebanese of different sects; promote social and political cohesion, with guarantees against the recurrence of the last Lebanese tragedy; generate common values, interests, and goals and give them expression in state laws and institutions such that all Lebanese enjoy equal rights and opportunities; forge a common perception of the national interest and public good; and (while respecting pluralism) be effective in bringing about needed change by solving problems that are the inevitable product of political life in any society.

Fortunately, such a political system need not be invented. Secular democracy is a form of governance that has withstood the test of time, constituting the solid foundation of the most advanced, stable, and integrated states where the rights of individuals are respected. It is the political system most suitable to the establishment and maintenance of a modern state.

In Lebanon, only secular democracy can provide the discourse likely to bring members of different sects to a durable agreement on national objectives and policies. The interest or voice of one sect cannot be the interest and voice of all Lebanon's citizens, nor can a mere totality of the contradictory interests and objectives of all the sects constitute a common "national" interest and objective; the entire history of modern Lebanon (not only the sixteen years of war) has sadly proven this. The solution offered by secular democracy is the only one capable of creating one Lebanese cause, of attracting Lebanese of all sects, of giving meaning to the sacrifices suffered and lives lost, and of facilitating the emergence of a stable, independent country.

Is the establishment of a secular democratic system in Lebanon achievable? Scholars who have studied successful democratic experiences have identified certain factors that contribute to the emergence of a democratic system.[9] Most of these factors were present in Lebanon, accounting for the relative success of its prewar democratic experience. Two factors, however, undermined this relative success: (1) Lebanon's vulnerability to intervention by outside forces opposed to democracy, and (2) the divisive effects of subcultural pluralism.[10]

As noted earlier, it is the confessional system that has rendered Lebanon vulnerable to foreign intervention. The country's disintegrated society facilitated and guaranteed the success of foreign intervention, not the other way around.

The only manifestation of subcultural pluralism in Lebanon occurs along religious lines. As Albert Hourani rightly observes:

> The division along religious lines is not a total division. There is a unity of language; all groups are Arabic-speaking, except for some Armenians.

> There is a similarity of popular culture, of manners, habits of life, cuisine, and even popular religion of the countryside; one can still find in the Lebanese mountains sacred springs and sacred trees on which votive rags are hung, the outward symbols of a divine presence.[11]

Even so, cultural homogeneity is not strictly necessary for a successful democracy. Democracy can survive and prosper despite extensive subcultural pluralism. However, when the solidarity within one subculture is strengthened by fear and mistrust of another subculture, and when the perception of common interests and identification with members of the other subculture are reduced to a level insufficient to maintain national cohesion, violence erupts and democracy collapses along with national unity.[12] When, on the other hand, the legal and institutional framework and the general political environment encourage development of emotional ties among members of different subcultures, social cohesion at the national level is strengthened and any tendency to resort to violence is reduced.[13]

The confessional system may foster ties among members of the same sect, but it encourages division and alienation among Lebanese of different religious subcultures. Its laws act as barriers to the development of transsectarian identifications and crosscutting loyalties that are integral to forging national cohesion and successful democracy.

OPPOSITION TO SECULAR DEMOCRACY

The real reasons why many politicians and some intellectuals oppose establishment of a secular democratic state are numerous, but their pretext is usually one: Secular democracy, they argue, is incompatible with Lebanon's deeply rooted (mostly religious) subculture. Three different variations on this theme, representative of the forces opposed to secular democracy, are critiqued below.

Samir Khalaf, arguing in favor of the confessional system, challenges the notion that "the underlying problem of any political system . . . is one of asserting and legitimizing the priority of the nation-state over the tribal and traditional loyalties."[14] He maintains that the confessional system embodies the primordial ties that are strongest and most enduring in Lebanese political life.

Khalaf recognizes the incompatibility between preservation of these primordial ties and the emergence of civil society. Indeed, he acknowledges that, under the prevailing system, Lebanon "is neither national nor civic." While Khalaf does not overtly embrace Ernest Renan's distinction between nations that emerge by destroying primordial ties through "human will, volition, and consent rather than sheer force, coercion or cruelty," and nonnational political units that "retained much of the so-called primordial and archaic identities," his argument seems to place Lebanon in the latter category.[15]

In a 1968 article, Khalaf states that "political modernization in Lebanon need not involve a clear transfer of sovereignty from primordial allegiance to secular and ideological commitments." He suggests that the values and historical traditions rooted in Lebanese culture may inhibit Lebanon from developing a rational, democratic state: "It is doubtful whether Lebanese society can ever be a duplicate of a rational, secular and egalitarian society based exclusively on achievement-oriented and universalistic criteria." Khalaf is suggesting, therefore, that it may not be possible to overcome or alter primordial ties in Lebanon. Moreover, he then goes on to credit the confessional system that embodies these ties with most of the benefits that Lebanon has experienced (including its prewar periods of prosperity and stability) while showing impatience with widespread criticism of the system.[16]

In this same article, Khalaf observes: "Primordial ties and loyalties are not as often assumed, an impediment to national solidarity and political unity. It is true that factors like kinship, fealty and religion may undermine or inhibit the growth of civil national loyalties, but they need not be detrimental in terms of the overall political stability in society."[17] In 1991, after sixteen years of war and destruction, he notes: "The political history of Lebanon appears to have degenerated, once again, into a history of communal conflict."[18] He acknowledges that confessional loyalties undermined "civic consciousness and commitment to Lebanon as a nation-state," and that "communal attachments and the network based on them may not so much dampen open radicalism as exacerbate it. Instead of acting as a buffer against militancy, as has been recently argued, they may provide individuals and groups with the determinations, resources, and legitimation to participate in collective violence. . . . Indeed, confessional loyalties have become so intense that they now account for much of the bigotry and paranoia permeating the entire social fabric."

If the current state of social disintegration is the result of sixteen years of "communal conflict," one might expect Khalaf to have lost faith in the political system that embodies these "primordial ties." This does not appear to be the case. He continues to back the confessional system, albeit with a vague subscription to some adjustments. As to the primordial ties, he states:

> Pathological as they may seem at the moment, such communal solidarities need not continue to be sources of paranoia and hostility. They could be extended and enriched to incorporate other more secular and civic identities. If stripped of their bigotism and intolerance, they could also become the basis for more equitable and judicious forms of power sharing and the

articulation of new cultural identities. Here lies the hope, the only hope, for an optimal restructuring of Lebanon's pluralism.

Unfortunately, Khalaf does not reveal how such solidarities can be "stripped of their bigotism and intolerance," or how this refurbishing could possibly be achieved within the confines of a confessional system.

Khalaf's advocacy for preservation of the confessional system has at least two fundamental flaws. First, it does not indicate how national unity—Lebanon's most pressing need, if it is to overcome its chronic crisis—is to be achieved. (I argue—in total opposition to this view—that preservation of the confessional system will only perpetuate the prevailing state of disintegration.) Second, by exaggerating the tenacity of "primordial ties," Khalaf downplays the feasibility of instituting a system that would encourage development of alternative ties and crosscutting loyalties compatible with the requirements of a secular democratic state. In my view, Khalaf's perspective—instead of promoting much-needed change—adds scholarly weight to arguments that stand as obstacles to change.

In contrast to Khalaf's support for confessionalism, Mahmoud Ayoub's opposition to secular democracy stems from his opposition to "Westernization," and his belief that religion in the Middle East plays, and should continue to play, an important role in social and political life. He is basically opposed to separation of religion from state. Safeguards for an individual's rights and freedoms, he proposes, should be limited to those granted him as a member of a group, with special respect for religion.[19] Ayoub's argument does not clearly indicate how much Westernization should be accepted and how much avoided, nor whether there should be a substantial reversal of the Westernization and secularization that have been taking place in the Arab Middle East, including Lebanon, since the early nineteenth century. No doubt Ayoub is aware that those who seek secular democracy as a solution to the Lebanese problem are not trying to sneak a novel concept into Lebanon (or the region) through the back door of politics. The societies he wants shielded from Westernization have already adopted Western political and legal concepts in the vast majority of their laws and institutions.

In addition to uniting the country and solving its problems, implementing secular democracy would widen the base of scientific and rational behavior in Lebanese social and political life. It is not clear why any society should deny itself helpful concepts and ideas that have become part of the human patrimony—especially the model offered by secular democracy, including the Universal Declaration of Human Rights, the greatest modern standard of social and political progress yet devised. The West itself knows the value of assimilation. It was the West that once upon a time absorbed the accumulated knowledge of Arab thinkers and scientists.

The argument that, in the Middle East, Islam is perceived and should

be applied as both a religion and a form of government cannot be convinc-
ingly made in the Lebanese case. By no stretch of the imagination can the
confessional system be considered an expression of Sharia.[20] On the other
hand, selective application of Sharia is not in conformity with any Islamic
religious theory. The fact that only a part of the Sharia is still applied in
Lebanon (and in many other Arab countries) has no justification in religious theory. It does, however, have a sociological explanation. Students of
legal sociology have long known that of all branches of law, family law is
the most resistant to change. This is all the more so in patriarchal societies
(like those of the Arab countries), and has been well demonstrated in the
Middle East—from the early reception of foreign laws under the Ottoman
Empire through to the present.[21]

Nevertheless, when awareness of the need to change meets a will to
change, one could expect that Islam would be as flexible with respect to
personal status and inheritance law as it has been with respect to other areas
of law. After all, total secularization has taken place in countries with overwhelming Muslim majorities.[22] In countries where Muslims were not a
majority, they sought separation of religion and state.[23]

A third view, represented here by the writings of Salim el-Hoss, stops
short of calling for full-fledged secular democracy. Instead the call is for
"political deconfessionalism." Salim el-Hoss is keenly aware of the relationship between confessionalism and the Lebanese problem. He rightly
observes that Lebanon's "salvation could be achieved with a formula for
the right kind of state," which could come about only through a "call for
democracy . . . the one platform to which there could be no articulate opposition."[24] He correctly asserts that the confessional system lacks resilience,
defies political accountability, negates equal opportunity among individuals, and has been antithetical to democracy. Nevertheless, el-Hoss considers political deconfessionalism to be sufficient change to correct Lebanon's
ills. He sees the contest between proponents of political deconfessionalism
and their adversaries in the following terms:

> The advocates of political deconfessionalism had on their side the full
> weight of argument for equality among citizens as a basic human right.
> Their adversaries countered at times with a disarming challenge calling
> for full secularization which would require the Muslims to abandon some
> of their religious tenets relating to marriage and inheritance.

El-Hoss goes on to explain that, unfortunately, some Christian members of the confessional establishment have, without the slightest commitment to secular democracy, reacted to proposals for political deconfessionalism with a call for full secularization. This tactic was designed to
frustrate and blunt the argument of the deconfessionalists, in order to preserve the confessional status quo. Regrettably, the attitude of some advo-

cates of political deconfessionalism has lent credibility to the fears spread by their opponents in the confessional establishment. It has also raised the suspicions of those who seek genuine reform.

Political deconfessionalism is without precedent in any democratic society. It is intended to keep outside the political and democratic process the laws governing inheritance, the family (the basic nucleus in the social structure), and the institutions for their application. According to this view, these areas would continue to fall within the exclusive control of the religious authorities of Lebanon's seventeen officially recognized sects. As such, the people's elected representatives would not be permitted to modify or unify these laws (which would remain protected by a sacred prohibition), regardless of society's interest in so doing.

Political deconfessionalism will not lead to democracy. It may lead to further fragmentation of Lebanese society, however, for the following reasons:

First, as a form of self-government whereby citizens are entrusted, directly or through their elected representatives, with choosing the laws and institutions that govern their lives, democracy is essentially secular. The premise underpinning democracy is that each member of the self-governing group is rational and morally autonomous. To deny people the right to participate in the process of choosing laws and institutions that govern very important aspects of their lives is to deny them the ability to develop as moral and social beings, and to prevent them from protecting and advancing their fundamental rights, interests, and concerns.[25] Consequently, one would be hard pressed to find a truly democratic society that is not secular.

Second, political deconfessionalism is totally incompatible with social integration, unity, and development of common interests and objectives (which are probably Lebanon's most compelling needs at this point in time). Rather, it preserves laws and institutions that breed the sectarian culture and frustrate the most effective form of social integration—the emergence of crosscutting loyalties among members of different religious groups (by way of marriage, for example).

Third, preservation of the vast discrepancies in personal status laws that govern Lebanon's officially recognized sects (which are presumed to comprise the totality of *one* Lebanese society) is not only incompatible with democratic practice, but also violates at least three articles of the Universal Declaration of Human Rights.[26] Moreover, it contravenes the Lebanese constitution, which avows the binding effect of this declaration "in every field without exception."[27]

Fourth, the argument that secularization would require Muslims to abandon some of their religious tenets ignores the following realities: (1) Every Muslim living in a democratic society where man-made laws apply indiscriminately to all members of society has in fact abandoned some of his religious tenets; and (2) Sharia can be selectively applied, meaning that some equally binding religious laws can be abandoned while others cannot. Moreover, in Lebanon's case, the current system of personal status laws can require Lebanese to abandon or compromise their religiosity, as exemplified by these social absurdities: (1) A potential spouse who undergoes religious conversion immediately before the marriage (in order to overcome a legal obstacle by the sect of the betrothed) expresses genuine conviction and commitment to the newly acquired religious tenets; and (2) Civil marriages between two Lebanese of different sects are recognized as valid if officiated outside Lebanon, but are not recognized if officiated on Lebanese soil. (Is this really a rational and logical national policy?)

Fifth, political deconfessionalism is bound to harden resistance to change by the chief beneficiaries and supporters of the confessional system, and to demoralize a large segment of society, leading to further fragmentation.

Key objectives of any political reform in Lebanon must be social cohesion at the national level, a common perception of the national interest, and a shared commitment to protecting that interest. The confessional system is the root cause of the Lebanese problem. It must be abolished.

The establishment of secular democracy will become a reality to the extent that the forces working for its achievement overcome the forces resisting it. Institutions and values underlying democratic practices take root and endure only to the extent they are adopted and protected by the people. Constitutional and legislative actions, and means for their effective enforcement, remain basic vehicles for change, but education and mobilization of public opinion are crucial to the ultimate success of any change. The role of the intelligentsia in creating awareness and support for the needed change cannot be underestimated.

In my opinion, the Lebanese intelligentsia—the main agents of any meaningful change, the interpreters and menders of the broken sociopolitical code of conduct—bear substantial blame for the lack of awareness concerning Lebanon's pressing need for change. Neither before, nor during, nor after the civil war did the intelligentsia or political elite sponsor rational and viable solutions to the Lebanese problem.

Resistance to abolishing the confessional system resides in the confessional establishment and some influential foreign powers, not in immutable cultural habits. It should be noted that prior to 1975, significant social and economic ties had developed among members of different religious groups. Urban life, secular education, and social and business associations had already eroded confessionalism to a considerable extent.[28] These integrating ties did not grow as a result of rational political or social planning; rather, they emerged in spite of the constraints imposed by a system that frustrated and discouraged their development.

In rational societies, laws are enacted to promote the common good and overcome the divisive effects of substantial differences. In Lebanon, confessional laws and institutions promote and perpetuate divisive values and practices. They undermine the development of the most effective social ties: family ties and crosscutting loyalties among Lebanese of all sects. Lebanon's sixteen years of war—and the country's prevailing condition—testify that replacing the confessional system with a secular democratic one is a matter of national survival.

NOTES

Those well versed in the tenets of democracy may find the title of this chapter redundant. I do not wish to imply there are forms of true democracy that are not secular, for I know of none. Rather, I wish to emphasize the secular nature of democracy, which I consider an effective solution to the Lebanese problem, as distinguished from secularization per se. While a secular rule may be undemocratic, as many dictatorships have well demonstrated, the converse does not hold. True democracy can only be secular. That is, to the extent that democracy is "rule by the people" (a form of self-government in which man, considered rational and morally autonomous, is entrusted with the decisions that control the management of his life in society), democracy is essentially secular.

1. These are the laws that govern matters relating to personal status such as birth, marriage, divorce, inheritance.

2. For further discussion of the Ta'if Accord, see the chapters by Joseph Maila and by A. R. Norton.

3. The Christian leadership has either opposed Ta'if (e.g., General Aoun, Raymond Eddé) or supported it half-heartedly. Nabih Birri and Kamal Jumblatt (representing the Shi'ite Amal and Druze PSP militias respectively) have expressed dissatisfaction with it. Only U.S., Saudi, and Syrian representatives constantly express their support for the accord's full implementation.

4. See discussions in Deirdre Collings and Jill Tansley, *Peace for Lebanon? Obstacles, Challenges and Prospects,* Working Paper no. 43 (Ottawa: Canadian Institute for International Peace and Security, May 1992).

5. See the Ta'if Accord, Caption 2: Political Reforms, section (g).

6. Ta'if Accord, Caption 2: Political Reforms, section (a).

7. Ta'if Accord, Caption 3: Other Reforms, sections (B), (b).

8. Ta'if calls for an increase in the number of members of parliament to 108 and requires that the electorate unit be the *mohafazah*. In the latest elections, members of parliament increased to 128 and the mohafazah was adopted as an electoral unit in certain regions of the country, while other regions used the *qada'*—to accommodate and guarantee the election of key confessional leaders. See the chapter by A. R. Norton.

9. For discussion of these factors see Tatu Vanhanen, *The Emergence of Democracy: A Comparative Study of 119 States, 1850–1979* (Helsinki: Finnish Society of Arts and Letters, 1984), and Robert A. Dahl, *Democracy and Its Critics* (New Haven: Yale University Press, 1989).

10. See Dahl, *Democracy,* pp. 254–264.

11. Albert Hourani, *Political Society in Lebanon: A Historical Introduction,* Inaugural Lecture of the Emile Bustani Middle East Seminar, 3 October 1985 (Cambridge, Mass.: Center for International Studies, MIT, 1986).

12. See Dahl, *Democracy,* p. 255.

13. Acting on behalf of the International Institute of Intellectual Cooperation (associated with the League of Nations), Albert Einstein asked Sigmund Freud for his perspective on ways to deliver mankind "from the menace of war." Freud's reply noted: "Anything that encourages the growth of emotional ties between men must operate against war. These ties may be of two kinds. In the first place they may be relations resembling those towards a loved object, though without having a sexual aim. . . . The second kind of emotional tie is by means of identification. Whatever leads man to share important interests produces this community of feeling, these identifications. And, the structure of human society is to a large extent based on them." *Pelican Freud Library* vol. 12.

14. In discussing Khalaf's position, I rely mostly on two articles: "Primordial Ties and Politics in Lebanon," *Middle East Studies* vol. 4 (1968), and "Ties That Bind: Sectarian Loyalties and Restoration of Pluralism in Lebanon," *The Beirut Review* vol. 1 no. 1 (Spring 1991). I also draw on his contribution to the CIIPS workshop series (1990–1991). The citation is from "Primordial Ties," p. 263.

15. See "Ties That Bind," p. 33.

16. All citations in this paragraph are from "Primordial Ties," pp. 241 and 261.

17. See "Primordial Ties," pp. 245–246.

18. Citations in the next two paragraphs are from "Ties That Bind," pp. 53–56.

19. See Collings and Tansley, *Peace for Lebanon?* p. 99. My comments on Ayoub's view are based on his contributions during the CIIPS workshop series, as well as personal conversations with him.

20. *The Shorter Encyclopedia of Islam* (Ithaca: Cornell University Press, 1965) defines Sharia as "the totality of Allah's Commandments relating to the activities of man, apart from those relating to ethics (*akhlak*) which are treated separately." As a technical term it is also referred to as "The Canon Law of Islam."

21. See Herbert J. Liebesny, *The Law of the Near and Middle East* (New York: State University of New York Press, 1975), p. 56.

22. Turkey is a glaring example of the total separation between religion and state. The explanatory note to the Turkish Civil Code of 1926, which replaced Sharia-inspired laws, stated: "The goal of legislation is not to maintain customs or beliefs having their origin in religion, but to assure the economic and social unity of the nation. Also, modern legislation must establish a separation between law and religion. . . . By separating the temporal and spiritual spheres, modern civilization has saved the world from many calamities and has given religion an imperishable place in the conscience of the believers. . . . For countries whose citizens belong to different religions, it is even more necessary to break with religion. Otherwise, it would not be possible to issue laws applicable to all citizens. On the other hand, if laws are enacted for each religious minority, the political and social unity of the nation will be broken." Quoted in Liebesny, *The Law of the Near and Middle East,* pp. 80–81.

23. See Halim Barakat, *Society, Culture and State* (Berkeley: University of California Press, 1992), pp. 270–271.

24. All citations for el-Hoss are from his comments at CIIPS workshops; see also his chapter in this volume.

25. See Dahl, *Democracy.*

26. Articles 2, 7, and 16.

27. Paragraph B of the Introduction, containing general principles that were added to the Lebanese Constitution as amended on 21 September 1990.

28. See Kamal Salibi, *A House of Many Mansions* (London: I.B. Taurus, 1988), p. 196.

19

Culture, Collective Memory, and the Restoration of Civility

Samir Khalaf

How can a fractured, plural society, beleaguered by protracted civil strife and entrapped in a tumultuous region, incorporate painful events of its past into its national identity and collective memory? The rhetorical tone of this query notwithstanding, it is not as florid or abstract as it may seem. It has concrete implications for efforts aimed at articulating and healing Lebanon's conflicting conceptions of itself and its troublesome past.

To commemorate a country's former glories, or those historic events that are sources of national pride and collective consensus, would be, one assumes, a relatively easy task. Had Lebanon's war, for example, been a heroic or redemptive experience through which Lebanon sought to recover its lost integrity and virtue, or transformed itself into a secular and more viable entity, or, better yet, had it been an experience that helped to bring the Lebanese people closer together, then there would have been no problem in embodying such a "glorious" national event in the country's collective memory.

Alas, the war—or *adath* (events) as it is often dismissed in colloquial argot—in both its origin and consequences has neither been a source of collective inspiration nor consensus. All wars are atrocious. The catalog of horrors spawned by the Lebanese war requires no further documentation. They have been chronicled ad nauseam and are now etched, thanks to the graphic imagery of the media, in our collective consciousness. The direct physical devastation of life and property and the associated sociopsychological damage are, by almost any measure, extraordinary. They are particularly galling in Lebanon's case precisely because they are not anchored in any recognizable and coherent set of causes, nor have they resolved the issues that might have sparked off the initial hostilities. In this poignant sense, the war has been wasteful and futile, ugly and unfinished.

There is a painful irony in this. The Lebanese have not only been reduced to hapless victims of catastrophic events beyond their control, they now face the menace of a demoralizing national image. Deservedly or not, this once vibrant republic, with more than a modicum of pluralist and democratic institutions, has degenerated into an ugly metaphor; a mere figure of speech to highlight the most foreboding encounters elsewhere in the world. "Lebanon" is only invoked to conjure up images of the grotesque and unspeakable.

The task of representing or incorporating such inglorious events and malign images into a nation's collective identity is highly problematic, but it needs to be done. Otherwise, the memory of the war, like the harrowing events themselves, would be trivialized and forgotten and, hence, more prone to be repeated.

Among all the disheartening consequences of the war, two are particularly relevant to this chapter, namely, symptoms of "retribalization" (apparent in reawakened communal identities and the urge to huddle in cloistered spatial communities) and second, a pervasive mood of lethargy, indifference, and weariness that borders at times on "collective amnesia." Both are understandable reactions that enabled traumatized groups to survive the cruelties of protracted strife. Both, however, could be disabling as the Lebanese now consider less belligerent strategies for coexistence. The issues underlying these problems can be restated in explicit terms: (1) Through what vectors and mediating agencies can resurgent, parochialized identities become the basis for the articulation of a political culture of tolerance? (2) Who is to mobilize and speak on behalf of those who are numbed and bereft of speech?

Let me pose the questions still a bit more graphically. Suppose we establish a war museum in Lebanon or erect a score of national monuments. What messages, artifacts, or symbols, if any, could crystallize events associated with the war or the new sociocultural realities and unify society around them? How is one to write or rewrite a coherent and unifying history of the war? How, in the words of Wagner-Pacifici and Schwartz, "is commemoration without consensus, or without pride, possible?"[1]

Discussing and analyzing such processes can tell us much about how culture and cultural meanings are produced, as well as how they become lodged in and assimilated into the collective memory of a society. In the case of Lebanon, they could also tell us how a society comes to terms with troublesome events of its past and how, by "celebrating" and memorializing these divisive and futile events, the process itself could become a source of moral unity and collective rejuvenation. The recent experience of Israel, particularly the processes by which those involved in the misadventure in Lebanon have come to rationalize their experience, is instructive.

Israeli officials, we are told, when speaking at ceremonies occasioned by the Lebanese war, extol their soldiers in words that are vivid and inspiring. Their remarks about the war itself, however, are vague and pointless. They affirm the war as a historical event but "deny it an elevated place in the national experience. The event is swallowed, as it were, but never assimilated. Such is the memory of 'Israel's Vietnam': a misbegotten cause nobly pursued."[2]

Clearly, there is nothing noble about the Lebanese war. It was a misbegotten experience in all its despicable dimensions. Nevertheless, it must be assimilated into our collective consciousness and transformed into an instrument for recovery and national solidarity. This preliminary exploration is a modest step in that direction.

Three vital but overlooked dimensions of this salient predicament will be briefly exposed. First, how can the collective memory or memories of the war, searing and divisive as they are, become instruments for recovery? Second, what role can culture, particularly urban design and other aesthetic sensibilities, play in rehabilitating and articulating a political culture of tolerance? Finally, how can such efforts reinforce prospects for the restoration of civility?

THE WAR AND COLLECTIVE MEMORY

Lebanon's checkered experience with civil unrest reveals a large residue of unresolved or unappeased hostility. Indeed, virtually all confrontations, even the bloodiest, were rarely resolved explicitly. Combatants entrapped in violent conflict generally find it psychologically dignifying to mystify the outcomes of hostility. Like other victims of protracted violence, they often opt to suffer the more "tolerable" cruelties of strife rather than the "intolerable" psychic wounds of defeat. The ethos of "no victor, no vanquished," so endemic to Lebanon's political culture, is an expedient strategy for such purposes. Hence, wars never seem to end, or are never permitted to end, with the unequivocal defeat or victory of one group over another. As a result, Lebanon (like Ireland, Bosnia, and other instances of so-called low-intensity conflict that also come to mind) can never freely will its entry or exit from war.

This is not, clearly, a benign predicament. Had any of the earlier episodes of political violence been more explicitly resolved, then the issues associated with each might have been more realistically recognized and addressed. In doing so, Lebanon might have been spared many of the trials and tribulations of subsequent turmoil. The Ta'if Accord, like earlier such covenants heralding a new, nonbelligerent order, offers only a temporary reprieve from the ravages of war. All the adversaries, including those whose interests are presumably being served by the accord, remain disillusioned. It suspends the fighting without addressing some of the basic issues or sources that provoked and sustained the violence.

This is not meant as a glib denouncement of Ta'if; its virtues and shortcomings are discussed elsewhere in this volume. I am not expecting Ta'if to be a Bill of Rights or a Magna Carta. It is, however, Lebanon's new covenant: a blueprint, a manifesto, as it were, to restore civility and transform the rhetoric of confrontation into a new architecture of peace and reintegration. In this regard, it is starkly deficient.

By a curious coincidence, as Ta'if was being pronounced, the Paris Charter was issued at the conclusion of the Conference on Security and Cooperation in Europe (CSCE) on 21 November 1990. One cannot but dwell on the difference between the two documents. Both, after all, were inspired by the same vision and felicitous hopes: the creation of a political culture of tolerance. The Paris Charter is concerned with the specters hovering over Europe today—political reintegration and economic cooperation in times of profound change and ferment, while preserving the ethnic, cultural, and religious identities of national minorities. Are these not also the problems that have plagued Lebanon for so long: political stability and integration, balanced economic growth, allaying the fears and grievances of communities, communal versus national identities, times of ferment, regional and international rivalries? The Paris Charter not only affirms its steadfast commitment to fundamental human values (i.e., democracy based on human rights and fundamental freedoms, prosperity through economic liberty and justice) but goes further to offer explicit guidelines for the future. Alas, there is little of this in Ta'if. Instead, perhaps for understandable reasons, it is excessively concerned with issues of political reform, power sharing, and administrative reorganization. Important as these are, they skirt or gloss over some of the sociocultural and psychological realities exacerbated by the war.

History and future generations will not be kind to us if, after sixteen years of protracted cruelties, the most we can come up with is a small change in the proportion governing parliamentary representation (now six to six rather than six to five). The accord, in this regard, is deficient and fickle. It is a flagrant misreading, a distortion of the underlying causes that drove the Lebanese to civil strife. It also rests on a grievous delusion: that recutting the political pie will cause economic disparities and sociocultural differences to disappear.

Let me briefly expose two such issues identified earlier—retribalization and collective amnesia—before moving on to consider how they can be mitigated and transformed into rehabilitative strategies. First, confessional sentiments and their supportive loyalties, even in times of relative peace and stability, can be effective sources of social support and political mobilization, but they are not, as Lebanon's fractious history amply demonstrates, unmixed blessings. While they can cushion individuals and groups against the anomie and alienation of public life, they can also increase the density of communal hostility and enmity. In Lebanon, such processes have been particularly acute largely because class, ideological, and other secular forms of group affiliation have been comparatively more distant and abstract and, consequently, of less relevance to the psychic and social needs of the uprooted and traumatized. Hence, the war has prompted more and more Lebanese to brandish their confessionalism, if we may invoke a dual metaphor, as both emblem and armor. Emblem, because confessional identity has become the most viable medium for asserting presence and securing vital needs and benefits. Without it groups are rootless, nameless, and voiceless. One is not heard or recognized unless confessional allegiance is first disclosed. It is only when an individual is placed within a confessional context that his ideas and assertions are rendered meaningful or worthwhile. Confessionalism is also being used as armor, because it has become a shield against real or imagined threats. The more vulnerable the emblem, the thicker the armor. Conversely, the thicker the armor, the more vulnerable and paranoid other communities become. It is precisely this dialectic between threatened communities and the urge to seek shelter in cloistered worlds that has plagued Lebanon for so long.

There is a curious and painful irony here. Despite the many differences that divide the Lebanese, they are all in a sense homogenized by fear, grief, and trauma. Fear, as it were, is the tie that binds and holds them together—three primal fears, in fact: of being marginalized, assimilated, or exiled. However, those fears also keep the Lebanese apart. This geography of fear is not sustained by walls or artificial barriers as one observes in other comparable instances of ghettoization of minorities and ethnic groups. Rather, it is sustained by the psychology of dread, hostile bonding, and ideologies of enmity.

The war in Lebanon, with its protracted sectarian-based violence, destroyed common spaces and reinforced proclivities to exclusive and seclusive spatial arrangements.[3] Massive population shifts, particularly since they were accompanied by the reintegration of displaced groups into more homogeneous, self-contained, and exclusive spaces, reinforced communal solidarity. Consequently, territorial and confessional identities began to converge. For example, prior to the outbreak of hostilities, 44 percent of all villages and towns included inhabitants of more than one sect. As Salim Nasr has shown, sectarian migration during the war harshly reshuffled this mixture. While the proportion of Christians living in the southern regions of Mount Lebanon (i.e., Shouf, Aley, Upper Metn) was 55 percent in 1975, it had shrunk to about 5 percent by the late 1980s. The same is true of West Beirut and its suburbs. Likewise, the proportion of Muslims living in the eastern suburbs of Beirut has also been reduced from 40 percent to about 5 percent over the same period.[4]

Expressed in spatial terms, if urbanization normally stands for variety, universality, mix, openness, then what has been happening in Lebanon, at least in a majority of areas, is ghettoization. In this sense the Lebanese are inverting what might be assumed to be the most typical course of evolution in social systems.

Social and intellectual historians are keen on reminding us that a fascinating transformation in the historical evolution of most societies involves their passage from a relatively closed to a more open system; membership, exit or entry, and access to privileges and benefits are no longer denied by virtue of limitations of religion, kinship, or race. Such openness accounts for much of the spectacular philosophical, artistic, and political emancipation of contemporary societies. It is in this sense that Lebanon stands today at a critical threshold. We either resist this inversion of the natural course of history, or we succumb to the repressive and pathological manifestations of exclusive communities hostile to any form of coexistence and tolerance.

In hindsight, one can readily understand the proclivity of the Lebanese, indeed of any traumatized or threatened group, to seek shelter in cloistered communities, especially during times of cruel, protracted, internecine, communal fighting. That this ghettoization occurred cannot be wished away or mystified. Now, in the war's aftermath, there is a danger that the war-induced geography of fear will persist. The coalition of confessional and territorial entities could be particularly potent in Lebanon: a more viable vector for political mobilization than kinship, fealty, or sectarian loyalties.

Second, the war has also generated a pervasive mood of what is labeled, for lack of a better term, collective amnesia. To survive the cruelties of war, the Lebanese psyche became deadened and numbed. Like other victims of collective suffering, the people became desensitized and overwhelmed by muted anguish and pain.

During the war, such callousness (often masquerading as resilience) served them well. It allowed them to survive, but also to inflict and rationalize cruelties on the "other." By distancing or cutting themselves off from the "other," they routinized the brutality of embattled communities and became morally indifferent to violence. People could engage in guilt-free violence and kill with impunity precisely because they had restricted contacts with their defiled victims. To a large extent, it is "the group boundaries," as Randall Collins tells us, "that determine the extent of human sympathy; within these boundaries, humanity prevails; outside them, torture is inflicted without qualm."[5]

That which enabled the Lebanese to sustain and survive the cruelties of civil strife is clearly disabling now that they are considering options for peaceful coexistence. Here again, Collins is quick to remind us that "the point is not to learn to live with the demons, but to take away their powers."[6] The issue, here as well, converges on who is to mobilize or speak on behalf of those whose painful experiences have left them numbed and bereft of speech.

THE SOCIAL TECHNOLOGIES OF PACIFICATION

What groups are most qualified to play such healing roles? Where, when, and with what does one commence the processes of healing and rehabilitation? Since many of the internal contradictions are exacerbated by unresolved regional and international rivalries, how is one to neutralize such external sources of destabilization? How much, after all, can be accomplished in reversing deeply embedded cultural or geopolitical realities rendered all the more incompliant by the war?

As a fragmented, diminutive state entrapped in a turbulent region, Lebanon will always be made more vulnerable by forces beyond its borders. This is the fate of many such tiny republics. To a large degree, Lebanon is destined to remain at the mercy of its neighbors' goodwill and the compassion of international organizations. Much can be done, however, by the Lebanese themselves to merit and consolidate such redemptive concerns. Furthermore, the task of reconstituting or reconstructing a society is much too vital to be left to politicians and vengeful militias. Concerted efforts must be made to broaden and incorporate the participation of other, thus far overlooked, elements.

I take my point here from Paul Rabinow's analysis of the sociocultural history of France between 1830 and 1930. He delineates the constellation of thought, action, and passions underlying what he terms the "social technologies of pacification" as tools for reforming and controlling the inherent antagonisms between space and society, forms and norms, that France was undergoing during that eventful century.[7]

Rabinow identifies a set of actors—ranging from aristocratic dandies, governors, and philanthropists to architects, intellectuals, and urban reformers—who were all infused with this passion to "pacify the pathos" and, consequently, who articulated a set of pragmatic solutions to public problems in times of crisis (e.g., wars, epidemics, strikes, etc.). Despite their divergent backgrounds, they shared two common perspectives: (1) bitterness about the institutional and cultural crisis of their society, and (2) an unshaken faith in positive science or the consolidation of power and knowledge in the production and regulation of a peaceful and productive social order.

One can easily find in Rabinow's analysis several persuasive examples of such successful consolidation. Urban designers, architects, intellectuals, and humanists of all shades and persuasions, along with other outraged but muted groups, are particularly qualified to play this role in Lebanon.

Willfully or otherwise, they have thus far been shunted aside and trivial-ized. They have to shed their timidity and reclaim the credibility of their professions and legitimate interests. By mobilizing aesthetic sensibilities and other artistic energies and popular cultural expressions in everyday life, they can do much to arouse the public to redeem its maligned heritage. More important, they can prod the Lebanese to turn outward and transcend their parochial identities to connect with others. City life, after all, is an ideal environment for acting out and working out personal and social con-flicts. Competitive sports, performing arts, reviving interest in national the-ater, museums, and efforts to rehabilitate the country's neglected land-marks and historic sites can do much in this regard.

Three added reasons justify why such groups are ideally suited today to articulate this new language and vision on behalf of their besieged com-patriots. First, a disproportionate number of such groups has been, for much of the war, in diaspora. Every culture has its own diaspora. Lebanon's trials with exile and dispersal have been quite acute. They were, however, also enabling. Mavericks, as the histories of itinerant populations tell us, rarely stay at home. The traditional Lebanese *mkari* (peddler), who wandered beyond the narrow confines of his bounded village, came back with tales, goods, and tidbits of the world beyond. We have today the mak-ings of a growing generation of global multiculturalists. Both established and younger cohorts of gifted professionals and entrepreneurs have been deepening and extending their skills and experiences abroad. Many are rightfully disillusioned, perhaps bitter, but they have not been rendered speechless by the harrowing events. They only experienced the war vicari-ously, from a distance. Hence, they have not been as numbed or cynical, nor do they harbor deep-seated hostility toward other groups. Second, though exiled, they have not severed their ties to or nostalgia for their native culture. They bring home comparative visions, not the alien con-structs of foreign "experts" imposed on unfamiliar and unreceptive milieux. Finally, by virtue of their multicultural sympathies, they are less likely to perceive their projects as efforts for privileging or empowering one group or community in opposition to another. Hence, they are more predisposed to transcend their parochialism as an antidote for doing away with the geography of fear and its demarcating lines and enclosures.

Pacifying Lebanon's pathos, though intricate, is not insurmountable. Much can be done to prepare for this blissful eventuality. Foremost, the Lebanese must be made to realize that massive postwar reconstruction and development can and must be accomplished without added damage to envi-ronment. Given its size, Lebanon clearly can ill afford any further environ-mental abuse. Scant and menaced, the country's dazzling landscape is, after all, its distinctive legacy, a source of national pride and resourcefulness. Indeed, other than the ingenuity of its human resources, the goodwill of its neighbors, and gratuitous guarantees of geopolitics, the country has little else to sustain its vulnerable existence. In an existential sense, there are two inescapable realities that equalize the Lebanese today: geography and fear. We have no choice but to invoke the captivating beauty of our country's habitat as an antidote to fear.

Much can be done to stop the defoliation of open spaces and to reconnect disinherited and denationalized groups with their country's national treasures and collective memory. Likewise, much can be done to assuage those roused with fear that they need not be fully appreciative of the "others" to be able to live with them. Some of the liveliest cities in the world are, after all, those that manage to live with tolerable conflict among diverse communities. Many in such places express strong aversions toward those with whom they do not identify, yet they recognize such differences as a given, something they must live with.[8] Louis Wirth, in his classic essay "Urbanism as a Way of Life," expressed this same reality when he declared that "the juxtaposition of divergent personalities and modes of life tends to produce a relativistic perspective and a sense of toleration of differences."[9]

Second, the Lebanese must be made to realize that the way we use space is also a reflection of our commitment and devotion to it. The more we live in a particular place, the more inclined we are to care for it. As concerned citizens, it is our vital interest to be involved in safeguarding, repairing, and enriching our experience of space. Consider what happens when a country's most precious heritage either is maligned or becomes beyond the reach of its citizens. This is precisely what has happened to many Lebanese. Their country's scenic geography, its plural and open institutions that were once sources of national pride and inspiration, things that made them a bit different from others and around which they weaved fantasies, have either become inaccessible, or worse, are being redefined as worthless.

Finally, the Lebanese must also be reassured that their territorial commitments are understandable and legitimate under the circumstances; so is their need to break away. Being spatially anchored reinforces their need for shelter, security, and solidarity. Like other territorialized groups, they become obsessed with boundary delineation and with safeguarding their community against trespassers and interlopers. The needs for wonder, exhilaration, exposure to new sensations, world views, the elevation of our appreciative sympathies—all enhanced through connectedness with strangers—are also equally vital for our sustenance. Recall our village mkari who, in a much different time and place, broke away, crossed barriers, and was a cultural broker of sorts precisely because he exposed himself to new sensations and contacts. He had no aversion to strangers. He wandered away from home but always managed to return. We need to revive and extend the ethos of the mkari as the prototype of an idyllic national character. With all his folk eccentricities, he epitomizes some of the enabling virtues of a "traveler" and not a "potentate."

Edward Said employs this polar imagery to construct two archetypes for elucidating the interplay between identity, authority, and freedom in an academic environment. In the ideal academy, Said tells us, "we should regard knowledge as something for which to risk identity, and we should think of academic freedom as an invitation to give up on identity in the hope of understanding and perhaps even assuming more than one. We must always view the academy as a place to voyage in, owning none of it but at home everywhere in it."[10] Are these not also the attributes or paradigms we should use in restoring a city (or the places and institutions within it) to render them more permeable for this kind of voyaging?

> The image of traveller depends not on power, but on motion, on a willingness to go into different worlds, use different idioms, and understand a variety of disguises, masks, and rhetoric. Travellers must suspend the claim of customary routine in order to live in new rhythms and rituals. Most of all, and most unlike the potentate who must guard only one place and defend its frontiers, the traveller *crosses over,* traverses territory, and abandons fixed positions, all the time.[11]

Ideally, this could well serve as the leitmotif of those entrusted with educational reform as well as cultural and political rehabilitation, that is, to create the conditions germane for transforming "potentates" into "travelers." When Barbara Ward implores us to find some way of making "ghettos" and all other cloistered spaces more respectable, she is in effect making a plea to keep them open—to facilitate voyaging, traversing, and crossing over. They should be, in other words, designed in such a way that people can move on when the need for communal support and shelter is no longer essential. Any form of confinement, in the long run, becomes a deprivation.[12]

We need to modify the image of the Lebanese as a spatially anchored creature, compulsively huddling and defending his domains (in the compact enclosures of family and neighborhood) against potential trespassers. He is also (or at least was until the war terrorized his public spaces) a creature of the outdoors. Design can do much to restore the conviviality of such open spaces. Street life is emblematic of urban provocation and arousal precisely because one lets go, so to speak, and drops his conventional reserves toward others. As Richard Sennett puts it, as "one goes to the edge of oneself, he sees, talks and thinks about what is outside. . . . By turning outward, he is aroused by the presence of strangers and arouses them." Sympathy in such instances becomes a condition of "mutual concern and arousal as one loses the power of self-definition." It is also in such instances that "differences" are reinforced without sustaining "indifference" to others.[13]

PROSPECTS FOR THE RESTORATION OF CIVILITY

The Lebanese at the moment, and for understandable reasons, seem bent on "retribalizing" their communal and spatial identities. This is not, as we have seen, unusual. In times of disaster, even in cultures aversive to propinquity, traumatized groups are inclined to reconnect with family, home, and community for security and shelter. Pathological as they now seem, such territorial solidarities need not continue to be sources of paranoia and hostility. If stripped of their bigotry, they could be extended and enriched to incorporate more secular and plural identities. There is still a faint hope, given the tenacious survival of religiously mixed communities, that the country might still evade this fateful crossover into that barbarous logic of enclosure and partition.

Even in times of fierce fighting, when all crossings between the two halves of Beirut were either cut off or hazardous, people continued tenaciously to cross over. Hence, differences between the two sides were "staved off," as Jean Makdisi put it, "by those sullen people who stubbornly cross over, day after day by the thousands, some to go work, others to visit friends and relatives, and many *just to make a point*"(emphasis added).[14] A more telling indicator of the resistance to succumb to pressures of partition are marked differences in real estate prices. Land values in religiously mixed areas, regardless of their aesthetic or urban quality, continue to be higher than in exclusive or homogeneous areas. So are the volume of construction activity and other manifestations of economic enterprise.

In these and similar symptoms of resistance to the logic of segregation lie the hope for an optimal restructuring of Lebanon's pluralism. (Pluralism, among other things, is also an antidote to collective amnesia.) This is not another elusive dream. Just as enmity has been socially constructed and culturally sanctioned, it can also be unlearned. Under the spur of enlightened planning and other schemes of spatial rearrangement and cultural rejuvenation, individuals can be resocialized to perceive differences not as dreaded symptoms of distrust, fear, exclusion, or seclusion, but as manifestations of cultural diversity and enrichment.

Despite all its ambiguities, Lebanon's troubled history with pluralism yields at least one unequivocal and sobering reality: Of all encounters with its many varied forms of spatial rearrangements—coexistence, guarded contact, integration—the political management of separate, exclusive, and self-contained entities has always been the most costly and short-lived. If it has been difficult for the Lebanese to live together, it is extremely unlikely that they can live apart. The calls for "cantonization," "federalism," or other "partitioning" and "dismantlement" schemes, like earlier such experiments, are byproducts of xenophobic fears and vengeful impulses. They are impelled by a merging of parochial interests and short-term political expediency. They should not be interpreted as genuine expressions of coalescing identities.

Lebanon's experience, treacherous and perplexing as it has been, is not all that unique. In considering the most supportive environment for the "good life," Michael Walzer arrives (after reviewing predominant socialist and capitalist ideologies in the nineteenth and twentieth centuries) at a similar conclusion. To "live well," he tells us, "is to participate with other men and women in remembering, cultivating and passing on a national heritage . . ." and that such a "good life" can only be realized in a civil society: "The realm of fragmentation and struggle but also of concrete and authentic solidarities where we . . . become social or communal men and women."[15] Walzer goes on to assert:

> The picture here is of people freely associating and communicating with one another, forming and reforming groups of all sorts, not for the sake of any particular formation—family, tribe, nation, religion, commune, brotherhood or sisterhood, interest group or ideological movement—but for the sake of sociability itself. For we are by nature social, before we are political or economic beings. . . . What is true is that the quality of our political and economic activity and of our national culture is intimately connected to the strength and vitality of our associations. Ideally, civil society is a setting of settings: all are included, none is preferred.[16]

Other equally sobering voices—Ralf Dahrendorf, George Konrad, Vaclav Havel—have made similar appeals for the restoration of civil society.[17] All three remind us that the task of reconstruction will require more than political reform, physical rehabilitation, and economic development. More compelling and problematic is the need to restructure basic loyalties. By its very nature this is bound to be a long and fragile process. Dahrendorf is perhaps most assertive: "It takes six months to create new political institutions; to write a constitution and electoral laws. It may take six years to create a half-way viable economy. It will probably take 60 years to create a civil society. Autonomous institutions are the hardest things to bring about."[18] In almost identical terms all three caution us that the reproduction of loyalty, civility, political competence, and trust in authority are never the work of the state alone, and the effort to go it alone—one meaning of totalitarianism—is doomed to failure.

Two parting thoughts: Now that the prospects for recovering Beirut seem imminent (indeed it is heralded as a momentous milestone presaging the new order), we must bear in mind, lest we be disillusioned again, that cities, civilizations, and citizenship share a linguistic and historical root. Where cities, great or small, are not hospitable to the multiplicity of groups, voices, and the interplay of viewpoints, civil society will always suffer. Second, creating such a political culture of tolerance demands, among other things, that every Lebanese today should change his perception of the "other." Only by doing so can we begin to transform the geography of fear into genuine, but guarded, forms of coexistence.

NOTES

1. R. Wagner-Pacifici and B. Schwartz, "The Vietnam Veterans Memorial: Commemorating a Difficult Post," *American Journal of Sociology* vol. 97 no. 2 (September 1991), p. 379.

2. R. Wagner-Pacifici, "The Vietnam Veterans Memorial," p. 380.

3. Militias often employed sectarian-based terror to compel the Lebanese to seek shelter in same-sect ghettos, as the chapter by Georges Corm elucidates at length.

4. Salim Nasr, "New Social Realities and Postwar Lebanon," in Samir Khalaf and Philip Khoury (eds.), *Recovering Beirut: Prospects for Urban Reconstruction* (Leiden: E. J. Brill, 1993).

5. Randall Collins, "The Three Faces of Cruelty: Towards a Comparative Study of Violence," *Theory and Society* vol. 1 (1974), p. 417.

6. Randall Collins, "The Three Faces of Cruelty," p. 416.

7. See Paul Rabinow, *France Modern: Norms and Forms of the Social Environment* (Cambridge, Mass.: MIT Press, 1989).

8. Claude Fischer, *To Dwell Among Friends: Personal Networks in Town and City* (Chicago: University of Chicago Press, 1982), pp. 206–240.

9. Louis Wirth, "Urbanism as a Way of Life," reprinted in Richard Sennet, *Classic Essays on the Culture of Cities* (New York: Prentice Hall, 1969), p. 155. Wirth's essay originally appeared in 1938.

10. Edward Said, "Identity, Authority and Freedom: The Potentate and the Traveler," *Transition* no. 54 (1991), p. 18.

11. Edward Said, "Identity, Authority and Freedom," p. 18.

12. Conversely, open urban spaces can also be rendered more congenial so as to cushion groups against the tempestuousness of city life.

13. Richard Sennett, *The Conscience of the Eye* (New York: Knopf, 1990), p. 149.

14. Jean Said Makdisi, *Beirut Fragments* (New York: Persea Books, 1990), p. 77.

15. Michael Walzer, "The Idea of Civil Society," *Dissent* (Spring 1991), p. 298.

16. Michael Walzer, "The Idea of Civil Society," p. 298.

17. Ralf Dahrendorf, "Has the East Joined the West?" *New Perspective Quarterly* vol. 7 no. 2 (Spring 1990); George Konrad, *Antipolitics* (New York: Harcourt Brace Jovanovitch, 1984); Vaclav Havel, *The Power of the Powerless: Citizens Against the State* (New York: M. E. Sharpe, 1985).

18. Ralf Dahrendorf, "Has the East Joined the West?" p. 42.

20

Peace for Lebanon?
Reflections on a Question

Deirdre Collings

Has the Ta'if Accord placed Lebanon upon the path to lasting, self-sustaining peace? Although the contributions to this volume have not removed the question mark, they have framed dilemmas inherent to the question.

The Ta'if Accord has muzzled most guns in Lebanon, but it cannot guarantee the achievement of long-term peace. Ultimately, Lebanon's future stability will not be dictated by the words in a document or constitution, but by the actors who shape the meaning of those words—the external players, the Lebanese entrusted with the state's governance, and the Lebanese people themselves. Despite the accord's deficiencies, the scope of its provisions underlines these external and internal prerequisites to lasting peace.[1] Externally, Lebanon's stability will be determined by the degree to which its legitimacy and sovereignty are respected by external actors. Internally, sociopolitical stability will be dependent upon whether the state's structures and its governance are perceived to be legitimate and are respected by internal actors.[2]

As this book has detailed, the overarching reason behind Lebanon's war was that neither of these two prerequisites was upheld. The volatile regional environment of the 1960s and 1970s produced a kaleidoscope of regional actors who were more than willing to pursue their own agendas on Lebanese soil. They did so as the external patrons of competing Lebanese actors who were eager clients, largely because of Lebanon's domestic instability. This instability resulted from rapid socioeconomic and demographic change in combination with mounting political disaffection and the ideological radicalization of the populace. Because of the weakness of the Lebanese state, domestic stability was largely dependent upon the solidarity of the governing elites and their respective abilities to command legitimate influence over their constituencies. By 1975, escalating external penetration and internal volatility proved too much for Lebanon's fragile governing elites to manage or contain. The result was the breakdown of elite solidarity and elite legitimacy in the eyes of their constituencies,[3] and the eruption of a seemingly irresolvable war, protracted by a plethora of shifting external and internal alliances.

It is perhaps not surprising that Lebanon's emergence from war (a process that began with the 1989 Ta'if Accord and was sealed with General Aoun's defeat in 1990) resulted from a combination of changes that occurred in the international, regional, and domestic environments. Of primary importance to the success of the Ta'if Accord, however, were the transformations in the external environment. The Document of National Reconciliation that Ta'if purports to represent was not implemented because Lebanese actors had reconciled their differences, or because the roots of Lebanon's domestic instability had been resolved. Regardless of the accord's intentions as envisaged by the Tripartite Arab High Commission or its Lebanese signatories, Ta'if's implementation proceeded because international and regional conditions permitted the ascendance of Syria as the single, overarching "patron" for Lebanon.[4]

This final chapter offers reflections on what our authors have to say about prospects for Lebanon's peace. It begins by surveying the lingering disruptive potential of the main regional actors. Although these external factors are important and will definitely affect Lebanon's quest for stability, they are largely beyond the control of the Lebanese. For this reason, the bulk of the discussion focuses on challenges residing in Lebanon's domestic arena that, Syrian penetration notwithstanding, the Lebanese do have some power to control. The discussion centers on a domestic issue identified by our authors as crucial to Lebanon's move toward a more stable sociopolitical order—deconfessionalization of its political system. My purpose is to render more explicit the differing ideas raised in Part 4 of this book, especially the posited relationship between deconfessionalization and democratization, in order to offer some perspective on Lebanon's prospects for realizing these objectives.

THE TA'IF ERA: LINGERING EXTERNAL STRAINS

Lebanon's Second Republic exists in a markedly changed external environment. The varied menu of external patrons willing to sponsor and arm Lebanon's many militias has diminished considerably. At a minimum, the decreased availability of external patrons will curb the flow of arms and competing regional agendas that exacerbated the levels of violence in the period prior to the *pax Syriana*.[5]

Lebanon's fate is still buffeted by an array of external actors. For example, Iran (through its sponsorship of Hizballah), Saudi Arabia (through its financing power and the Hariri connection), and the United States (as sole superpower, with influence over the entire region) all exert an impact on Lebanon, albeit in markedly different ways. As the chapters in Part 2 of this book emphasize, three actors continue to challenge directly Lebanon's ability to consolidate lasting internal peace: the Palestinians, Israel, and Syria.

Although the Palestinians are no longer an ideological or military challenge to Lebanon's internal stability or cohesiveness, they continue to pose perplexing political and humanitarian challenges.[6] As Rex Brynen notes, a genuine Lebanese consensus has emerged that "strongly opposes any return to the pre-1982 era of Palestinian influence." Thus, if the regional peace process results in some form of "return" for Palestinian refugees, then the Palestinian presence will become a relatively benign foreign policy issue for Lebanon. Should, however, the process resolve that Palestinian refugees stay in their host countries, the domestic debate over the nature and extent of Palestinian rights may become dangerously hot, especially if Lebanon's sectarian system remains intact.[7] It is important to note that the Ta'if Accord provides no guidance as to how the sensitive Lebanese-Palestinian relationship is to be managed or transformed.

Although Israel's agenda for Lebanon is markedly diminished since 1982, the country continues to bomb, occupy, and patronize (i.e., the SLA) the South. In July 1993, Israeli retaliation for Hizballah attacks and the death of Israeli soldiers in its "security zone" culminated in Operation Accountability, a one-week bombing campaign on southern Lebanese villages that left approximately 132 dead and 500 wounded, and caused 350,000 southern residents to flee the area. A cease-fire brokered by the United States sought to prohibit Hizballah attacks in northern Israel, but said nothing of attacks launched in the "security zone." Before the ink was dry, Hizballah had killed eight more Israeli soldiers in the zone, prompting Israeli retaliation (on a much smaller scale) against villages in the Bekaa.

Israel's declared motive for Operation Accountability was to create a massive exodus from South Lebanon to put pressure on the Lebanese government to restrain Hizballah. Following the cease-fire, Lebanese Army units deployed southward, alongside certain UNIFIL positions, but the Lebanese government stated its refusal to prohibit acts of resistance against Israeli occupation (i.e., inside the "security zone"). Moreover, on a popular level, the jury is still out as to whether Israel's operation will result in Hizballah's alienation, or enhanced popularity.[8] In the short run, however, it is clear that Israeli-incurred destruction—in complete violation of international law—has multiplied Lebanon's socioeconomic problems and swollen the ranks of displaced persons, turning back the clock on Lebanon's slow crawl to restabilization.[9]

The Ta'if Accord decrees unequivocal support for UN Resolution 425 and Israel's withdrawal. Indeed, in the wake of the Gulf War there was fleeting hope that "even-handedness" in the "new world order" would dictate that the same energy that was applied to routing Saddam from Kuwait would be used to remove Israel from Lebanon. This hope, of course, ignored the vagaries and interests that still structure international relations and dictate the United Nations selectivity as a law-upholding body. Nevertheless, the issue of Israel's occupation of Lebanon is being discussed at the regional peace talks.

In this regard, Don Peretz suggests that if Israel's involvement in Lebanon is now restricted to its security concerns, then arrangements emerging from the regional peace process—if it is successful—should eventually settle the issue. However, as Amery and Kubursi warn, Israel's security concerns may be a guise for its hydrostrategic designs on Lebanon's water resources. If this latter argument is correct, the Lebanese government may be faced with a powder-keg decision: Should the country's water be used to solidify external peace (i.e., with Israel) or internal peace (i.e., for development of its previously neglected southern region)?

Syria's more or less unrivaled patronage is a mixed blessing: on the one hand it better insulates Lebanon from the fomenting penetrations of other external powers; on the other hand, it compounds domestic discontent especially among those who feel "conquered" by the pax Syriana. The dark side of Syrian insulation, therefore, is Lebanon's inability to offset Syrian preponderance. This issue, as many of our authors have detailed, has immense repercussions on Lebanon's domestic environment.

The Ta'if Accord did contain a measure of assurance that Lebanon would not be abandoned to Syria completely, by providing for the continued involvement of the Tripartite Arab High Commission in Lebanon's recovery (especially with respect to Syria's armed presence). This "Arab guarantee," as Maila tells us, was a crucial factor behind the Lebanese deputies' decision to climb on board the Ta'if train in 1989. Many of the participants in the first round of the CIIPS workshops (September 1990), while cynical that the commission would act as mediator, were at least hopeful it might. As events have unfolded, their cynicism was visionary.[10]

This is not to argue that Syria reigns unrestrained in Lebanon. Syria's recent Western turn (prompted by the disappearance of its Soviet patron, its domestic economic imperative, and the opportunity presented during the Gulf War) is one factor behind the U.S. green light for Syria's ascendancy in Lebanon in 1990.[11] Should the U.S.-Syrian relationship hold, Syria may be more beholden to Western watchfulness, thereby augmenting Lebanon's room to maneuver.[12] In this sense, as Hudson argues, it is the United States, and not Syria, that is the "key external actor shaping Lebanon's future." Nevertheless, as Hudson points out, while the United States possesses leverage—in theory—to influence Syrian action in Lebanon, in practice it "indulges . . . Syria's continuing presence. . . ." For the time being at least,

Lebanon is squarely, if not completely, in Syrian hands, for better or for worse.

Syria's "special relations" with Lebanon, as codified in the 1991 Treaty of Brotherhood and Cooperation and the 1991 Defense Pact, are far more intimate than many Lebanese would prefer. As Paul Salem observes, for the time being Syria's presence in Lebanon is such that "all [domestic] policy is foreign policy." Most Lebanese, however, grudgingly accept that good relations with Syria are axiomatic.[13]

Lebanese optimists, while mindful of the extreme asymmetry of the current Lebanese-Syrian relationship, concede that it need not be a one-way flow from Damascus to Beirut. The fact that some surprises were allowed to occur in the Lebanese elections[14] and that Rafiq al-Hariri was permitted to become prime minister, is perhaps indicative of an opening. CIIPS workshop participants generally agreed that the Lebanese could better influence Syria's preponderance by exploiting the current window of relative calm to redress some of the country's domestic ills, thereby initiating the process of forging genuine domestic reconciliation.

In this regard, despite the negative domestic fallout that Syria's presence provokes, its insulating effect has a positive domestic consequence: it allows the Lebanese to focus better on their internal problems. Throughout the war, external intervention served to obscure the domestic reasons for the war;[15] the breathing space afforded by Ta'if permits Lebanon's internal sources of instability to be perceived better and (perhaps) rectified.

In sum, Lebanon's fate as it is shaped by external pressures and influences will largely be determined by the regional peace process. Here, however, Lebanon admittedly exerts very little influence. Whatever happens among the major players at the table—which for Lebanon means Syria, Israel, and the Palestinians—will reverberate powerfully on the Lebanese domestic scene; Lebanon will be left either to evolve with, survive, or submit to the consequences. Although the results might work in Lebanon's favor, the possibility is real that "Lebanon may end up on the table rather than at it."[16]

Assuming that, for now, Lebanon is unable to exert any meaningful control over shaping its external environment, and that the key to limiting the country's exposure to external penetration is through domestic cohesion, it is worthwhile to focus on certain internal challenges embodied in the daunting task of domestic consolidation.

THE TA'IF ERA: DOMESTIC CHALLENGES

Notwithstanding valid concerns about the Ta'if Accord's legitimacy as a document of genuine national reconciliation,[17] it does contain important directives that target longstanding sources of domestic instability, namely, socioeconomic imbalances relating to uneven regional development (see chapters in Part 3) and sociopolitical disaffection centering on the country's sectarian political system (see chapters in Part 4).

Many of our authors analyzed Ta'if's provisions in this regard; their assessments were both positive and negative, although discussions of the latter often criticized the way in which the accord was implemented rather than the text of the accord per se. Charif, for example, commends the accord's provisions for equitable regional development and the related aspect of administrative decentralization;[18] both clauses hold promise for invigorating the state's political legitimacy in the eyes of the formerly disinherited. This relegitimizing effect, however, will be dependent upon the degree to which the provisions are actually implemented. As Charif laments, to date, little energy has been dedicated to the task.

With respect to structural change, Ta'if specified numerous political reforms. One in particular became centerpiece to the new constitution: "The abolition of political confessionalism shall be a basic national goal. . . ."[19]

Our authors had much to say about the issue of Lebanon's deconfessionalization; many considered this as an important step toward relegitimizing Lebanon's political system. Given the importance of this issue, the remainder of this chapter will explore and expand on our authors' views on two questions: Is deconfessionalization an important prerequisite to the restoration of internal political legitimacy? What are the barriers to achieving this goal? The first part of the discussion focuses on their arguments in favor of deconfessionalizing Lebanon's institutions. The second part examines their perspectives on how this should be achieved (i.e., on mechanisms for deconfessionalization) and questions whether institutional change alone can provide for a stable democracy in Lebanon.

Deconfessionalization and Institutional Legitimacy

El-Hoss and Khairallah make the specific argument that Lebanon's confessional system impeded governmental accountability and was—by definition and function—antidemocratic, unrepresentative, and alienating.

Conceptually, their condemnation of the confessional system is grounded in the liberal democratic principle that considers the individual— the citizen rather than the community—as the sovereign building block of sociopolitical order. They argue that Lebanon's confessional system, which apportions political representation among groups, subsumes the individual into the group and is therefore antidemocratic.[20]

Historically, their perspective rejects the idea that Lebanon's sects are an "organic social reality," an argument well supported in this volume by Ayoub and Corm. Both these authors argue that the historical manipulation of Lebanon's communal groups by outside actors (i.e., the Ottoman and European colonial powers) changed the communal social character of intergroup relations into more politicized and sectarian forms.

Nevertheless, despite the artificiality of Lebanon's received sectarian institutions, they did change internal sociopolitical relations and, to some degree, the psychology of intergroup relations. Local leaders colluded in Lebanon's formal sectarianization, aware that sectarian institutions would buttress and expand their local power bases. They developed a vested interest in maintaining and reinforcing this system.[21]

This combination of changed social relations and the vested interest of those who were empowered by sectarian structures meant that the sectarian political system, once in place, took on a life of its own. Formalized sectarianism, which encompassed both political and judicial institutions, compelled Lebanese citizens to define themselves more and more on the basis of their sectarian affiliation. One's sect became one's social identity, regardless of one's individual beliefs. So powerful was this association that domestic conflicts that had little to do with intersectarian differences often came to be perceived in sectarian terms.[22]

This is not to say that Lebanon's sectarianism-reinforcing institutions produced completed closed structures of coexistence; despite the constraints, the system was opening up from the mid-1960s onward, propelled by numerous forces that challenged the relevance and representativeness of Lebanon's sectarian structures (an important point that will be returned to below). The outbreak of war in 1975, however (which was fomented by factors far beyond Lebanon's internal instabilities), reversed this process of incipient opening. As one observer noted: "Instead of changing a regime to better represent the people, [the war changed] the people to better accommodate the regime."[23]

Corm's analysis details the process by which this forced accommodation took place. The militia-run war system embodied a pathological extension of the sectarian-based logic underpinning the country's political institutions. Just as the political system accorded representation on the basis of one's sectarian affiliation rather than one's individual beliefs, so too did the warlords "cleanse" areas and kill people on the basis of their ascribed identities. Thus, the mantle of legitimacy was seized by armed groups claiming to represent and protect their sects. Their actual, popular, legitimacy, however, was highly questionable; often it was forged through violence and maintained by fear—especially the war-induced fear of the "other," which prompted belief in the need for protection.

In terms of the sectarian psychology of the population, the war prompted a retribalization effect (as Khalaf details).[24] However, militia-orchestrated sectarian cleansing, which compelled the psychological and physical ghettoization of the country and its citizens, also demonstrated the false consciousness of sectarian identities. In particular the intrasect muzzling (i.e., assassinations and disappearances of those who spoke against the militias' legitimacy) and prolific intrasectarian fighting (which resulted in more deaths than intersectarian warfare)[25] helped to destroy the power of Lebanon's sectarian myths (i.e., that sects constituted an organic social reality). Moreover, as popular disenchantment with the militias grew, civilian protests against the war and its logic increased.

The legacy of Lebanon's war embodied a dynamic whereby "imagined" communities tore apart existing communities: Lebanon's sectarianism destroyed the very communities it was supposed to protect. In many ways, therefore, the perversities of war undermined any lasting belief that Lebanon's sects are organic.

Khairallah and el-Hoss concur that the legitimacy of a state's institutions is dependent upon their ability to be perceived as broadly representative. Hence they consider deconfessionalization as an important step toward relegitimizing Lebanon's state institutions in the eyes of the populace. In this regard, Ta'if's provisions extend constitutional recognition to the assertion that the sectarian political structure is not an inherently stable institutional formula for Lebanon. The corollary to this is an implicit recognition that Lebanon's sects are not its organic social reality, and that power sharing among sects is not, therefore, a sincerely democratic or legitimate form of representation.

Barriers to Deconfessionalization

While most of our authors acknowledge the need to deconfessionalize Lebanon's institutions, they also outline three barriers that may derail any progress toward achievement of this basic national goal.

First, they note the deconfessionalization paradox embodied in the Ta'if-bequeathed constitution. The constitution's decree to eventually abolish political confessionalism is hardly new; both the 1926 constitution and the 1943 National Pact referred to the sectarian system as transitional. Although the Second Republic's constitution goes beyond previous rhetoric by proposing concrete steps to facilitate the transformation, it also entrenches sectarian principles and procedures in more explicit terms than the previous constitution (as Maila details).

Second, our authors question the intentions of those who are to carry out deconfessionalization: Is it likely that those whom the system empowers will work faithfully toward their own disenfranchisement? A principal mechanism for facilitating deconfessionalization is Ta'if's provision for Parliament to establish a national committee that will devise measures to guide the political transition. Khairallah's critique of this latter mechanism is noteworthy: "[Ta'if] gives the confessional establishment an unguided, nonbinding, open-ended mandate to abolish itself."

A third crucial, but less tangible, barrier resides in the nature of

Lebanon's current political and social reality: Will institutional change, alone, achieve a functionally deconfessionalized system? An additional question (given the linkage made between deconfessionalization and democratization) is: Will institutional deconfessionalization result in a functionally more democratic system? Many of our authors, directly or indirectly, address key aspects of these questions. It is therefore useful to render this debate more explicit by highlighting certain of the tensions running through the chapters by Khairallah, el-Hoss, and Khalaf, with the specific point of examining the prospects for deconfessionalization and exploring the relationship among institutional reform, political deconfessionalization, and democratization.

Khairallah's analysis of the dysfunctional aspects of the sectarian system leads him to call for its rapid and complete abolition. Institutional transformation, he argues, will result in Lebanon's transition into a liberal, democratic state. Implicitly, his argument suggests that deconfessionalization of Lebanon's institutions (both political and judicial) is the necessary and sufficient condition to eradicate sectarian divisions among the populace. Once the state provides the opportunity, the Lebanese will assume their role as individual citizens of a functionally democratic state.

In making his argument, Khairallah takes to task the writings of Samir Khalaf, whose sociological perspective focuses on certain social underpinnings of the sectarian structure, and hence its tenacity. Unfortunately, Khalaf takes a different tack in this volume, and does not develop his analysis of Lebanon's traditional sociocultural fabric. It is for this reason that I take the liberty of outlining certain elements of Khalaf's perspective (which he develops elsewhere) in the discussion to follow.[26] For now, let us observe that Khalaf's previous works argue that even if Lebanon's confessional system were to be abolished tomorrow, it would not cure many of Lebanon's antidemocratic features; other informal features of Lebanon's social fabric would hinder the emergence of a liberal democratic order.

Midway between these two extremes sits el-Hoss, who attests that Lebanon's political life should be deconfessionalized, but argues that this process must be undertaken gradually. El-Hoss's gradualist approach implies that demobilization of sectarian feelings and the mobilization of democratic practices cannot be imposed by fiat.[27] In CIIPS workshops, el-Hoss answered Khairallah's call for immediate abolition: "We do not want secularism to become another sect in Lebanon. Progress towards secularization must be done through democratic reform and persuasion, to encourage people to share this conviction." Sensitive to the polarizing potential of rapid, top-down secularization, el-Hoss argues that secularism must become less of a political dogma and more of a grassroots force for change, if it is to become the basis for a viable sociopolitical order.

The scope of this discourse and the differences that emerge highlight two interrelated dimensions of the deconfessionalizing process. On the one

hand, as Khairallah argues, is the need to deconfessionalize Lebanon's formal institutions in order to relegitimize state institutions and depoliticize
the sectarian aspects of identity. On the other hand, as el-Hoss and Khalaf
note, is the need to take account of the informal tendencies within the wider
social fabric. Our authors raise two points in this regard. First is the need to
demobilize sectarian-based perceptions that, despite their artificiality, have
acquired both social and political relevance. Second is the need to consider
other aspects of traditional Lebanese society that are not sectarian per se
but, in dynamic interaction with outside interference and Lebanon's sectarian-based institutions, have functioned to buttress sectarian tendencies on
both the formal and informal levels. It is this second point that is developed
in Khalaf's previous writings.

Whereas Khairallah condemns the organic sectarian tones of Khalaf's
1968 view of Lebanese sociopolitical fabric, a close reading of Khalaf
reveals other aspects of his perspective, namely the society's norms of
familialism, *wasta* (intermediary or go-between), and patron-client networks. These informal norms are important because, on a broad level, they
call into question the applicability of the liberal, democratic model to
Lebanese society. That is, these informal norms could compromise the formal democratic functioning of any political system—even one that is thoroughly deconfessionalized. As such, they also question the "deconfessionalization will result in democratization" equation. Because Khairallah has
raised the point, the following discussion will render explicit parts of
Khalaf's analysis that are omitted in Khairallah's critique.

First, however, we consider the relevance of sectarian feeling at the
informal level of people's perceptions. We have seen that Lebanon's sixteen years of militia rule catalyzed different dynamics. While fear prompted a "retribalization" effect, disgust with militia actions (and the harsh reality of intrasectarian bloodbaths) prompted growing appreciation of
sectarianism's false consciousness. The aftermath of the war further con-
founded things, as militia leaders were appointed to the post-Ta'if government of national reconciliation (thereby upholding their supposed legitimacy as sectarian representatives).[28]

Nevertheless, a growing number of Lebanese tend to consider that
deconfessionalization is an important goal:

> It could be that many of us did not fully appreciate the pluralism which
> permeated Lebanon's political and cultural life before the war. The time
> has come to defend and strengthen this pluralism by democracy, which in
> the Lebanese case now means recognizing individuals—versus family,
> region and confession—and institutionalizing the political and legal
> equality of Lebanese as citizens by the installation of a secular state.[29]

To some extent this task continues to be met with resistance at the popular level. For example, certain sectors of Lebanon's Christian population are highly uncomfortable with the prospect of deconfessionalizing the system, especially in light of Syria's preponderance and the rise of Hizballah.[30] As for Khairallah's call to usurp personal status laws from confessional jurisdiction, this too would meet with immense resistance (especially from Hizballah members of parliament). As a result, el-Hoss's measured approach would seem to be less destabilizing than Khairallah's immediate abolition. Gradual transformation in the institutional structures (in good conscience) may allow for the gradual recalibration of sectarian perceptions (and fears) on the social level.[31]

Over and above the sectarian-perception question, however, are other variables within the social fabric that may compromise the end goal of deconfessionalization, that is, rendering Lebanon more democratic (in Khairallah's liberal democratic sense). For the purposes of this discussion, three features, highlighted by Khalaf's previous work, will be mentioned: the functionally extended family, wasta, and patron-client relations.[32]

Khalaf points to the family (not the sect) as the basic social unit in Lebanon.[33] The importance of the functionally extended family is relevant to the issue of sectarianism and deconfessionalization, because kinship and sect often mutually reinforce each other.[34] This is especially true in Lebanon because, as Khairallah points out, all aspects of personal status and family law are under the jurisdiction of the various religious authorities, which serve to reinforce allegiances to both the extended family and the formal sectarian organization of the country.[35]

A second traditional feature of Lebanese society relates to the well-entrenched wasta system, which serves important functions for resolving conflicts and for accessing life's amenities:

> One needs a *wasta* in order not to be cheated in the market place, in locating and acquiring a job, in resolving conflict and legal litigation, in winning a court decision, in speeding governmental action, and in establishing and maintaining political influence, bureaucratic procedures, in finding a bride. . . . The *wasta* procedure is complex, its rules varied depending on the sphere and nature of activity, whether it is legal, familial, economic etc.[36]

Shared belief in the wasta norm is the fundamental glue that holds together the third most important and ubiquitous feature of Lebanese society: the patron-client relationship. The patron-client relationship refers to the reciprocal exchange of favors for personal allegiance. As Khalaf notes, this is neither a contractual nor rational relationship but is sustained by "personal commitments and a system of political obligations in which a powerful local leader [za'im, plural zu'ama] is owed the personal loyalty of followers and servile dependents."[37] Khalaf, like other analysts of Lebanese sociopolitical relations, contends that

> To a large measure, much of the sociopolitical history of Lebanon may be viewed as the history of various groups and communities seeking to secure . . . patronage: client groups in search of protection, security and vital benefits, and patrons seeking to extend the scope of their clientage. Within such a context . . . the *wasit* . . . promises greater access to opportunity, needed services and protection [and] emerges as the most prized and viable political actor. Likewise, patron-client ties become one of the most fundamental of all social bonds to hold the society together. . . . Both parties . . . have a vested interest in maintaining this kind of mutually beneficial transaction.[38]

Khalaf details the impressive social welfare benefits of the patron-client relationship but also notes its drawbacks at the political level, when judged by the rational criteria that are supposed to characterize the autonomous functioning of state institutions and government. When, in the context of elections, the za'im ensures his political success by mobilizing his client base for votes, it sets in motion the whole system of mutual obligations and personalism. Thus, the za'im's followers pledge support not for a political program but for the person. In return, the newly elected state official delivers the spoils of his position to his loyal supporters. As Su'ad Joseph notes: "The *za'im* played out his role in the state structure not to develop the state, but to maintain his position and that of his clients."[39]

A full stop is necessary here to make an important refinement in this discussion. By highlighting Khalaf's analysis of the role of family, wasta, and patron-client relations, I am not advocating a quasi-biological argument concerning Lebanon's immutable sociopolitical culture. Khalaf himself clarifies that these features do not "comprise the entirety of Lebanese political relations." I will make this clarification more direct. These characteristics are not unique to Lebanon. For example, the term "amoral familism," which has been used to describe the functionally extended activities of family in Lebanon,[40] was first coined to describe sociopolitical patterns in Italy, and has been recently applied to present-day Poland;[41] all three societies have emerged from completely different political and cultural histories.[42] Moreover, these characteristics are also evident in the "rational" government systems of the West. I am reminded here of a longstanding "truism" in Canada for those seeking employment: "It is not *what* you know, but *who* you know." Our focus in this book, however, is Lebanon, and the point to be made is that through Lebanon's particular historical experience—including colonialism and the more recent war with its imperative for refinement of survival strategies—wasta and patron-client relations, rather than being a lubricant of the political system, have become a salient component of its substance. It is a matter of degree, therefore, but an important matter. With this clarification in mind, let us briefly consider Khalaf's analysis of these sociopolitical characteristics on Lebanon's political life.

Khalaf's writings detail how institutionalization of patronage blurs the distinction between public office and private concerns, severely constraining the state's ability to function in an autonomous manner: elections are not contested on issues of program or policy but often reflect intense and bitter conflict between competing extended families; politicians are more engaged in distributing funds and "squabbling over patronage rights and boundaries" than in formulating broad policy issues of national or civic importance. Real civic concerns, which would necessitate "some disregard and favour of clients" are ignored.[43] Moreover, the power of the patron-client system is such that access to political power is dependent upon working within its rules: "Politicians in Lebanon rise or fall more on the size of their clientage and competence at dispensing personal favours than on their merit in articulating and coping with public issues and problems."[44]

Khalaf's sociological perspective is relevant to the discourse on Lebanon's deconfessionalization and democratization in several regards. First, he points to the mutually reinforcing aspects of Lebanon's sectarian institutional system and the traditional sociocultural patterns of the extended functional family and patron-client networks. Second, he suggests that the personalistic, vertical nature of patron-client networks means that many government officials have little imperative (or latitude) to focus on civic concerns, and Lebanese citizens have little incentive to develop a sense of civic consciousness or responsibility toward the state. Thus, abolishment of the confessional system would not guarantee the transformation of Lebanon's political life into a "state-citizen" or "state-party-citizen" relationship; rather the "state-zu'ama–client community" relationship could well persist.[45]

If we accept Khalaf's observations, then transcendence of Lebanon's "antidemocratic" features will require more than the deconfessionalization of state institutions; it will also require transformations in Lebanese sociopolitical perceptions and relations: fairness and accountability at the state level must be mirrored and reinforced by the civic responsibility of those to be governed.

Khalaf's focus on the mutually reinforcing aspects of sectarian institutions and the wider social fabric leads him to hold little faith in the prospects for Lebanon's deconfessionalization. While his analysis of the variables (and their tenacity) deserves careful consideration, one could (as Khairallah does) contend his deterministic conclusion.

For example, despite the symbiosis of Lebanon's formal and informal relations, immense changes were undermining the closed vertical aspects of the sociopolitical system prior to 1975. Beginning in the 1960s, growing numbers of educated and mobilized Lebanese were disillusioned with their political system's particularist character.[46] Indeed, on the eve of 1975 more authentic political parties were emerging, such as the Lebanon Democratic Party, supported by a burgeoning, educated middle class; recruitment into

trade unions had also increased tremendously.[47] These trends, harbingers of
a move toward a more secularized, open, civil society in at least part of the
population, indicate that change was possible, despite the constraints of
vested political interests in the sectarian system and the wider social fabric
that tended to buttress it. Moreover, certain pressures in the early 1970s
were causing fundamental changes in the Christian, Shi'ite, and Sunni communities related to the weakening of the hold on power by the traditional
zu'ama.[48]

We have already noted, however, that the war reversed many of these
developments. While the war affected the society's sectarian consciousness
and divisions, it also inevitably influenced other aspects of Lebanese society. If we concur that Lebanon's social fabric contains variables, above and
beyond politicized sectarianism, that bar the prospects for a functionally
deconfessionalized (and democratic) sociopolitical system, it will be
important to assess how these have been affected by the war and its aftermath. No such comprehensive analysis has yet been undertaken; moreover
it is far too early to assess any long-term transformations in the Lebanese
social fabric. For illustrative purposes, however, the final section contains
some highly preliminary observations on possible areas of flux at the informal level.

PERSPECTIVE

The first national elections of the Second Republic witnessed a number of
fundamental changes wrought by the war: the diminished importance of
traditional leaders; a trend toward less sectarian political platforms; and a
broad-based desire by many voters for meaningful social and economic
reform.[49]

The unsuccessful showing of the traditional leaders who ran (Kamal al-
Asad, for example) suggests that many traditional patron-client relations
have broken down. To some degree, this is a consequence of the war,
wherein militia hegemony and cantonization meant that the militias became
the source for many services inside their realms, often usurping functions
from traditional leaders.[50] (Non-governmental organizations also played a
vital role; see the discussion that follows.) However, militia "patronage," as
we have seen, was both imposed and largely linked to the economic necessity of their "clients"; in many cases, it caused only hostility among the
populace, not fealty. With militia actions now largely contained, there is
perhaps an opening for the government to become the new service
provider, thereby relegitimizing itself in the eyes of the populace and
diminishing their need to seek personal patrons.

The government is aware of its imperative to assume this role. As confirmed by two Lebanese MPs in August 1993, the government has been try-

ing "to improve the quality of living conditions and provide social benefits so people would transfer their allegiance from groups such as Hizballah and other political parties to the central government."[51] However, as noted, the government's success in ameliorating Lebanon's social injustices has been minuscule at best. In fact, it is Hizballah, flush with external resources, that is expanding its social following by assisting Lebanon's impoverished (especially in the South and Beirut slum areas): Hizballah's success in the elections stems primarily from its effective grassroots outreach to people in need.

Moreover, even should the government rally to extend its administrative outreach, this, alone, will do little to transform Lebanon's "undemocratic" sociopolitical features unless those charged with administering state policy, themselves, relinquish the wasta rules—that is, unless services are provided to all citizens regardless of wasta, socioeconomic status, region, religion, or politics. The prospect for such a transformation appears dim, indeed.

In the opening days of the Second Republic, corruption (the negative political extension of the social wasta norm) was at an all-time high.[52] There are many reasons for this; perhaps the most obvious is that wasta became an essential survival strategy during the war[53]—for both citizens and government officials alike. Indeed, recent studies suggest that although many Lebanese consider corruption to be both rampant and highly undesirable,[54] they have also "come to regard small routine bribes with some equanimity, as a kind of tax or tariff."[55]

A number of MPs elected in 1992 have spoken forcefully against government corruption: "Corruption and weakness in the government is reflected in the same tendencies within the civil service and encourages reliance on *wasta* in the wider society, especially given the economic devastation."[56] This MP considered that the vicious circle will only be broken through governmental and civil service reform: "We cannot stop this at the wider social level. The government must set the example, and stick to it."

The Ta'if Accord has bequeathed administrative changes that, if implemented in spirit, should provide checks and balances that may break the back of the political wasta syndrome, by routing its political relevance. Moreover, during Lebanon's sixteen years of war, many Lebanese have thought carefully about the kinds of administrative reforms that would facilitate this process. A plethora of solid proposals is now in existence—as the chapters in this book exemplify.[57]

The Hariri government has attempted to fight corruption and to redeem the civil service in the eyes of the public. An example is Hariri's effort to draft a law that would lift the immunity of government employees in order to perform a thorough administrative review. However, by the time the law was finally enacted in February 1993, it contained significant amendments that undermined its principal objective (the amendments "limit the time frame within which immunity is to be lifted, and insure that administrative review is carried out by the bureaucracy itself").[58] Thus, despite the goodwill of many in the government, barriers to reform remain, especially because some of those entrusted with reform have vested interest in the status quo. Relying solely on change to occur from above, therefore, may not be the most effective strategy for fundamental transformation of the system.

Nevertheless, the imperative for institutional reform toward a more democratic and open system may be pushed by agitation from below, from Lebanese society. To illustrate the possibilities, we survey four elements that may push the reform process: municipal elections, socioeconomic changes, the activities of nongovernmental organizations, and changes in the functionally extended family.

Municipal elections, last held in 1967, offer a potential vehicle for the people to have a greater say in government, and for government structures and services to be extended more directly to the people. Such elections hold promise for engendering a popular, vested interest in the state. Moreover, broadened participation in government may provide a transitional mechanism that will lessen the tenacity of sectarian-based power sharing[59] and abet the process of enhancing popular support for the government:

> Participation is as useful a way to get at the vital needs and perceptions of each community as it is to respond to the national need for government renewal. . . . The danger of local government is . . . that it has the same potential as national government to disregard its social, economic, and political responsibilities and to arrogate to itself a sort of "top-down" approach to action. But this is a danger inherent in all government, and it is up to the Lebanese, as any political community, to exploit the current level of political consciousness in each region of the country to demand real participation. This participation must begin with local elections . . . but ultimately will depend upon each area's holding local as well as national officials accountable for their actions.[60]

Municipal elections, therefore, provide a conditional opportunity for expanding Lebanon's democratic potential. Municipal government, if it functions as a responsible intermediary between the center and the people, could provide a legitimate channel through which to articulate grievances and demand action.

Municipal elections may also be a step toward the realization of the Ta'if Accord's promise for the equitable development of Lebanon's outlying regions. If the government fails to act on the new constitution's promises, the newly empowered residents of these regions may agitate for state presence and government action. As Charif's chapter notes, Lebanon's previously neglected regions were invigorated during the war (see his discussion of "reverse rural migration"), resulting in the socioeconomic empowerment, political consciousness, and rising expectations of the residents. These residents, therefore, may embody a second force for change from below.

A third force pushing for institutional change and governmental action is found in Lebanon's numerous nongovernmental organizations. Detailed discussion of the role of Lebanon's NGOs is beyond the bounds of this chapter.[61] It suffices to observe that the war prompted a proliferation of NGOs to meet the needs of the population—some from within traditional groups, some as the benevolent arms of militias, and some with a secular orientation, providing services and relief on the basis of need. While NGOs of the latter type abound, here we will merely cite one type: the NGOs that emerged in response to the needs of the handicapped—a growing sector of the population whose war-incurred needs transcend both family and sectarian lines.

The war demonstrated the capabilities of Lebanon's NGOs to provide for and sustain Lebanese society. In the war's aftermath, while continuing to provide vital services, NGOs are undergoing the transition from relief to mid- and long-term development work. A 1993 workshop on Lebanon's reconstruction and rehabilitation underlined that Lebanon's enormous post-war needs require a national plan to be developed and implemented through the collaborative effort of the government, NGOs, and research bodies. All three have crucial roles to play: the government, with its (potential) capacity to develop a coordinated countrywide framework; the NGOs, with their grassroots knowledge, access, and facility for implementation; and research bodies, with their ability for data gathering, analysis, and advice (the building blocks for any coherent national plan).[62] The NGOs, however, may play an additional vital role. To the degree that the NGOs involved in this collaboration challenge the dominant social order—i.e., whose identity and function represent a common solidarity based on the needs of citizens rather than those whose identity and function are grounded in religious or family affiliation—they could serve as an incremental force, pushing institutional reform and strengthening civil society.

The fourth variable that may push for sociopolitical change resides in the war-induced flux within the solidarity of the functionally extended family, especially as embodied in the expectations and perceptions of the "war generation."

The ravages of war (as Khalaf details) enhanced the solidarity of the family. Indeed, in many ways, the insularity provided by the strength of family was key to the mental and physical survival of most Lebanese during the war. The war, however, has wrought consequences that are beyond the capability of the family to mitigate, even through its extended networks. For example, we have already mentioned the handicapped. In 1993, approximately 10 percent of the population is in need of facilities that the family is not able to provide. Neither are the NGOs able fully to address these needs. As Riad Tabbarah, dean of public health at the American University of Beirut, has stated: "Although NGOs are active in meeting their needs, the problem is too massive. What is required is state-provided services across the country. The government's focus on reconstruction, however, is limited to physical rebuilding, rather than developing new, accessible buildings and facilities adapted to the current needs of the population. Social aspects are sorely absent from plans for reconstruction, questioning their relevancy for all Lebanese in the long-term."[63] Another, similar, example relates to Lebanon's drug problem: "We have no idea how huge the problem is, largely because the family tends to hide the problems. We do know that it is significant: the drug of choice among the young is heroin; valium addiction is a problem for many women."[64] A third problem relates to psychological difficulties resulting from exposure to the war.

The handicapped, drug addiction among the young, and psychological trauma are consequences of the war that afflicted Lebanese society across the board, regardless of sect. All three will require effective, countrywide programing and services that only a state can effectively orchestrate. In this sense, the families of those affected, in solidarity with relevant NGOs, may push from below—demanding the state to provide for all its citizens.

A related aspect of change within the family resides in the expectations and perceptions of the war generation. As one observer has commented:

> A whole new generation has grown up in the war. It is deeply suspicious of both the traditional leaders and the warlords. It refuses to be reduced to family, regional or confessional identities. It has been silenced and crushed under the roar of bombs. This generation will speak a new and sincere language . . . [and will] articulate their aspirations and vision for a new Lebanon.[65]

The long-term effects of social transformation will probably only become evident with the maturation of the war generation, its children, and its children's children. Moreover, the war has taught the Lebanese the importance of civic consciousness: plans to reform the educational system and curricula call for the mandatory inclusion of civics classes. Lebanon's coming generation may embody a motor for fundamental transcendence of Lebanon's formal and informal patterns that have limited the prospects for "citizenship" within the sociopolitical order.

*   *   *

Lebanon's potential for transition to a more internally stable order will be calibrated through the dynamic interaction of institutional reform from above, with informal changes from below. In this sense, the state's relegitimation in the eyes of its citizens will depend on more than its ability to provide for basic human needs; for the long term, it must also provide institutional devices that ensure and protect basic human choices.

Fundamental transformation, as the essays in this book indicate, will meet with many barriers. The reforms embodied in the Ta'if Accord represent a preliminary, but insufficient, step in the process. Whether the government is able and willing to implement Ta'if's reforms in spirit remains a question. Syria, too, will likely try to scuttle any initiative for profound change in the sociopolitical order.[66] Nevertheless, should the Lebanese state, against all odds and entrenched interests, manage to create institutions capable of accommodating the changing reality of the social fabric, it will have taken a vital step toward ensuring its long-term stability through peace, not war.

NOTES

1. See the chapter by Maila in this volume.

2. Internal legitimacy, therefore, means that accountability of governance is reflected by a sense of civic responsibility emanating from those who are to be governed.

3. A detailed and prophetic analysis is Michael Hudson's *The Precarious Republic* (New York: Random House, 1968). For insight into the process of elite-constituency breakdown, see Michael Johnson, *Class and Client in Beirut: The Sunni Muslim Community and the Lebanese State, 1840–1985* (London: Ithaca Press, 1986).

4. As Daoud Khairallah argues: "Despite appearances, whatever semblance of normalcy, stability or recovery Lebanon enjoys at present is the direct consequence of the Syrian government's determination, in a suitable international environment, and cannot be attributed to the spirit of reconciliation the Ta'if Accord is presumed to have produced among the Lebanese." In Collings and Tansley, *Peace for Lebanon?* Working Paper no. 43 (Ottawa: CIIPS, 1992), pp. 21–23. This working paper also contains discussion of the conditions that permitted Syria's ascendance in Lebanon, as does the chapter by Maila in this volume.

5. Of course, Israel is still involved in explicit patronage of the SLA. Iran, too, is active in Lebanon, but its working condominium with Syria has greatly restrained its latitude.

6. See the chapter by Sayigh in this volume.

7. The Palestinian refugees, mainly Sunni Muslims, would alter the sectarian balance in Lebanon if they were given citizenship.

8. See Jim Muir, "Israeli Attacks Unite Lebanese," *The Christian Science Monitor* (2 August 1993); Susan Sachs, "Attacks Prove to be Boon for Hizballah," *New York Newsday* (2 August 1993).

9. As two Lebanese members of parliament stated during a visit to Washington: "All our [recent] efforts to create jobs and create a proper social climate have been seriously hindered. . . . [Israel's actions have] enhanced the arguments of adversaries of the peace process." Statement made during press conference and briefing in Washington by Nassib Lahoud and Imad Jaber on 4 August 1993.

10. For clarification see the chapter by Maila in this volume.

11. See the chapter by Maila in this volume, as well as Paul Salem, "An

Overview of American-Lebanese Relations," *The Beirut Review* no. 5 (Spring 1993), pp. 53–82.

12. In this volume, Abukhalil notes that Syria's strategy for control in Lebanon has become more "subtle." For analysis of Syria's move toward greater liberalization and the West, see Raymond Hinnebusch, "Syria: Calculated Decompression as a Substitute for Democratization" (paper presented at the Conference on Political Liberalization and Democratization in the Arab World, Montreal, 1993).

13. See the chapter by Salem in this volume. Also see Deirdre Collings and Jill Tansley, *Peace for Lebanon?*

14. Some analysts contend that Syria's apparent aversion to Hizballah is not genuine, but is part of the Asad regime's disinformation campaign; see Marius Deeb, "Shi'a Movements in Lebanon: Form, Ideology, Social Basis and Links with Iran and Syria," *Third World Quarterly* vol. 10 no. 2 (April 1988), pp. 683–698.

15. This obfuscation was such that some Lebanese insist that Lebanon's problems were solely the result of external conspiracies to dismantle the state.

16. See Salem's chapter in this volume.

17. As noted, Ta'if's implementation proceeded because of regional and international prerogatives, not because Lebanon's domestic issues were resolved. Although Faris has observed that the accord's contents did not emerge in a vacuum (the proposed domestic reforms were mostly taken from previous reconciliation attempts), it is important to note that these previous proposals were negotiated by various elite and/or militia actors on the Lebanese scene. Given the growing gap between Lebanese political actors and the populace, it could be argued that the reforms do not necessarily reflect a poplar consensus. Moreover, as Maila highlights, the Ta'if document was drafted by outside players; when it was presented to the Lebanese deputies at al-Ta'if they had little margin of maneuver to alter the document's contents. In addition, the very representativeness of these deputies is questioned because they had held their positions since 1972. This latter point, raised in the CIIPS workshops, was answered by Clovis Maksoud (a workshop participant): "Although the representativeness of the MPs might be in question, their legitimacy, which derives from parliament's continuity and its international recognition as a state institution, was not. The goal of Ta'if was to restore the state, and unlike the militia leaders, the MPs had maintained their allegiance to the state even when it was completely marginalized." See Collings and Tansley, *Peace for Lebanon?* For details of the compromises incorporated into the accord, see *The Beirut Review* vol. 1 no. 1 (Spring 1991), pp. 119–172.

18. Preamble to the new constitution, Clause g, states: "The even development among regions on the educational, social, and economic levels shall be a basic pillar of the unity of the state and the stability of the system." Administrative decentralization is also detailed in a provision that was not incorporated into the new constitution. For text of these provisions, as well as background on the debates surrounding the issue of decentralization, see the annotated version in *The Beirut Review* vol. 1 no. 1 (1991).

19. Preamble to the new constitution, Clause h, and Section F: *On the Abolition of Political Confessionalism.*

20. For clarification, see the chapter by el-Solh in this volume.

21. In CIIPS workshops, el-Hoss noted that sectarian polarization was always greater at the political level than at the social level, because of vested interests, not "organic" hatreds. However, social sectarianism was augmented by the colonial-bequeathed educational institutions and the Ottoman-instituted personal status laws.

22. Michael Hudson's detailed analysis, in *The Precarious Republic,* of Lebanon's 1958 crisis is illustrative: "The insurrection of summer 1958 . . . disrupt-

ed political, social and economic life, but did not degenerate into a confessional struggle until well after a political settlement had been reached. At that point, however, and for a full month afterward, there was a rash of incidents with distinctly sectarian overtones. Although most of them may have been matters of personal vengeance and isolated aggression, they were sufficient to remind Christians and Muslims of their mutual fears of persecution" (p. 90). For further discussion of the sectarian coloring that came to override personal, kinship, or class rivalries, see Su'ad Joseph, "Muslim-Christian Conflicts in Lebanon: A Perspective on the Evolution of Sectarianism," in Su'ad Joseph and Barbara Pillsbury (eds.), *Muslim-Christian Conflicts: Economic, Political and Social Origins* (Boulder, Colo.: Westview Press, 1978); Samih Farsoun and Walter Carroll, "The Civil War in Lebanon: Sect, Class and Imperialism," *Monthly Review* vol. 28 (1976), pp. 12–37; Halim Barakat, *Lebanon in Strife: Student Preludes to the Civil War* (Austin: University of Texas Press, 1977).

23. Fawwaz Traboulsi, "Confessional Lines," *Middle East Report* (January–February 1990), p. 10.

24. Corm describes the process whereby militia terror tactics caused the population to internalize the militia's sectarian-based logic, resulting in eruptions of communal hysteria. Khalaf focuses on the protective aspects of ingroup identification (see his discussion on identity as "emblem" and "armor" in this volume).

25. See American Task Force for Lebanon, *Working Paper: Conference on Lebanon* (Washington: 1991), p. 19.

26. The unfamiliar reader may be surprised at Khairallah's dismissal of Khalaf's perspective, especially given Khalaf's contribution to this volume in which he conjectures that the war's trauma might have been mitigated had it resulted in the country's transformation into a "secular and more viable entity." This statement appears to contradict Khairallah's pigeonholing of Khalaf as one who considers Lebanon's sectarian system to be the organic reflection of a sectarian society. It is true that the ambiguities (and at times contradictions) running through Khalaf's discourse leave him open to such a reading. However, as the discussion below reveals, Khalaf's 1968 formulation focuses more on the society's norms of familialism, personalism, and patron-client networks and how these interact with the society's more recent sectarian divisions. For detailed development of Khalaf's perspective, consult his series of essays published in book form, *Lebanon's Predicament* (New York: Columbia University Press, 1987), which contains his 1968 essay cited by Khairallah.

27. In his chapter, el-Hoss contends that democratic rules are a necessary but insufficient condition for democratic political change, because "a perfectly sound democratic process is not conceivably attainable under the prevailing circumstances in Lebanon." He observes that Lebanon's democratic functioning has been compromised by "sectarianism, regionalism, and political feudalism or traditionalism. These phenomena are endemic to the country's body politic, and have hampered the inculcation of democratic values when confronting issues and problems."

28. See Corm's chapter in this volume.

29. Traboulsi, *Middle East Report* (1990), p. 10.

30. It is not deconfessionalization per se that is feared, but the possible hidden agenda behind this institutional change. See el-Hoss's comments in this volume.

31. Khairallah's argument against gradualism is grounded in the equally pragmatic argument that step-by-step abolition will provide so many disruptive opportunities to those who wish to scuttle the process that the transition will never happen. That Lebanon has been waiting to abolish sectarianism for sixty-seven years is fodder for Khairallah's view.

32. See Khalaf's essays in his *Lebanon's Predicament*. Sources that develop

similar or related insights are Malcolm Kerr, "Political Decision Making in a Confessional Democracy," in Leonard Binder (ed.), *Politics in Lebanon* (New York: John Wiley & Sons, 1966); Su'ad Joseph, *Muslim-Christian Conflicts*; and Samih Farsoun, "Family Structures and Society in Modern Lebanon," in Louise Sweet (ed.), *Peoples and Cultures of the Middle East,* vol. 2 (New York: The National History Press, 1970), pp. 257–307.

33. As Khalaf explains in his 1968 essay on "Primordial Ties and Politics" (reprinted in *Lebanon's Predicament*, pp. 102–120): "Kinship has been, and is likely to remain, Lebanon's most solid enduring tie. The extended patriarchal family . . . has demonstrated remarkable resiliency as a unit of social organization. . . . The family, not the individual is the basic social unit. To a large extent a person's status in society, his occupation and social and political prestige are defined by it" (pp. 104–105). Khalaf describes the far-reaching implications of the extended family for the political life of the country: "The persistence of kinship rivalry and the political dominance of prominent families has, on the whole, been more dysfunctional. . . . Political alliances, parliamentary blocs and opposition fronts are still predominantly initiated and sustained by personal and not ideological considerations" (p. 109).

34. As Su'ad Joseph clarifies: "A kin gathering is usually simultaneously a sect gathering. This means that kinship can be used to mobilize people for sectarian organizations and a sectarian perspective" (*Muslim-Christian Conflicts*, p. 29).

35. As Farsoun notes: "A functional, reciprocal, mutually reinforcing dependence of the kinship and confessional organization exists in Lebanon" ("Family Structure and Society in Modern Lebanon," p. 293).

36. Farsoun, "Family Structure and Society in Modern Lebanon," p. 270.

37. Khalaf, "Primordial Ties," p. 112.

38. Khalaf, *Lebanon's Predicament*, p. 76.

39. Su'ad Joseph, *Muslim-Christian Conflicts*, p. 80.

40. Farsoun, "Family Structure and Society in Modern Lebanon," p. 265.

41. Elizbieta Tarkowska and Jacek Tarkowski, "Social Disintegration in Poland: Civil Society or Amoral Familism?" *Telos* no. 89 (Fall 1991), pp. 103–109.

42. See also the discussion by Anatoli Kaminski in his *An Institutional Theory of Communist Regimes* (San Francisco, Calif.: ICS Press, 1992), which highlights the endemic normative pattern of patron-client relations in the former Soviet Union.

43 . Khalaf, *Lebanon's Predicament*, p. 87 and p. 103. Khalaf lists other delegitimizing side effects: "Endemic corruption, bribery, graft, nepotism, executive and administrative incompetence, private interference in public decisions and quid pro quos all suggest that private and particularistic ends are being promoted at the expense of public and universalistic expectations" (p. 232).

44. Khalaf, *Lebanon's Predicament*, pp. 87–88.

45. Michael Hudson's 1968 assessment is noteworthy: "Even if there were no religious cleavages in present-day Lebanon, there would still be a politics of clique and balance, and there would still be formidable traditional barriers to building a positive identity with the national state" (*The Precarious Republic,* p. 21). Hudson goes on to note: "The parochialism manifest in Lebanon's family, community, and sectarian structures pose severe environmental adversities for political modernization . . . which requires centralization, greater governmental intervention, and rationalized procedures. . . . It limits the capacity of the political instrumentalities to induce significant change. As long as there are few elements seeking radical change, the problem is manageable, and the stability produced by Lebanon's neotraditional system has thus far thrown a veil of affluence over the sores of discontent. Whether or not Lebanon's uneven prosperity can alone control the demands for change arising from social mobilization is an open question" (pp. 33–34).

46. As Michael Hudson concluded in 1968: "There is evidence to suggest that an increasing proportion of the population . . . can be mobilized into legitimate, open and routinized political activity, particularly if the appeal were moderate and progressive" (*The Precarious Republic*, p. 329).

47. See discussion in Collings and Tansley, *Peace for Lebanon?*

48. The alienation of the population residing in Beirut's "Belt of Misery" illustrates this breakdown. Charif explained the reasons behind Shi'ite migration from the countryside to the slums around Beirut, noting that this area became a major recruiting ground for militiamen once the war broke out. These suburban slum dwellers were further marginalized because their internal migration severed them from the insulating mechanism of the patron-client system. As Michael Johnson has detailed, Shi'ite immigrants to the suburbs were not registered to vote in Beirut. As a result, Beiruti zu'ama "refused to perform services for them, and their own zu'ama were singularly inept in dealing with the changed nature of their clientele" who, divorced from the effective structures of zu'ama control that existed in their villages and living in depraved conditions, were "susceptible to the radical appeals of Nasserist, socialist, and, very significantly, Marxist organizations." See Michael Johnson, "Popular Movements and Primordial Loyalties in Beirut," in Talal Asad and Roger Owen (eds.), *Sociology of "Developing Societies" in the Middle East* (New York: Monthly Review Press, 1983), p. 192.

49. See the chapter by Norton and Schwedler in this volume.

50. See, for example, Lewis Snider, "The Lebanese Forces: Their Origins and Role in Lebanese Politics," *Middle East Journal* vol. 38 no. 1 (Winter 1984), pp. 1–35.

51. "Lebanese Parliamentarians Assert: Israel Strengthened Extremists," release by the American-Arab Anti-Discrimination Committee (August 1993), based on press conference and briefing in Washington by Lebanese MPs Nassib Lahoud and Imad Jaber.

52. Personal interviews conducted in October 1992 with various Lebanese MPs elected in the 1992 elections. One MP stated that "Corruption is no longer a matter of small favors or baksheesh; it now has the power to change governmental priorities, leading the government down avenues that it should not go. It has caused the corruption of independent analysis and thinking."

53. A Lebanese playwright, Ziad Rahbani, has captured this postwar wasta-mania with a highly apocalyptic view of Lebanon's future. His play, *Of Dignity and Stubborn Folk*, portrays a Lebanon finally freed of foreign influences, but racked by internal social decay. Among his many cynical scenes, one focuses on the Lebanese sitting around and bragging about their wasta. Perhaps appreciating Rahbani's vision, the Lebanese daily *al-Hayat* commented that "Rahbani is like those animals who feel the earthquake before it happens."

54. See opinion poll data in *The Beirut Review* no. 4 (Fall 1992), pp. 162–165.

55. Maroun Kisirwani, "Lebanese Bureaucracy Under Stress," *The Beirut Review* no. 4 (Fall 1992), pp. 29–42.

56. An off-the-record interview with a newly elected MP. Also of note is that one of Hizballah's election platforms was to fight government corruption.

57. See, in particular, the contributions by Salim el-Hoss, Nasser Saidi, and Ahmed Sbaiti.

58. See "Waiting for Springtime," (editorial) *The Lebanon Report* vol. 4, no. 3 (March 1993), p. 3.

59. Decentralization by way of municipal elections "would help tone down confessionalism in politics because local decisions would be taken in a fairly pragmatic atmosphere, focussing on recognizable local needs and interests. In contrast,

national politics have often fallen prey to ideological or confessional demagoguery and rhetoric, which has had negative effects at the local levels" ("LCPS Conference on Decentralization," (editorial) *The Lebanon Report* vol. 4, no. 2 (February 1993), pp. 7–8.

60. Ronald D. McLaurin, "Change, Crisis, Catharsis, Political Renewal and Political Participation in Lebanon," *Middle East Insight* vol. 7 no. 5 (1991), pp. 24–29. For additional insight on municipal elections see LCPS, *Postwar Institutional Development in Lebanon: An Assessment and Strategy for Foreign Assistance* (Beirut, February 1992).

61. For detailed discussion, see Mona Assaf, *Foreign Aid to Wartorn Lebanon, The Role of NGOs* (unpublished research paper, Beirut, 1988); Ghassan Sayyah, *Potential and Constraints upon NGOs in Lebanon,* and Kamel Mohanna, *Rôle des ONG au Liban* (papers presented at a conference in Ottawa, June 1993 entitled Reconstruction, Rehabilitation and Reconciliation in The Middle East: The View from Civil Society); and LCPS, *Postwar Institutional Development* (Beirut, 1992).

62. For further discussion see the conference report by Deirdre Collings, *Reconstruction, Rehabilitation and Reconciliation in the Middle East* (Ottawa: Middle East Working Group, September 1993).

63. Interview, Beirut, October 1992.

64. Interview with Riad Tabbarah, Beirut, October 1992.

65. Traboulsi, "Confessional Lines."

66. As the chapter by Abukhalil in this volume notes, Syria's power in Lebanon is guaranteed by the divisions separating the Lebanese: "Syrian policy in Lebanon consistently sought to prevent a decisive victory by any of the Lebanese combatants. By not allowing any one party or faction to control Lebanon, Syria upheld its own political and military prominence."

Appendixes

Appendix A Major Peacemaking Attempts, 1975–1989

	Constitutional Document (C.D.)	Lausanne Conference (L.C.)	Tripartite Agreement (T.Ag.)	Ta'if Accord
Legislative				
Number of seats	99	120	198	108
Seat distribution: Muslim/Christian	50/50	50/50	50/50 during transition period; thereafter, sectarian proportions abolished.	50/50
Electoral district	No change	Not defined	Mohafazat	Mohafazat
Term of speaker	1 year renewable	2 years renewable	2 years renewable	Same as the term of Parliament, which after two years may withdraw its confidence from the speaker.
Executive				
Appointment of prime minister	Elected by Parliament	Same as C.D.	Appointed by president following binding parliamentary consultations.	President names prime minister in consultation with speaker following binding parliamentary consultations.
Formation of council of ministers	Prime minister holds consultations and forms government in agreement with president.	Same as C.D. Absolute majority of Parliament required to override presidential veto of government makeup.	Same as L.C. 55% of Parliament required to override presidential veto.	Same as C.D. No mention of what happens if prime minister and president disagree.
Powers of council of ministers	No change	Final executive and administrative authority in the state. President serves as member and chairman. Council can override presidential veto of decrees and draft laws.	Executive authority lies in the council of ministers. Can override presidential veto. President can attend certain sessions of the council but cannot vote.	Same as T.Ag. President can attend any session of the council of ministers but cannot vote.
Decentralization	Reinforces administrative decentralization.	Transfers numerous administrative functions to local authorities.	Same as L.C.	Broad administrative decentralization.

Confessionalism in administration	Abolishes confessional appointments except for first grade posts.	Same as C.D.	Same as C.D. during transition period. Afterwards, practice is abolished.	Same as T.Ag. but length of transition period is not specified.
Future of Sectarian System	Confirms sectarian distribution of three presidential posts.	Calls for drafting of a new constitution within one year. Future of sectarian system not dealt with.	After first elected Parliament, sectarianism to be abolished according to a timetable proposed by council of ministers to Parliament. Measure becomes effective automatically if it is not legislated by the term of the third elected Parliament.	Abolishment of political sectarianism is declared a fundamental national objective. Calls on first elected Parliament to form a national committee to propose the necessary measures. No timetable specified.
New Institutions				
Supreme council to try presidents and ministers	Yes	Yes	Yes	Yes
Supreme constitutional court	Yes	Yes	Yes	Yes
Supreme council for planning and development	Yes	The Council for Development and Reconstruction was established in 1977.	See L.C.	See L.C.
Economic and social council	—	Yes	Yes	Yes
Senate	—	To be considered	To be established	To be established following election of nonsectarian-based Parliament.
Lebanese-Syrian Relations	—	—	Distinctive relations. Strategic complementarity at all levels.	Distinctive relations. Coordination and cooperation at various levels. Sovereignty and independence of each to be respected.

Prepared by Hani A. Faris.

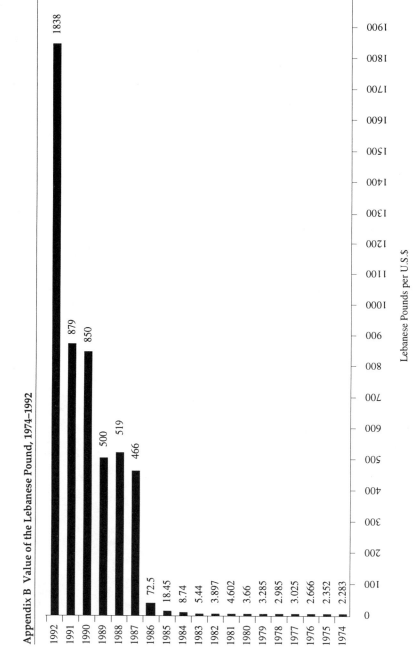

Appendix B Value of the Lebanese Pound, 1974–1992

Source: Wall Street Journal year-end figures, 1974–1992. Prepared by Augustus Richard Norton and Jillian Schwedler.

Appendix C Chronology, 1860–September 1993

1860   War in Mount Lebanon between Druze and Christians leaves 11,000 Christians dead. French troops land in Beirut to protect Maronites.

1861   The major European powers and the Ottomans establish the *Règlement Organique* decreeing Mount Lebanon a *Mutassarrifiyya*—a privileged administrative region within the Ottoman Empire under international guarantee.

1914–1918 Ottoman rule in Syrian region collapses. British and French divide Syrian provinces as mandates between themselves. Present-day territory of Lebanon falls under the French mandate.

1920   French create Greater Lebanon by annexing to Mount Lebanon and Beirut the outlying provinces to the north, south, and east.

1932   Last official census in Lebanon (as of mid-1993).

1943   Following British and Free French capture of Beirut from Vichy forces (1941), France promises full independence for Lebanon.

            Bishara al-Khoury (Maronite leader) and Riad al-Solh (Sunni leader) reach unwritten agreement, the National Pact, to allow the country to proceed to independence.

1946   French troops leave Lebanon.

1948   First Arab-Israeli war as state of Israel declares independence. Palestinian refugees flee, mainly to Lebanon and Jordan.

1958   Civil war breaks out in Lebanon. President Camille Chamoun invokes Eisenhower Doctrine to call in the U.S. Marines.

            Head of the army, Fouad Shehab, takes over presidency and commences a comprehensive program of socioeconomic reform.

1964   Palestine Liberation Organization (PLO) founded.

1967	Third Arab-Israeli war. New wave of Palestinian refugees enters Lebanon.
1968	In retaliation for Palestinian guerrilla attack in Athens, Israel blows up Middle East Airlines fleet at Beirut Airport.
1969	Lebanon signs Cairo Accords regulating Palestinian actions in Lebanon.
1970–1971	Jordanian Army defeats Palestinian armed organizations. Many Palestinian civilians and leaders flee to Lebanon. PLO relocates its headquarters to Beirut.
1973	Fighting between the PLO and the Lebanese Army.
	Fourth Arab-Israeli war.
1974	Arab League recognizes the PLO as the sole legitimate representative of the Palestinian people.
1975–1976	A series of incidents—government repression of a labor strike, rightist attacks on Palestinians in Beirut—triggers clashes between the Lebanese National Movement and the Lebanese Front.
	Syria sends Palestine Liberation Army (PLA) troops into Lebanon. Foreign Minister Abdul Halim Khaddam of Syria arrives in Beirut to try to arrange a compromise.
	Frangieh announces a program of limited reform (1976 Constitutional Document).
	Lebanese Army disintegrates.
	Syrian troops enter Lebanon at the request of President Frangieh to prevent a victory by the LNM.
	Saudi Arabia calls for an Arab summit (Riyadh Conference) to discuss Lebanon; Riyadh resolutions passed at Cairo Summit, formally ending the Lebanese civil war (Two-Year War).
1977	Assassination of LNM leader Kamal Jumblatt.
	Shatura Agreement between Lebanese President Sarkis, Syria, and the Palestinians reviving the Cairo Accord of 1969.

1978   Clashes between Syrian troops and Lebanese Front.

Israel invades Lebanon, occupying the southern part of the country up to the Litani River. UN Security Council passes Resolution 425 calling upon Israel to withdraw from Lebanon. Israeli troops pull back, but create a self-declared "security zone" along the border, placing the zone under the command of Major Sa'd Haddad and his Israeli-controlled rebel forces. UNIFIL forces take up positions in South Lebanon.

Syrians heavily bomb the Christian sector of East Beirut.

1979   Renewed fighting between Syrians and Phalangists.

Major Haddad shells UNIFIL forces and prevents Lebanese Army from reasserting control in the South.

Israel launches a number of air raids against Palestinian positions in South Lebanon.

1980   Syrians withdraw from Christian areas of Beirut.

Israel continues to launch raids into Lebanon.

President Sarkis develops fourteen-point proposal for national reconciliation (not implemented).

Right-wing Phalange (Kata'ib) militia, under Bashir Gemayel, crush their former allies, the Chamounists.

1981   Haddad shells UNIFIL troops.

Fighting in Zahle between Phalangists and Syrian soldiers.

Israel shoots down Syrian helicopters. Syria installs SAM missiles in Bekaa; Israel demands their removal.

Begin wins Israeli elections.

Israel resumes heavy bombing of Lebanon. Palestinians engage in cross-border attacks into Israel. Israel bombards Beirut.

1982   Israel renews air strikes against Palestinian camps in Lebanon; PLO shells northern Israel. Israeli ambassador in London is shot.

Israel invades Lebanon; attack culminates in massive bombing of Beirut. PLO evacuates to Tunis. U.S. Marines land in

Beirut as part of the Multi-National Force (MNF). Syrian troops evacuate Beirut as part of the cease-fire agreement.

Bashir Gemayel is elected president. MNF troops withdraw from Lebanon. Bashir Gemayel is assassinated. Phalange militia conduct massacres of Palestinians at Sabra and Shatila refugee camps. U.S. Marines ordered back to Lebanon. Inauguration of Amine Gemayel.

1983   U.S. Embassy in Beirut bombed. United States brokers May 17th Agreement between Israel and Lebanon. U.S. naval vessels shell Souq al Gharb. U.S. barracks bombed; MNF attacked.

Israel unilaterally withdraws from Shouf Mountains to new front lines north of Sidon. War of the Mountains ensues as the Phalange militia and Lebanese Army troops of President Amine Gemayel clash with Druze militias backed by Syria.

Lebanese hold first "reconciliation meeting" in Lausanne.

1984   United States and MNF withdraw from Lebanon. Shi'ites take control of West Beirut. Militant Islamic groups take Western hostages.

Lebanese leaders meet at second reconciliation meeting in Geneva. Abrogation of May 17th Accord.

1985   Israel announces three-stage withdrawal from Lebanon.

Beginning of the War of the Camps, as Syrian-backed Amal militia besieges Palestinian refugee camps.

Syrian-sponsored Tripartite Agreement attempts to obtain political consensus among main militia leaders in Lebanon.

1986   Tripartite Agreement is repudiated. Samir Ja'Ja' ousts Hobeiqa from command of Lebanese Forces. Israeli bombardments of Palestinians refugee camps.

Syrian troops enter West Beirut for the first time since 1982.

1987   Fighting between Amal militia and pro-Arafat factions of the PLO in West Beirut. Syrians increase military presence. Syria intervenes to end War of the Camps.

Assassination of Prime Minister Rashid Karameh.

1988   Intra-Shi'ite fighting between Amal and Hizballah for control of Beirut's southern suburbs; additional Syrian troops deployed.

Following end of Gemayel's term, Lebanon fails to elect a new president. Rival governments established: General Aoun (appointed by Gemayel) in East Beirut; Salim el-Hoss in West Beirut (successor to Rashid Karameh).

Israeli air strikes within fifteen kilometers of Beirut.

1989   Continued fighting between rival Shi'ite militias, Hizballah and Amal. Fighting in East Beirut between Ja'Ja's Lebanese Forces and General Aoun's army units. Aoun launches War of Liberation against Syrian armed presence in Lebanon.

Arab League Summit at Casablanca establishes Tripartite Arab High Commission (heads of state of Saudi Arabia, Morocco, Algeria) to create a comprehensive solution to end the Lebanese conflict. Following a cease-fire, Lebanese parliamentarians assemble in Ta'if, Saudi Arabia, to finalize the accord.

Ta'if Accord officially adopted. The UN Security Council voices unanimous support.

1990   Deadlock between General Aoun (government centered in East Beirut) and Ta'if government of Elias Hrawi over the Ta'if Accord.

Continued Amal-Hizballah fighting. Renewed, intensive fighting between Ja'Ja's Lebanese Forces and General Aoun's army units in East Beirut. Continued Israeli shelling of targets in South Lebanon.

Gulf crisis erupts as Iraq invades Kuwait.

Lebanese Parliament officially adopts Ta'if's constitutional amendments. Implementation begins. General Aoun declares amendments null and void.

Hrawi government ousts General Aoun with Syrian military backing. Disarming of militias begins.

Amal and Hizballah sign peace treaty, brokered by Syria and Iran (although clashes continue through 1991).

1991   Implementation of Greater Beirut Plan continues. Lebanese
              Army continues process of reestablishing control over large
              parts of country. Formation of a new cabinet (Government of
              Reconciliation); appointment of deputies (including many
              militia leaders) to fill vacant seats and raise the number of
              deputies.

              Lebanon and Syria sign Treaty of Brotherhood, Cooperation,
              and Coordination, establishing a formal structure for close
              relations between the two countries.

              Israel steps up bombardment of Palestinian targets in South
              Lebanon. Assaults are the largest since the 1982 invasion.

              PLO leader Yasir Arafat reaches agreement with Lebanese
              government concerning PLO armed presence. PLO fighters
              hand over military hardware to authorities.

              Army troops round up pro-Aoun activists.

              Lebanese Parliament approves General Amnesty Law (for war
              crimes, except political murder and killings of diplomats and
              clergymen). Aoun leaves refuge in French embassy; departs
              for France.

              South Lebanon erupts in violence as Hizballah forces strike
              against Israeli and SLA targets; Israel responds with massive
              bombing sorties.

1992   Ongoing fighting in South Lebanon between resistance forces
              (i.e., Islamic Resistance Movement, Palestinian forces, Amal,
              Lebanese National Resistance Front, Lebanese Communist
              Party, SSNP) and SLA/Israeli forces. Katyusha rockets also
              fired into northern Israel.

              Lebanese officials announce refusal to negotiate with
              Palestinians until conclusion of the Arab-Israeli talks.

              Ministry of the Interior grants Hizballah license to become a
              political party.

              Israeli helicopter gunships assassinate Hizballah secretary
              general, Sheikh Abbas Musawi, along with his wife and child.

              Sheikh Hassan Nassrallah unanimously elected new Hizballah
              secretary general.

              Israel overruns UNIFIL positions to attack South Lebanese
              villages.

Shi'ite Amal movement reelects Nabih Birri as leader.

Nationwide labor strikes are observed as 10,000 people march in Beirut. In May, more strikes and a civilian riot erupt over deteriorating economic conditions. Prime Minister Omar Karameh and his cabinet resign; President Hrawi appoints Rashid el-Solh as prime minister.

LF head Samir Ja'Ja' loses to George Sa'ade in Kata'ib elections.

Interfactional Palestinian fighting and assassinations between Abu Nidal's Fatah Revolutionary Council (FRC) and Fatah.

Government begins to recover certain public properties held by various militias.

Amid dissension, Lebanon holds parliamentary elections for first time since 1972. Christians stage a successful boycott in predominantly Christian sectors within Mount Lebanon, the South, and Beirut districts; withdrawal of candidates in Kisrawan requires rescheduled byelection. Hizballah candidates score major gains at the polls.

Teachers and members of confederation of trade unions observe various strikes to oppose deteriorating socioeconomic conditions.

Lebanese-Saudi billionaire Rafiq al-Hariri is designated prime minister and forms new cabinet.

Amal leader Nabih Birri, following his sweeping electoral victory in the South, is elected Speaker of Parliament.

Israel deports 417 Palestinians to Lebanon; Lebanon refuses to accept them. Deportees set up camp in "no-man's-land" close to the SLA zone.

1993
(to
September) Lebanese Army continues to expand its territorial area of operations (including southern suburbs of Beirut).

UNWRA staff and employees strike to protest the issuing of new identity cards to Palestinian refugees in Lebanon.

UN Secretariat General declares the situation in Lebanon to be "normal"; permits UN employees to bring families.

Ongoing attacks between Hizballah and Israel/SLA in South Lebanon; some resistance attacks also launched against northern Israel.

Amended version of government's draft law lifting immunity of government employees (to conduct administrative reform) is implemented; Hariri declares amendments may render law useless.

Hizballah officials expand contacts with Maronite representatives.

U.S. Secretary of State Warren Christopher visits Beirut.

World Bank approves U.S.$175 million loan to Lebanon, first in fifteen years.

Public school teachers and Lebanese University professors stage strikes to improve working conditions.

Ongoing reconciliation initiatives between Druze and Christian representatives.

Interfactional fighting continues between Palestinian mainstream Fatah organization and FRC.

High-level Kata'ib delegation goes to Damascus; meets with Syrian VP Khaddam.

United States fortifies ban on U.S. travel to Lebanon by increasing restrictions.

Resistance attacks against SLA zone prompt massive retaliation by Israel against South Lebanon, which in turn prompts Hizballah rockets into northern Israel. One week of intensive bombing of approximately 100 Lebanese villages leaves more than 132 dead, 500 wounded, and causes approximately 350,000 southern residents to flee the area. Cease-fire brokered by U.S. Secretary of State Warren Christopher. Following the cease-fire, Lebanese Army units deploy alongside some UNIFIL positions in the South. Israel declares purpose of attack to create massive civilian exodus of the South to "pressure the Lebanese government" to rein in Hizballah. Throughout August, Hizballah continues to fire into Israeli "security zone," and Israel retaliates with (smaller scale) airstrikes.

Syria President Hafiz al-Asad declares that anti-Israeli resistance in South Lebanon must be maintained and improved.

The Lebanese Army receives $1.8 million of military equipment from the United States.

Syrian National Social Party member Nasri Khoury is appointed first secretary general of the Syrian-Lebanese Higher Council.

PLO representative in Lebanon, Shafiq al-Hout, suspends his participation in the PLO executive committee in protest against the organization's approach to the Middle East peace talks.

Amid growing dissension within and criticism of the Lebanese government, Prime Minister Hariri threatens to resign; Syrian vice president Khaddam arrives in Beirut and declares that Hariri will remain in office until the end of President Hrawi's term.

During a fund-raising tour of Arab states, Prime Minister Hariri secures renewed commitments for portions of the $500 million aid fund promised to Lebanon by Arab League states.

As Israel and the PLO move closer to mutual recognition, Palestinians in a number of refugee camps in Lebanon stage protests against the "Gaza-Jericho first" proposal; Foreign Minister Fares Bouez declares that any Israeli-PLO agreement must make provision for the return of Palestinian refugees residing in Arab countries; Nearly half of the 400 Palestinians expelled from the occupied territories in late 1992 return home.

Lebanon rejects the Israeli peace proposals on South Lebanon presented at the bilateral talks in Washington.

Israeli Prime Minister Yitzhak Rabin and PLO chairman Yasir Arafat sign the "Gaza-Jericho first" agreement in Washington.

Despite a ban by the Lebanese government on protests, an anti-"Gaza-Jericho first" rally in Beirut's southern suburbs results in the death of eight participants; Hizballah stages a large anti-government demonstration during the burial of the slain protesters.

Lebanon and Syria sign four bilateral agreements covering agriculture, social and economic affairs, health, and the movement of individuals and goods.

President Hrawi issues a strong warning concerning the dangers of the settlement Palestinians in Lebanon.

At a meeting in Washington, Prime Minister Hariri is informed that the United States will not lift its travel restrictions to Lebanon, open a consulate in Beirut, or allow Middle East Airlines to land in the United States.

Index

About the Contributors

As'ad Abukhalil is assistant professor of political science at California State University and a research assistant at the Center for Middle Eastern Studies at the University of California at Berkeley.

Mahmoud Ayoub is professor of Islamic studies at Temple University in Philadelphia.

Hussein A. Amery is an assistant professor of geography at Bishop's University.

Rex Brynen is assistant professor of political science and chair of the Middle East studies program at McGill University.

Hassan Charif works with the United Nations Economic and Social Commission for Western Asia in Amman, Jordan, and is a member of its special task force for the reconstruction of Lebanon.

Deirdre Collings is undertaking her Ph.D. in the Global Security Programme at Cambridge University.

Georges Corm is an independent financial consultant and is a forme ─── ──── fessor of economics and political science at the Lebanese Univers'

Hani A. Faris is research associate with the Institute of University of British Columbia.

Salim el-Hoss, reelected to the Lebanese Parlia several times as prime minister of Lebanon.

Michael C. Hudson is professor of internationa and the Seif Ghobash Professor of Arab Studies

Daoud L. Khairallah, a lawyer, is adjunct professor at Georgetown University Law Center.

Samir Khalaf is visiting professor of sociology at Princeton University and research associate at the Center for International Studies, M.I.T.

Atif A. Kubursi is professor of economics at McMaster University.

Joseph Maila, cofounder and editor of the journal *Cahiers de l'Orient,* is assistant director of the Institut d'Etudes Economiques et Sociales (Paris) and professor at the Université Saint Joseph (Beirut).

Augustus Richard Norton, professor of political science at Boston University, is currently the director of a major research project, "Civil Society in the Middle East," housed at New York University.

Don Peretz recently retired as professor of political science at the State University of New York at Binghampton.

Nasser H. Saidi was appointed as first deputy to the governor of the Central Bank of Lebanon in May 1993.

Paul Salem is assistant professor of political science at the American University of Beirut, director of the Lebanese Center for Policy Studies (LCPS), and editor of *The Beirut Review* (semiannual) and *The Lebanon Report* (monthly).

Rosemary Sayigh, an independent social researcher and writer, is a specialist on Palestinians in Lebanon.

Ahmed A. Sbaiti is president and CEO of Al-Shall International USA, an international brokerage firm. From 1983 to 1985 he served on the board of directors (as director of the project finance department) of the Council for Development and Reconstruction (CDR) in Lebanon.

Jillian Schwedler, associate program officer for civil society in the Middle East project, is completing doctoral work in the Department of Politics, both at New York University.

Raghid el-Solh, a member of the governing board and the research committee of the Centre for Lebanese Studies in Oxford, is codirector of its Project for Democracy Studies in the Arab Countries.

About the Book

———— · ————

Although Lebanon is no longer at war, its long-term stability remains hostage to myriad political, economic, and regional problems. This book serves as a comprehensive survey of developments in Lebanon following the 1990 peace accord.

The authors examine the roles of Syria, Israel, and the Palestinians, as well as the internal challenges facing the Lebanese in their attempts to reconstruct their polity, economy, and society. They also outline areas in which the international community can, and should, play an active role in Lebanon's restabilization.